Health Management Information Systems

Theories, Methods, and Applications

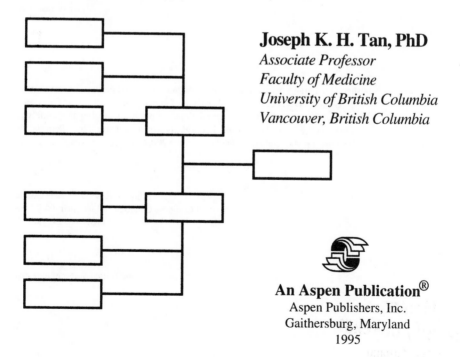

Joseph K. H. Tan, PhD
Associate Professor
Faculty of Medicine
University of British Columbia
Vancouver, British Columbia

An Aspen Publication®
Aspen Publishers, Inc.
Gaithersburg, Maryland
1995

Library of Congress Cataloging-in-Publication Data

Tan, Joseph K. H.
Health management information systems: theories, methods, and applications/
Joseph K.H. Tan.
p.   cm.
Includes bibliographical references and index.
ISBN 0-8342-0613-7
1. Information storage and retrieval systems—Health services administration.
2. Management information systems. I. Title.
[DNLM: 1. Management Information Systems.
2. Health Services—organization & administration.
W 26.5 T161h 1995]
RA971.6.T36   1995
362.1′068′4—dc20
DNLM/DLC
for Library of Congress
94-47453
CIP

Aspen Publishers, Inc., grants permission for photocopying for limited personal or internal use.
This consent does not extend to other kinds of copying, such as copying for general
distribution, for advertising or promotional purposes, for creating new collective
works, or for resale. For information, address Aspen Publishers, Inc., Permissions
Department, 200 Orchard Ridge Drive, Suite 200, Gaithersburg, Maryland 20878.

Editorial Resources: Jane Colilla
Library of Congress Catalog Card Number: 94-47453
ISBN: 0-8342-0613-7

Printed in the United States of America

1   2   3   4   5

To my beloved wife, Leonie, and son, Joshua, for their patience and inspiration;
My relatives for their understanding and encouragements; and
My friends for their support and assistance.

Table of Contents

Foreword

In this age of exploding technologies and information superhighways, students, health professionals, and managers need more than ever to understand health management information systems. To do so they need to understand the theories and methods underlying their structures and limitations, and the range of their applications not yet tapped in most places. Take the seemingly simple example of word processing software. It has insinuated itself into virtually every desktop computer. Nearly every desktop of health professionals now sports a computer with at least this software if none other. Health professionals use few of the capabilities of these word processors, even those who use them daily for routine writing tasks. If word processing software is so underemployed, consider spreadsheets, database management packages, statistical packages, and other generic productivity software. All these productivity tools await a new fifth generation of user-friendliness to put their wider range of capabilities to work. That new generation is here.

Joseph Tan describes the generations of health management information systems and the latest generation of expert systems that could change this underutilization. He takes pains in the early chapters to convey an appreciation of the health management information systems that have built the platform for new technologies. Artificial intelligence and expert systems software hold promises for taking information systems to new heights of decision-making support for managers. Health informatics and telematics hold the parallel prospect of integrating health information systems in more seamless and accessible ways.

One platform on which Dr. Tan builds his account of the oncoming information era is systems theory. "Viewing the health service industry from a systems perspective," he notes, "provides valuable insights into the functioning and structure of the present system." His development of those insights from the systems perspective puts this book in the forefront of both health care and information science. He uses the perspective to examine data systems and subsystems, management functions and roles, and systems development methodologies in subsequent chapters.

Finally, Tan outlines some of the issues for the future on the basis of projections and assumptions concerning the reform or renewal of health care systems. These include new criteria of effectiveness, and the fate of the total quality management paradigm.

The graphics in this book demonstrate a feature of desktop information technology. Combining new information systems and concepts with new communications technology has opened new horizons in management productivity, mobility, independence, and competitiveness. Those who have been the early adopters of these systems, technologies, and concepts have opened the doors of the health care system to new possibilities, new efficiencies, and new accountability.

—Lawrence W. Green, DrPH
Professor and Director
Institute of Health Promotion
University of British Columbia
Vancouver, British Columbia

Preface

Over the years, computerized information systems have become increasingly important in the management of health service delivery. Today, many hospitals and other health organizations have information system departments and managers to handle the continuously increasing flow of information. As a result, many universities are incorporating undergraduate and graduate courses on health information systems as part of their curriculum in health administration programs. Thus, it appears that there is now a growing need for organized materials that will provide students and practitioners alike with state-of-the-art coverage of this field. This book is an attempt to fill such a need by offering students an integrated discussion of issues surrounding the application of modern information technologies in the context of the evolving North American health services delivery system. In addition, the book serves to provide general readers and health administrators with updated information on technological advancements that are applicable to today's evolving health care environment.

The discipline of health management information systems (HMIS) utilizes many theories and concepts developed in other fields, in particular, the management information systems (MIS) field. This book therefore adapts MIS theories and concepts to fit within a health service delivery system perspective. Overall, topics covered in this book in HMIS include systems theory; information flows and data management; systems development methodologies; components of modern information technology such as hardware, software, databases, electronic data interchange, and communication systems; advanced information system applications such as group decision support systems and expert systems; management information technology planning and infrastructure; information resource management; administration of end-user computing; and total quality management processes.

The key strength of *Health Management Information Systems: Theories, Methods, and Applications* is that it provides an integrative framework that covers and links this wide variety of interesting topics in health informatics within the context of modern-day health service delivery systems. The book is organized into five parts. Part I provides an introduction to the field. Part II focuses on HMIS theories and methodologies, including systems theory, information theory, management concepts, and systems development methodologies. Part III of the text discusses HMIS technologies and applications and their roles in supporting the health service delivery industry. Part IV deals with HMIS administration and impacts. Part V provides the readers with a look at the growth of HMIS beyond the 1990s.

Accordingly, this book will serve well as a comprehensive reference source to health care executives who are presently working in the information system and telecommunication field or other related areas. More specifically, the book is designed to be used at advanced undergraduate or introductory graduate level programs in health service management. To this end, the chapters have been developed to introduce students to current information technology applications that facilitate health planning, administration, and evaluation. Many citations are provided throughout the book for those who might be interested in and further motivated to studying a particular topic in more depth. More generally, the topics of discussion are drawn from important pieces of past and contemporary work on health management information systems that are based on a thorough review and accumulation of ideas and concepts published in books, peer-reviewed journals, and other literature sources. As such, this book is a resource that can be a useful addition to the library of any student in health service management.

This book is generally suitable as a text for a one-semester graduate or a two-semester advanced undergraduate course in health management information systems and may also be used in conjunction with additional cases and materials dealing with specialized knowledge domains for specialty HMIS courses (e.g., Medical Informatics). This book presumes that students have no prior experience or knowledge of computer-related issues. Readers are, however, assumed to have a working knowledge of the different aspects of the health service industry. Many hospitals and other health service delivery organizations already rely on computers to store and process information, and to support their health service delivery activities. Therefore, cases illustrated in this book are abstracted or adapted from many "real life" examples throughout the North American Health Service Delivery System.

Acknowledgments

I am indebted especially to several University of British Columbia colleagues who have guided and shaped my thinking in the design and development of this work: Izak Benbasat, who introduced me to the thinking and concepts of Management Information Systems (MIS) and has since continued to sharpen my interest in its applications to human information processing; Sam Sheps, who has served as my mentor in the field of health care and epidemiology; Robert Modrow, who has contributed greatly to expanding my thinking about the integrative function of MIS in health organizations and real-life practices; and John Milsum, who has enlightened me to the need and importance of emphasizing a general systems perspective for health administration education, a theme under which I have attempted to bring together the ideas and thoughts expressed in various parts and chapters of this book.

Even so, special acknowledgment is due to the library work, searches, contributed materials, detailed summaries, reviews, corrections, suggestions, editing, and changes made to the original work by the 1992/93 and 1993/94 classes of the University of British Columbia's Masters in Health Administration (MHA) Program, as well as by several of my PhD students and research assistants, without whose help the current work would not have been completed in a timely fashion. To name each and every one of these students and assistants would run the risk of missing someone important, but the abilities and selfless contributions of a number of individuals should be especially recognized: Lief Ahrens, Terrence Fan, John Hanna, Marilynne Hebert, John Ko, Mieke Koehoorn, Denny Kwan, Hector Leon, and Otamere Omoruyi.

Next, I also would like to express my appreciation to the many colleagues from whose communications and discussions of parts and pieces of the manuscript I have benefited; especially, Donald Amoko (University of British Columbia), Charles Austin (University of Alabama), Stuart Boxerman (Washington University), Paul Chapin (Royal Inlands Hospital), Gerardine DeSanctis (Duke University), Lawrence Green (University of British Columbia), Robert Gold (University of Maryland), Clarke Hazlett (University of Alberta), Roger Kropf (New York University), Richard Kurz (Saint Louis University), Lawrence Nestman (Dalhousie University), Dennis Protti (University of Victoria), Donna Royston (Association of University Programs in Health Administration), Thomas Wan (Virginia Commonwealth University), Randy Wong (Mission Memorial Hospital), Richard Woo (St. Vincent's Hospital), David Uffelman (Health Care Management Review), and Dean Uyeno (University of British Columbia).

I am also very grateful to the staff of Aspen Publishers, Inc., for their support and guidance throughout the project. In particular, I wish to thank Jack Bruggeman, Associate Publisher; Sandy Cannon, Acquisitions Editor; Jane Colilla, Associate Editor; Amy Martin, Developmental Editor; and Laura Smith, Production Manager; for all their encouragement and care in the preparation and production of this work. The reviewers of the earlier drafts of this manuscript have also helped shape the work to its present form.

To all these individuals, and to my family, friends, and relatives, I offer my thanks for the positive support provided to me throughout the incubation and preparation process. Much of the value of this final version of the text is due to their assistance, but I alone bear responsibility for any errors or omissions that can be found between the covers.

Part I

Designing a Blueprint for Health Management Information Systems: The HMIS Discipline

Chapter 1

Health Management Information Systems: An Introduction

LEARNING OBJECTIVES

---

1. Distinguish HMIS from MIS.
2. Characterize the problem(s) addressed by the HMIS discipline.
3. State the need for a managerial perspective in HMIS education.
4. Identify basic functions of a health information processing system.
5. Justify HMIS knowledge and skills expected of health administrators.
6. Rationalize the organization of this book within an HMIS framework.

INTRODUCTION

> *The deficiency of the simple data processing system is that it fails to tell management all sides of the story.*[1]

In its broadest sense, a health management information system (HMIS) encompasses diverse concepts and methods from many related fields. The beginning of the HMIS discipline may be traced to many roots, including general systems research, information economics, management science, information system development methodologies, computer science and communication theory, medical computing, health organization behavior, health policy, and health services research. The subjects of this book are HMIS theories, methods, and applications. It therefore draws freely from and synthesizes relevant concepts embedded in many of these fields.

This chapter introduces the reader to HMIS as an emerging discipline. To this end, it relates HMIS to its origins. Its primary goal is to show how the domains of HMIS knowledge constitute the interface of knowledge among diverse fields of study. As in the well-known adage "The whole is more than the sum of its parts," the HMIS discipline must entail, because it is interdisciplinary, synergistic concepts that are scattered in many of its reference disciplines, and thereby justifies its existence as a separate discipline. We begin this chapter by considering a few key HMIS-related concepts.

TOWARD A BROAD DEFINITION OF HMIS

We have seen that the HMIS discipline may be conceived as an emerging discipline with many roots, involving a synergy of concepts and methods from a host of reference disciplines. Each of these reference disciplines contributes some philosophical perspectives and principles to the field. For instance, the discipline of computer science and communication technology is seen to provide the technological framework or know-how for designing HMIS. In contrast, the field of organizational and behavioral science has provided the HMIS discipline with the strategic framework and techniques for successful management and implementation of computer-based health information systems. Similarly, medical computing and management science have contributed to the HMIS discipline an array of tools and methodologies for analyzing and optimizing data flows and techniques for simulating complex processes in health service delivery. Lastly, the field of information economics has contributed significantly to the theoretical basis for cost-benefit and cost-utility evaluation of HMIS technologies.

As a field in itself, HMIS is built upon the following four key concepts and their interrelationships:

1. Health
2. Organization management
3. Information management
4. Health management information systems

Health is the end-purpose of all HMIS designs and applications. It defines the problem that is to be addressed by the HMIS discipline. Specifically, the ultimate goal or overall purpose in applying state-of-the-art HMIS solutions is to improve the health status of the populace (i.e., including curative and preventive health) and to enhance the delivery of health services for targeted patient populations.

Organization management indicates the need for a managerial perspective in developing HMIS applications for health service organizations. Briefly, the concept of organization management refers to the act of mixing and blending various health organizational resources such as health capital and finances, health personnel, health technology, and health information in a way that best accomplishes a set of predetermined goals and objectives within the context of an evolving health care environment.

Information management essentially shifts our attention back to health data and health information processing as the basic building blocks for developing HMIS. To achieve the set of predetermined goals and objectives of their organizations more effectively, health managers must rely on health data and health information processing. More importantly, they point to the need to view health information as an organizational resource that must be properly managed to yield expected benefits in the context of present and future health care environments.

Health management information systems presuppose that the science and art of the HMIS discipline can be firmly established and distinguished from those of its reference disciplines only on the basis of a framework that absorbs the many insights and interactions inherent in any health organizational information system project or application. Moreover, the term "system" indicates that the concept of HMIS is necessarily encompassing and must be expandable in scope to include a hierarchy of concepts, including linkages among these various concepts.

A more formal definition of HMIS is given later. For now, we will explore the implications of each of the four concepts discussed as they relate to the HMIS field. They can be viewed in different contexts (environmental, organizational, and technological) and can be shown to link intricately with each other, internally or externally to the organization, as shown in Figure 1–1.

For example, HMIS is linked to health as the environmental context that is external to the organization, whereas it is linked to information management and organizational management within the framework of the organizational context. Since the environmental, organizational, and technological contexts form the major underlying themes for understanding HMIS, the relationships (linkages) among HMIS and the contexts are significant in impact. In this book, we will not only study the various HMIS-related concepts separately but, more importantly, investigate in depth the interrelationships among these concepts both within the organizational context and in the broader technological and environmental contexts.

HMIS versus MIS

In advocating HMIS as a discipline, we are reminded of the long historical struggle of management information systems (MIS) to detach itself from other, more established disciplines (e.g., management science) before it was recognized as an independent field of study. Indeed, even as recently as the early 1980s, the MIS discipline was still characterized as a "theme."[2,3] One of the major difficulties facing MIS researchers and academics that have persisted is the lack of clarity of the many definitions in the MIS field.[4-6]

The identity problem of HMIS is even more pervasive than that of MIS. HMIS is a discipline that is built largely upon the application of MIS concepts to health

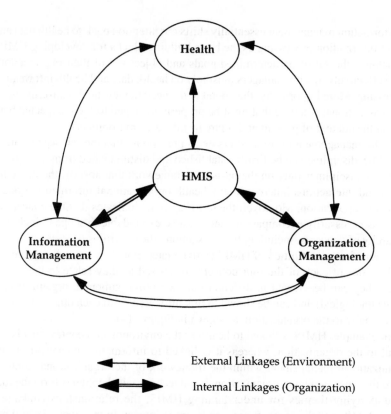

Figure 1–1 A Broad Conceptualization of Health Management Information Systems (HMIS)

sciences, as is apparent in many of the acronyms used in the two respective fields.[7-9] Unless and until HMIS educators and researchers build a cumulative tradition of their own in terms of theories, methodologies, and applications, they must and constantly do draw on new ideas and concepts that are current in the MIS field. Of course, this is not to say that there are no specialized concepts and terms that apply only to the field of health care and medical computing and do not belong to the overall MIS field; for example, terms such as "informatics," "medical informatics," or "health informatics" are considered foreign to the field. Thus, it is the "health" concept that uniquely distinguishes the field of HMIS as a specialty field within MIS.[10,11]

Table 1–1 summarizes the major differences between the HMIS and MIS fields. As shown, the objects of cognition, object systems, subspecialties, and related

Table 1-1 Characteristics of the Health Management Information Systems (HMIS) versus the Management Information Systems (MIS) Disciplines

Characteristics	HMIS (A Specialty of MIS)	MIS
•Object of Cognition	• Clinical & Health Management Decision Making	• General Management Decision Making
•Object of Systems	• Health Delivery Systems - Patient Populations - Health Providers - Third Parties	• Organizational Systems - Consumer Populations - Business Professionals - Corporations
•Subspecialties	• Medical Informatics • Dental Informatics • Pharmacy Informatics • Nursing Informatics	• Management Technology • Management Support Systems • Data Processing • Office Automation • Telecommunications
• Reference Disciplines	• MIS • Health Sciences • Information Science	• Behavioral Science • Computer Science • Management Science • Information Economics

disciplines of HMIS are more specialized and are derived substantially from the more general MIS field.[12,13]

Problems Addressed by the HMIS Discipline

Basically, the different terms used to describe the field of HMIS reflect different perspectives of what the area should cover. Yet, one way to set a boundary for the HMIS field and to judge its maturity as a discipline is to try to answer the following few important questions:

- What is (are) the problem(s) addressed by this field?
- Why has (have) this (these) same problem(s) not been attended to by scholars trained in one of the core disciplines, for example, one of the reference disciplines of HMIS?
- How do we draw a distinction between solutions provided by the HMIS field and those suggested by its reference disciplines?

Although it appears impossible to constrain the many overlaps of the HMIS field with other core disciplines, it is clear that the key problem that engulfs HMIS domains is the application of automated solutions to problems and concerns in the health service delivery industry. More specifically, we may characterize the HMIS problem as one that pertains to the use of organizational computing, information systems, and advancing technological solutions to solve mounting problems of productivity, cost containment, and quality management in the delivery of health services. In short, the problem addressed by HMIS lies largely in the overlaps of the MIS field, the health sciences, and organization science. It is also these kinds of overlaps that continually create the need for a growing number of subspecialties in HMIS, including medical informatics, dental informatics, pharmacy informatics, and nursing informatics.[14]

What this implies, then, is that HMIS thinking and approaches are most appropriate to those problems that have not been successfully or effectively addressed by many of the better established core disciplines such as behavioral sciences, computer science, management science, information economics, medicine, pharmacy, dentistry, and allied health disciplines. Figure 1–2 shows that the HMIS discipline has emerged through addressing problems at the interface of a mix of clinical and nonclinical sciences.

Accordingly, the application of HMIS solutions to health service problems must take into account the unique nature of the interdisciplinary aspects of the field. Moreover, the goal must be to achieve improvements in the health of individuals and more generally, the efficient, effective, and excellent delivery of health services (see Chapter 5). Indeed, as early as 1980, Lincoln and Korpman recognized the difficulties that existed with computer applications in health care. In their classic paper, "Computers, Health Care, and Medical Information Science," they argued that the goals for medical information science, although easy to state, are difficult to achieve for a number of reasons:

> First, it has proved insufficient merely to adapt information processing procedures and programs of proved success in other fields, largely because of the complexity of the medical context, the diversity of medical data, and the vagueness, disparity, and variety of health care objectives. . . . The procedural rigidities of computer systems often stand in the way of appropriate medical information processing and may generate additional clerical work to meet actual requirements. . . . The goal of MIS [in this case, medical information science] is to resolve the apparent dissonance between the rigid structure of computer logic and the often inherently ambiguous structure of medicine. The materials are the full range of patient care data and their applications. . . . The methods employed encompass a wide range of disciplines, including not only information processing and communications but also the management, behavioral, and fundamental sciences.[15]

Moving to an example in the context of the HMIS field, the implementation of a computer-based utilization care plan system for effective patient data management is complex because it involves the coordination of dozens of highly skilled health professionals, including physicians, nurses, nurse-secretaries, and secretar-

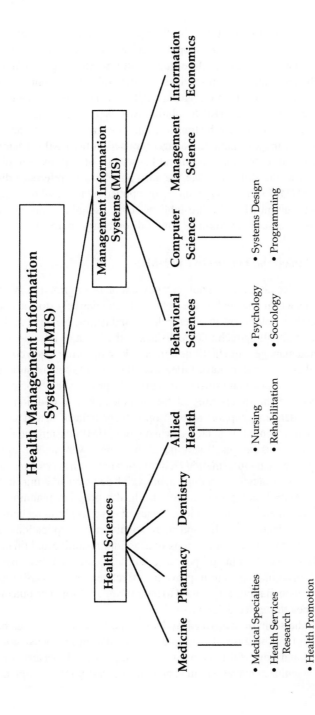

Figure 1-2 The Interdisiciplinary Aspect of the Health Management Information Systems (HMIS)

ies; paramedics such as dietitians and physiotherapists; administrative clerks; social workers; hospital managers; and support service personnel such as housekeepers and maintenance workers.[16] More importantly, whether the system ultimately results in better quality health services will determine the extent to which its implementation may be considered a success. All of the investments, including time, money, and energy into the HMIS solution, will be questionable if the returns cannot, in one way or another, be translated into better "health." To achieve this kind of successful transformation, managers trained in the HMIS discipline should not only have at least a mix of general knowledge of various core disciplines but also possess the skill to bridge the gaps among these reference disciplines. That is why HMIS solutions are not easily applied by those whose educational training has been limited to a well-established core discipline. Hence, HMIS concepts and skills necessarily encompass a multidisciplinary approach.

The Need for a Managerial Perspective in HMIS

Over the past few decades, the technological evolution of information systems (IS) in organizations within the health care field has been relatively slow and sporadic compared to IS development in other fields of industries. Nolan et al. have noted that this rather appalling technological slack is the result of a failure to involve health service managers in HMIS design and development.[17] As well, they stress that hospital administrators have failed over the years to secure sufficient funding for HMIS developmental projects, in particular, projects that would have a significant impact on the functioning of the organizations. In addition, they found very little evidence of support among top management of health service organizations for actively involving end-users in ongoing HMIS design and developmental efforts. This was because many health managers were unable to perceive the benefits of applying information technologies in health service managerial activities such as strategic planning, managerial decision making, health service utilization control and management, and health program planning and evaluation. Moreover, there was also an inadequacy of expertise in IS technology in health service organizations to develop more sophisticated applications. Accordingly, apart from entry-level applications such as administrative and financial systems for efficient record keeping purposes, very little attention has been paid to applying information technologies to improve the effectiveness of organizational and managerial decision making with regard to monitoring performance outcomes and the quality of health service delivery.

In recent years, the scenario described by Nolan and his colleagues has been changing gradually, first, because of the rapid proliferation of inexpensive user-friendly computers and powerful personal workstations; second, because of the growing interest of senior management in achieving successful HMIS implementations; and, third, because senior managers are becoming more knowledgeable about and better trained in computers and management information systems these days. Thus, it has been predicted, for example, that the potential growth of IS applications within the health service industry during the coming years will probably be greater than in most other industries.[18] Therefore, management should not and cannot afford to stand aside by leaving the job of designing, developing, and implementing computer-based information systems in the hands of IS specialists alone. By doing so, they may allow the resulting HMIS applications to center around the technology and not organizational requirements. As such, the importance of adopting a management perspective in health information system implementations should not be underestimated.

Indeed, Dr. Gary Filerman, past president of the Association of University Programs in Health Administration (AUPHA), once argued that "information systems management ranks with financial management as a central skill for optimal administration of the health service organization," and it is seen to be "essential for quality improvement, for technological assessment and for every aspect of productivity organization."[19] Tan sees the need for a managerial focus in HMIS to be strongly fostered by three factors: (1) the unmet need in the health service sector as many administrators have yet to acquire the knowledge and skills for aligning IS effectively to support strategic planning, general management, and routine problem solving; (2) the emergence of the view that information is an organizational resource to be managed; and (3) the emergence of chief information officer (CIO) positions in health service organizations.[20]

In the words of D.J. Protti, director of a Canadian health information science undergraduate program:

> Information is the common link binding the organizational subparts. As organizations grow in size and complexity, the need for better and more timely information and for improve decision-making techniques becomes critical. Recent advances in computer and communications technology are making it practical to integrate the planning and control of operations across functional areas and geographic distances. Concurrent with these developments is the recognition that information is a resource which should be subject to managerial planning and control in the same way as other resources such as land, labor and capital. The recent appointment of Vice-President and Assistant Vice-Presidents of Information Systems in three Canadian hospitals is testimony to this view.[21]

Accordingly, the purpose of this entire work is to contribute substantially to the need for an integration of MIS content into the health administration curriculum.[22] Having covered the implications of "health" and "organizational management" concepts, we now turn to what constitutes the basic functions of "information management" as they relate to the core areas of HMIS designs and development. We will do this by focusing on the health information processing (HIP) model.

BASIC FUNCTIONS OF A HEALTH INFORMATION PROCESSING SYSTEM

Historically, all information systems, including health management information systems, are built on the foundation of the data and information processing model. From a health information management and processing perspective, the basic functions of an HMIS may be perceived in terms of eight featured characteristics or elements.

1. Data acquisition
2. Data verification
3. Data storage
4. Data classification
5. Data update
6. Data computation
7. Data retrieval
8. Data presentation

The schematic representation of Figure 1–3 depicts specifically these eight elements that together define a typical information processing system. The first two elements (data acquisition and verification) of the information processing system focus on the data input phase, whereas the third through the sixth elements (data storage, classification, update, and computation) of the model concentrate on the data management or processing phase. It must be noted that the elements in the data management phase need not be sequential in process; they can be executed at any point within this phase. The last two elements of the information processing system (data retrieval and presentation) correspond to the data output phase.

Data acquisition involves both the generation and the collection of accurate, timely, and relevant data. Data are the raw materials of an information processing system. The process of data generation in a computer-based system is normally achieved through the input of standard coded formats (e.g., the use of bar codes), thereby allowing rapid mechanical reading and capturing of data. The process of data collection differs from that of data generation in that data can be entered directly at their sources (e.g., the use of a point-of-care bar code scanner), thereby enhancing data timeliness, validity, and integrity.

Data verification involves the verification and validation of gathered data. It is important to note that the quality of collected data will depend largely on the au-

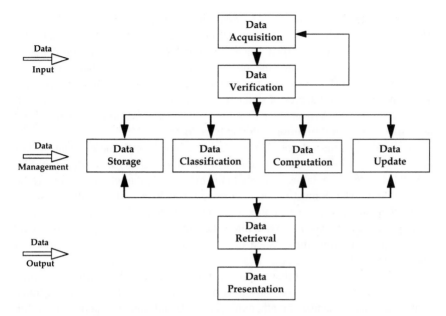

Figure 1–3 Basic Functions of a Health Information Processing (HIP) System

thority, validity, and reliability of the data sources. The Garbage In Garbage Out (GIGO) principle is an important factor to consider in the data verification process; data containing inaccuracies and inconsistencies should be detected as early as possible in the system to allow immediate corrective measures to be taken. This will minimize the eventual costs of system data errors.

The preservation and archiving of data may be regarded as part of the data storage function, a third element of the information processing system. Memory (i.e., a physical storage system) and indexing (i.e., the selection of key words or terms to determine major subject areas) are primary means of amassing data. When accumulated data are no longer actively used in the system, a method to archive the data for a certain period is usually advisable and may sometimes be mandatory, as when it is required by legislation.

A closely related element to data storage is data classification (or data organization). It is a critical function for increasing the efficiency of the system when the need arises to conduct a data search. Moreover, imposing a taxonomy on the data that have been collected and stored provides greater understanding of how the data will be used. Most data classification schemes are based on the use of certain key parameters. For example, data referring to a patient population may be classified and sorted according to various diagnostic classification schemes such as the widely accepted *International Classification of Diseases, 9th Revision, Clinical Modification* (ICD-9-CM).[23] Such an organized patient data system is useful for conducting a case-mix analysis since it comprises a set of diagnostic codes of 14,000 patient classifications. Indeed, the particular taxonomy that is used will have a powerful influence on the way that the data may subsequently be exploited. This is because a high degree of semantics is implied in any particular data classification. Crowe and Avison noted that if the wrong classification is chosen, a great deal of potentially useful information may be lost.[24]

New and changing information is accounted for through the element of data update. The dynamic nature of the data and HIP model calls for constant monitoring. Allowance for updating changes in the event of a transaction's occurring assumes that the HMIS must maintain currency (timeliness) of data already stored within the system. The concept of processing a transaction (i.e., updating the database or data file whenever an event alters the current state of the system) is critical for ensuring data timeliness. Such updates can be either on-line (real-time) or batch processed.

Data computation is another important function of an information processing system. This function involves various forms of data manipulation and data transformation such as the use of mathematical models and statistical applications, linear and nonlinear transformation, and completely or partially random processes.[25] Computational tasks allow for further data analysis, synthesis, and evaluation so that data can be used for strategic purposes besides tactical or operational use.

Data retrieval is a critical element in the information processing system. This function is concerned with the processes of data transfer and data distribution. The data transfer process is constrained by the time it takes to transmit the required data from the source to the appropriate sink (or agent) for use or presentation. A key problem in data transmission is the existence of noise (i.e., distortion) that is both internal and external to the HIP system. The data distribution process ensures that data will be accessible when and where they are needed. There must also be ways to ensure that unauthorized users are not allowed to access the data in the system. This is normally achieved through the institution of data security and access control mechanisms such as the use of passwords and other forms of user identification. One significant criterion to be considered in the data retrieval function is the economics of producing the needed information. Many early information processing systems (particularly, large mainframe hospital information systems) were far too costly to operate and the costs were simply not justified relative to the value of information that was finally produced.

The last element of the information processing system to be discussed is data presentation. This function has to do with how users will interpret the information output generated by the system. In situations where only quantitative managerial decision making is expected, summary tables and statistical reports may be all that is needed. However, most managerial decision making involves both quantitative and qualitative components. The use of presentation graphics for qualitative managerial decision making is particularly emphasized in current information processing systems, since they appear to provide a better intuitive feel of data trends and patterns. Tan and Benbasat have presented a theory to explain and predict the human processing of graphical information that is valuable to guide HMIS designers in the matching of presentation graphics to tasks.[26]

To illustrate the eight information processing functions just described within the context of a health organization information management and control system, we will use the example of a computerized patient medical record system that is also supported with bedside terminals. In this system, data acquisition comprises the generation and gathering of daily notes on symptoms, treatments, diagnoses, progress notes, discharge summaries, registration of orders for laboratory tests, operations, anesthesia, and other sources of information such as patient demographics and physicians' findings. The coding of the data to be automated is usually limited to specific elements, fields, and records.

Exhibit 1–1 illustrates an abstract of a patient medical record that could be implemented on a microcomputer system for use in monitoring patient medical conditions and treatments in a health service organization. As for data verification, the system relies on the ease with which the coded data may be mechanically processed and properly decoded. In many cases, standard forms and standard terms are used in recording patient data to ensure and enhance data integrity and consistency. Some clinics or hospitals still employ data clerks to inspect and verify data input manually, but many computerized patient record systems have built-in capabilities to reject invalid data inputs through the use of range checks (e.g., specifying a patient's age to fall within a verifiable range of classification) and other means (e.g., using batched totals).

After data input, the data are kept securely (data storage) in a database and usually on a magnetic medium (e.g., disk or tape). This is to ensure that the data are accessible to the health service providers on any subsequent visits by the same patient. A master patient index (MPI) is used to identify the exact location of a specific patient record. This type of data classification also allows for easy processing and regular updating by most provider organizations. Updating and maintenance of the data (data update) to ensure timeliness and integrity can be carried out either interactively or on a daily basis through batch processing. For example, many hospitals collate their daily census through batch processing around midnight. Additional data processing functions that are often applied include data analysis and synthesis to transform and combine various elements of the input data into useful and meaningful information (data computation). The data retrieval function ensures that the appropriate end-users (e.g., physicians and nurses) have access to or are provided with accurate, timely, and relevant information from the system. This has to do with centralization-decentralization issues and the nature of systems architecture distribution. The distribution of information to end-users

Exhibit 1-1 A Sample Abstract for a Computerized Patient Medical Record System

1. Patient Medical Insurance Number: _____	3. Date of Admission: / /
2. Patient Name: _____	4. Date of Discharge: / / Mo/Day/Yr:

| 5. Sex:
   - Male   ☐
   - Female   ☐

6. Birthdate: __ / __ / __

7. Tel. No.: ___ ___ ___

8. Next of Kin: _____

9. Address: _____

10. Admission Source:

   - Admitting   ☐
   - Emergency   ☐
   - Outpatient   ☐

11. Location
    of Patient: _____ | 12. Discharge Status:

Alive:
   - With Approval   ☐
   - Against Notice   ☐

Death:
   - Autopsy   ☐
   - No Autopsy   ☐

Transfer to:
   - Other Institution ☐
   - Home   ☐

13. Type of Death:
   - Anesthesia   ☐
   - In Operating Room ☐
   - Postoperative   ☐
   - Other   ☐

14. General Remarks:

_____ | **PROCEDURES**

15. Principal Procedure:
   a. _____ Date: / /

16. Additional Procedures
   a. _____
   b. _____
   c. _____

17. History/Physical:

   _____

18. Laboratory:

   _____

19. Radiology:

   _____ |

PHYSICIANS	**DIAGNOSIS**

20. Principal Specialist: _____
 	
Second Specialist: _____
 	
Family Physician: _____
	21. Principal Diagnosis: _____
	
	22. Additional Diagnosis:
	   a. _____
	   b. _____
	   c. _____

typically occurs through the imposition of a system of user identification and authentication. Ultimately, data presentation in the context of the preceding example is concerned with generating reports that are easy to read and interpret for use in patient care–related decision making.

The simple information processing system illustrated in Exhibit 1–1 is representative of a lower level HMIS whose functions may be limited to facilitating operational level thinking. Many real-world HMIS applications are even more sophisticated and are capable of providing high-level assistance beyond data tracking and activity monitoring. Examples of these more sophisticated HMIS applications will be the topics of later discussion. Note, however, that the phrase "a health information processing or management system" does not only emphasize the technological aspect or the hardware, software, and communication capabilities of the system. Although it is true that the types of HIP systems we will cover in this book are probably state-of-the-art computerized systems, one incorrect assumption often made is that an information system may be viewed as the equivalent of a computer system. There is a critical distinction. An information system is a human/machine system with emphasis placed on designing the system to suit every aspect of the user(s), whereas a computer system is merely an electronic black box equipped with a selected range of hardware, software, and firmware capabilities (see Chapter 7). In other words, it is not only "high tech" that is of interest in the application of an HMIS but both "high tech and high touch"—an outcome of systems thinking application, which is a paramount theme throughout this book.

WHAT HEALTH ADMINISTRATORS NEED TO KNOW ABOUT HMIS

A general survey of the IS literature in both the management and health care domains yields the following major conclusions about what health administrators should know about HMIS as an intellectual discipline[27]:

1. The HMIS discipline, like any other discipline, must be founded on well-tested theories and methods to be recognized as such; therefore, health administrators need to acquire a sound understanding of the conceptual foundations of HMIS.
2. Although the HMIS discipline must necessarily include hardware, software, and communications concepts, the environment in which the discipline is most likely to blossom for health administrators differs substantially from that of mainstream computer science and communication technology.
3. The success of HMIS as a discipline from a health administrator's perspective must ultimately rest on the bridging of technical and managerial skills to improve health service delivery within the context of current and future health care environments.

It is evident that the future HMIS is one that requires continuous adaptability and flexibility so as to accommodate rapid changes in the health service delivery system. As such, new HMIS applications must be able to provide information not only for solving administrative and clinical decision making in single hospital settings but for multiorganizational utilization of health care resources. This can be achieved, for example, through the integration of administrative and clinical information, such as in the design and development of HMIS applications for organized health delivery systems or managed care. Yet, regardless of the complexity of future HMIS development, the design and implementation of a successful HMIS must still be based on the three fundamental aspects of HMIS described previously and elaborated in the next few sections.

Building on Conceptual Foundations of HMIS

What holds the HMIS discipline together are its theories and methodologies. The field of HMIS embodies general systems theory,[28] information theory,[29] theories of human problem solving and decision making,[30] and organizational behavioral theories.[31] It is difficult, if not impossible, within the limited space of this book to undertake any substantial discussion of all published theories in HMIS. Our attempt here will be to concentrate on a few landmark theories while providing honorable mentions of or references to other relatively significant contributions.

With theory in place, methodology determines the level of abstraction, revision, and implementation of theory in real life in order to design and deliver a successful HMIS that is acceptable to end-users. For example, IS development is universally described by a traditional life-cycle model (see Chapter 6), and thus it is this life-cycle concept that essentially provides the foundation for understanding the practice of HMIS.[32] Today, there are hundreds and even thousands of methodologies that have been derived one way or another from the traditional life-cycle concept. Formed through the interactive evolution of theory, technology, and practice in the field, methodologies serve as an essential toolbox for each stage of HMIS development.

In summary, theories and methodologies represent two essential aspects to understanding the founding principles of the HMIS discipline; it is therefore in the interest of HMIS educators to recognize the importance of these two domains of knowledge and practice in their mission of effectively training health service administrators for information management.[33]

Balancing Technological Expertise and Organizational Skills

Like any IS discipline, the discipline of HMIS must necessarily include computing technologies and their applications. This is made evident by the growing number of HMIS curriculum models suggested for North American graduate and undergraduate health administration and information science programs.[34–38] Yet, many of these models have also warned about the need to train individuals with a balance of knowledge and skills in hardware and software systems as well as in organizational and human behavior theories.

Put simply, a curriculum in HMIS must fundamentally differ from that of mainstream computer science and communication technology because of the environment in which the discipline is taught, the employment environment for the graduates, and the depth of technical expertise expected of the graduates.[39] In designing an effective HMIS curriculum, the environment for teaching MIS concepts should thus be one of health administration, and the working environment should be one of interaction between health organizational functions and computer technology, rather than an emphasis on technical skills alone. Therefore, the technical expertise required or expected of health administrators should enrich administrators' ability to develop and implement an information system and telecommunication infrastructure for an organized health service delivery system based on information requirement assessments and strategic planning considerations.

IS technology has been undergoing rapid expansion and change not only because of the great competition among vendors and developers of the technology, but because of the increasingly urgent and varied demands of the market. With such diversity and change in the field of IS technology, emphasis laid upon technical skills in current HMIS education programs should follow a pattern or methodology reflecting the dynamic principles and methodologies associated with the technology. The point here is that the effective health service administrators of the future will have to be at ease with rapid changes, the continued growth of information system functions and capabilities within their organizations.

Emphasizing Health Administration and Impacts

The use of theories and methodologies in defining the boundaries of the HMIS discipline is not only crucial for applying key aspects of various established disciplines in a directed and purposeful way, but critical for making the health administrator the master and not the servant of technology. The glitter and attractiveness of sophisticated technologies will always have a way of distracting the health service administrator from the main issues of health administration. Therefore, an important question to be asked by health administration students engaged in the study of HMIS is, What area of HMIS knowledge is most critical in the practice of health administration?

We have seen that successful health administrators must be able to bridge both technical and managerial skills in applying information technology solutions to improving health service delivery within the context of current and future health care environments. The study and advancement of HMIS can therefore be considered as the study and advancement of the administration of IS within the health organization and its impacts on individuals, work groups, and community organizations. These end-effects of the implementation of HMIS technology are the end-effects of all the considerations embodied in the HMIS discipline. Thus, in considering HMIS administration and its impacts, the whole of the HMIS area is brought into consideration.

In summary, a key question to be asked in the study of HMIS is what the role and responsibilities of a top-level IS executive (i.e., a CIO) in a health organization should be in light of the ever changing health care environments. After all, this is precisely the underlying rationale for training health administrators in IS concepts and their applications in practice.

HMIS AND THE ORGANIZATION OF THIS BOOK

Although there may never be an agreement about the scope and boundary of the HMIS field, the literature appears to advocate a view that draws broadly from a total systems perspective. The following definition of HMIS is therefore suggested as representing an integrated perspective of this broad and complex field. A health management information system (HMIS) is "the application of a total systems perspective in linking relevant theoretical principles with practical methodologies for the effective administration (i.e., planning and management) of information technologies and their applications to improving health service delivery within the context of current and future health care environments."[40]

In this book, there are three identifiable components in the HMIS field that are significant for the development of an HMIS framework: (1) HMIS theories and methodologies, (2) HMIS technologies and applications, and (3) HMIS administration and impacts. Figure 1–4 provides a visual representation of these three facets or modules of the HMIS framework. In the next chapter, we will discuss each facet of this integrated framework for the HMIS field. For now, we will use the framework to organize the content of the various parts of this book.

The HMIS Framework in the Context of This Book

A visual representation of the integration of various facets of the HMIS framework and the various parts of this book is given in Figure 1–5. As shown in the figure, the HMIS framework is applied in organizing Parts I through V of this book. Part I, which includes this and the next chapter, provides a blueprint of the HMIS discipline. Part II focuses on the conceptual foundations of the field by introducing the reader to classical and contemporary HMIS theories and methodologies. Part III directs the discussion to HMIS technologies and applications, and Part IV deals with critical issues of HMIS administration and impacts. Part V concludes by viewing the framework in the light of future HMIS developments.

One suggested use of the framework is to make discussions of definitional issues easier to understand by providing an overall schema for technical and specialized terms, phrases, and acronyms. This allows the reader systematically to gather

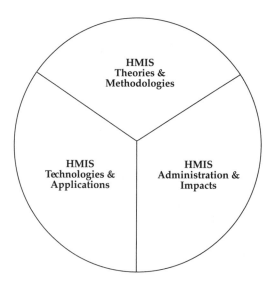

Figure 1–4 Three Facets of the Health Management Information System (HMIS) Discipline

a collection of concepts related to various subareas of the HMIS discipline. Terms (e.g., "data," "information," and "knowledge"), phrases (e.g., "HMIS planning," "HMIS design," and "HMIS implementation"), and acronyms (e.g., electronic data processing [EDP], management support systems [MSS], office information systems [OIS], and strategic information systems [SIS]) that are used throughout this book may be indexed pertaining to different parts of the HMIS framework. The relationships among these terms can therefore be more easily understood by fitting them into the different facets of the framework. To this end, Part I is an attempt to conceptualize the various aspects of the HMIS field using an integrated framework.

Part II: HMIS Theories and Methodologies

Part II, which focuses on HMIS theories and methodologies, consists of Chapters 3 through 6. These chapters are placed near the beginning of the book because they provide the founding principles for the field. Figure 1–6 provides a diagrammatic representation of Part II. Chapter 3 discusses the systems approach, elements of systems theory, and an integrated organizational model for the North American Health Service Delivery System (NAHSDS). It also applies systems thinking to the analysis of health information problems within the context of

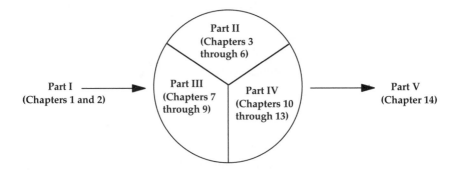

Part I - A Blueprint of the HMIS Discipline
Part II - HMIS Theories & Methodologies
Part III - HMIS Technologies & Applications
Part IV - HMIS Administration & Impacts
Part V - The Future HMIS Developments

Figure 1–5 The Organization of This Book with Respect to the HMIS Framework

NAHSDS. It essentially provides a theoretical basis for an integrated perspective of HMIS to facilitate solutions to key problems and issues faced by other health service organizations today. As shown in Figure 1–6, a systemic view and an integrated perspective of HMIS help to construct a framework for understanding how the combination of data resources (Chapter 4) and organizational management processes (Chapter 5) can lead to effective HMIS designs and development (Chapter 6).

Therefore, Chapters 4 through 6 each deal with some very fundamental concepts of HMIS. Chapter 4 concentrates on the relationship between data and information, discusses theories of information and communications, and demonstrates the application of health organizational information system modeling through the use of information flow diagrams and flow charting. This chapter is therefore mainly concerned with understanding the basic components of HMIS that will serve as resources (input). Chapter 6 focuses on HMIS designs and development. It takes a historical approach to the evolution of HMIS development methodologies and discusses criteria that can be used to choose among various competing methodologies. Developmental methodologies from system development life cycles (SDLC) and prototyping to contemporary models (e.g., CASE) will be part of the discussion. Hence, the concern focuses on the actual implementation aspects of HMIS (output).

Chapter 5 essentially bridges the gap between Chapter 4 (input: data resource) and Chapter 6 (output: HMIS design and development) by bringing into focus many of the key management concepts that are relevant to transforming data into

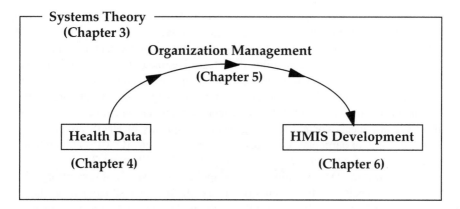

Figure 1–6 Overview of Part II (Chapters 3 through 6)

a functional HMIS. It presents health service managerial roles and functions as a basis for organizational HMIS designs.

Readers who have only marginal (or no previous) exposure to the HMIS field are therefore strongly urged to complete the reading of Part II before proceeding to other parts of the book. Those who want to gain a stronger foundational knowledge of HMIS are advised to read the top-rated MIS journals, for example *Information Systems Research, Management Science, MIS Quarterly,* and *Decision Science* for pursuing additional information. A good starting point for the reader is to go through the Notes at the end of each chapter and select those articles that appeal most.

Part III: HMIS Technologies and Applications

Part III focuses on the technological development of health information systems and its application in health service organizations from a contemporary perspective. It includes Chapters 7 through 9 and provides the link between the past and the future of HMIS with regard to technological advancement.

Chapter 7 provides an introduction to various existing and emerging HMIS technologies and discusses their applications to support the health service delivery industry. It essentially surveys the different types of "automated support" to highly structured (i.e., operational) tasks performed in a health service organization. Chapter 8 focuses on expert systems (ES) technology and other applications of artificial intelligence to the health service delivery industry. It also covers HMIS applications for assisting clinical decision making and complex administrative problem solving. It therefore represents the kind of technology support for consultative decision making and other semistructured or unstructured tasks.

Figure 1–7 provides a diagrammatic representation of how Chapters 7 and 8 are related. It also brings to our attention the integrative role of Chapter 9 (in relation to Chapters 7 and 8), which moves into more advanced topics of health informatics and telematics by concentrating on the integration of health organizational service delivery with integrated technologies and networks. Chapter 9 therefore provides a context for the growing complexity of HMIS products for managed care, in particular, case-mix information systems (C-MIS) and clinical management information systems (CMIS). Together, Chapters 7 and 8 in sequence show how HMIS solutions may be applied increasingly at various organizational task levels (i.e., from well-structured to ill-structured situations), and how these solutions and others with a more leading-edge perspective may be understood and integrated for future HMIS designs and development (Chapter 9).

To appreciate Part III thoroughly, the reader should become knowledgeable about widely used word-processing (e.g., WordPerfect, MsWord), spreadsheet (e.g., Excel, Lotus), graphics (e.g., Aldus Freehand, Harvard Graphics), and communication (e.g., ProComm Plus, MacLink Plus) software. As computer literacy among the general population grows with the influx of the user-friendly interfaces that have appeared in the health computing marketplace, the reader should find Part III illustrative and informative. Part III therefore is intended to guide the reader in applying state-of-the-art information technologies for health organizational problems.

Part IV: HMIS Administration and Impacts

The major issues in HMIS administration and impacts are addressed in Part IV, which comprises Chapters 10 through 13. Specifically, Part IV examines HMIS strategic planning (Chapter 10), HMIS resource management (Chapter 11), HMIS

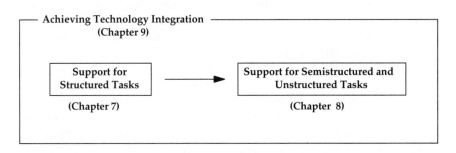

Figure 1–7 Overview of Part III (Chapters 7 through 9)

implementation (Chapter 12), and HMIS evaluation (Chapter 13). Figure 1–8 summarizes the relationships among various chapters of Part IV.

Since HMIS planning and management focus on linking the objectives and strategies of the information system group of the health service organization to corporate missions and goals, Chapter 10 introduces various approaches for achieving such a strategic alignment. Among other things, the concept of critical success factors (CSF) is identified as an approach for eliciting the information requirements of an organization or agency from the views of senior management, and as a tool for designing the health organizational management information technology infrastructure (MITI).

Chapter 11 expands on the discussion of managerial roles and functions (see Chapter 5) and focuses on how these roles relate to the management of information and technological resources in health service organizations and agencies. It therefore provides a framework of HMIS administration for putting together the various chapters in Part IV. Chapter 12 focuses on the HMIS implementation process and provides details on how management can help ensure that this process will be a pleasant and meaningful experience for both end-users and systems personnel. It provides the link between the concept of strategic planning and alignment (Chapter 10) and the concept of achieving total quality management (TQM) (Chapter 13) within the framework of HMIS administration. The last chapter of Part IV prepares the reader to put HMIS in the perspective of TQM for systemwide processes (Chapter 13), which is the purported goal of many, if not all, organized HMIS implementations.

No readings can replace the experience to be gained through real-life participation in HMIS development and implementation projects. Nevertheless, in a classroom setting, cases and examples provide a good alternative to real experience since they are an effective way to elicit and promote critical analysis of the pre-

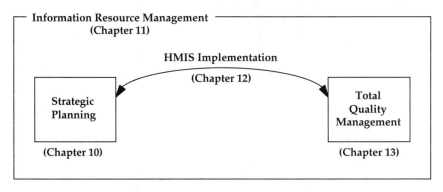

Figure 1–8 Overview of Part IV (Chapters 10 through 13)

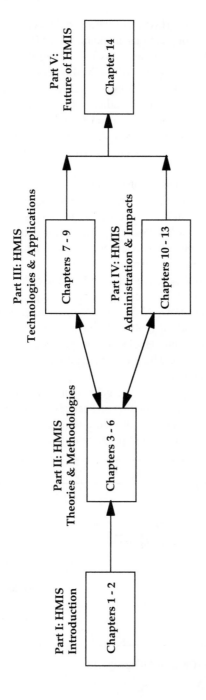

Figure 1–9 Relationships among Various Parts of This Book

sented issues. Minicases that are often drawn from real-life cases are therefore provided at the end of each chapter to encourage the reader to consider further how the issues presented in the discussion may relate to actual practice.

CONCLUSION

This chapter started out with a broad definition of HMIS and then gradually arrived at the analysis of a framework for the HMIS field. This framework is essentially the basis on which the various parts of this book are organized. It is hoped that this chapter has given the reader an overview of HMIS that is broad enough to accommodate future developments in the field and yet specific enough to facilitate the understanding of the book's organization. In other words, this chapter is intended to serve as a road map of the HMIS field for the reader. Altogether, the book examined HMIS from three broad angles: theories and methodologies (Part II), technologies and applications (Part III), and administration and impacts (Part IV). The relationships among these parts are summarized by Figure 1–9.

Briefly, Part II covers the foundational theories and methodologies of HMIS, which are in turn the fundamental building blocks of both Parts III and IV. For instance, data flow diagrams (DFDs) introduced in Part II can express the flow of information in a health service organization in explicit terms; this in turn will facilitate understanding of how and where various technological advancements can be applied for enhancing the delivery of health services (Part III) and assist in the actual strategic planning for and management of a state-of-the-art HMIS infrastructure (Part IV).

In retrospect, HMIS has emerged over the years to become a specialty in MIS dealing specifically with efficient and effective information management systems in the health service delivery industry. Today, it has blossomed into a critical discipline that is different from such traditional disciplines as computer sciences. Nevertheless, full recognition of HMIS as a discipline of its own ultimately depends on the continued development of a cumulative tradition of its own, including theories, methodologies, and applications.

CHAPTER QUESTIONS

1. What do you see as the major contributions of a core discipline such as epidemiology or biostatistics (which is taught in many health administration programs as a required course) to the field of HMIS?

2. Define the term "organization management" and state why a management imperative in the health service organization context appears to be strongly advocated in the development of an HMIS curriculum.

3. How is HMIS different from MIS? How are they similar?
4. Why is a balance of technical skills and organizational know-how important for HMIS training and education? How does this relate to evolving health information as an organization resource?
5. What, in your view, is the future of the HMIS field?

MINI CASE 1
TAKING THE LEAD IN HMIS TECHNOLOGIES AT
METROPOLITAN GENERAL

You have been hired as an assistant consultant to advise Metropolitan General Hospital on the application of advancing computer-based information technologies. Currently, the hospital has a mainframe computer in its data center, and every physician who has practicing privileges at the hospital can have access to a microcomputer terminal that is linked to the mainframe.

The chief executive officer (CEO), who is newly hired and has no formal training in information systems, has, however, been receiving complaints from these physicians that the current system focuses only on managerial efficiency, not clinical decision-making effectiveness.

MINI CASE QUESTIONS

1. Imagine that you have been asked to brief the new CEO in the discipline of HMIS. In no more than 100 words, summarize what HMIS is: its reference disciplines, problems faced, and topics discussed by the discipline. Remember also to distinguish HMIS from hospital information system (HIS).
2. What are some of the clinical versus managerial components of the computer-based system installed at Metropolitan General? What then do you think the physicians were complaining about?
3. How would you address the CEO's concerns? Suggest functions of applications of a health information processing system that will enhance the clinical performance of the current system.

CHAPTER REVIEW

Health management information systems is an emerging discipline. Although it encompasses concepts derived from various core reference disciplines and fundamental sciences, it has emerged to address issues specific to the requirements of health planning, administration, and management. In order to fulfill the vision inherent in HMIS, one must therefore take a management perspective in HMIS education. Students of HMIS must be taught to apply information technologies in health service managerial activities. This defines the need for a central skill for the optimal administration of any health service organization. As a result, administrators must be required to possess specific skills and a defined knowledge base in HMIS. From this one can build a foundation in the HMIS discipline and validate theories and methodologies based on real-life applications.

More specifically, HMIS is built on the foundation of health data and the health information flow model. This model integrates theory and practice and is a basic building block of HMIS knowledge development. The model describes various data functions and elements of an information processing system, including data acquisition, data verification, data storage, data classification, data computation, data update, data retrieval, and data presentation. The implementation of effective HMIS requires an integral balance between technological expertise and organizational skills without a compromise for one over the other. This provides a clear definition of HMIS for the health administrator, who then becomes the master of technology and not its servant.

NOTES

1. J.D. Aaron, Information Systems in Perspective, *Computer Surveys* no. 4 (1969) 213–236.

2. P.G.W. Keen, MIS Research: Reference Disciplines and a Cumulative Tradition, *Proceedings of the First International Conference on Information Systems* (December 1980): 9–18.

3. G.W. Dickson, Management Information Systems: Evolution and Status, *Advances in Computers* 20 (1981): 1–37.

4. Keen, MIS Research, 9–18.

5. Dickson, Management Information Systems, 1–37.

6. G.B. Davis and M.H. Olson, *MIS: Conceptual Foundations, Structure, and Development* (New York: McGraw-Hill Publishing Co., 1985).

7. C.J. Austin, *Information Systems for Health Services Administration,* 4th ed. (Ann Arbor, Mich: Health Administration Press, 1992).

8. R. Kropf and J.A. Greenberg, *Strategic Analysis for Hospital Management* (Gaithersburg, Md: Aspen Publishers Inc., 1984).

9. R. Kropf, *Service Excellence in Health Care through the Use of Computers* (Ann Arbor, Mich: Health Administration Press, 1990). A review of this book has been published in *Hospital & Health Services Administration* 38, no. 1 (1993): 159–161.

10. J.R. Mohr, Teaching Medical Informatics: Teaching on the Seams of Disciplines, Cultures, Traditions, *Methods of Information in Medicine* 28, no. 4 (1989): 273–280.

11. J.H. Milsum and C. A. Laszlo, From Medical to Health Informatics, *Methods of Information in Medicine* no. 23 (1984): 61–62.

12. Mohr, Teaching Medical Informatics, 273–280.

13. H.J. Seelos, The Science of Medical Information Systems, *Journal of Medical Systems* 16, no. 4 (1992): 171–175.

14. K. Hannah, *Introduction to Nursing Informatics* (New York: Springer-Verlag, 1993).

15. T.L. Lincoln and R.A. Korpman, Computers, Health Care and Medical Information Science, *Science* 210, no. 4467 (1980): 257–263.

16. J.K.H. Tan et al., Utilization Care Plan and Effective Patient Data Management, *Hospital & Health Services Administration* 38, no. 1 (1993): 81–99.

17. R.L. Nolan et al., Computers and Hospital Management: Prescription for Survival, *Journal of Medical Systems* 1, no. 2 (1977): 187–203.

18. J.K. Kerr and R. Jelinek, Impact of Technology in Health Care and Health Administration: Hospitals and Alternative Care Deliver Systems, *Journal of Health Administration Education* 8, no. 1 (1990): 5–10.

19. G.L. Filerman, The Administration of Health Services in the Twenty-First Century. Bernard Snell Lecture and Scholarship Fund, Department of Health Services Administration and Community, Faculty of Medicine, University of Alberta Hospitals, 1990.

20. J.K.H. Tan, Graduate Education in Health Information Systems: Having All Your Eggs in One Basket, *Journal of Health Administration Education* 11, no. 1 (1993): 27–55.

21. D.J. Protti, Health Information Science: What Is It? Is It Computing Science? Unpublished Paper, University of Victoria, Victoria, BC, 1990, 3.

22. B.T. Malec and C. J. Austin, Editorial, *Journal of Health Administration Education* 8, no. 1 (1990): 1–4.

23. ICD-9-CM is a US Public Health Service official adaptation of a system for the classification of diseases and operations. The original system was developed by the World Health Organization (WHO) for the purpose of indexing hospital records. See T. C. Timmreck, *Dictionary of Health Services Management* (Owings Mills, Md: National Health Publishing, 1987): 306.

24. T. Crowe and D.E. Avison, *Management Information from Data Bases* (Basingstoke: The MacMillan Press, 1980).

25. G.M. Weinberg, *Rethinking Systems Analysis and Design* (Boston: Little, Brown & Co., 1982).

26. J.K.H. Tan and I. Benbasat, Processing Graphical Information: A Decomposition Taxonomy to Match Data Extraction Tasks and Graphical Representation, *Information Systems Research* 1, no. 4 (1990): 416–439.

27. Tan, Graduate Education, 30.

28. K.E. Boulding, General Systems Theory: The Skeleton of Science, *Management Science* (April 1956): 197–208.

29. C.E. Shannon, A Mathematical Theory of Communication, *Bell System Technical Journal* (1948): 370–432, 623–659.

30. A. Newell and H.A. Simon, *Human Problem Solving* (Englewood Cliffs, NJ: Prentice-Hall, 1971).

31. R.M. Cyert and J.G. March, *A Behavioral Theory of the Firm* (Englewood Cliffs, NJ: Prentice-Hall, 1963).

32. D.E. Avison and A.T. Wood-Harper, Information Systems Development Research: An Exploration of Ideas in Practice, *Computer Journal* 34, no. 2 (1991): 98–112.

33. S.B. Boxerman, Commentary, *Journal of Health Administration Education* 8, no. 1 (1990): 36.

34. Protti, Health Information Science, 3.

35. Tan, Graduate Information, 27–55.

36. D. Zalkind and B. T. Malec, The National Survey of Health Administration Program Graduates on Management Information Systems Education, *Journal of Health Administration Education* 6 (1988): 315–335.

37. D.J. Protti, A New Undergraduate Program in Health Informatics, *AMA Congress '82 Proceedings*, ed. C. Lindberg (Masson Publishing, 1982): 241.

38. C.J. Austin and B.T. Malec, An Ideal Curriculum Model, *Journal of Health Administration Education* 8, no. 1 (1990): 53–61.

39. J.F. Nunamaker Jr., et al., eds., Information Systems Curriculum Recommendations for the 80s: Undergraduate and Graduate Programs: A Report of the ACM Curriculum Committee on Information Systems, *Communications of the ACM* 25, no. 11 (1982): 781–805.

40. Tan, Graduate Information, 33.

Chapter 2

The HMIS Framework: Theories, Methods, and Applications

LEARNING OBJECTIVES

1. Review major facets of the HMIS framework.
2. Identify key developments in HMIS theories and methodologies.
3. Formulate a theoretical model for HMIS.
4. Devise a methodological plan for HMIS.
5. Suggest a classification of HMIS technologies and applications.
6. Identify key issues in HMIS administration and impacts.
7. Suggest methods for evaluating progress in the HMIS field.

INTRODUCTION

> *The relationships among the ideas are not yet clear, nor has the wheat been adequately separated from the chaff. It is hard to tell who started what, what preceded what, and which is method and which theory.*[1]

In this chapter, our purpose is to provide a multifaceted conceptualization of the entire HMIS field. This exercise is important because it is intended to put HMIS theories and methodologies in perspective with other aspects and domains of the HMIS field; more specifically, this will help to identify and clarify the technological significance and practical implications of HMIS theories and methodologies. Just as pieces of a puzzle need to be put together before the meaning conveyed by the various pieces may be properly interpreted, this general framework will assist readers in keeping sight of the total picture as they go about systematically gathering, processing, and interpreting bits and pieces of the HMIS puzzle.

In Chapter 1, a threefold taxonomy of health management information systems was proposed.

1. HMIS theories and methodologies
2. HMIS technologies and applications
3. HMIS administration and impacts

Tan has described this clustering of ideas as three facets of the HMIS famework.[2] In this chapter, each of these facets is elaborated. The focus of discussion will be on significant past and current contributions to HMIS theories, methods, and applications.

It is important to recognize that the three facets of HMIS do not represent isolated islands of knowledge or development in HMIS; rather, they are intricately connected to one another, hence the need to view the entire field as a synergy of these facets. For instance, the "intertwined" relationship among them can be demonstrated by our discussion on key theoretical developments in each of the three HMIS domains throughout this chapter. These theoretical developments are important to a better understanding of the relationships among HMIS domains; for example, how are HMIS technology and applications related to HMIS administration and impacts? The discussion therefore extends and details the conceptualization of the HMIS field provided in Chapter 1. Whereas Chapter 1 traces the development of the field to its origins, this chapter takes the reader through a tour of current developments and ends with a closer look at key criteria determining progress in the field.

HMIS THEORIES AND METHODOLOGIES

In this section, our focus is on major developments in HMIS theories and methodologies. Figure 2–1, adapted from Tan, shows an upper and lower bound curve to convey the limited growth of HMIS theories and methodologies over the last several decades.[3] As knowledge and practice in HMIS progress over time, the boundaries of these curves will expand outwardly. The top left corner of the figure shows that much research and hypothesis testing is still needed to advance the theoretical bases of the discipline, whereas the bottom right corner shows that past experience with real-world HMIS applications is often useful in augmenting our methodological skills and improving our understanding of the art of successful HMIS implementation. In other words, developments in HMIS knowledge and practice are contingent on the advancement of theories relevant to HMIS on the one hand and on the development of methodologies relevant to health systems analysis on the other.

In this section, our discussion will focus mainly on the life cycle of the HMIS modeling process, the transformation of real-world problems into implementable HMIS solutions. Because of space limitation, we ask that the readers bear with us whenever there is a need to brush through a series of theoretical frameworks and

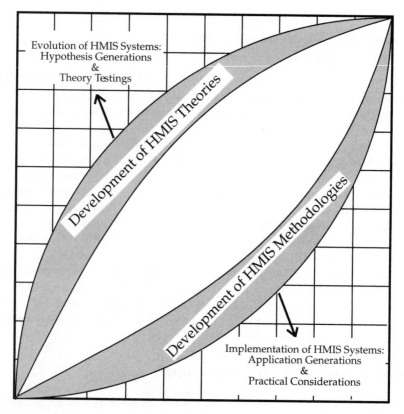

Evolution of HMIS Systems:
Hypothesis Generations
&
Theory Testings

Development of HMIS Theories

Development of HMIS Methodologies

Implementation of HMIS Systems:
Application Generations
&
Practical Considerations

Figure 2–1 Limits of Growth in Theories and Methodologies within the Health Management Information Systems (HMIS) Field

methodological ideas. We purposely keep the details aside in order to focus on the main issue, which is identifying the critical problem from an HMIS theoretical and methodological perspective, or viewing the organization through HMIS "sunglasses." Interested readers who wish to do further research into HMIS theories and methodologies will find the Notes at the end of each chapter a valuable resource.

A Theoretical Framework for HMIS

Very often, the first few questions that come to mind in discussing HMIS theoretical perspectives are the following: What is a "theory"? Is there a theory of health management information systems? What is the purpose of having such a theory? At this point, it is reasonable to conclude that numerous theories exist and that these theories pertain to different aspects of HMIS, as will be seen in the discussion throughout this chapter. Therefore, we may confidently assume at this point that a common HMIS theoretical perspective has yet to be established.

Conceptually, HMIS activities may be conceived of as a set of multifaceted goal-setting and goal-seeking processes. In Chapter 1, it was pointed out that the purpose of all HMIS activities is to improve health service delivery and, ultimately, health. This transformation of HMIS activities into health was seen as the product of a multistage interactive process: (1) health managerial interventions to set goals and objectives and to take actions for achieving these goals and objectives (corresponding to a conceptual world model); (2) health information processing functions to translate health managerial decisions and actions into health information needs and health management information flow processes (corresponding to a logical world model); and (3) synthesis of all actions (human or machine) into a complex but physically implementable health management information system model (corresponding to a physical world model). These processes are captured in a three-worldview model, which includes :

1. Conceptual worldview
2. Logical worldview
3. Physical worldview

Figure 2–2 shows a schematic representation of the three worldviews and their interrelatedness, which provides a simple theoretical model for the HMIS modeling process. The interaction of these "worldviews" resembles a natural train of thought to explain the "abstract-to-concrete" HMIS honing process. Part II (Chapters 3 through 6) explores the details embedded in each of these worldviews.

First, the "conceptual world," which is the closest representation of the "real world" (that is, the health service delivery system) with all of its complexity, is ill structured and apparently very abstract. It embodies the conceptual reality in which empirical problems and needs are observed and interpreted by humans. In other words, this is the point where empirical reality is gradually translated into mental concepts and articulated as human ideas. The representation of these problems and their interrelationships is necessarily still very complex as they are often the product of an interplay of many poorly defined "variables" that are frequently difficult, if not impossible, to measure (see Chapter 3). In fact, the meaning of these variables and their relationships is often subject to multiple interpretations depending on a manager's or analyst's view of the world. However, in this beginning step of HMIS modeling, elements of real-world problems and their interrelations have been removed from highly dynamic environments in which economic, political, legal, social, and technological variables are constantly evolving.

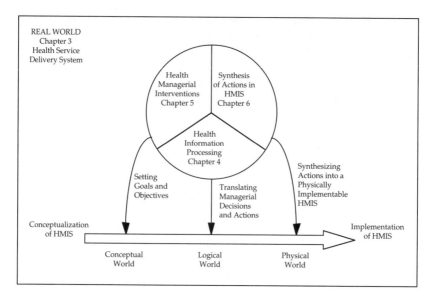

Figure 2–2 Three Schematic Worldviews of the Health Management Information Systems (HMIS) Process

---

The next transitional stage is the "logical world." The purpose here is to move from a mental representation of abstract ideas and concepts to a logically defined and formalized model. This is the stage where all of the stakeholders (including upper and middle health service management, analysts, and end-user representatives) attempt to go beyond working out an acceptable interpretation of the real-world problems: they move toward a model of the organizational situation. Therefore, the most "logical" HMIS model is expected to prevail in dealing with the perceived problems.

From an HMIS perspective, concepts and variables of the "conceptual" world have now become operationalized into a "logical" model, and the complex but observable phenomenon in question is now reduced to a paper-based information flow model (see Chapter 4). In short, these variables and their relations are now translated into corresponding data objects (i.e., entities) and linkages (i.e., relationships). The resulting models formed during these transformational stages are still many, each of which may be relatively abstract compared to the physically implementable and concrete models belonging to the final schematic world. Indeed, it is often the human elements of the HMIS modeling process (specifically, the participation of end-users in the HMIS design process) that will make this part of the modeling process extremely challenging for both management and analysts.

Last of all, the "physical" world, which is the ultimate reflection of real-world problems and solutions, is represented in the highly structured but limited information technology context. As noted, the objective here is to achieve a functional health information processing system. The immediate product is anticipated to be a computer-based "prototype" that adequately captures the "logical" design model. In fact, the HMIS design models produced in the "logical" world may or may not be totally transportable into the "physical" world: for example, it may be advisable to create a much more comprehensive and complex logical model but then to push for physical implementation of only parts and pieces of the overall model depending on the availability of organizational resources and technical expertise. This last schematic world is where machines and technology reign: it is the technical aspect of HMIS, which makes this portion of the model essentially a computer programming application (see Chapter 6).

Apparently, the distance between the "conceptual" and the "physical" world is separated by various stages of "logical" transformation. There is no reason to expect different analysts to choose the same route of "logical" transformation; this explains why essentially different types of HMIS solutions can and may be proposed, even for the same problem. This implies that there can be as many HMIS applications as there are conceptualizations and interpretations of the real-world phenomena to be modeled. More importantly, the roles and functions of health management in linking all three worldviews determine whether HMIS solutions may be achieved successfully (see Chapter 5).

These are specific theories, models, and paradigms that clearly belong to and are encapsulated within each of the three worldviews described. For instance, "systems theory," which is discussed in Chapter 3, is an ideal philosophy based on the conceptual world. The complexity of the conceptual variables and their interrelationships can often be viewed and analyzed by using systems thinking and a general systems approach.[4] It may be important for the reader to note that the conceptual worldview interfaces largely within the environmental context of HMIS. Similarly, "information theory," which is discussed in Chapter 4, will provide a formal basis for modeling activities within the "logical" world; these activities relate mostly to the design of a meaningful and valid information flow model based on an identified set of conceptual variables and their relations. Corresponding to the broad environmental context of the HMIS conceptual worldview, the logical worldview interfaces within the organizational context of HMIS. Lastly, there are numerous theories and methods that are relevant to the modeling process within the "physical" world. One such theory is the stages-of-growth (SOG) model,[5] which will be discussed in a later section. Here, we will only note that the physical worldview is largely applied within the technological context of HMIS. We turn now to devising a plan for choosing among HMIS development methods for actualizing the HMIS models in a physical sense (see also Chapter 6).

A Methodological Plan for HMIS

Although the three-world schematic view model provides a general theoretical perspective of how one goes about translating real-world problems into implementable HMIS solutions, it does not address the issue of choosing among alternative methodologies. However, by extending the theoretical model just described, the choice of methodologies becomes relatively straightforward. That is, different "worldviews," in which the problem-solution stage belongs, may be matched appropriately to different methodological approaches by using a contingency philosophy.

The range of HMIS tools, techniques, and methods that are highly appropriate for each of the three schematic worldviews is summarized in Table 2–1. Evidently, when the problem-solution is classified as belonging to the "conceptual" realm, HMIS techniques and methods that are available to analysts can include detailed observations, searching of records and sampling, case studies, telephone surveys, interviews, heuristics, intuitive judgments, rich pictures, and soft systems methodology (SSM). SSM methodology is well documented and illustrated in many sources.[6-8] The argument for classifying SSM as a methodology for the "conceptual worldview" is that it is concerned precisely with moving from the real world to the conceptual world. Checkland, who originated SSM, noted that the methodology is based on systems thinking.[9] He also advocated the use of rich pictures as a means of recording the unstructured problem situation encountered in the real world. Rich pictures are discussed and illustrated in the next section.

If the problem-solution set falls into the next category (i.e., the "logical" world), then techniques of data flow diagramming (DFD), entity-relationship (ER) modeling, and data dictionary (DD) will provide excellent tools for analysts to construct the "logical" design required. Chapters 4 and 6 discuss several of these and other tools and related techniques. The use of ER diagrams is discussed later; DD is discussed in Chapter 6. Compared to rich pictures, these tools and techniques are

Table 2–1 A Methodological Plan for HMIS Three-World Modeling Process

Schematic Worlds	HMIS Tools, Techniques, & Methodologies
Conceptual World	Sampling, Case Studies, Surveys, Heuristics, Intuitive Judgments, Rich Pictures, and Soft Systems Methodology (SSM)
Logical World	Data Flow Diagramming (DFD), Entity-Relationship (ER) Diagramming, Modeling, Data Dictionary (DD), and Multiview
Physical World	Client/Server Technologies, Graphical User Interfaces (GUI), Multimedia, Application System Shells, Visual Programming Languages, Computer-Aided Software Engineering (CASE), and Object-Oriented Programming

somewhat less user-friendly, but they do allow the problem(s) to be well specified since the process of diagramming is better structured (i.e., with the use of standardized symbols). Indeed, they serve a different purpose. There may be as many DFDs and ER diagrams generated for the same problem-solution set as there are analysts or HMIS design teams. Multiview, a methodology that brings together all of these various tools and techniques (see Chapter 6), also provides a good methodological approach for the transition between this stage and the next stage of modeling.

Finally, the physical implementation of a problem-solution set may be supported with the use of numerous tools, techniques, and methodologies. Advanced examples of such tools and techniques are client-server technologies, graphical user interfaces (GUI), application generators (AG), application system shells, object-orientation, UNIX, multimedia, visual programming languages, and automatic code generators. Computer-aided software engineering (CASE), prototyping, and structured programming approaches, many of which are discussed more fully in Chapter 6, are types of methodologies that are both applicable and relevant at this stage.

Altogether, analysts should be aware that they will have to rely heavily on their personal experience in choosing among and determining the most appropriate tools, techniques, and methodologies to use in each case. Nonetheless, it should be pointed out that a methodology that may be suitable for designing large-scale mainframe computer-based applications may be totally unsuitable for developing small-scale microcomputer-type applications; similarly, a technique that is suited to be used with conventional (e.g., Cobol, Pascal) programming may be poorly suited to be used with object-oriented (e.g., C++, Smalltalk) programming.

There are many other theoretical and methodological contributions that are also instrumental to the development of the HMIS field, and these will be highlighted and discussed throughout this and other chapters. At this point, we will discuss rich pictures, an innovative technique that has assisted many HMIS analysts in gaining a handle on defining "unstructured" and "fuzzy" problem situations.

The Rich Pictures

From a methodological viewpoint, the rich picture is a convenient tool for documenting themes or issues for an ill-defined problem situation, specifically for soft and fuzzy issues.[10] It is an innovative diagramming tool that does not subscribe to any standards (or a particular convention). It uses the language and terminology of the environment and shows how various pieces of a problem situation are perceived as relating to each other by those who developed the picture. The aim of the rich picture is to record the problem situation as a whole, that is, in a "holistic" fashion without limiting it to the agenda or biases of key actors and decision makers.

For instance, in a multicommunity health promotion project (MCHPP), several health promotion programs and activities are developed for community residents through the mobilization of an interdisciplinary team of health professionals such as physicians, administrators, social workers, public health officers, and nurses, as well as other volunteer participants. The efficient and effective sharing and use of information are therefore crucial to the success of MCHPP. To document the parties who share information, and to illustrate their perceived concerns and problems, we can use a rich picture.

Figure 2–3 is a rich picture of MCHPP, illustrating the various parties who share the information pool, as well as the various tasks and concerns encountered in this project. A rich picture is therefore a communication tool between the analysts and all potential users of the system. It is constructed in no particular order but may begin, for example, by writing the names of major subsystems in the center of the page; other symbols are then drawn to represent the people and entities within and outside these various subsystems. Arrows may be used to show relationships, and meaningful icons may be incorporated into the diagram to show special events (e.g., using a pair of scissors to show conflicts or "problems"). The ultimate objective of the rich pictures is therefore to flag or identify potential problems embedded in the system, to brainstorm for avenues to relieve these problems, and to relate the problems to potential HMIS solutions.

Entity-Relationship (ER) Diagrams

Entity-relationship (ER) diagrams are widely used for designing and managing databases to show relationships among entities, especially when there is a large number of instances (e.g., John Smith or other individuals wanting to get involved) in a specific entity (e.g., "Participant"). Focusing on "things" about which data must be recorded (entities or objects) and the relationships among them, ER diagrams provide a high-level architectural view of, say, a computer database. Moreover, they assist in the identification of various ways to divide the database into subject databases for use in distributed systems. If there are problems or if changes are to be made in the database, ER diagrams can offer great assistance in finding the problems and making the changes. ER diagrams are great tools for logical modeling of HMIS problem-solutions.

Figure 2–4 shows a simple ER diagram describing the key entities and relationships to be captured as information in a database for use by MCHPP. It shows the participants, health promotion supervisors, health promotion programs, and events as the major entities for which data are to be collected. As we can see, boxes are used in ER diagrams to show data items or entities, and lines to show relationships between data items and entities. One-to-one, one-to-many, or many-to-one relationships, as well as many-to-many relationships, can be indicated by

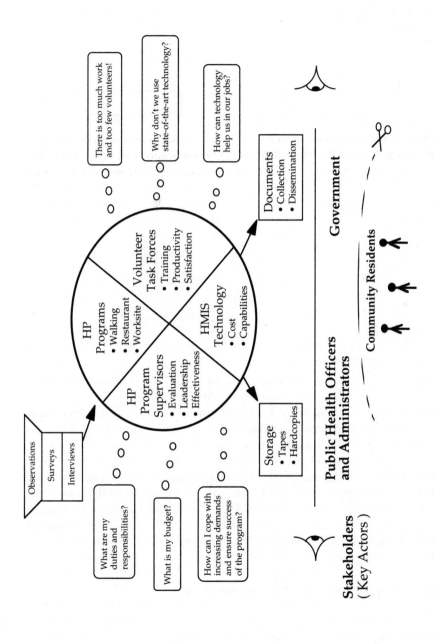

Figure 2–3 A Rich Picture of a Multicommunity Health Promotion (HP) Project (MCHPP)

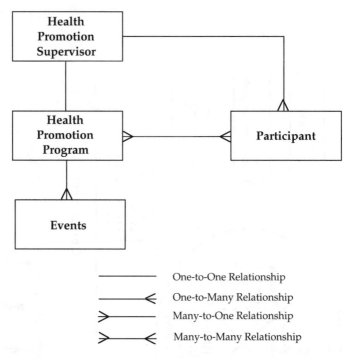

Figure 2–4 An Example of an Entity-Relationship (ER) Diagram for the Multicommunity Health Promotion Project (MCHPP)

using ER diagrams. See Figure 2–4 for illustrations of these relationships. It is interesting to note that less conventional forms of ER diagrams also allow either-or and other optional relationships to be depicted.

This completes our discussion of the first module of the HMIS framework, HMIS theories and methodologies. The next module to be discussed is HMIS technologies and applications. Unlike the slow development of HMIS theories and the somewhat limited changes in HMIS methodologies (since these methodologies can be consolidated into just a few themes),[11] advances in the domain of HMIS technologies and applications are exceedingly rapid and difficult to keep abreast of, even for experts in this field.

HMIS TECHNOLOGIES AND APPLICATIONS

The evolution of HMIS technologies and the range of existing and developing HMIS application profiles are featured in this section. Two taxonomies are presented: (1) a classification of HMIS technologies and (2) a classification of HMIS applications. Figure 2–5 details this module of the HMIS model.

Historically, progress in hardware, software, and user-interface technologies has emphasized the improvement of data processing (DP) technology. More recently, the emphasis has shifted to advancement in office automation (OA) and teleprocessing (TP) technology. This trend is indicated on the left vertical axis of Figure 2–5.

From a health management perspective, DP technology implies the automation of routine data processing to support administrative and patient care operations, for example, the processing of patient medical records and the computerization of managerial and financial accounting systems to solve everyday business problems of health organizations such as hospitals and health maintenance organizations

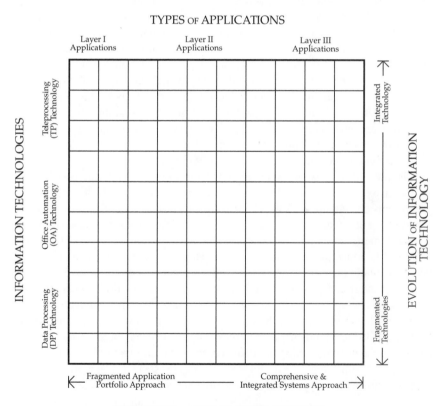

Figure 2–5 A Multiclassification of HMIS Technologies and Applications

(HMOs). In contrast, OA technology is concerned with the automation of office systems to reduce the expenditure of time and effort of knowledge workers including clerical staff, management, and professional workers. Common examples of OA applications include word processing, voice messaging systems, desktop publishing, and use of optical scanning devices. Lastly, TP technology is distinguishable from the other two technologies in its focus on the electronic processing of transmitted data, text, or voice information from one source to another. Examples include electronic messaging, faxes, teletext, and electronic data interchange (EDI) applications.

Although many health organizations and agencies have continued to maintain separate islands of DP, OA, and TP technologies, McFarlan et al. have suggested that the gaps among these technological islands are closing.[12] Among the reasons they cited for this trend were (1) the large capital outlay that is normally required for the separate technologies to operate in parallel, indicating that there is a potential for economies of scale to be achieved through integration; (2) the scarcity of available technical expertise, skills, and resources, suggesting that the same pool of technologists may be used to solve similar problems encountered in projects related to any one of the technologies; and (3) the limitations of products based only on a single technology, implying that the physical integration of two or more of these technologies may be deemed desirable to end-users trying to achieve a greater payoff. In addition, the push for health service integration in responding efficiently and effectively to today's patient expectations and social needs is yet another driving force behind such a trend. In fact, the trend of technological integration is evident in many future-oriented HMIS applications, including artificial intelligence (AI) and expert systems (ES) applications in health care (see Chapter 8). Other examples include telecommunication-oriented applications,[13] health group decision support systems (GDSS), and other integrated office products (see Chapter 9). Future technology is therefore predicted to increase in capacity as well as merge the functionality of several previously separate sets of functions (see Chapter 14). Thus, the move from a fragmentation of technologies to an integration of technologies is depicted on the right vertical axis of Figure 2–5. We now move to a suggested classification of the wide spectrum of HMIS applications.

Previous attempts made in classifying the range of HMIS applications were limited by the technology at the time.[14-16] Essentially, these classifications described HMIS developments as moving along three levels of sophistication according to the degree of integration and communication capabilities built into the systems: (1) individual stand-alone systems addressing the specific needs of single departments or specialties, for example, laboratory systems, pharmacy systems, and accounting systems (Class A); (2) hospital information systems (HIS), which cross departmental and specialty boundaries but are based institutionally; these applications are administratively oriented and have a communication network superimposed on them, for example, test order transmission systems and integrated ancillary applications (Class B); and (3) HMIS applications oriented toward patient medical recording and the computer linkage of patient information; such applications may also have communication networks superimposed on them, for example, fully integrated ancillary systems and patient database linkage systems (Class C). The major difference between Classes B and C is in their structures: that is, Class B uses administrative or fiscal systems as a base, whereas Class C uses the patient medical record as a base.

It is safe to claim that almost all hospitals today are beyond the stage of Class A sophistication since these applications are only useful for solving subsystem level business problems in a health service organization. The bulk of these systems include financial and managerial accounting and "stand-alone" clinical information systems, which to a large extent collect, store, and manipulate the hospital financial data, drug inventory, or laboratory test results as subsystem applications. There is a need to maintain these systems separately, and duplication of patient data is also necessary. Any linkages that are required between the subsystem data sets and applications must be made manually. These traditional applications are of little interest to us today because of their inadequate designs and poor user interface.

Class B applications may be further subdivided into two levels: Level 1 sophistication, which includes an admission-discharge-transfer (ADT) subsystem and a data collection message switching subsystem; and Level 2 sophistication, which maintains some archival structure for retaining the patient medical record of orders, results, and progress notes in addition to all the capabilities of a Level 1 sophistication. On the one hand, the HIS implementation scenario for Level 1 involves on-line terminals to be placed throughout the health service organization for order entry, communication of the order, and batch processing of captured charges (i.e., the system is cleared of the charges daily and the only information that is kept permanently for patients is their demographic or census data, which are maintained by the ADT system). On the other hand, the scenario for Level 2 will provide the capability of solving specialized problems related to one or more clinical units and departments of the health service organization in addition to all Level 1 capabilities; Level 2 therefore allows medical record storage and retrieval, computer-assisted clinical decision making, computer-assisted medical instrumentation, and other clinical service applications such as research and patient education. As such, Class B, Level 2 systems can generate medication schedules, nursing care plans, and cumulative laboratory results and have the potential to provide the data linkages necessary for case-mix determination. Class C sophistication can perform just about the same functions and has the same capabilities and potential as Class B, Level 2, although an integrated database approach is taken. Many HMIS implementations in health organizations today are at the various stages of sophistication just described, depending on the technological leadership that is advocated by these organizations.

In this book, the acronym HMIS is used rather than HIS to move away from the narrow view of hospital-based systems as implied in the Ball-Boyle classification described.[17] Our suggested taxonomy, which is depicted in the top horizontal axis in Figure 2–5, is based on current thinking[18] and corresponds to the six stages of Nolan's Stages-of-Growth (SOG) model, presented next.

Nolan's Stages-of-Growth (SOG) Theory

Nolan's Stages-of-Growth (SOG) theory, which has evolved over the decades and has been widely discussed in mainstream MIS literature, provides a way to explain and to predict the historic growth patterns of computer applications within the health service industry.[19] According to the latest version of the theory,[20] there are six stages and five shifts in a typical cycle for an organizational growth in data processing maturity (see Figure 2–6).

1. Stage I (Initiation)
2. Stage II (Contagion)
3. Stage III (Control)
4. Stage IV (Integration)
5. Stage V (Data administration)
6. Stage VI (Maturity)

The computer technology is introduced into the organization mostly for transaction processing purposes during Stage I. Although the cost of installation may be high, there is little need for management to exercise tight control as the cost of the computing operation is kept relatively low at this stage by the restricted range of applications. Stage II sees computer use going beyond transaction processing to more sophisticated applications as more and more users become familiar with the technology. There is a need to increase resources that result from growing costs and growing enthusiasm for all types of applications. Given that not all users will have experience with data processing applications, a specialist is usually required to maintain the rate of growth, and management begins to feel the pressure to tighten up control on technological expenditures.

Budgetary restraints force management to institute strict control and set efficiency standards for systems development during Stage III. An environment of management information planning and control is set up. Growth levels off and fewer applications are being developed as management begins consolidating the use of computing technology. End-users are also made accountable for using the technology in a cost-effective manner. In Stage IV there is continued proliferation

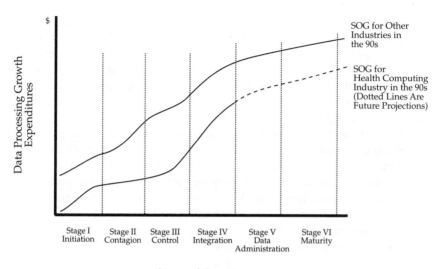

Figure 2–6 The Stages-of-Growth (SOG) Theory As Applied to the Health Computing and Other Industries

of applications but in a more structured and organized fashion; for example, on-line databases are used to upgrade existing systems. Planning and control are formalized and the focus is on systems integration. Duplication of systems is eliminated and fragmentary applications are combined.

The concept of information as a corporate resource begins to sink into the organizational mind-set during Stage V. Data administration functions are created to manage and control organizational data resources. This stage of growth also takes into account that appropriate management control exists to ensure that systems are effectively developed. Organizations reaching Stage VI will have technology and management processes integrated into an effective functional entity. Systems personnel and end-users have joint responsibility for data resources. However, it is the CEO or the chief information officer (CIO) who will take the leadership in strategic data planning and information resource management (see Chapter 11).

For the health service delivery industry, the growth patterns of computer applications are believed to have been curtailed during Stages II to III by the lack of funding and technological expertise faced by many health service organizations. Consequently, many hospitals and other health service organizations are seen to limit their growth to Stages I and II for a long time, with few applications that go beyond the administrative and financial systems. In recent years, there has been renewed technological growth in the health service sector as hospitals and other health service organizations are finding new ways of funding their HMIS projects. This has led them through a repeat of Stage II and into Stage III. The availability of on-line database technology and the affordability of powerful microcomputer workstations have also provided greater incentives for growth in HMIS applications in the health service industry. Since this resumption of growth, several health service organizations are today experiencing the pressure to begin consolidating and managing that growth (Stage IV), as shown in Figure 2–6.

The SOG theory has provided many hospital and health service executives with a general framework for HMIS strategic planning. With the move to cheaper telecommunication services and the demand for patient data linkages, many health service delivery organizations are entering the growth stage of integration (Stage IV) and data administration (Stage V). Health service organizations that did not pay particular attention to their HMIS potential in the last several years must begin to take a good look at what other organizations with experience in HMIS are doing if they are to keep up with the industry trend.

A New Taxonomy of HMIS Applications

Parallel to SOG, we see three different layers in our new taxonomy of HMIS: (1) Layer I applications, which emphasize stand-alone financial-oriented systems, simply correspond to the traditional islands of technology in an isolated fashion (Stages I and II); (2) Layer II applications, which emphasize networked patient-oriented systems, correspond to the current trend in data sharing systems in which a mix of technologies is used in a connected fashion (Stages III and IV); and (3) Layer III applications, which emphasize future-oriented systems, correspond to truly integrated technological products designed primarily for gaining professional image, better market share, and service excellence (Stages V and VI).

Table 2–2 provides examples of various HMIS applications that relate to each layer and differentiate among the characteristics of the application layers. Layer I applications are limited by the lack of connectivity to each other. They include Class A hospital information systems (HIS) and other related administrative and clinical applications. Layer II applications do allow data sharing among systems but are not yet truly integrated.[21,22] HIS of Class B Level 1 are therefore part of these applications. Layer III applications are truly integrated systems and include, for example, Class B, Level 2 HIS and Class C HIS multihospital case management (CM) information systems; clinical management information systems (CMIS); community information systems (CIS) with an integrated health database management systems (HDBMS) component; integrated health-oriented telecommunication systems; and integrated decision support and expert systems. Several of these systems are introduced briefly in the next section and all of them will be discussed more fully throughout the book.

Table 2–2 Examples of HMIS with Respect to the Layered Classification Scheme

Classification	Features	Examples
Layer I Application	Stand-Alone Financial-Oriented Systems	Class A HIS: Hospital Accounting Systems, General Ledger, Drug Inventory System
Layer II Application	Networked Patient-Oriented Systems	Class B HIS: Admission-Discharge-Transfer (ADT), Drug Order Entry Systems, Patient Record Systems
Layer III Application	Integrated Future-Oriented Systems	Class C HIS: Integrated Patient Records, Case Management Systems, Integrated Health Database Systems, Integrated Decision Support and Expert Systems

On the basis of our analysis, therefore, it is evident that the application maturity for the different layers of HMIS applications moves through several stages, beginning normally with a fragmented application portfolio (i.e., Stage I of the SOG model discussed earlier) and ending with a more comprehensive and integrated one (Stages II through VI). This is depicted on the bottom horizontal axis in Figure 2–5. Because applications of an integrated nature will replace traditional ones in the years ahead, the significance of exposing the readers to case management systems (CMS) at this time cannot be overstressed as they must begin to think beyond the use of HMIS applications in traditional hospital settings. Admittedly, these systems are inevitably the hospital information systems of the future since they provide flexible, efficient, and effective management of systemwide case-based data flow. In designing future HMIS applications then, it is important to note that the scope and complexity of integrated information systems requirements are contingent on the scope and complexity of the various subsystems of the organized health service delivery system for which it is intended. As a consideration, HMIS planning today must take into account the growth of managed care in the health service industry. This is reflected in the growing need for complex integrated clinical and financial systems and that for greater information sharing among multiple health service organizations. Therefore, the future generation of HMIS applications will not only be expected to have the capacity to allow for major changes in the data reporting structure, but to have enough built-in flexibility to accommodate any future expansions. CMS and related types of applications are discussed in greater details in Chapters 9, 11, and 14.

Even so, there is the need to balance the tendency (especially among practitioners) to overemphasize issues of HMIS technologies and state-of-the-art HMIS applications. As noted in Chapter 1, particular attention should be paid by health administrators to the more critical human and social aspects of HMIS implementation. Since the technical competence of health administrators depends on the number of years of experience with computing technologies, any level of more elaborate technical competence than basic word processing and analytic spreadsheeting skills will be difficult, if not impossible, to achieve during their first few years on the job (unless, of course, they have been previously trained). It is therefore advisable that health administrators focus on developing those technology management skills that will be absolutely essential for them to oversee an HMIS project from beginning to end.

Classes of HMIS Applications

In this section we highlight a number of HMIS applications to provide an overview of the wide range of uses and the variety of problem contexts in which the applications of HMIS solutions have been considered meaningful and significant. Detailed descriptions of these systems are available in the various chapters as referenced. The few HMIS applications highlighted are

- Hospital information systems (HIS)
- Expert systems (ES)
- Case management systems (CMS)
- Health database management systems (HDBMS)
- Group decision support systems (GDSS)

Hospital information systems are among the oldest types of HMIS applications (see Chapters 4 and 7). They have always been considered an integral part of medical informatics. According to Orthner, HIS have traditionally been oriented to the administrative and business tasks of a hospital using large centralized mainframe computers.[23] Over the years, these systems have begun to shift their emphasis to providing integrative medical and clinical information support services through the use of a variety of computers that are linked with high-speed communication networks.

Expert systems are knowledge-based computer systems whose purpose is to provide expert consultations to end-users for solving specialized and complex problems (see Chapter 8).[24] Reeves et al. discuss a health care benefits adviser system that provides employees of the George Washington University with the expert consultation that they need to choose among alternatively managed care provider services.[25] Tan et al. discuss the use of EMPOWER/Canadian Health software as an ES for the computer-assisted planning and evaluation of community health programs.[26]

Case management systems are a family of information systems that can be regarded as the HIS of the future. They have evolved in recent years as a result of the growing trend of integrating health service delivery both vertically and horizontally (see Chapter 9). Vertical integration concerns the coordination of clinical care for a given person across providers or provider organizations, whereas horizontal integration has to do with the linking of institutions providing essentially the same type of clinical services such as a multihospital organization. Case-mix (C-M) applications are especially important for serving today's health care environment as they provide the flexibility and capability of integrating clinical and financial data. CMS include case management (CM) information systems, case-mix information systems (C-MIS) and clinical management information systems (CMIS); they are discussed in Chapters 9 and 11. For the next generation of CMS, electronic linkages of clinical and financial data that join patient and providers across "the continuum of care from the patient's home to the work setting, to many possible sites of contact within the delivery system" must be developed.[27]

On-line health database management systems technology has been used extensively in health care (see Chapter 11). HDBMS refers to a depository of logically organized facts and figures with querying facilities. A typical example is the automated patient medical record system. Whether the modality used to deliver health service is a solo practice, a group practice, a hospital, a freestanding health research center, an HMO, or another organized health delivery mechanism, HDBMS allows the organized storage of related patient and provider data into fields, records, and files.[28] COSTAR,[29] which is a computer-based record system for ambulatory patients served by the prepaid Harvard Community Health Plan (HCHP), is an example of HDBMS.

Group decision support systems involve the use of an interactive, computer-based system that facilitates the search for solutions to semistructured and unstructured problems shared by a group of decision makers. Chapter 14 provides a discussion of the application of GDSS technology for health service delivery settings.

HMIS ADMINISTRATION AND IMPACTS

In this chapter, we have so far covered HMIS theories and methodologies and HMIS technologies and applications. However, even if the management of a health organization all share the same vision and level of conceptualization of "the perfect" HMIS for their organization and know exactly what kinds of technology should be employed, and how and when they should be employed, real-life experience has taught us that there will very likely be problems involved in the implementation and operation of the HMIS. Why?

In practice, the blame usually lies in the management's neglect of HMIS administration and impact, which are the main concerns of this section. Here, we will first take a look at the process of innovation diffusion, next at the core areas of HMIS administration and impact, and finally at achieving effective HMIS administration and the criteria to be considered in assessing HMIS impact. In terms of innovation diffusion, we will take a brief look at one of the landmark contributions to HMIS theory, one that is closely related to the S-curve phenomenon of the SOG theory discussed previously: Rogers's innovation diffusion theory.

Rogers's Innovation Diffusion Theory

As with any new discipline, the rate and patterns of growth are expected to follow the well-known S curve of innovation diffusion.[30] The innovation diffusion growth curve typifies the stages of adoption of knowledge and practice in a new field. For example, the teacher who adopts a new teaching-learning method on the basis of his or her own recognition and awareness of the desirability of this method will adopt it before others in the community. The first adopters of the new model are the innovators. Others who follow will then become early adopters. They will not have access to all of the information that the innovators have about the new model. Therefore, early adopters tend to regard innovators as experts and will readily adopt the practices that these experts recommend. An additional link to this chain is classified as the early majority, who are then followed by late adopters. Figure 2–7 shows the diffusion curve that is likely for growth in HMIS knowledge and practice.

As shown in Figure 2–7, we are among the so-called early majority for the diffusion of HMIS knowledge and practice. This implies that the potential for an expansion of HMIS knowledge and practice over the next several years is projected to be especially high. Therefore, the time appears right for us to begin consolidating our past knowledge and experience in the area and to identify gaps for future research and development. The purpose of this work is to do just that.

Core Areas of HMIS Administration and Impacts

Previously, we noted that the success of the HMIS implementation process largely depends on the level of support from the senior management in those key administrative and managerial aspects of HMIS projects (Chapter 1). Here, we identify four subareas where special attention must be given to achieve successful HMIS implementations vis-à-vis managerial goals and objectives: (1) strategic information systems (SIS) planning, (2) information technology (IT) management, (3) impact on individual motivation and other group behavior, and (4) impact on organizational change. The importance of these four subareas in the HMIS model is reflected in their being placed graphically at the central core of the HMIS model as depicted in Figure 2–8. We will discuss the first two subareas under HMIS administration and the last two under HMIS impacts.

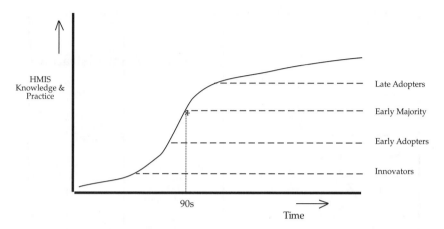

Figure 2–7 The Diffusion of Health Management Information Systems (HMIS) Knowledge and Practice

Effective HMIS Administration

One of the most critical aspects of understanding HMIS administration (i.e., HMIS planning and management) is the realization that goals of senior management and information system people within a health service organization or agency must be strategically aligned (Chapter 10). Essentially, this implies that the mission of the information systems group must relate fully to the core vision of the health service organization, and vice versa. To accomplish this, strategic information system (SIS) planning and information technology (IT) management must be properly and effectively implemented.

Over the years, the trend of HMIS planning and management was characterized by a continual shifting of responsibilities and power from systems professionals to end-users. More recently, this trend has attracted the attention of top management because of the growing acceptance of the notion that information is a corporate resource and should be properly managed just like any other resources such as land, labor, or capital.[31,32] Traditional approaches to IS planning begin by designing a blueprint for an entire MIS and then setting out to implement it. Problems that have been attributed to this approach include the risk involved with new technology, the costly financial outlays, and the resulting problems of systems management, which apparently are not insignificant.[33]

More recent approaches call for limiting this strategy to the initial phase of data analysis and then to the design of a systemwide management information technology infrastructure (MITI).[34,35] An assessment of the environment should also precede the formulation of a strategic information system plan (SISP). In general, the

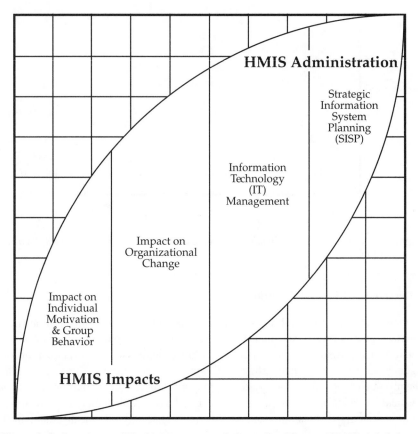

Figure 2–8 Core Areas of Health Management Information Systems (HMIS) Administration and Impacts

SISP entails an evolutionary development of the HMIS infrastructure, which is guided primarily by a systemwide data analysis to support all aspects of modeling the organizational information needs. Experience has taught us that no single approach is best; rather a mix of approaches is often suited to most organizations since the various approaches deal with different aspects of planning (see Chapter 10).

Successful HMIS implementation requires not only discrete SISP but also effective IT management. Briefly, IT management from a health management perspective is the management of the entire HMIS capacity of an organization. Ideally, IT managers would want to ensure that technology and information resources are adapted to meet the needs of organizational functions and activities best

(Chapter 11). There are two kinds of transitions taking place today that are defining a broader scope for IT management. First, the increased complexity of the health care environment and the rapid rate of change in the capabilities of information technology will make the process of IT management increasingly more complex and difficult. It is known, for example, that the knowledge and skills pertaining to the management of routine data processing of even an experienced DP manager cannot be easily transferred to cater to the growing need for the management of OA and TP technologies because of the different types of workers and computing facilities that are involved in these other technologies. Second, the need to fit information systems culture with organizational culture and the need to align information systems management philosophy with organizational philosophy demand new responsibility and executive supervision of technological integration projects (see Chapters 5, 10, and 11). The need for senior management level involvement in IT management is best reflected in changes of IS activities occurring within technologically leading health service organizations, including, for example, the rapid merger of mainframes and microcomputing platforms, the implementation of CMS and case-mix applications[36] through the integration of clinical and financial databases, and the production of integrated multimedia technology products. McNurlin and Sprague provide an excellent source of reference for discussing IT management in practice that can easily be adapted to today's health service organizations.[37]

Assessing HMIS Impacts

The last aspects of the HMIS model to be discussed are the impacts of HMIS implementation on individual motivation, group behavior, and organizational change (see Chapter 12). The primary objectives of HMIS implementation are to reduce operational costs and to improve the quality of patient care (see Chapter 13). After all, the promise of computerization is to make information handling more efficient by reducing the amount of costly errors and unnecessary delays, as well as to project an improved professional image by relieving health care workers of tedious reporting activities so they can concentrate on patient care.

At the individual level, it is critical to know whether the introduction of an HMIS will improve the productivity and decision-making effectiveness of the end-user. For example, it can be argued that traveling health executives who are equipped with a cellular phone and an automated directory of all potential contacts on a portable or hand-held computer will be better able to perform their duties irrespective of their whereabouts. At the work group level, HMIS implementation requires the sharing of data and the coordination of activities among different individuals belonging to the same work group.

An efficient computerized patient medical record system (see Chapter 1) for use in an organized health care system, for example, is one that can contain and integrate all of the information regarding the patient and keep track of the various stages of patient treatment at any time so as to accommodate the schedules of clinicians and specialists who may want to see the patient. An integrated database system that is linked to the different subsystems of the organized service delivery system with on-line updating capabilities that are supported cooperatively by all the clinical subsystem units can be used to achieve this level of data timeliness and integration. Therefore, the immediate step required to advance the current state of IS in health service organizations is to take a broad-based approach to designing the organizational HMIS; such a developmental effort will necessarily encompass the cooperation of analysts, technicians, managers, and users (including all associated clinicians and health professionals).

Any HMIS implementation will produce some form of organizational change— change in the organizational structure, change in the level of computing competence required of current and new employees, and change in the information flow and reporting behavior of the organization. On this note, managing change is fast becoming one of the most critical tasks of health managers today. Closely related to this concept of managing change is total quality management (TQM), a process for ensuring that all HMIS implementations will be guided by the goals of user empowerment and high-quality service performance. Common criteria that may be used for judging quality in the context of TQM for HMIS include (1) leadership, (2) information and analysis, (3) planning, (4) human resource utilization, (5) quality assurance of HMIS products and services, (6) quality of results, and (7) customer satisfaction.[38]

In summary, to ensure that high performance is achieved or maintained in the application of HMIS within health service organizations, the chief information officer (CIO) or health information systems manager must have the appropriate knowledge, skills, and attitudes to address the many issues of HMIS implementation discussed here.

MEASURING PROGRESS IN THE HMIS FIELD

After discussing the theoretical, methodological, technological, and administrative aspects of HMIS, we have largely completed our detailed introduction to the framework for the study of HMIS. However, what we have discussed so far focuses on either the past or the present: we have yet to devise a "guidepost" for future HMIS developments. In this section, our attempt is to devise such a guidepost to measure future progress in the HMIS field.

From our previous knowledge and experience with many areas of applied and social sciences, it may be argued that progress in a field such as HMIS can and has to originate from three primary sources: (1) the development of meaningful theories and theoretical models within the field, including attempts to import well-established theoretical perspectives from other reference disciplines; (2) the application of sound methodological traditions and approaches that are based on cumulative real-life experience and empirical research; and (3) the continued demonstration of the practical benefits and utility of the HMIS field to individuals, organizations, and society. In short, progress in the HMIS field is dependent on contributions that have theoretical significance, methodological soundness, and practical utility.[39] In other words, progress in the HMIS field depends on continued developments in the three facets of HMIS identified in our model.

With regard to theoretical significance, the interdisciplinary aspect of HMIS runs the risk of encouraging scholarship and research in areas that are sometimes considered confusing, fragmentary, and marginal to well-established disciplines. Apart from the need to rely heavily on other disciplines for theoretical conceptualization and clarification, there is also the difficulty of attracting our best minds to work in an area that is devoid of its own theories and where problems are still far from being defined.[40] For example, some areas of current research in HMIS that must rely on theories from other reference fields are (1) the study of end-user behavior in computer-based HMIS interaction[41] (using behavioral science as a reference discipline), (2) the evaluation of HMIS benefits[42] (using economics as a reference discipline), (3) the development of HMIS technologies[43] (using computer science as a reference discipline), and (4) the modeling of HMIS applications[44] (using management science as a reference discipline).

Although it has been pointed out that there is nothing wrong with, and no restriction to, borrowing theories from reference disciplines,[45] it may be argued that true progress in a discipline begins "at home": that is, once we have adopted a theoretical perspective in HMIS, we can clearly endorse and define for ourselves those issues that deserve our utmost attention and those that do not. This is indeed one of those important areas where more attention should be given to broadening the appeal of HMIS as an intellectual discipline. Perhaps, all that is needed at this point is a simple theoretical model. Ultimately, it is hoped that a "theory" of HMIS will be able to spark greater excitement and unity among researchers in this area, to provide guidance to continuing growth in the field, and to inspire future theoreticians to add to our knowledge and understanding of HMIS.

A second but equally fundamental problem in this rapidly growing but eclectic field is the need to consolidate the large number of methodologies that have been advocated for HMIS designs and development. As Zani remarked with respect to early management information systems (MIS) designs: "No tool has ever aroused so much hope at its creation as MIS, and no tool has proved so disappointing in use."[46] The same comment is also true of HMIS, especially in the application of HMIS methodologies. Experience in the field has demonstrated that many consultants and vendors have failed to dissolve the rising problems of cost-effectiveness and quality in health service delivery in spite of their many attempts to provide efficient and user-friendly HMIS solutions. Indeed, part of the reason why HMIS practitioners have not been able to satisfy user health information needs may be that they are overly concerned with the tools, techniques, and methodologies that are available rather than with the nature of management decisions and how these tools, techniques, and methodologies may be appropriately applied to support the making of those decisions. In this regard, much research is still needed to unveil the matching of ideal methodological approaches to different types of HMIS problems. For now, we may be able to get by with a simple "methodological plan." It is hoped, therefore, that the publication of this work will inspire serious students in HMIS to begin conceptualizing the meaning of HMIS problem-solution sets to HMIS methodological approaches.

The current lack of theoretical focus and methodological know-how in HMIS explains why progress in this field has been relatively slow over the years; ideally our suggested changes will turn this around. But what about the practical utility of the area? One of the reasons why HMIS is being taught in the colleges and universities is its very strong practical appeal. To maintain this orientation, HMIS theories and frameworks must pay special attention to real-world activities and their formulation must not be mere abstract or axiomatic exercises. Consequently, the entirety of the HMIS field must be conceptualized and the various pieces of the HMIS puzzle must be related to practice. This book uses numerous examples and mini cases that are abstracted from real-life instances whenever possible and appropriate.

Taking into account all of the issues raised here, the theoretical models and frameworks discussed in this book are simply intended to serve as starting points to allow readers to contribute their own thoughts to the advancement of theory, methods, and applications in this field.

CONCLUSION

Our analysis of the HMIS field reveals that it is rapidly growing and has much potential for new contributions. Recent research in HMIS is reported at conferences, and results or findings are published in peer-reviewed journals, government publications, and other information sources (e.g., statistical reports and trade magazines). These additional information sources are particularly useful for those who are interested in a more specialized area of the field. Readers are therefore

TYPES OF APPLICATIONS

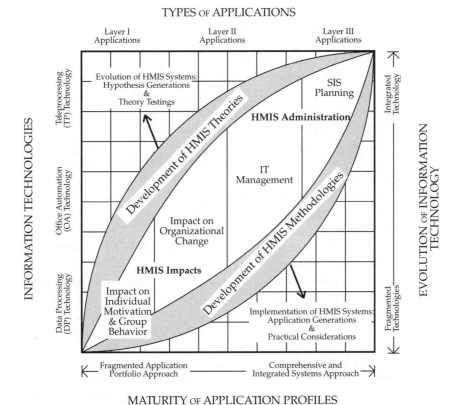

MATURITY OF APPLICATION PROFILES

Figure 2–9 The Health Management Information Systems (HMIS) Framework

encouraged to search for additional readings and sources of materials other than those provided by the references cited in this book.

Figure 2–9 gives a diagrammatic representation of the framework for the overall HMIS field. It summarizes our discussion of how various facets of HMIS contribute to its current development and composition. As we can see, the framework for the overall HMIS field is composed of the different modules discussed in great detail in this chapter.

It is now the responsibility of the reader to take the next step in advancing the HMIS field. Chapter 14, the last chapter, attempts to help readers accomplish this mission by making them more aware of future developments. It is therefore hoped that this book will help spark excitement in this area, provide guidance for continued research interest in this territory, and inspire significant future contributions to theories, methods, and applications in the HMIS field.

CHAPTER QUESTIONS

1. Provide an example of a theoretical model in the field of administrative and behavioral science that would be useful to explain the "black box" of the HMIS modeling process.
2. What is the role of theory and methodology with respect to the practice of HMIS? State specifically how the HMIS field is tied to practice and health managerial functions.
3. What are the strengths and weaknesses of the classification of HMIS applications as advocated in this chapter? Can you think of an alternative classification scheme?
4. What do you see as the possible diffusion patterns of HMIS knowledge and practice in the next 10 years?
5. What are the values and benefits of using a model such as the HMIS framework to structure the design and development of an HMIS for a health service organization?

MINI CASE 2
HEALTHLINK SERVICES FROM CAREPLAN, INC.

Telemedicine is a growing phenomenon in many organized health service delivery systems. Careplan, Inc. is experimenting with a prototype telephone-based "patient decision support" referral service known as Healthlink that will be available to all eligible subscribers who are insured patients. Healthlink is an innovative information support and referral service system that allows subscribing patients to phone in to ask specific questions about their health or to gain access to clinical consultations and referrals.

Each time a patient initiates a call, the system requests specific information to identify that the call is a valid one. Through the use of a touch-tone signal, the system will monitor and direct all calls to appropriate points of contact. For instance, if the customer is new to the system and has never been registered in it, the system will direct the customer to a recorded message on how a potential patient may subscribe to the service. For subscribers to the service, Healthlink allows health-related questions to be answered by a general nurse, who will refer the problem to a supervisory nurse or a general physician if necessary. All consultations with patients are noted interactively through the use of a computerized patient record and billing system.

The regular insurance payments made by the patients or their employers will cover all consultations that do not result in physical examinations, diagnostic tests, or surgical operations. If the patient referral results in such activities, a percentage of the fees will be borne proportionally by the insured, employer, or the government, depending on the nature of the contract. Patients who have no history of such claims will continue to enjoy a low premium rate, which is set biannually.

MINI CASE QUESTIONS

You are an MHA (Masters in Health Administration) graduate who has been exposed to concepts of managed care and health management information systems. Careplan, Inc. decided to ask you for an interview as a consultant to this project. During the interview, the following questions were raised:

1. Where would you put Healthlink in the context of the HMIS model described in this chapter? How is the idea related to each module of the model?
2. Do you think Healthlink is an innovative idea? If so, how can you ensure successful diffusion of this idea in today's health service delivery industry?
3. What are the informational, technological, and managerial implications of Healthlink?

Discuss briefly how you would address each of these questions, drawing from your training and experience and knowing that management of Careplan, Inc. is ready to give you the contract if you can convince them of your competency.

CHAPTER REVIEW

Just as there has been little success reported among educators in the design and development of a general MIS curriculum, there appears to be a similar, perhaps even greater, problem with the design and development of a general HMIS curriculum. This is because HMIS, like MIS, is an eclectic field built upon concepts drawn from many core disciplines. Moreover, HMIS, unlike MIS, has received somewhat less attention from educators and researchers because of its relatively shorter history as an academic discipline.

The slow advancement of theories relevant to HMIS and the unorganized development of methodologies relevant to health information system development have resulted in limited progress for HMIS knowledge and practice. The rate of growth will follow the criteria defining innovation diffusion. Accordingly, this rate is expected to accelerate in the next several years. To this end, two of the most important items to include in an agenda for ensuring the future growth of HMIS as an intellectual discipline are the need to pay attention to theory and the need to consolidate the large number of methodologies in this field. In this chapter, a simple theoretical model and a methodological plan of HMIS were used to provide a starting point for discussion.

The integration and cumulation of HMIS theories, methods, and applications discussed throughout this book are provided in the form of a general HMIS model. HMIS is portrayed from an integrated perspective by subdividing the field into three important domains: (1) HMIS theories and methodologies, (2) HMIS technologies and applications, and (3) HMIS administration and impacts. Directions for developing a cumulative tradition in HMIS are discussed in terms of this framework.

NOTES

1. H.J. Leavitt and T.L. Whisler, Management in the 1980s, *Harvard Business Review* 36, no. 6 (1958): 41–48.

2. R.L. Nolan, et al., Computers and Hospital Management: Prescription for Survival, *Journal of Medical Systems* 1, no. 2 (1977): 187–203.

3. J.K.H. Tan, Graduate Education in Health Information Systems: Having All Your Eggs in One Basket, *Journal of Health Administration Education* 11, no. 1 (1993): 27–55.

4. Ibid.

5. R. Dubin, *Theory Building* (New York: Free Press, 1969).

6. P.B. Checkland, *Systems Thinking, Systems Practice* (New York: John Wiley & Sons, Inc., 1981).

7. M.J.S. Harry, *Information and Management Systems* (London: Pitman Publishing, 1990).

8. D.F. Avison and G. Fitzgerald, *Information Systems Development: Methodologies, Techniques, and Tools* (Oxford: Blackwell Scientific Publications, 1988).

9. Checkland, *Systems Thinking*.

10. Harry, *Information and Management Systems*.

11. Avison and Fitzgerald, *Information Systems Development*.

12. F.W. McFarlan, et al., The Information Archipelago—Maps and Bridges, *Harvard Business Review* 60, no. 5 (1982): 109–119,

13. M.D. McDonald and H.L. Blum, *Health in the Information Age: The Emergence of Health Oriented Telecommunication Applications* (Berkeley, Calif: Environmental Science and Policy Institute, 1992).

14. M.J. Ball, Computers: Prescription for Hospital Ills, *Datamation* 21, no. 9 (1975): 50–51.

15. M.J. Ball and T.M. Boyle, Hospital Information Systems: Past, Present, and Future, *Hospital Financial Management* 34 (1980): 12–24.

16. C.J. Austin and W.J. Harvey, Hospital Information Systems: A Management Perspective, *Frontiers of Health Services Management* 2, no. 2 (1985): 3–36.

17. Ball and Boyle, Hospital Information Systems, 12–24.

18. D.J. Ferrand, et al., An Integrated Analytic Framework for Evaluation of Hospital Information Systems Planning, *Medical Care Review* 50, no. 3 (1993): 327–366.

19. Nolan et al. Computers and Hospital Management, 187–203.

20. R.L. Nolan, Managing the Crisis in Data Processing, *Harvard Business Review* (March–April 1979): 115–126.

21. J.K.H. Tan, et al., Utilization Care Plan and Effective Patient Data Management, *Hospital and Health Services Administration* 38, no. 1 (1993): 81–99.

22. L.K. Lichtig, *Hospital Information Systems for Case Mix Management* (Albany, NY: Delmar Publishers, 1986).

23. H.F. Orthner, Ten Years of Medical Informatics, *Computer Methods and Programs in Biomedicine* 25, no. 2 (1987): 73–85.

24. J.K.H. Tan, et al., The Application of Expert System Technology to Community Health Program Planning and Evaluation, University of British Columbia, Vancouver, BC.

25. P.N. Reeves, et al., Expert Systems: A New Technology for Increasing Decision Makers' Effectiveness and Efficiency, *Hospital Topics* 66, no. 4 (1988): 10–13.

26. J.K.H. Tan, et al., Expert System Technology.

27. S.M. Shortell, et al., Creating Organized Delivery Systems: The Barriers and Facilitators, *Hospital and Health Services Administration* 38, no. 4 (1993): 447–466.

28. L.E. Perreault and G. Wiederhold, Essential Concepts for Medical Computing, in *Medical Informatics: Computer Applications in Health Care,* eds. E.H. Shorliffe and L. E. Perreault, (Reading, Mass: Addison-Wesley Publishing Co., Inc., 1990): 117–150.

29. G.O. Barnett, *Computer Stored Ambulatory Record (COSTAR),* NCHSR Research Digest Series DHEW, 1976, as referenced in D.A.B. Lindberg, ed. *The Growth of Medical Information Systems in the United States, D.C.* (Toronto: Health and Company, 1979).

30. E.M. Rogers, *Diffusion of Innovations,* 3rd ed. (New York: Free Press, 1983).

31. J.I. Cash, Jr., et al., *Corporate Information Systems Management: Text and Cases,* 2nd ed. (Homewood, Ill: Richard D. Irwin, Inc., 1988).

32. S.L. Jarvenpaa and B. Ives, Information Technology and Corporate Strategy: A View from the Top, *Information Systems Research* 1, no. 4 (1990): 351–376.

33. S.C. Blumenthal, *Management Information Systems* (Englewood Cliffs, NJ: Prentice Hall, 1969).

34. D.E. Avison and A.T. Wood-Harper, Information Systems Development Research: An Exploration of Ideas in Practice, *Computer Journal* 34, no. 2 (1991): 98–112.

35. C.H. Sullivan, Systems Planning in the Information Age, *Sloan Management Review* 27, no. 1 (1989): 3–11.

36. J. Federowicz, Hospital Information Systems: Are We Ready for Case Mix Applications?, *Health Care Management Review* 8, no. 4 (1983): 35–41.

37. B.C. McNurlin and R.H. Sprague, Jr., *Information Systems Management in Practice,* 2nd ed. (Englewood Cliffs, NJ: Prentice Hall, 1989).

38. H.R. Shrednick, et al., Empowerment: Key to IS World-Class Quality, *MIS Quarterly* 16, no. 4 (1992): 491–505.

39. The need for theoretical significance, methodological soundness, and practical utility of HMIS knowledge motivates the phrase "Theory, Methods, and Applications" used in the title of this book.

40. G.B. Davis, et al., The Future of Information Systems as an Academic Field: Your Fate in 1998, in *Proceedings of the Ninth International Conference on Information Systems,* J.J. DeGross and M. H. Olson, eds. (Minneapolis, 1988).

41. J.K.H. Tan. Health Graphics: Using Computer-Generated Faces for Representing Heart Health Data, *International Heart Health Conference Abstracts* (Victoria, BC: 1992): 16.

42. W. Redekop and J.K.H. Tan, Diagnostic Utility and Cost-Utility of Magnetic Resonance Imaging and CSF Oligoclonal Banding in Multiple Sclerosis, *International Society of Technology Assessment in Health Care (ISTAHC) Abstract* (Vancouver, BC, 1992).

43. Tan et al., *Expert System Technology.*

44. J. Milsum and J.K.H. Tan, *Health Systems Analysis: Theory and Applications Using Spreadsheets,* Faculty of Medicine, University of British Columbia (1992).

45. Davis et al., The Future of Information Systems.

46. W.M. Zani, Blueprint for MIS, *Harvard Business Review* 48, no. 6 (1970): 95–100.

Part II

Laying the Conceptual Foundations for Health Management Information Systems: HMIS Theories and Methodologies

Chapter 3

Elements of Systems Theory: Toward a Systems Perspective of Today's North American Health Service Delivery System (NAHSDS)

1. Describe systems theory.
2. Identify basic elements of systems theory.
3. Apply systems thinking to the North American health service delivery system (NAHSDS).
4. Classify systems models.
5. Apply systems modeling to organizational problem finding and decision making.
6. Rationalize an integrated organizational model of the NAHSDS.

INTRODUCTION

No man is an island entire of itself; every man is a piece of the continent,
a part of the main;
If a clod be washed away by the sea, Europe is the less, as well as if a
promontory were,
as well as if a manor of thy friend's or of thine own were;
any man's death diminishes me, because I am involved in mankind,
and therefore never send to know for whom the bell tolls; it tolls for
thee.[1]

In the same vein as in John Donne's famous poem, an individual is a part of, and influenced by, the immediate community, which in turn is a part of and influenced by society, and ultimately, humanity. This type of reasoning is the essence of systems theory.

Systems theory has been around for a long time. It originated in studies in communication and cryptography spawned in the desperate and frenzied atmosphere of World War II and grew into a powerful conceptualization tool. Essentially, it provided insights into everything from the structure of the ball-peen-hammer assembly line to the interactions of states and nations. The concept of systems has since then played an increasingly critical role in contemporary science. During the post–World War II period, considerable research has been conducted on systems theory and its potential applications in all segments of our society.[2] In particular, this is true for business and health management information scientists, for whom systems planning, management, and evaluation are the principal subjects of study.[3]

The nature of systems theory, and such cybernetic concepts as feedback, proved to have relevance beyond phone systems and computers. But it is only in this generation that some of the work in the field of systems theory has significantly impacted on the North American health service delivery system (NAHSDS).[4] The evolution of the traditional health service delivery facility into a highly complex system, with many new organizations, structures, and supporting entities, requires one to view this entire order by using a systems approach. This allows one to gain a valuable holistic insight into the basic structure, components, and function of the present and ever-evolving health service delivery system. Through such a broad understanding, the role of health management information systems (HMIS) as related to the NAHSDS will become more defined (i.e., in terms of its effects on various facets of the health service industry).

In view of the multiplicity of interconnected organizations within the NAHSDS, general systems theory provides an excellent tool of analysis and conceptualization of the system. The goal of this chapter is, therefore, to provide an overall discussion of the elements of systems theory and to explore their applications to health service delivery in general, and NAHSDS in particular, within the context of HMIS design and development.

GENERAL SYSTEMS THEORY

The general systems theory, also termed "cybernetics," is most successful when it combines the analysis of individual parts of the system with the study of the interactions among these parts. The theory begins from the empirical observation that all systems, in whatever disciplinary domain, share certain important similarities in their underlying structure and exhibit some common behavioral patterns. Moreover, in every system, the whole is greater than the sum of its parts. For example, the combined action, as in human-machine interaction, is more significant in total emergent effect than the sum of the separate effects.

All systems have objects and attributes. Objects constitute the components of a system, whereas attributes are the properties of these objects. Specifically, an attribute is an abstract descriptor that characterizes and defines the component parts

of the system. For instance, in a health service facility, objects of the bed allocation system can include actual beds, patients, health service providers who attend
to the patients, and the computer that stores, analyzes, and provides the bed allocation information. The attributes describing the object "patient" may include, for
example, the patient's condition, gender, and age and the time the patient needs a
bed. Figure 3–1 shows the basic objects of a bed allocation system and their interactions in a health service delivery institution.

A system combines all the objects and their attributes and defines the relationships among these objects, enabling the parts to add up to some greater unity
rather than simply constituting an unplanned assemblage of objects. Indeed, relationships of objects may be planned or unplanned, and formal or informal. In our
bed allocation system, the percentage of beds allocated to children, adults, and the
elderly is a planned relationship. Conversely, the particular percentage of beds
allocated to children immediately after an unexpected measles outbreak among
children in the community is an unplanned relationship.

A concrete system is one in which at least two elements are tangible objects,
whereas an abstract system is one in which all the elements are concepts. Languages and philosophical systems are abstract systems, whereas the bed allocation
system is a concrete one. In an abstract system, the elements are created by definitions and the relationships between them are created by assumptions. These abstract systems are subjects of study of the "formal sciences." In a concrete system,
on the contrary, the establishment of the existence and properties of elements and
the relationships among them are empirically observed. These systems are subjects of study in the realm of "nonformal sciences."[5] HMIS, since its study involves the establishment of the existence and properties of elements that are empirically observed, can be considered a concrete system in the context of a
nonformal science. Therefore, the emphasis of our discussion will be made in reference to a nonformal or social science.

Systems Unity and Environment

By definition, a system is a set of interrelated elements. It is a unified or integral
reality in its own right, composed of at least one other element in the set. Each
element connects to every other element, directly or indirectly, and no subset of
elements is unrelated to any other subset (see Figure 3–1).

As a direct consequence of the inherent concept of unity within systems theory,
a system must have a unity of purpose in the accomplishment of its goals, functions, or desired outputs. In other words, a system must have its own identity and
be able to differentiate itself from external events, objects, or other such subsystems outside certain definable boundaries. For example, our bed allocation sys-

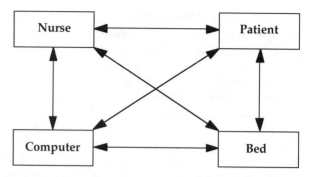

Figure 3–1 Basic Components of a Bed-Allocation System in a Health Service Facility

tem is differentiated from other such systems in the health service facility by its unified goals and defined boundaries. This constitutes an independent system, whereas an assemblage of people waiting in the lobby of the health service facility normally do not, since these people do not have a unified purpose and are themselves not much different from, say, others walking into and out of an office building.

Outside the definable boundaries of a system is its environment. This environment has a set of elements with relevant properties that are not part of the system, but a change in any part of the environment can effect a change in the state of the system. For example, a decrease in transfer payments from any private or public funding agency has a resultant effect on the functioning and quality of service provided by a health service facility. This is similar to the human anatomy, where insulin and glucagon can effect a change in the biological state of the system. One cannot ignore the dynamic nature of systems. An important point to remember is that the state of a system at any moment in time contains a set of relevant properties restricted to that time frame. Consequently, our bed allocation system functions in the environment of a health service facility. However, other systems of the health service facility, such as an outpatient clinic, may affect the bed allocation system, which, in turn, may affect the pharmacy department and the laboratory unit.

Although concrete systems and their environments seem to be objective, an element of subjectivity is introduced when particular configurations are being dictated by the analyst. Time is a key factor affecting the state of a system's environment. For instance, although the HMIS in a general hospital when it is first implemented may serve the same overall purpose as other such systems, its organization, level of sophistication, and interactions with these systems are likely to be very different after several years of operation.

Systems Structure

The structure of a system ranges from simple to very complex. An example of a simple system may involve the input of a single resource, a conversion process, and the output of a single product or service. As depicted in Figure 3–2, the patient admission process of a nursing home is an example of a simple system. Inputs to the system consist of elective admission requests from physicians, current bed availability, admitting department resources, and other emergency admission requirements. The conversion process includes a set of actions in which the admitting clerks collect information from referred patients, match patient requirements to available beds, and make room assignments. Output of this simple system comprises patients admitted to the facility or patients who are asked to go elsewhere. This output may then become the input for the planning of several other functional systems such as nursing care and diagnostic services.

In contrast, the relationships among system components in health service delivery organizations tend to be very complex. The intricate network of complex relationships that constitutes most social systems often makes it difficult to describe simple causal (i.e., cause-and-effect) relationships among individual components of the system. This phenomenon of system complexity aptly captures the statement that the whole (system) is greater than the sum of its parts. More importantly, causal relationships are dependent on the definer's perspective. The same phenomenon is defined in terms of different systems and environments by different observers. For example, the patient admission process of a nursing home system may be described from an information resource management perspective, as was illustrated by our simple case example. If the same system were viewed from a governmental program funding and regulatory perspective, however, it would be necessary to collect utilization and cost data and to determine the costs associated with the processes involved during the admission stage and other stages of the

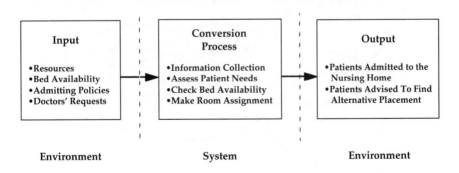

Figure 3–2 Patient Admitting Process of a Nursing Home

home health service program. Output of the system would have comprised some sort of mechanisms to provide regular program reporting to serve as feedback to the government on the effectiveness of the program in order to justify its continued funding.

In addition to the difficulty of establishing causal relationships, complex systems are also defined by their hierarchical or nested structure of subsystems, each having some meaningful function while interacting to produce the overall system. Large systems in health service organizations can be divided into several subsystems, and these subsystems in turn are subject to further subdivision in a nested fashion. For instance, a community hospital can be broadly divided into a patient care subsystem, support services subsystem, and community relation subsystem, as shown in Figure 3–3. The support service subsystem may in turn be considered as being composed of a data processing subsystem, a housekeeping subsystem, and a patient accounting subsystem.

The hierarchical or weblike structures of subsystems will reflect a hierarchy or network of goals embedded in the total system. The goals of a community health service delivery system, for example, are dictated by the platform of the presiding government who represents the voice of the people in that community. The goals of a hospital are, on the contrary, specified by its governing board members. Moreover, there may not be clear distinctions between the goals within a system hierarchy. In effect, the narrower goals of the subsystems may be viewed as subsets of the broader goals of the entire system. In the context of health service organization management and HMIS, the narrow subsystem goals are mainly goal-seeking (i.e., they relate to actualizing preset objectives), whereas the

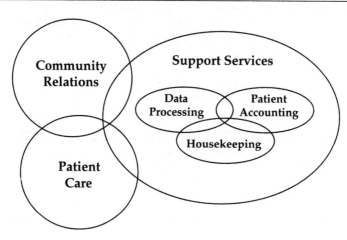

Figure 3–3 Boundaries of Various Subsystems within a Health Service Organization

broader goals of the entire system are primarily goal-setting (i.e., they relate to conceptualizing and aligning total system-subsystem objectives).

Systems Interactions

A major element identifying the holistic behavior of a system is the nature of interactions among its subsystems and between the system and the environment. Systems whose only goal is to maintain self-viability are called closed (autotelic) systems.[6] A closed system is one that is not affected by its environment: it is completely self-contained. In a closed system, elements in the systems do not interact with elements in the environment in which they are immersed. Hence they are autonomous. Figure 3–4 shows that the internal processes of an autotelic model (i.e., interactions within a closed system) are not generally affected by the larger system (i.e., social context of the system).

An open system is one that is influenced by the external environment. In other words, elements in an open system do interact with, and are influenced by, factors outside this system. Typically, open systems may be described as those systems that incorporate the standard triad: input(s), process(es), and output(s). The output from the system may be classified as either intermediate or final; intermediate output is one that is needed to produce the final output but itself is not the final output, whereas final output is the end-product of a system or subsystem. Moreover, the output at any one stage may then serve as input at another, essentially repeating the same process cycle at a different level.

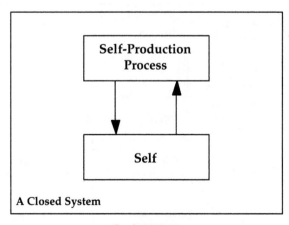

Figure 3–4 A Closed (Autotelic) System Model

Briefly, an open system is therefore one that has an environment and interacts with it. Every living organism is essentially an open system. It maintains itself in a continuous inflow and outflow, a building up and a breaking down of components, never in a state of absolute or static equilibrium. From a health systems perspective, the bed allocation system in an ambulatory care institution is an example of an open system because it interacts with the many facets of its environment and its functioning depends on the health needs and well-being of its surrounding community.

Open systems are often referred to as intelligent systems since they are and can be drastically influenced by external factors. If we extend the scheme in order to include several subsystems, we then get a "network" consisting of nodes (representing subsystems) that are connected by arrows (representing process flows). The integration of both open and closed system views is summarized in the scheme depicted in Figure 3–5. Complex systems are those systems that result when a closed system is combined with an open system. The term "heterotelic model" may sometimes be used to describe such a system.[7]

Alternatively, the output of a system may be used to regulate the input of the same system by comparing the actual output with a reference standard or a desired output. Any resulting discrepancy or error discovered by this comparison can then be used to determine the corrective or regulatory action necessary to return actual performance to the desired level. With the corrected or regulated input, the whole process is then repeated. The homeostatic mechanism of the body to regulate tem-

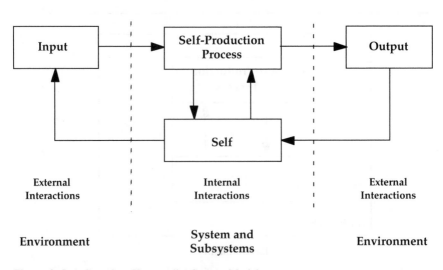

Figure 3–5 A Complex (Heterotelic) System Model

perature is a prime example. This mechanism is termed feedback control and is illustrated in Figure 3–6 for our bed allocation system.

The logic of the functioning of the feedback control system is similar to the homeostatic mechanism in humans whereby blood glucose levels are regulated by secreting glucagon when sugars are decreased or by secreting insulin when they are increased. Positive feedback is the process by which a difference between actual output and desired (or reference) output is increased through repetition. This type of process is relatively rare in biological systems and is generally of little concern in systems theory. Negative feedback, the process by which discrepancies between the desired and the actual output are reduced or eliminated through adjustments of the conversion process, is prevalent in biological systems. Through the use of this feedback mechanism, resource utilization and output production can be constantly adjusted or adapted to the desired level.[8] In our health service delivery system, for example, the government and third-party payers can act as a feedback control element by gathering information about resource utilization and outputs. The control element will then help decide whether or how the system should be changed in the future to achieve the desired outcomes.

Adaptation of the feedback mechanism inherently carries the notion of "optimization," that is, of achieving an operation that takes into account the needs to meet demand and to conserve resources. Analytical optimization depends on establishing a pertinent criterion or objective function whose value can be maximized or minimized, depending upon the context. Unfortunately, in practice, it is often difficult to quantify many of the outputs of the health service delivery system such as quality of life and improvement of well-being since only quantifiable variables can be used in a numerical optimization analysis. The type of management that occurs within the negative feedback structure is, therefore, already a form of optimization. However, the concept of optimization usually implies a more holistic view of the problem. In particular, it involves a trade-off or balance between the benefits of fine-tuning system performance and the increasing costs required in the process. For instance, increasing the inventory of a particular drug in a nursing home may decrease the cost of reordering and the risk of short supply but may correspondingly increase the holding cost and the risk of medication "expiration." If the benefits and costs can be expressed in monetary terms, this trade-off can usually be shown explicitly as an inverted-U-shaped curve.[9] Figure 3–7 shows a typical inverted-U-shaped curve that is characteristic of the trade-off between costs and the quantity of drug inventory for a health service facility.

Systems Behavior

The behavior of systems objects can be broadly classified as either deterministic or probabilistic. The objects of deterministic systems function in completely

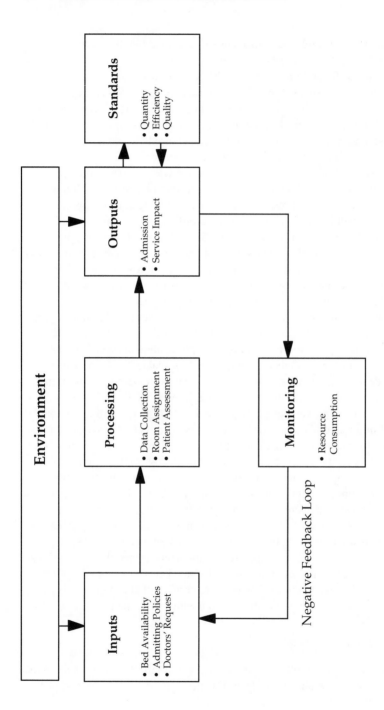

Figure 3–6 The Bed Allocation System: An Open System with Feedback and Control

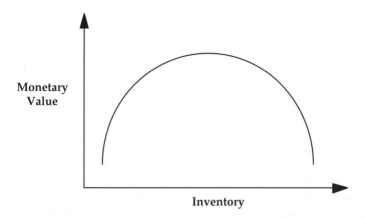

Figure 3–7 Trade-Off between Costs and the Quantity of Drug Inventory of a Health Service Facility

predictable or definable relationships, whereas those of probabilistic or stochastic systems do not. Such completely predictable relationships are characteristic of certain mechanical systems but never of human or most biological systems. For example, in a hospice, an establishment that provides for the terminally ill, the bed allocation system becomes probabilistic since bed availability cannot be entirely predicted. Predictions for probabilistic systems are based on probability laws and are therefore meaningful only for long-term trends.

A system event (or transaction) is a change in one or more structural properties of the system (or its states) over a period of specified duration. System events can also be classified as either static or dynamic. A static (one-state) system is one that lacks events, whereas a dynamic (multistate) system contains various events whose states change over time (i.e., transactions occurring over time). For example, the utilization rate of certain diagnostic devices in a health maintenance organization (HMO), an establishment that is designed to help maintain wellness through early detection and prevention of health problems with predetermined fees, may exhibit dynamic behavior over time. A homeostatic system is a static system whose elements and environments are dynamic, that is, a system that retains its state in a changing environment through internal adjustments.

Three common patterns of time-behavior in systems are of major practical importance in health service. These are statistical constancy, growth and decay trends, and rhythmic or oscillatory behavior.[10]

Statistical constancy, or steady-state (equilibrium), refers to a time-varying behavior characterized by a functional constancy with a superimposed randomness. Such patterns may be caused by complex self-regulatory, or homeostatic, mechanisms. For example, an intravenous drip represents a functionally constant addition to a patient's system on a macroscopic scale but when examined microscopically exhibits momentary changes of data that may be the result of stochastic variations.

The increase in the proportion of people over 65 years is a growth trend that carries significant utilization implications for the NAHSDS. In recent years, incidences of acquired immunodeficiency syndrome (AIDS) have increased due to irresponsible use of contaminated hypodermic needles, frequent casual and unprotected sexual contacts, and uncontrolled transmission of tainted blood products. Such trends can often be characterized, over time, by an exponential curve, which is well known for its constant double-time (in the case of growth), or half-life (in the case of decay). Over a longer time, however, there is usually a "softening" of the exponential growth or decay trend, resulting in a sigmoid curve (or S curve).

Oscillatory or rhythmic behaviors occur throughout the health service system in examples ranging from heartbeat to patient admissions cycles, from diurnal body temperature changes to nursing duties. These oscillations can arise as a result of external environmental factors or from within the system itself because of contributory forces inherent in the system's components and structure. Furthermore, when examined in detail, the periods of these oscillations seldom stay exactly the same. They tend to fall in close ranges in very dynamic systems.

Even so, the behavior of a system must still be characterized by some stability and equilibrium if it is to continue functioning in a changing environment. For instance, a sudden outbreak of childhood diseases such as mumps and measles in a community requires hospital bed allocation systems to adapt to this sudden change. This adaptation must retain the basic rules and defined relationships within the system's elements to prevent the system from collapsing. In other words, the procedures involved must be general enough to accommodate a variety of unexpected environmental changes but must also retain basic characteristics of structural and functional integrity.

THE NORTH AMERICAN HEALTH SERVICE DELIVERY SYSTEM

In both local and national settings, the provision of health services in North America is very complex in structure and function. To understand the functioning of all individual components and their collective interrelationships, a systems approach can be employed to view all of these components as parts of a total system, that is, the North American health service delivery system (NAHSDS).

To adopt such an approach, all the elements of systems theory must be considered. Integral components such as unity, external environment, subsystem structure interactions, and behaviors will come into play when attempting to understand and model the complexity of NAHSDS systematically.

Open System

The NAHSDS comprises a variety of organizations that are continually evolving. Despite an evolution into a complex structure with weblike interactions among its component organizations, the entire system as a whole does have at least one unified goal: to improve the health conditions of the general (sometimes selected groups of) populace. Analogous to the NAHSDS is the educational system, which also attempts to improve the literacy of North Americans in general. Consequently, these unified systems also distinguish themselves from other systems in North American society such as the market exchange system, the judicial system, and the transportational system.

Without doubt, the NAHSDS exists within the environment of our society. Accordingly, various sociopolitical factors such as government policies or local decisions do affect the operations of the system. For example, changes in the fiscal policies of United States and Canada that are due to changing economic conditions can often bring about changes in the functioning or organization of the health service delivery system. Taken as a whole, the NAHSDS, with its interactions with its physical environment, is by definition an open system.

Because it is an open system, the NAHSDS is constantly under the influence of various factors, among which the following are considered the chief determinants of population health:[11]

- Organizational factors
- Environmental factors
- Biological and behavioral factors

Organizational factors relate directly and internally to health service organizations and therefore fall within the realm of health management control. Examples include cultural factors, technical factors, structural factors, psychosocial factors, temporal factors, and managerial factors. These are summarized in Exhibit 3–1.

Among the factors that influence the NAHSDS, environmental factors are the most prevalent and these factors may be defined as factors extrinsic to the health service delivery system and outside the realm of health management control. From a total systems perspective, these factors include politics, laws and regulations, economics, demographics, sociological factors, cultural factors, education, and technology. These factors are detailed in Exhibit 3–2.

Biological factors are the basic characteristics and processes of human biology; behavioral factors relate to a person's life-style. Thus, disorders such as high blood pressure and hypercholesterolemia can be inherited and are attributable to human biological processes. In contrast, disorders such as hypertension and myocardial infarction may often be attributed to an unhealthy life-style, which is be-

Exhibit 3–1 Organizational Factors That Influence the Population Health

Organizational Factors	Examples
Cultural factors	Goals and values of the organization, comprising not only the cultural values and goals of internal organizational members but also a merging of these values and goals with those of the broader external environment described below
Technical factors	Know-how, and technologies of an organization to carry out tasks in achieving its goals and objectives
Structural factors	Formal organizational design and supervisor-subordinate reporting relationships as well as other formal organizational characteristics such as specialization, professionalism, and authority that have been derived from the works of Weber and others (12)
Psychosocial factors	Informal organizational groups and the informal interaction between individuals and groups, thus contributing to a "people climate" that dictates individual behavior and motivation, status and role relationships, and group dynamics (13)
Temporal factors	Incidental or sudden occurrences arising at any point in time with unpredictable outcomes, which must be resolved in order to avert major problems or collapse such as temporary labor disputes, breakdown of electrical and water supplies, and food poisoning in the cafeteria
Managerial factors	Managerial roles, responsibilities, and activities that are the central factors of the organization as these affect the coordination of the different parts of the organization to ensure its efficient and effective functioning (14)

Exhibit 3–2 Environmental Factors That Influence the Population Health

Environmental Factors	Examples
Politics	Governmental initiatives, policies, and changes in political interests and orientations due to changes in governments such as U.S. President Clinton's health care reform policies
Laws/regulations	Governmental rules and regulations and enforcement of federal and provincial legislative acts such as the Freedom of Information Act and Protection of Privacy Act
Economics	Governmental fiscal policies and changes in economic climate of the countries such as recessionary and antiinflationary pressures; examples include fiscal restraint and lowering of the prime lending rates to encourage economic growth
Demographics	Changing population demographics from growth and increase in elderly population as well as changing institution direction as seen with mergers and new forms of organizations appearing in the North American health service industry
Sociological factors	Reforms in health care industry such as greater privatization, regionalization, globalization, and general changes in management thinking across North American society as seen in the North American Free Trade Act
Cultural factors	Changes in North American culture such as pressures for greater patient involvement and improved quality of care
Education	Need for more information to be made available to providers and purchasers of health services such as Canadian Freedom of Information Act and growth in health promotion education
Technology	Technological advances and diffusion of innovative technologies such as advancing medical and managerial technologies, for example, imaging techniques, automated voice systems, CT scanners, and team management approaches

havioral. High cholesterol food intake, smoking, and excessive drinking are examples of unhealthy life-style.

Together these diverse and often unpredictable factors influence the functioning and continual evolution of the NAHSDS. The system is therefore inevitably dynamic in nature, and a stochastic or probabilistic component of this dynamic nature of the system, which should not be unheeded, is self-evident.

Subsystems Interactions

As noted earlier, the NAHSDS has a complex structure. When viewed from a systems approach, each of these broad factors or components of the system may be viewed as either an independent subsystem or a narrower component of other subsubsystems. The linkages among the components can be either hierarchical or network.

In particular, the decentralization of health service institutions has been a general trend in North America for the past several years. The functions of the traditional government-funded hospitals are now increasingly being performed by ambulatory care institutions, nursing homes, hospice agencies, and home health services and, in some cases, supplemented by health maintenance organizations (HMO), preferred provider organizations (PPO), and individual practice associations (IPA). HMO have been described previously in this chapter in the discussion of systems behavior. On the one hand, a PPO has a network of providers under contracts to offer services to policyholders for a prenegotiated fee schedule, but unlike HMO patients, PPO policyholders are only encouraged to use, and not locked into, the preferred provider. On the other hand, the IPA functions similarly to the HMO and the PPO, but IPA providers are reimbursed on a "fee-for-service" basis and the subscriber is restricted to using only these providers in the IPA.[15]

The corporatization of the medical or organized health service delivery system is more prevalent in the United States than in Canada. However, a modified version of managed care is conceptually operative in Canada, and a model of that description may be found in current literature.[16] Moreover, as an outgrowth of this trend, each organization or institution in the larger managed care system has also become more decentralized because of further specialization of services provided by the individual department.

Each subsystem or organization within the NAHSDS has its own goal or purpose, distinct from the goals or purposes of other such subsystems, and the interactions among the various subsystems often arise primarily to supplement the functioning of the individual subsystems. However, the unified goal of the entire system should also be reflected in the interactions among the various subsystems.

As a consequence of the trend of decentralization and specialization, a patient's medical information may be disseminated in various subsystems, thus creating a problem for case management (CM) and directly threatening the unified goal of the entire system.

To alleviate this problem for CM, effective communications and interactions among the subsystems become increasingly crucial. In the health service delivery setting, those interactions can be either vertical or horizontal. Vertical interactions are those that take place among subsystems in the same field but in different positions in the hierarchy, whereas horizontal interactions are those of subsystems of different fields. For example, decisions made in association with the administrative subsystem of the same hierarchy are vertical interactions. The concerted effort of specialists, occupational therapists, physiotherapists, and nurses on the care of a patient is an example of horizontal interaction.

Often, such interactions function as negative feedback mechanisms. A typical input to the system may be an increased demand for a particular health service program, driven by various factors, as introduced in the previous section. The conversion process would then include various vertical and horizontal interactions among various responsible subsystems to produce a desired output such as an increase in the program services. The amount and quality of the increased service would then be influenced by environmental factors, which would determine the degree to which the output should be changed.

Local Subsystems

In a local setting, the systems approach can also be applied to further our understanding of the functioning of a health service delivery organization. According to Ackoff, an organization is a purposeful system that contains at least two purposeful elements that have a common purpose.[17] The term "purposeful" here refers to the fact that the same outcome can be produced in different ways in the same state (internal or external) and different outcomes can be produced in the same or different states. A purposeful system is one that can change its goals under constant conditions, and one that can select ends as well as means to achieve its goals. In this regard, human beings are the most familiar examples of such systems.

On a local level, the actual functioning of an HMO in terms of HMIS designs and development can also be examined by using systems theory. Conceptually, an HMO is usually designed to help maintain wellness through early detection and prevention of health problems. Many HMOs contract with hospitals and physicians to perform services for predetermined fixed fees that are paid in advance. When viewed within a systems perspective, as in Figure 3–8, inputs of an HMO

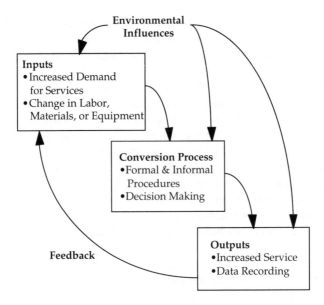

Figure 3–8 The Functioning of a Health Maintenance Organization (HMO) from a Systems Perspective

may typically include an increased demand for services requested from the hospitals, physicians, or other funding agencies. Changes in the availability of labor, materials, or equipment may also act as inputs to the system.

These inputs normally undergo a "conversion process" through both formal and informal procedures and are then followed by management decision making. Here, the use of a health management information system (HMIS) is likely to be most intense during the management decision-making process. Various kinds of information on the utilization of resources such as equipment, the availability of professional help, and the operational costs can then be drawn from existing HMIS applications to play an important role in managerial decision making. Accurate estimates can also be made by using HMIS information rather than relying on intuitive feelings or conjectures about possible outcomes of feasible alternative solutions.

The output of the conversion process is usually the execution of decisions made by the managers, such as providing a particular service, changing the price charged for a service, or altering the current resource distribution pattern. Moreover, these outputs are by no means the end-product. Very often, these outputs may signal the need for further changes in the data collected by the information systems. On the basis of these changes in the HMIS, the adequacy of the services provided, the quality of care, patient impact, staff satisfaction, and efficiency of resource distribution can all be periodically evaluated. Put simply, the HMIS would be designed to provide meaningful information comparing system performance to predetermined standards as specified by the health service institution (e.g., the HMO).

If there is a discrepancy between the actual provision of a new service and the desired level, decisions may be required to increase the provision of the service through a feedback control mechanism. In general, these control mechanisms may include education and training, procedural changes, personnel changes, incentive programs, or even disciplinary actions. These decisions are then converted into an actual output through a conversion process similar to the one mentioned previously or can in turn create additional demands for related services, thus repeating the entire cycle.

SYSTEMS MODELING

According to Senge, systems thinking is a conceptual framework, a body of knowledge and tools that have been developed over the past 50 years, to make the complete patterns clearer and to help us see how to change them effectively.[18] An important step in the systems approach to decision making is, therefore, the development of models that are used to obtain valuable insights into the behavior of a system.

The meaning of the term "model" and the usefulness of models in decision making are best understood through a number of important considerations that focus on model classification. First, models attempt to imitate systems by capturing their major components and interactions. By referring to a model, valuable insights into the behavior of the system being modeled can be obtained. Second, models are representations or abstractions of actual objects or situations. They show the relations and interrelations of action and reaction, of cause and effect, in operational situations. Third, models can be conceptually regarded as substitutes for the real systems. Thus, instead of investigating and experimenting with the real system, the model can be studied and interrogated, usually with less risk, time, and resources needed. Finally, models are caricatures of reality. If the models are good, then, like good caricatures, they portray, though perhaps in a distorted manner, some of the features of the real world. The main role of a model is thus not to explain and to predict as to formulate thinking and to pose sharp questions. Models, by definition, are not expected to be a complete substitute for real systems.

Models can be broadly classified into several types.

- Conceptual models
- Iconic models

- Analog models
- Symbolic models

These are depicted in Figure 3–9. On a smaller scale, for example, at an administrative level, several different kinds of models may coexist to assist or support decision making.[19]

Briefly, conceptual models are those formed through our experience, knowledge, and intuition. These may be mental, verbal, or descriptive in form and are essentially abstractions based on our experience. "Mental models" are deeply ingrained assumptions, generalizations, or even pictures or images that influence how we understand the world and how we take action. Mental models are normally ill defined and not easy to communicate. Verbal models are better structured than mental models but are still difficult to transmit. Descriptive models represent a higher level of conceptualization and may be articulated and communicated. For example, a crude conceptual model of a hospital visit from a patient's point of view may involve such steps as referral by the primary physician, admission by the hospital, further diagnosis (or confirmation of diagnoses), treatment, and release.

Iconic models are those that resemble what they represent, although the properties of an iconic model may not be exactly the same as those of the real system it represents. Iconic models include physical and pictorial models. Physical models are constructed from concrete, tangible materials. Pictorial models are images of

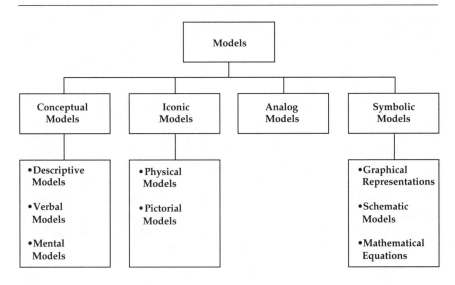

Figure 3–9 A Classification of Models

objects and provide description rather than explanation. The three-dimensional architectural prototype of a hospice agency is an example of a physical model; an artist's drawing of the hospice agency is a pictorial model.

Analog models are those that are built to act like real systems, even though they look different from what they represent. An artificial kidney dialysis machine that provides life support is an example of an analog model. These models employ one set of properties to represent some other set of properties possessed by the real system.

Symbolic models are those that use symbols to designate the components of a system and relationships among those components. These are abstract models in which symbols are substituted for systems characteristics. These kinds of models usually take the form of graphs, schematics, and mathematical equations. Graphical models are normally used to represent growth, flow, or activities. Schematic models are obtained by taking an idea or an event and reducing it to a chart. Mathematical models are symbolic models that employ the language of mathematics. They differ from all other "natural" models in that they are informational models expressed solely in a logical, mathematical, analytical, or numerical relation. For instance, a mathematical equation that attempts to simulate the amount of utilization of an HMIS in a typical day for an HMO may be regarded as part of a mathematical model. Furthermore, mathematical models often employ variables, constants, and parameters. Constants, as the term implies, always have fixed values, whereas parameters can have arbitrarily assigned values. Variables assume different values while the model is run or calculated. A variable is exogenous when it is determined by conditions in the environment and endogenous when it is determined by the system.

Since models are attempts to imitate systems, and organizations are systems that run through rational decision making, the close relationship between systems modeling and decision making cannot be overemphasized. Systems models are therefore sometimes simply referred to as decision models. From an HMIS perspective, one of the most important levels at which organizational systems should be modeled for analysis of its information resource needs is at the individual organizational and interorganizational level. It is certainly the level of systems thinking that should be understood by HMIS students, and thus the next section is an attempt to apply systems modeling as a tool for understanding the difficulty of identifying problems (i.e., problem finding) in the context of health service organizations.

Problem Finding via a Systems Perspective

The general systems approach to problem diagnosis focuses on systems as a whole, as opposed to looking at their individual parts. It is concerned with the total-system performance (i.e., from a holistic perspective) rather than with the performance of each individual component. As a result, the relationships among parts of systems, that is, how the parts interact and fit together, are of great interest and importance. The rationale is that in an imperfectly organized system, even if every part performs to its potential, there is no guarantee that the total system will meet its overall objectives.

As a direct result of continuing specialization over the years, health organizational service provision today contains some very fundamental problems that need to be addressed. These basic problems arise essentially from the duplication and fragmentation of services provided. For example, an individual with a particular ailment will first contact a family physician. The physician will proceed with history taking, perform a general examination, and arrive at an initial diagnosis. Given the hypothetical complexity of the ailment, the physician will order specific tests in an attempt to confirm the diagnosis. In all probability, the patient will be requested to visit another center (Referral A), where the ordered tests will be conducted. Upon arrival at the testing center, the patient is often required to undergo a similar type of preliminary medical history check. Already we see the duplication of a service that has previously taken place, as shown in Figure 3–10. This duplication is both costly and time consuming. Moreover, a second visit to the physician may be required just to follow up on the test results. Under certain circumstances, the physician may not have the expertise to treat this patient further, and a referral to a specialist may be required (Referral B). At this point, another cycle of patient-physician interaction has been created.

Our current system is therefore serviced by inefficient and ineffective information reading and reporting, which in turn have resulted in fragmentary clinical decision making. In the system described, it is rather clear that the impediment to accurate and relevant information flow among various subsystem components is a major problem. Once this is defined, we can then use systems modeling to help find possible solutions and to test the efficacy of these possibilities, with various limitations.

Nevertheless, finding the problems or their causes is not always an easy task because of the complexity of today's health service organization systems. Accurately defining and pinpointing the problems inherent in complex systems is an area where system modeling can be very helpful. This simply implies that health service managers should have an "explanatory model" of how the system or the particular subsystem works before making hypotheses on what could have gone wrong. Such tools as the rich pictures and the entity-relationship (ER) diagrams introduced in Chapter 2, as well as the data flow diagrams (DFD) to be described in Chapter 4, can be used to express ideas and link concepts. Sound understanding of the behavior of individual components of the subsystem and the interactions among these components is therefore crucial when making these hypotheses. This

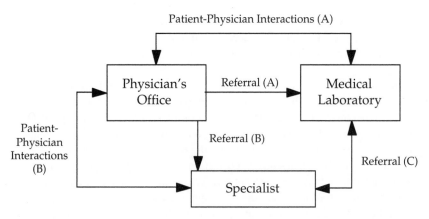

Figure 3–10 Life Cycles of Patient-Physician Interactions and Referrals

brings us back to the importance of systems theory and various kinds of system models described earlier.

Problem Solving Using a Systems Approach

We have just observed that one major problem existing in the NAHSDS is the impediment to the flow of needed information among various subsystem components, which in turn leads to the duplication of information gathering activities in various subsystems.

In this regard, it may be suggested that since the duplication of information is an inefficient exercise, only one source should be allocated to take care of initial data gathering. This concept is precisely optimized by database technology (see Chapter 11). The data collection process in such a system, however, should be thorough. More importantly, in order to prevent fragmentation of service provision within an organized system, HMIS needs to be integrated. Electronic linkage of information allows for a continuum. Integration must occur through a multidimensional process: vertically, horizontally, and even diagonally.

Indeed, Gilles et al. argued that clinical integration of services is key to enhancing system performance in our health service organizations.[20] The idea of clinical integration outlines the coordination of patient care services within the functional activities and operating parameters of a health service delivery system, as identified in the preceding example of physician-patient interactions. The ideal HMIS design is to take a holistic approach to service integration so as to support the entire added-value chain of health service delivery effectively. When applying systems modeling to solving specific organizational problems of duplication and fragmentary services, an efficient next step after the identification of the "problems" is therefore to develop an electronic monitoring system that is capable of generating relevant feedback and control information from a series of linked databases.

With the dramatic decrease in the cost of information technology, it is not difficult to envision the possibility of integrating existing systems at multiple delivery sites (see Chapter 9). The specific kinds of coordination of care also depend on the specific cases and the degree of cooperation or interventions of physicians. In other words, the coordination of care and the degree of integration of health services should involve clear-cut categorization of users or consumers of various services, which, in this case, is essentially a case management approach (this concept will be discussed in greater depth throughout the book).

In addition to ongoing case data collection, the behavioral characterizations (statistical constancy, growth and decay trends, and rhythmic or oscillating behavior) of subsystems described earlier in this chapter are powerful ways of understanding the changes occurring throughout various parts of the system. These characterizations will also provide a foundation for understanding and applying computerized systems modeling. As noted earlier, systems philosophy provides a holistic approach for visualizing and comprehending a decision problem in a rational and objective way relative to the information made available. At the heart of systems thinking is the idea that problems are seen in their entirety, through time.

At this point, it is possible to extend our discussion of systems modeling from the level of a group of isolated health organizations to the entire network of the NAHSDS. Indeed, this is best accomplished by our further understanding of the fundamental structure of NAHSDS through some broader theoretical organizational model, which is described next.

TOWARD AN INTEGRATED ORGANIZATIONAL MODEL FOR NAHSDS

Undoubtedly, the NAHSDS has undergone revolutionary changes in the past century, with particularly dramatic reforms in the last few years. Mainly in the United States, but also to some extent in Canada, the dominance of the independent, solo practitioner in combination with the independent voluntary hospital has given way to many other forms of health service provider organizations. These changes are frequently cited in recent health service literature and have significant implications for the discussion, examples, and cases used throughout this book.

To date, numerous other theories have been aimed at rationalizing one or more key aspects of the changing health service sector in North America. Often, these efforts have occurred in a rather piecemeal fashion. Although each of these theories may provide a sharper understanding of a particular trend of change, few can provide a general organizational framework upon which a holistic understanding of the entire system can be built. Richard Scott, a professor of sociology at Stanford University, recently proposed a general organizational framework within which various changes in the health service delivery industry may be viewed, interpreted, and explained. The discussion in the following section draws largely from his work.[21]

A Three-Tier Organizational Model

The rationale for discussing Scott's general theoretical framework on health service organizations instead of the narrower, more specific theories focusing on one or two particular facets is a direct consequence of the general systems theory discussed earlier. An important concept in systems theory is that the entire system is more than the mere sum of its parts. Hence, having a broad understanding of the whole system will greatly facilitate the rationalization and understanding of specific trends or changes occurring in the system.

Figure 3–11 presents Scott's layered organizational model for the health service industry. It identifies three definable levels of organizations.

1. Organizational environments
2. Organizational fields and populations
3. Organizational sets and organizations

In this model, organizational environments constitute the most general and comprehensive level of health service delivery organizations and organizational sets and organizations constitute the smaller units.

Organizational environments comprise both institutional and technical environments. The institutional environment consists of the symbolic systems that we as social beings develop to input meaning to our world: these symbolic systems also determine the parameters within which individuals and collective forms operate. In modern societies, symbolic systems have become highly differentiated around particular sets, making it necessary to identify the "culture" of an institutional environment. The technical environment refers to the network of knowledge systems and technical apparatus that supports the efficient and effective transformation of inputs into outputs. The technical environment is concerned with quality and efficiency, that is, how well the valued activities are performed.

The intermediate level of comprehensiveness and organizational structure identified is organizational fields and populations. DiMaggio and Powell propose that the concept of organizational fields refers to organizations that, in the aggregate, constitute a recognized area of institutional life or social activity.[22] Organizational fields contain several diverse organizational populations. The traditional view of

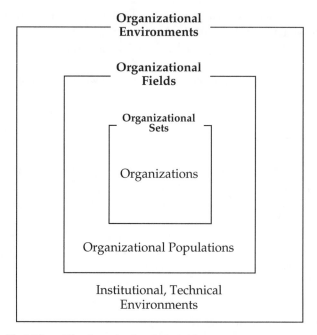

Figure 3–11 A Three-Tier Organizational Model for the Health Service Industry

organizational populations focuses on the fate of a particular organizational form as it is created, is reproduced (diffused), falls into decline, and is then succeeded by a different organizational form.[23,24] However, population ecologists have also advocated examination of the linkages between organizations and wider systems, thus shifting the focus from the fate of a particular organization to the changing distributions of organizational forms (for example, the decreasing prevalence of the independent solo practitioner) in our case.

In the most specific level of the model are organizational sets and actual organizations. Here, organizational sets refer simply to the specific collection of organizations providing the critical sources of inputs, and markets for outputs, required for organizational survival. For instance, an HMO (or a private hospital), in association with its medical supply companies, insurance companies, and nursing homes, each itself an organization, may be regarded as an organizational set.

An Integrated Organizational Model of the NAHSDS

As we have seen earlier, the health service delivery system is, in general, an open system in which the system and the environment are constantly and mutually affecting each other (heterotelic). Moreover, we can gain further insight into the system by viewing it as an integrated system within the three-tier organizational model described earlier. In the most comprehensive level of organizational environments, the institutional environment of the open system of health service delivery is predicated on several fundamental theories about how these services are to be organized and administered. The profit or nonprofit nature of organizations, the reliance on market conditions, and the extent to which management enhances its power at the expense of health service professionals are all manifestations of these fundamental concepts. It is also through these ideas that it is possible and useful to talk about the "culture" of health care, which, according to Scott, refers simply to "activities that surround efforts to cure and care for the ill."[25]

In the next level, the technical environment of the health service delivery system emphasizes outcome controls with the available technology. During the period 1950–1980, the combination of high levels of public funding for medical research and third-party reimbursement policies in North America supported the adoption of a "technological imperative"—that is, the idea that advancing medical technologies, regardless of cost, questions of priority, or optimal allocation of resources, should be made available to all physicians for the benefit of their patients.[26] Although the application of new technologies does improve the quality of health services on average, there is also increasing evidence of resulting ineffectiveness (or redundancy) and inappropriate diffusion of medical technologies.[27]

All of these factors have helped increase the cost of health care. With the gradual tightening of governmental budgets in recent years, numerous health service organizations have shifted their focus to cost containment and increased efficiency. The traditional core service providers of HMOs and hospitals have started downsizing to increase efficiency. Numerous small outpatient or rural clinics, as well as home health care and ambulatory care institutions, have grown tremendously in number and in size. In this regard, HMIS is expected to play an increasingly crucial role as a continuous skeleton linking various health organizations providing care for the same individuals. Shortell et al. have noted and identified the development of an information system infrastructure for improving quality and cost performance of the organized health service delivery system and for generating useful data for external stakeholders as a key challenge to achieving greater levels of integration of health services.[28] These issues will be discussed more fully in other parts of this book (see Chapters 9 and 11).

The organizational field of the NAHSDS includes within its domain not only the focal organizations providing core services, such as hospitals and HMOs, but also those diverse organizations, such as medical associations and health service financing administrations, that support and control these activities. Organizational fields also vary in their degree of structure. The health service delivery field, in particular, has exhibited a higher level of structuring earlier than many other industrial sectors in North America. The stability and order evident in many health service organizations reflect, in general, a professionally imposed division of occupational labor rather than managerial design and influence.[29] Nevertheless, structural isomorphism within the organizational field of health service delivery, as well as mutual awareness and interaction, has been encouraged as funding has become more centralized in recent decades.

"Inhabiting" the organizational field of health service delivery are various kinds of organizational forms or populations. These populations or forms include (1) hospitals and multihospital systems, (2) different forms of medical practice, (3) HMOs, (4) home health agencies, (5) rural primary care centers, and (6) renal dialysis facilities. The NAHSDS has seen a shift in the dominance of each of these organizational forms. This is a direct result of differentiation and specialization of particular tasks carried out in smaller facilities and of horizontal and vertical merging of organizations. The independent solo practitioner in combination with the independent voluntary hospital, once dominant forms of service provision, are gradually being replaced by groups of practitioners in combination with market-oriented hospital systems. As well, an array of other health service provider organizations of smaller scale are surfacing abroad.

The most specific level of organization of the NAHSDS comprises organizational sets and actual organizations. This is the level where the general trends mentioned actually operate within various health service organizations. Various systems at work within an organization are often affected by changes in other organizations in similar fields. In many cases, the output of a process from a similar organization is actually used as the initial input into various systems of such organizations. For instance, the early discharge of an inpatient from a hospital may be accompanied by home health services for a specified period offered by a different agency.

In extending the ideas of systems modeling to the NAHSDS, it is hoped that Scott's three-tier organization framework has provided readers with a descriptive model of the NAHSDS that is both revealing and illustrative of the application of general system theory.[30] The examples, mini cases, and illustrations used throughout this book have drawn freely from this understanding of the structure of NAHSDS.

CONCLUSION

A model of an organization has been used as a method of illustrating the application of general systems theory, as well as providing a foundation for HMIS design and development in the context of NAHSDS. The NAHSDS is an open system, constantly affected by changes in governmental policies and regional demography. Its subsystem structure includes hospitals, independent practitioners, nursing homes, hospice agencies, home health services, and, particularly in the United States, health maintenance organizations (HMOs), preferred provider organizations (PPOs), and individual practice associations (IPAs).

After viewing the whole health service delivery system, it is clear that an ideal HMIS should not only be able to provide a convenient tool for aiding administrative and clinical decision-making processes within a health service organization but should also be able to generate a continuous information backbone to facilitate case management. The reader should keep in mind that efficient and effective information processing and HMIS design and development cannot be realized without paying particular attention to systems theory in general, and health service organizational models in particular.

CHAPTER QUESTIONS

1. Explain in terms of the elements of systems theory the functioning of a drug inventory system.
2. Distinguish between open and closed systems. Why is the North American health service delivery system (NAHSDS) more appropriately considered as a complex rather than just an open system?
3. Identify factors that are critical to changing some aspects of the NAHSDS. What mechanisms are there to drive these changes?
4. What are analog models? Provide an example of how they can be applied to describe an HMIS.
5. How is Richard Scott's three-tier organizational model for the NAHSDS related to general systems theory?

MINI CASE 3
ACHIEVING A PAPERLESS OFFICE AT WELLINGTON MEDICAL CLINIC

With shock and surprise many physicians learned in the 1980s that they must change the way they do business. Competition for patients, increasing government regulation, and the rapidly escalating risk of litigation force physicians to seek modern remedies in office management.[31]

The Wellington Clinic in Nanaimo, British Columbia, has been automating information management for about 15 years. At the heart of the automated management is COMPRO, a software package that is used for the following functions:

- Patient registration with demographic data
- Full medical record keeping

- Private or third-party billing
- Reconciliation of payments
- Physician profile reporting
- Electronic mailing
- Word processing and spell checking
- Hand-scanned data entry
- Research training

The automation is then completed with three dial-in modem lines and a computerized telephone system called Ultracom, supplied by British Telecom Equipment. These functions together have helped the Wellington Medical Office approach a paperless office. As a direct consequence, medical office assistants waste no time filing paper charts.

In summary, the use of this computer system for information management in the clinic has dramatically increased the productivity of the office staff: about 220 patients a day are handled by the equivalent of 7.5 full-time staff members. As a result of the technology, the medical office assistants can be relatively easily trained to do all of the jobs in the office, allowing them to cover for each other's absences. They love their jobs, and physicians, too, enjoy their freedom to spend more time dealing with people instead of chasing paper. The quality of patient care has therefore also greatly improved: everybody wins.[32]

MINI CASE QUESTIONS

1. Where does the Wellington Medical Clinic belong in Richard Scott's theoretical organizational model for NAHSDS?

2. What trends have been witnessed in the past few decades in the operation of health service delivery organizations like the Wellington Medical Clinic?

3. Outline various subsystems in the clinic whose operations have been partially or fully automated.

4. Does each of these subsystems have a unified goal? How do these goals relate to those of the entire system of the clinic?

5. With reference to your answers to Questions 2 and 4, decide whether systems applications have helped the Wellington Medical Clinic in overcoming challenges faced by similar health service organizations. If so, how?

CHAPTER REVIEW

Systems theory has played an increasingly significant role in contemporary science in the information era. Viewing the health service industry from a systems perspective provides valuable holistic insights into the functioning and structure of the present system and helps better define the role and organization of the health management information systems.

A system is a set of interrelated elements. An open system is one that interacts with its environment, as do most real-life systems. The structure of a system may involve a hierarchy network of subsystems, each with its own unified purpose that ultimately contributes to the functioning of the entire system. The functioning of the subsystems can also vary in complexity. The simplest process involves a triad: an input, a process, and an output. More complicated functioning may involve a series of conversion processes, feedback mechanisms, and the channels through which the environment can exert its influence.

Systems can be classified as either deterministic or probabilistic. The deterministic or stochastic nature of systems can often be revealed through the time-varying or dynamic behaviors exhibited by most systems, which in the short run generally fall under the categories of statistical constancy, growth and decay, oscillation, and quasi-periodicity. In the long run, these trends also tend to be "smoothed," characterized by slower growth or decay and a stabilization in oscillatory patterns.

Systems models attempt to initiate and simplify real systems to an easily understandable scale. Models can be broadly classified into conceptual models, iconic models, analog models, and symbolic models. In particular, symbolic models usually take the form of graphs, schematics, and mathematical equations. In the health service delivery system, models are commonly used to aid organizational decision making and public policy analysis, often employing the techniques of mathematical optimization and simulation.

A contemporary theoretical organizational model can be applied when analyzing the current NAHSDS. In this model, three organizational levels are identified: (1) organizational environments, (2) organizational fields and populations, and (3) organizational sets and organizations. Conceptually, major changes that took place during the past few decades can also be rationalized on different levels of organization within this integrated model of the NAHSDS.

NOTES

1. J. Donne, Meditation 17 (1620), in *Adventures in English Literature* (San Diego: Harcourt Brace Jovanovich, Inc., 1985), 243–244.

2. F.E. Kast and J.E. Rosenzweig, General Systems Theory: Applications for Organization and Management, *Academy of Management Journal* (December 1972): 447–465.

3. V.T. Dock, et al., *MIS: A Managerial Perspective* (Palo Alto, Calif: Science Research Associates, Inc., 1977).

4. W.R. Scott, The Organization of Medical Care Services: Toward an Integrated Theoretical Model, *Medical Care Review* 50, no. 3 (1993): 271–303.

5. R.L. Ackoff, Towards a System of Systems Concepts, *Management Science* 17 (1971): 661–671.

6. *Random House Webster's College Dictionary* (New York: Random House, Inc., 1992).

7. Ibid.

8. C.J. Austin, *Information Systems for Health Service Administration,* 4th ed. (Ann Arbor, Mich: Health Administration Press, 1992).

9. J.H. Milsum and J.K.H. Tan, *Health Systems Analysis: Theory and Applications Using Spreadsheets,* Faculty of Medicine, University of British Columbia (unpublished, 1992), 39. Much of the discussion in this chapter is drawn from earlier drafts of this work.

10. Ibid.

11. B.B. Longest, *Management Practices for the Health Professional,* 4th ed. (Norwalk, Conn: Appleton & Lange, 1990).

12. M. Weber, *The Theory of Social and Economic Organization,* trans. A.M. Henderson and T. Parsons (New York: Oxford University Press, Inc., 1947).

13. J.T. Ziegenfuss, Jr., *The Organizational Path to Health Care Quality* (Ann Arbor, Mich: Health Administration Press, 1993).

14. G.O. Eni and J.K.H. Tan, Going North on a North-Bound Trail: A Model for Achieving Health Management Goals and Objectives, *Health Services Management Research* 2, no. 2 (1989): 146–154.

15. R.M. Hodgetts and D.M. Cascio, *Modern Health Care Administration,* 2nd ed. (Dubuque, Iowa: Brown & Benchmark, 1993).

16. M.B. O'Neill, et al., Modifying Managed Care for the Canadian Health System, *Annals of CRMCC* 26, no. 6 (1993): 349–352.

17. Ackoff, Towards a System, 661–671.

18. P. Senge, *The Fifth Discipline: The Art and Practice of the Learning Organization* (New York: Doubleday Currency, 1990), 7.

19. N. Sharif and P. Adulbhan, *Systems Models for Decision Making* (Bangkok: Asian Institute of Technology, 1978).

20. R. Gillies, et al., Conceptualizing and Measuring Integration: Finding from the Health Systems Integration Study, *Hospital & Health Services Administration* 38, no. 4 (Winter 1993): 467–490.

21. Scott, The Organization of Medical Care Services, 271–303.

22. P.J. DiMaggio and W.W. Powell, The Iron Cage Revisited: Institutional Isomorphism and Collective Rationality in Organizational Fields, *American Sociological Review* 38 (April 1983): 147–160.

23. M.T. Hannan and J. Freeman, The Population Ecology of Organizations, *American Journal of Sociology* 87 (March 1977): 929–964.

24. H. Aldrich, *Organizations and Environments* (Englewood Cliffs, NJ: Prentice Hall, 1979).

25. Scott, The Organization of Medical Care Systems, 271–303.

26. I.L. Bennett, Jr., Technology As a Shaping Force, in *Doing Better and Feeling Worse: Health in the United States* (New York: W.W. Norton & Co. Inc., 1977), 125–133.

27. P.J. Neumann and M.C. Weinstein, The Diffusion of New Technology: Costs and Benefits to Health Care, in *The Changing Economics of Medical Technology* (Washington, DC: National Academy Press, 1991), 21–34.

28. S. Shortell, et al., Creating Organized Delivery Systems: The Barriers and Facilitators, *Hospital and Health Services Administration* 36, no. 4 (1993): 447–466.

29. E. Freidson, *Professional Dominance: The Social Structure of Medical Care* (New York: Aldine, 1970).

30. Scott, The Organization of Medical Care Systems, 271–303. The author acknowledges the revealing discussion with Robert Modrow, a close colleague, on the practical significance of Scott's work to problem finding and problem solving at the health service organizational level.

31. M. Petreman, The Automated Medical Office, *Canadian Family Physician* 36 (August 1990): 1417–1419.

32. Ibid.

Chapter 4

Fundamentals of Information Concepts: Data versus Information, Information Theory, Information Flows, Health Statistics, and Hospital Information Systems

LEARNING OBJECTIVES

1. Differentiate between "data" and "information."
2. Delineate desirable characteristics of information for health managerial decision making.
3. Identify elements of information theory.
4. Demonstrate the use of data flow diagrams and flow charts for depicting information flows.
5. Identify prime sources of health data and health statistics.
6. Provide a model of the state-of-the-art hospital information system as an HMIS in an actual care-giving environment.

INTRODUCTION

What can managers realistically expect from computers other than a pile of reports a foot deep dumped on their desks every other week?[1]

In our previous discussion, we saw that a health service organization may be regarded as a collection of interacting subsystems. These interactions involve not only communications and networking among different subsystem elements but also interacting elements. Information was seen as the common link among interacting elements within an organization. This flow of information within a health service organization is the distinguishing feature of a health management information system (HMIS), which in turn is a prime example of the combined application of systems theory, organization management, and information management concepts discussed in earlier chapters.

The health service industry is information intensive. With the proliferation of information system technology (IST) and the increasingly vital role that information plays in health service organizations, it is useful to view a health service organization in terms of the flow and processing of health information.[2] How data are processed into information and how the available tools or techniques may be used for managing and understanding information flows are two fundamentals in the development of a health service organization and a management information system (MIS). In analyzing the structure and dynamics of MIS in any health service organization, the following series of questions can be asked from an information processing perspective:

- What are prime sources of information that can serve as inputs to the HMIS system?
- What are the desirable characteristics of information that can support health managerial decision making?
- What are the mode of transmitting and the process of transforming from one channel to another?
- What control mechanism exists for processing and transmitting information in a health service organization?
- What criteria may be used to judge the usefulness of the information outputs from an HMIS system?

This chapter attempts to provide answers to this series of questions. From a health policy and managerial decision-making perspective, information and information systems can be viewed collectively as a health resource to be managed efficiently, effectively, and productively. Information is necessary to support intelligent policy and health managerial decision making. The collection and distribution of valid, reliable, and timely information are critical to the development, growth, and survival of most, if not all, organizations and should be the primary focus of all health information managers. In order to provide the needed information, standard methods and procedures for documenting, processing, and evaluating information flows, such as those to be covered in this chapter, have to be followed.

To illustrate the sources and nature of information and how it flows within a health service organization, this chapter differentiates between data and information, explores some desirable characteristics of information, identifies elements of information theory, and discusses some fundamental concepts within the field of HMIS. The integration of these concepts may be found in the design and development of a state-of-the-art hospital information system (HIS) illustrated near the end of the chapter.

DATA VERSUS INFORMATION

In everyday language, the terms "data" and "information" are often used interchangeably. However, these two terms tend to have very different meanings to computer scientists and MIS specialists. Whereas "data" are perceived as unstructured, raw facts, or facts resulting from empirical observations of physical phenomena,[3] "information" may be thought of as "data" that have been processed into a form that is both meaningful and useful in prospective or current decisions and actions.[4,5] The concept of producing useful, structured information from unstructured raw data may be traced to the Latin origins of the word "information," derived from the verb *informo,* meaning "to give form to."

An analogy often drawn in discussions of data and information is the relationship between raw material and finished products in a manufacturing context. For example, in an automobile production line, a series of processes takes place in which the parts (i.e., raw material) are gradually assembled and eventually transformed into a car. The finished products from one division (e.g., assembly) often go on to become the raw material for another section within the whole organization (e.g., sales division). Thus, what may be considered "information" for one source may be raw "data" for another. Therefore, differentiating between "data" and "information" emphasizes the fact that some form of meaningful processing (i.e., assembly) takes place before the raw data from one source (e.g., the data entry clerk) become useful information for another (e.g., the health manager).

To illustrate the concept of information as "meaningful data" further, let us consider a list of numbers: 67, 78, 95, 73, 81, 67, 77, 75. By themselves, these numbers have little significance to the reader as they are presented (that is, as a set of raw data). Possible interpretations of this series could include such diverse views as a random set of numbers, the percentage grades of an examination, or perhaps the relative humidity of an operating room in a health service organization at various times. Once these numbers are "processed" in some manner, however, they tend to become more meaningful and useful (that is, yielding greater informational value). For example, providing a context and a mean calculation for the eight numbers would reveal that 75.5 is the average percentage of, say, the HMIS course grades in a midterm examination, or possibly the average relative humidity of an operating room over the last 8 days. Here it is the interpretation through processing and context that determines the usefulness of the data as information to the user.

Moreover, viewing information as "meaningful" data has significance. First, meaningful "information" is a relative concept, relative to the situation, to the time when a decision is made, and to the decision maker and his or her background and history. Information that is considered important in one situation may be relatively useless in another, even to the same decision maker. Second, information and decision making are closely intertwined: that is, information is useful for decision making when and only when decision makers can have direct (or indirect) access to it. Finally, the value of information is established when it is used in the process of decision making. Figure 4–1 shows that available, relevant, and high-quality information is critical to the generation of meaningful and significant decisions.

As an example, the "value" of a weather forecast (information) of strong wind and a severe thunderstorm the next day will be "established" through its role in the staff's (user's) decision whether or not a planned outdoor activity for a long-term care facility will take place. The information has little value when no particular choices or decisions need to be made on the basis of the information provided. For instance, if the outing was not planned to take place outdoors, the forecast might be irrelevant information to the organizer. Accordingly, information has economic value only to the extent that it reduces the decision maker's (or the user's) uncertainty about a future decision or action to be taken.

Because of the significance of information to decision makers, the objective of an HMIS design should be to provide the right information that is needed for making particular sets of decisions. To ensure that this objective is adequately met, HMIS designers must ensure that the appropriate data are available, valid, reliable, and consistent in terms of integrity and quality. In addition, the HMIS designed must permit the exchange of information between various processing systems (data independence) and the channeling of relevant information to appropriate decision makers on a timely basis (data management and control).

DESIRABLE CHARACTERISTICS OF INFORMATION

Once the "raw" data are collected, they are then processed into the form required. As we have seen, the usefulness of information depends directly on the context in which it is used to assist decision making. Nevertheless, on a broader level, there are certain characteristics of information that are desirable for all useful health management information processing systems. These are summarized as follows:

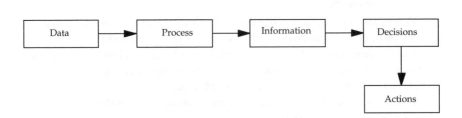

Figure 4–1 A Simple Information Processing System

- Useful information is accurate (error-free) and verifiable. This means that one can check to make sure that the information is correct, for example, by verifying multiple sources for the same information. It is worth noting that the accuracy of information directly depends on the accuracy of the data collection process. For example, similar data recorded by two departments within a health service organization can be cross-referenced to ensure their accuracy and consistency.
- Good information is characteristically composed of relevant and intelligently processed data. This means that the data must be processed according to predesigned plans so as to be relevant to the purpose they are to serve. Bed occupancy rates, for instance, would be relevant to nursing in calculating work load statistics.
- Timeliness and comprehensiveness are two characteristics of useful information. Timely information is current, fresh, and new. Comprehensive information covers all the relevant aspects of a system that are important for decision making. Hospital administrators need current and relevant facts to ensure appropriate responses to specific situations. In this way, both long- and short-term trends can be incorporated into management plans and decisions.
- Good information must be action-oriented and targeted to performance. To assist health managers directly in decision making, the information to be collected should be relevant to predetermined goals and objectives. The information should not be only facts about current situations, it should be as future-oriented as possible. Gathering information that supports, and is directly linked to, the organization's strategic plan will enhance prospective progress to the delineated goals and objectives.
- Useful information should be sensitive and unbiased in order to provide meaningful comparisons. It should not be collected or analyzed to justify forecasts or meet selfish needs. The motivation of the department or individual collecting or reporting the information should always be taken into account to ensure a complete picture (and not just a favorable or self-promoting perspective).
- Economic viability is another desirable characteristic of good information. When performing an analysis, the usefulness and benefits of the health information should exceed the cost incurred in collecting and processing the information. Reports that consume more human resources than the value of information being collected (i.e., the gain that can be reaped by being informed) need to be reassessed for appropriateness and evaluated on a cost-benefit or cost-recovery basis.
- Useful information should also be simple and easy to interpret; this means that the information system should not be overly complex. Sophisticated and

detailed information may not always be needed or helpful. In fact, use of excessive information has been found to cause cognitive overload, in which case the decision maker is unable to identify what is truly important. Hospital board members are often flooded with detailed information during board meetings, preventing them from effectively helping the CEO.

- Lastly, reports generated from an HMIS should be as uniform as possible to be useful for interdepartmental and intradepartmental comparisons over time (trends). Format of the information presented (i.e., graphs, tabulated categories) can be a critical factor in the management of a decision maker's time. Consistency and hence familiarity of formats used within and between organizations can enhance information sharing and exchange.

The desirable characteristics of information essentially imply that there are certain expectations for the functions of any working HMIS. More specifically, for an HMIS to be able to generate information with the desirable characteristics listed, the HMIS must first be able to carry out two important functions: (1) to separate the important, relevant information from the unimportant and irrelevant, and (2) to condense the "filtered" information into even more concise form within a short period. The second function here is especially important in view of the mounting evidence that information managers in most arenas are suffering from an overabundance of irrelevant information instead of a lack of relevant information.[6]

Factors that hinder these two important processes of isolation and condensation may arise for various reasons. Yet they generally tend to reside in these three broad areas:

1. Inability of health managers to specify their information needs
2. Misfit between technical and organizational designs
3. Error in communication

Planners and managers of health service delivery organizations who have yet to develop a working explanatory model of the decision process or the subsystem investigated may not be able to specify which information they require. They will be likely to gather as much information as possible, even information that is only marginally related to the domain of concern, before making a decision. In this case, the function of the HMIS of differentiating between important and unimportant, relevant and irrelevant information is hindered.

The misfit challenge refers to the fundamental discrepancies between the various functions and processes in the HMIS (in terms of data collection and information reporting) and the normal operation of the health service organization. For instance, the data computation ability of the HMIS may not be adequate to produce the kind of rigorous analysis demanded by management. This often creates additional work load for health professionals and directly affects both the perceived value and the acceptability of HMIS to the users. The normal functioning of the HMIS may be hindered even if there are no problems in these areas. In such cases, it is often the delivery of the "refined" information that breeds trouble. For example, problems may reside in the transmission of electronic signals or in some external electromechanical interfaces.

With regard to the possibility that some health service managers may have to devise a working model to help them specify the right kind of information needed from the HMIS in decision making, the systems approach and systems modeling techniques described in Chapter 3 provide a useful and practical tool for problems analysis. In terms of the misfit of the organizational structure and the technical design of the HMIS, strategic planning and strategic alignment, as described in Part IV, will offer a way to eliminate such mismatches. To understand where errors in the delivery of information can occur, information theory, which is our next topic of discussion, provides the necessary know-how.

ELEMENTS OF INFORMATION THEORY

Information theory is a collection of mathematical estimations, based on probability, that are concerned with methods of coding, decoding, sorting, and retrieving information.[7] This theory supports a framework that investigates the likelihood of a given degree of accuracy in the transmission of a message through a channel that is subject to probable failure or noise. Information theory was originally developed by Norbert Weiner,[8] a well-known mathematician, as a result of his study of cybernetics in the late 1940s. His contention remains that any organization is held together by the possession of means for acquisition, use, retention, and transmission of information.

As used in the mathematical theory of communications, information has a very precise definition: it is the average number of binary digits that must be transmitted to identify a given message from the set of all possible messages to which it belongs. If there are a limited number of possible messages that have to be transmitted, it is possible to devise a different code to identify each message. In turn, the message may be composed of alphanumeric characters, complete sentences, or certain predefined codes.

Although much of the subsequent research related to information theory focused primarily on the mathematical aspect of communications, the theory also provides important nonmathematical insights into the design and operation of an HMIS from a communication perspective. Within any communication system, the transmission of any form of information essentially flows from a given source to a chosen destination. There are five major components of all information communications systems, as shown in Figure 4–2.

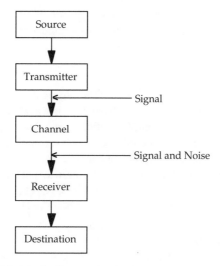

Figure 4–2 A General Model of a Communication System

1. Information source
2. Transmitter
3. Channel
4. Receiver
5. Destination

The Information Source

The information source in a communication system has the initial role of selecting the particular piece of information, or message, that is to be transmitted. In order for a meaningful transmission to occur, the underlying language, or code, must represent the message. The set of characters to be used on a microcomputer keyboard and the vocal sounds of the English language for a spoken message are examples of communication codes.

The Transmitter

The transmitter has an encoding function that converts the message into a medium that can be transmitted over the required distance. The generation of electronic signals for transmission via cabling or radio waves by keyboard strokes and the generation of muscular signals for speech production by brain activities are typical examples of transmitters within a communication system.

The Channel

The communication channel provides the physical conduit or medium necessary for the information to flow over distance. Air waves and electrical cables are communication channels. A communication channel, as a physical process, can include the addition of noise and distortion to a signal. Distortion is caused by a known (even intentional) operation that can be corrected by an inverse operation. Noise refers to random or unpredictable interference that tends to reduce the purity of the signal and the fidelity with which the message is transmitted. In practice, no channel can be made absolutely noise-free, although many techniques are used to reduce noise to an extent that is satisfactory for practical purposes. Examples of noise are voltage surges and meteorological disturbances in electronic transmissions and unintended sounds and echoes in speech transmission.

The Receiver

The receiver converts the message from its transmitted form to a state permitting its reception. Thus a human listener converts sound waves into nerve impulses in the inner ear, whereas a microphone receiving the same sound waves converts them into electrical signals. In microwave transmission within a computer network, the receiver apparatus converts the message back into computer-compatible electronic signals for use by other computers.

The Destination

The destination is the final stage of reception, in which the received form is decoded to provide a meaningful message. For instance, a patient's health record received in English sounds or written words may have little or no meaning to a practitioner who knows only French. Technically, the information is present in the message; however, given the ability of the receiver, it cannot be decoded.

Feedback is an additional component of most communication systems. A feedback loop can check how successfully a message has been transmitted from the original source to the destination sink. If the system has been unsuccessful in transmitting the correct message or information, a feedback mechanism may provide the means to have the information transmitted.

The obvious performance criterion of a communications system is the fidelity with which an encoded and transmitted message is received and decoded, and the associated reduction of any noise or distortion causing uncertainty of information.

Although all communication systems are imperfect, those depending on human voice alone are perhaps especially vulnerable. As we have seen, to enhance efficiency in the communication of information, the noise and distortion of data should be reduced if the communication channel is to maintain the fidelity of the transmitted message and to reduce the uncertainty. However, improving the efficiency in communications is only one aspect of information management; other aspects relevant to improved performance in the health service setting include cost-effectiveness, appropriateness, and service excellence (see Chapter 5).

To illustrate a typical communication system, we can look at a situation involving an instructor and a student. The "source" of information may be the instructor who chooses the message to be relayed. The "transmitter" refers to the instructor's voice and hand gestures. These signals are passed through the "channels" of sights and sounds. Interference, such as voices from the other students and other background sound, may be considered "noise" within the system. The message is then converted by the eyes and ears of the listening student, who is the "receiver." The endpoint or "destination" is the student's mind. Additionally, if the message is not sufficiently understood or received, the student has to reverse the communication process (feedback) to request clarification or further information.

This simple example demonstrates how a relatively routine information processing system, such as a class lecture, can be mentally broken down into a manageable series of communication stages. In a health service organization, the amount of data and information flowing through the system is typically enormous. A considerable amount of time and effort is therefore required to understand and document this flow. Since the advent of computer systems, many techniques and tools have been created to document organizational information flows better. By using appropriate tools, HMIS designers and specialists can graphically depict organizational information flows on paper quickly and effortlessly. In the next section, we discuss information flows in health service organizations and present an overview of two HMIS design tools commonly used for systems analysis: data flow diagrams and flow charts.

INFORMATION FLOWS

In a health service context, identical information can exist simultaneously in many different formats. For instance, a physician's order may exist as a thought, a set of written words, or some electronic configuration in a computer. Yet, in transmitting information, it is the final form of the information being transmitted that is pertinent, rather than the physical means of accomplishing the transmission. Examples of different transmission methods include manual or pneumatic delivery of multipart paper form; telephone, teletype, or telecopier; electronic messaging system and computerized hospital information system (HIS) via networking.

In an attempt to understand the various interacting flows of a health service delivery system or other similar system, the variables of concern may be divided functionally into (1) materials, such as food and anesthetics; (2) energy, both electrical and human; and (3) information, such as oral messages and computer transmissions. Such a classification involves some ambiguities as one type of variable may be transformed into another. In any case, all three categories have the common feature of HMIS analysis that their states, conditions, flows, or quantities can be represented by the concept of information flow. In other words, whatever the purpose and state of an element, its essential systems characteristic is the information that it brings to bear on the system's processes. It is then the changes in the nature of the information flows that determine how information contained in the different variables is modified or transformed via various processes.

In short, all health service institutions, whether small community hospital wards or a national health system network, have a bewildering array of interacting variables that can be expressed as changes in information flow. The extent to which various information is to be included, transformed, and transmitted from one part of the system to another is limited only by the decision about what's important and what's not. From a health service management perspective, information on the mineral content of a community hospital's water, for example, may be trivial to a facility manager deciding on the number of bed closures and the global greenhouse effect may be too all-encompassing to be practically useful. Managing the content and flow of information well can be a critical, if not an essential, characteristic of an organization that succeeds in today's health care economy.

For health service planners and administrators to be able to manage the content and flow of information in a health service organization or in other health projects, knowledge of how to express the complex interactions among various subsystems or components in simple terms becomes an important prerequisite. Numerous tools exist in this arena to assist health service managers and HMIS analysts. In fact, we have already seen two of these tools in Chapter 2: rich pictures and ER diagrams. The rich picture comes in handy when documenting themes or issues for "soft," ill-defined, or fuzzy problematic situations. The objective of the rich picture is to record the problem situation in its entirety, without confining it to the agenda or biases of key actors. One of its advantages is that it employs the language and terminology of the environment and shows how various pieces involved are related to one another. ER (entity-relationship) diagrams are particularly useful when there is a need to relate various entities in a system. Such relationships may be one-to-one, one-to-many, or many-to-one and many-to-many relations, as described in our previous discussion on ER diagrams. ER diagrams are frequently used in illustrating the structures of databases and distributed systems.

This chapter will introduce two more tools in HMIS design: data flow diagrams (DFD) and flow charts. DFD are meant to capture the essential features of existing HMIS systems or future information systems. They are top-down hierarchical diagrams that can provide successive levels of details and are particularly useful in documenting data flows and processes in a system. To emphasize a specific pathway of the flow of some piece of information from a starting point to the final destination (and temporarily ignoring other simultaneous information flows), flow charts are particularly useful. In essence, flow charts are like road maps: they show the logical relationships of system components. Again, no one particular tool is superior: the choice of the HMIS design tool to be used must rely critically on the knowledge and skills of the HMIS designer.

Data Flow Diagrams

One of the most popular and frequently used techniques is the DFD. Alternate techniques, which are similar and often interchangeable, are referred to as information flow diagrams, node diagrams, block diagrams, data flow graphs, or even bubble charts. Like many other techniques, the DFD provides a standardized approach to systems documentation as well as aids in the development of future system designs. DFDs are useful for documenting the logical design of an information system by graphically showing how data flow to, from, and within an HMIS, as well as the various processes that transform the data into meaningful and useful information.

The main purpose of DFDs is to break down a system into manageable levels of detail that can be visualized, first, at a very general (abstract) level and then gradually in greater detail, in a process termed "leveling" or "top-down analysis." For example, a walk-in clinic serving the medical needs of the community could review its overall services by sequencing the steps a patient would take to access any or all of its services. The staff's corresponding actions and flow of information can then be listed and categorized to clarify the center's operations. Thus, a large complex information process is first depicted as a context diagram. Each subprocess can also be subdivided into successive levels of "detailed" DFDs with corresponding subsystem details. This ability to expand and contract levels of details (leveling) as needed, depending on the particular requirements at that moment, is what makes DFDs such a valuable and flexible information flow documentation technique.

In formalizing a DFD, the basic schema of inputs, processes, and outputs introduced in Chapter 3 becomes essential. To operationalize this relation for computer or HMIS solution, two different aspects, variables and processes, can be utilized. Variables here refer to the data flows: the inputs and outputs. A variable must be defined specifically before any formal analysis of the system can take place. Examples include patients who are admitted daily and drugs that are prescribed weekly. In contrast, the processes are defined by algorithmic relations or other computations and are the mechanisms for making changes to the variables over time. In essence, a DFD is a network representation of a system, which itself may exhibit varying degrees of automation.

As shown in Figure 4–3, DFD are constructed by using four basic symbols.

1. Arrows
2. Rounded boxes
3. Open boxes (rectangles with three sides)
4. Rectangular boxes

Arrows represent the movement of data (with directions) between processes, data sources (sinks), and data stores (files). Arrows are therefore used to denote data flows. Each data flow arrow should be labeled to indicate the type of data involved, for example, "admission notification (phone)" and "chart package," as shown in Figure 4–4.

Rounded boxes in DFD represent the operational transformation (processing action) of input data flows to output data flows. Labeling of these processes typically involves verb clauses such as "Prepare patient chart package" and "Review and implement physician's orders for work requests," as shown in the example.

Open boxes are used in DFD to represent data stores: repositories of data used in the system. Examples of data stores are files, databases, microfiches, and binders of paper reports. In Figure 4–4, "patient charts" are an example of data stores.

Data sources or external entities, represented by rectangles, are the entities that lie outside the system and serve as a source or destination of data. Patients, labora-

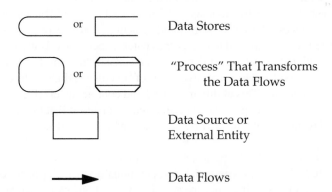

Figure 4–3 Conventional Data Flow Diagram (DFD) Symbols

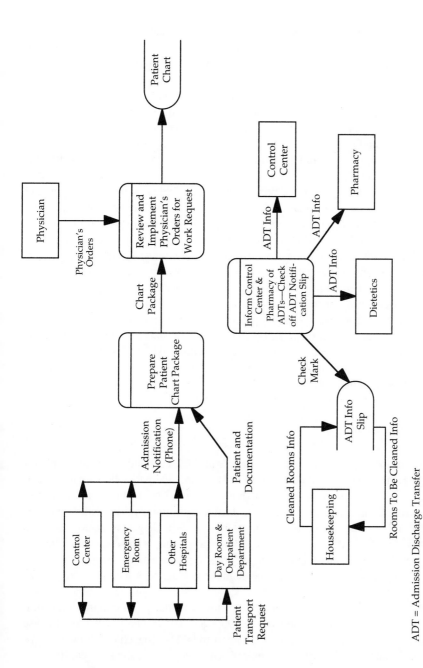

ADT = Admission Discharge Transfer

Figure 4-4 Surgical Interdepartmental Data Flows at a University Hospital

tories, wards, customers, banks, and even employees may be regarded as external entities. These data sources (or sinks) help define the boundary of the system. In our case, the emergency room, the pharmacy, and the dietetics department are examples of data sources.

To illustrate the use of DFDs, we will examine an actual application in the health service field. Figure 4–4 illustrates the flows of data involved in a surgical department at a university hospital. As we noted, DFDs can be used to provide both overall and detailed views of an HMIS. Details can be limited so that there will not be too much detail in any one DFD, which could make understanding the diagram difficult.

What takes place within one box (process) in a DFD can be shown in greater detail by using another DFD. For instance, the process "Review and implement physician's orders for work requests" in Figure 4–4 can be expanded in more detail by using another set of DFDs, as shown in Figure 4–5. In other words, these two figures are "leveled" in terms of context and details: Figure 4–4 is a more general overview of the data flows of the entire system, and Figure 4–5 breaks down a process (from the previous figure) into its substituent subprocesses. These two figures together can give a very accurate picture of various subsystem interactions involved in a typical surgical procedure at the university hospital, yet each also has its special functions. The broad overview provided by Figure 4–4 greatly facilitates higher-level decision-making activities like strategic planning; the more detailed view provided by Figure 4–5 is more suitable for operational and tactical decision making.

Flow Charts

In addition to DFDs, many other analytic tools and techniques are available for use in HMIS designs and development. These include paper flow charts, document flow diagrams, critical path method (CPM), GANTT charts, and Petri networks (see Chapters 12 and 13). Among the more commonly used tools in both the public and private sectors of many industries are flow diagrams. A flow diagram (or flow chart, as it is commonly called) is a graphic representation of the sequence of steps that an organization performs to produce some output. The output may be a physical product, a service, some information, or a combination of the three.

Most people associate flow diagrams with computer programming. Indeed, it was the computer programmers of the 1960s and 1970s who popularized the use of flow charts in the business world. Similar to DFDs, flow charts show the steps in a procedure by using various symbols, with arrows indicating logical flow and diamond boxes indicating a decision process that branches in one or two ways.

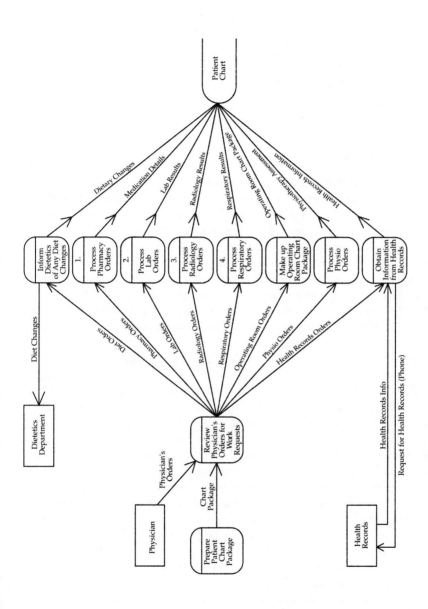

Figure 4–5 The Process of "Review and Implement Physician's Orders for Work Request" in Detail

Many groups or individuals often adapt the symbols of a flow chart to accommodate their specified needs. Although there are literally dozens of specialized symbols used in flow charts, most are built from the following basic set of symbols:

- Activity symbol (rectangle)
- Decision symbol (diamond)
- Terminal symbol (rounded rectangle)
- Flow lines (arrows)
- Document symbol (square)
- Database symbol (cylinder)
- Connector (circle)

The activity symbol is a rectangle that indicates a single step in a process. A brief description of the activity can be shown inside the rectangle, such as "Inject tuberculin" or "Read chest X-ray," as in Figure 4–6. The decision symbol is a diamond that designates a decision or branch point in the process. The description of the decision or branch is written inside the symbol, usually in the form of a question. The answer to the question determines the path that will be taken from the decision symbol, and each path is labeled to correspond to the appropriate answer. For instance, in our example, the diamond is labeled "Are there redness and swelling of the skin?" If there are, then the patient proceeds directly to have a chest X-ray; if not, the patient is shown to have no previous contact with the tuberculosis pathogen.

The terminal symbol is a rounded rectangle that identifies the beginning or the end of a process, by having either "Start" or "End" inside this symbol, as in Figure 4–6. Flow lines (arrows) are used to represent the progression of steps in the sequence. The arrowhead on the flow line indicates the direction of the process flow, as in Figure 4–6. The document symbol is a square with the bottom right-hand corner "torn" away. The document symbol represents written information pertinent to the process. The title or description of the document is shown inside this symbol. A pharmaceutical inventory order form is an example of a document.

The database symbol represents electronically stored information pertinent to the process. The title or description of the database is shown inside the symbol. For instance, an inventory database may be accessed to process an inventory order accurately and efficiently. The connector is a circle used to indicate a continuation of the flow diagram. A letter or number is shown inside the circle. This same letter or number is used in a connector symbol on the continued flow diagram to indicate where the processes are connected.

Figure 4–6 is a flow chart depicting the various steps a patient suspected of having tuberculosis (TB) would normally have to go through in a health service delivery system. Note that diamonds can be decisions that lead a branch back to

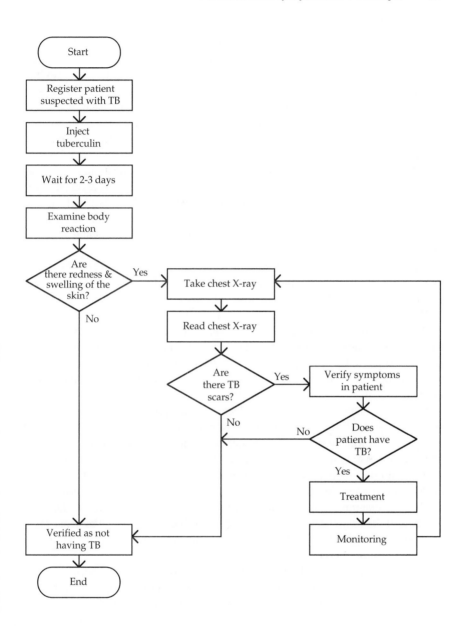

Figure 4–6 A Flow Chart of Procedures for Individuals Suspected of Having Tuberculosis (TB)

repeat an earlier step, thus creating a looping sequence. As in DFD "leveling," flow charts can be developed in multiple levels to aid in building a common understanding of the process and in problem solving. Here, the "high-level" flow chart (one that shows a larger, broader picture) for a particular process is called a "system" flow chart. Detailed flow charts can be constructed from each of the rectangles established in the system flow chart. Through this hierarchy of flow charting, an organization can build a complete, accurate pictorial description of the process inherent in its HMIS design.

In formatting a flow diagram within a health service organization, it is important to elicit the support of the staff to generate the diagram. This is especially true if the diagram has been drawn by an outside consultant who is not perfectly informed about all aspects of the organizational operations. Verification of the accuracy of the flow diagram should be made at all managerial, departmental, and staff levels.

Figure 4–7 uses a flow chart format to show how a flow diagram can be developed from scratch. Usually, flow charts are constructed so that the general direction is from left to right or top to bottom; otherwise, a snakelike layout will make the flow of the process difficult to follow. The criteria for the decisions indicated by the diamond-shaped symbol need to be shown in all instances, even by referring to supporting documents where the detailed criteria are spelled out. For instance, "Approved" decisions may refer to the criteria by which each instance is judged to be acceptable or unacceptable as set out in a separate but detailed reference document.

It is crucial that the flow diagram reflect the actual process that is in place in the work environment. Realistic consideration must be given to the fact that not all managers will wish to disclose every step or subprocess that actually takes place because of obvious redundancy or waste of resources. To this extent, flow diagrams and other tools may limit the user's ability to obtain optimal results. To counter this barrier, the atmosphere in which teams or organizations construct accurate flow diagrams must be conducive to honest and open responses. The overall goals of the exercise will need to take precedence over personal or departmental desires or motivations if the tool is to be useful and to generate additional meaningful information.

Although adapting the flow chart or diagram to meet the needs of specific groups or tasks can be advantageous, nonstandardized tools may in fact impede the desired information transfer to the user. For instance, one of the more frequently encountered "nonstandard" modifications of arrows in DFDs and document flow diagrams is showing arrows in both directions on one line. The standard approach would be to indicate two arrows separately. Such a modification may not identify subtle but important differences in the data being exchanged.

Other modifications documented in the literature include using dotted/dashed lines to indicate uncertainties about the connection and placing various groupings

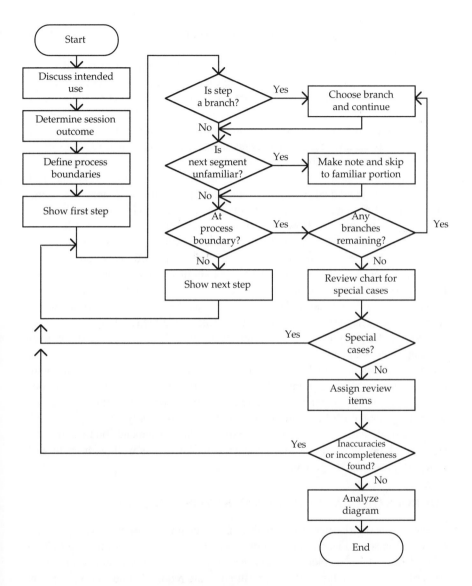

Figure 4–7 Flow Diagram Construction Steps

of processes within boxes to indicate their special closeness or purposes. Ways to overcome the risk of impeding information through tool modifications are to use standardized methods as much as possible and carefully evaluate any modifications to the tools in a formal and consistent manner. Modifications must be communicated clearly to all users within an organization and must represent a useful and meaningful transformation.

In health service organizations, both DFDs and flow charts can be utilized in numerous quality improvement efforts (see Chapter 13). DFDs excel in capturing the essential features of an existing system or a future system. They allow a top-down hierarchical design that provides successive levels of details and thus are useful in areas such as data flow and process documentation. In general, DFDs give a broad overview of the system concerned and are excellent tools at the levels of strategic planning and interdepartmental interactions within an organization.

The flow chart is a versatile tool with applications in nearly every phase of problem-solving and quality improvement tasks. Its use may be extended to training or orientation seminars for new staff within a health service organization. The pictorial presentations of flow diagrams enable communicators to reach across various cultural, educational, and language barriers that may exist in the workplace. Such barriers can block information transmission, partially or completely, if the channel for the information presented is only in verbal (oral or written) form. Because flow charts are more concerned with the steps and sequence of steps (from start to end) of a particular process, they tend to ignore other simultaneous flows of data. They are, as a result, an excellent tool at the level of procedural or operational designs but may not be particularly useful for high-level strategic or interdepartmental planning.

The reader should now have a good sense of the variety of tools, together with rich pictures and ER diagrams (Chapter 2), available to express the interactions among various components of a system. As mentioned, there are some cases where more than one of these tools are suitable; in others only one may be necessary and sufficient. As noted, the choice of tools largely depends on the analyst's skills and knowledge, the health managerial objectives, as well as the nature of task activities to be supported.

SOURCES OF HEALTH DATA AND STATISTICS

As we have seen earlier, data can be transformed into information when they are processed in some meaningful fashion. This particular process of transformation depends directly on the needs of the user and the statistical techniques employed. Nevertheless, certain types of basic health data are required almost universally by health service organizations using a manual or automated process of information generation to support planning and decision making. Such data generally fall into the following categories:[9]

- Health status statistics
- Health resource statistics
- Environmental statistics

Health Status Statistics

Health status statistics include population statistics, vital statistics, and morbidity statistics. Population statistics describe the size, composition, and growth of the population. This information is invaluable in planning and delivering health services. The main goal of the health service delivery system is to maintain and improve the health status of the people. Hence all health statistics must be related to an accurate statistical description of the population. The number of characteristics varies, depending on the purpose, but in most cases a basic population data set should include age, sex, race, profession or employment status, residence, and family composition. This information helps to identify high-risk groups, locations in need of services, and potential problems and to evaluate the effectiveness of existing programs.

Vital statistics are compiled from birth, death, marriage, and divorce information. It is the oldest and most developed form of health statistics. The vital statistics reporting system is based on legal documents: birth, death, marriage, and divorce certificates. For this reason, a higher quality of data collection than in other types of health statistics is required. Also, the issue of standardization of forms and definitions is less of a problem for vital statistics than for other categories. Vital statistics can provide a great deal of information about the health status of a population. Mortality statistics provide important indicators of the prevalence of specific diseases; birth certificates may provide valuable insights into the health of infants. Moreover, the data contained in the vital records can be very important to health planners and administrators for evaluating programs and determining environmental health hazards.

Morbidity statistics refer to the incidence of ill health in the population such as communicable diseases, chronic diseases, and other illnesses or ailments. On a local level, however, morbidity data are not readily available. Local health departments often publish statistics on communicable diseases such as tuberculosis, venereal disease, and typhoid. Statistics on other types of morbidity are more difficult to collect. The most important sources of morbidity statistics are physicians. When available, morbidity statistics are used to determine the health status of the population. Along with vital statistics, morbidity statistics become more valuable when they can be linked to specific population groups, thus facilitating the identification of high-risk groups who can then be reached through special programs.

Health Resource Statistics

Health resource statistics include statistics on health care personnel, facilities, and services. A major resource of the health service delivery system is its workers. The number of different professionals in the field is rapidly growing, and it is important for policy planners and administrators to have specific information about these professionals. A basic labor force data set includes the total number of staff in a health organization, a professional population profile, licenses and certifications, facility affiliations, services provided, a patient population profile, and the number of patients served. A major type of labor force statistic is the doctor-to-population ratio. Care must be taken in interpreting collected data. For example, an acceptable ratio is 1 doctor for every 1,500 people. This statistic, though frequently used, can be misleading. The type of physician must be specified, as well as the population breakdown by age and gender. When this is done, the acceptability of the ratio of 1 to 1,500 usually does not hold: a large number of females in a population indicates a higher need for obstetricians and gynecologists, children need pediatricians, and elderly adults require specialized palliative services.

Health facilities statistics are collected and published by a number of organizations, including hospital associations and government agencies. A major problem of facilities statistics is that each association tends to use a different way to describe the facilities listed. Also, the data are usually provided by facility administrators, who, for various reasons, might not accurately describe their organization's utilization of facilities. Like the doctor-to-patient ratio, the population group used in the evaluation should be known. What might be a proper ratio for the elderly may not be appropriate for the younger population group.

Health service statistics describe the delivery and receipt of health services by the population. They facilitate analysis of the level of service through which particular health problems are addressed. The most commonly found form of data on health services is the medical case abstract. The individual health service provider, however, should not have to take the responsibility for maintaining a long historical base of detailed data from medical case abstracts. As the operational needs for data of a health service provider can be defined with reasonable specificity, statistical abstracts of historical data will serve long-term needs more efficiently.

Environmental Statistics

Formerly called public health statistics, environmental health statistics provide data on health hazards, including noise, pollution, and deficient sanitation. They are extremely important in the prevention of health problems through various medical and nonmedical interventions by defining, more clearly, the causes of existing health problems. Statistics in this field can be obtained from government agencies that are responsible for regulating health and safety. Again, a major problem is linking environmental statistics with the populations affected, or, even more difficult, with mobile populations that have been affected.

Figure 4–8 summarizes the various sources of health statistics and epidemiological data commonly used in databases that are parts of a layered HMIS. Above all, since one of the primary objectives of an HMIS is to generate relevant and

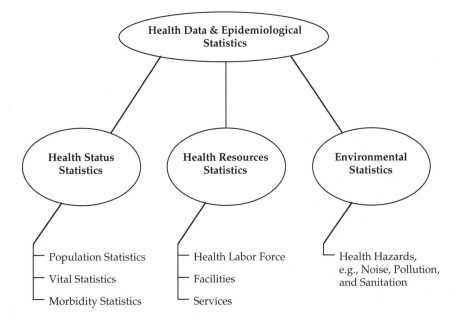

Figure 4–8 Summary of Various Sources of Health Data and Epidemiological Statistics

useful information in the context of health service planning and decision making, the quality of the information generated can also be an indicator of the performance of the system as a whole.

A MODEL FOR STATE-OF-THE-ART HOSPITAL INFORMATION SYSTEMS

Our knowledge of systems theory, information theory, and various kinds of commonly derived epidemiological data and health statistics allows us now to turn to designing a portfolio for a model hospital information system (HIS): that is, an HMIS in the context of a hospital environment.

As a result of the complex environment in which hospitals function, there is a growing need for health service planners to obtain timely and accurate information, as we have seen previously. At the same time, there exists a significant amount of duplication of health services, primarily caused by impeded information flow. In addition, there is a growing trend toward decentralization and distributed systems. All these factors point increasingly to the need for (1) ability to combine a variety of data sources into an integrated database, (2) ability to interrelate applications with linkages through an organizational database, (3) ability to transfer data among applications and share common data, (4) ability to accommodate physicians' actions with a range of medical data required for the various phases of a patient treatment, and (5) the option to shift among applications as the user chooses.[10] Incidentally, these are some advantages offered by a state-of-the-art integrated HIS over the traditional stand-alone systems. We shall therefore focus on the application portfolio for such an integrated HIS.

Zviran proposes an application portfolio with four major functional groups that cover all core issues of hospital management.[11]

1. Administration
2. Patient management
3. Facilities management
4. Medical applications

These functional groups may be translated in real terms into four major subsystems of the integrated HIS framework. In other words, there could be four modules in the HIS, each with its own data collection, computation, and retrieval abilities and each contributing (but with limited access) to a primary memory storage device.

Each module is proposed to have under its "umbrella" a collection of application programs for specific procedures or operations. For instance, the administrative module may have its own accounting subsystems, financial subsystems, inventory management subsystems, equipment management systems, and general management systems, all specifically adapted to the hospital environment; the facilities management module may include subsystem applications for laboratory management, radiology management, operating room management, blood bank management, and pharmacy management; the medical applications may include computer aided diagnosis, medical reference and bibliography management, and medical research subsystems (e.g., analysis, comparison, and evaluation of alternative treatments and outcome patterns). As for the patient management module, since it is needed for most health organizations and not just hospitals in particular, we will discuss it in more detail.

The patient management module should, at the outset, be the chief source of all information needed by the health organization about a patient, both personal and clinical. To perform this function, this module needs to encompass the functions of traditional admission/discharge/transfer (ADT) systems, possibly including many manual appointments and hospitalization scheduling "systems" that are still in use today. In order to collect all the clinical information about patients, this module needs to have data entry and retrieval functions for medical records (ideally featuring coded diagnoses and only a few verbal descriptions) and clinical procedures. This requires that the module be linked to both the central, primary patient record storage; computerized nursing stations; and possibly physicians' offices. To complete the repertoire, the module should have a monitoring subsystem to collect and analyze outputs from such monitoring devices as electrocardiograms (ECG) and electroencephalograms (EEG), also with a direct link to nursing stations and the primary patient record storage.

Figure 4–9 summarizes the proposed application portfolio of an integrated HIS. It is worth noting that the subsystems or modules in the proposed portfolio are not meant to be separate islands of computerization, but instead modular applications that can feed data into and retrieve information from the central, primary storage of patient data in the HIS. Some of these subsystems can even be directly linked to enhance the operation of a particular department. For instance, the pharmacy department of a hospital may need to use applications from the pharmacy management subsystem and at the same time be linked to the clinical subsystem (to obtain prescriptions from physicians) and to the monitoring system (to monitor the effects of medication on patients). In this case, the pharmacy department will be using applications under two different modules of the integrated HIS.

Lastly, one needs to build into such a system some form of system authentication such as the use of layered passwords for ensuring data access, privacy, and security. In other words, different users should be able to access or make changes only to data captured in their respective user views depending on the authority of the users as identified by the system. A discussion of this issue in more depth is included in Chapter 11.

CONCLUSION

Frontiers of the medical field are advancing at an ever-increasing pace. As a result, the amount of patient information required by health organizations and professionals to provide high-quality care soars rapidly. At the same time, stringent budgetary measures have put enormous pressure on the health service delivery industry to tighten cost control mechanisms. These changes have in turn dramatically increased the importance of an effective HMIS in producing information with numerous desirable characteristics and reducing the need for duplicated services in the health service delivery system.

This chapter has introduced the reader to various elements of information theory, methods of documenting information flows, and various other aspects of health data and information. Now equipped with these fundamental and yet very practical concepts of health information, the reader should be able to design an HMIS by focusing first on health data that can be effectively collected and processed to obtain the information needed by health professionals. The application portfolio proposed for the state-of-the-art HIS is an example to provide the reader

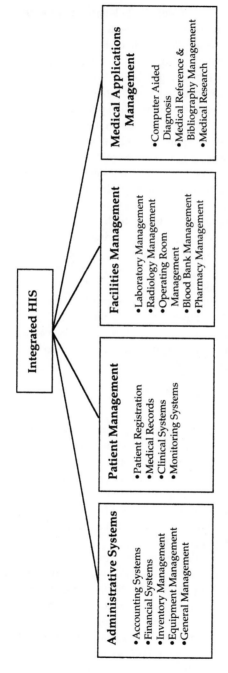

Figure 4–9 An Application Portfolio for an Integrated Hospital Information System (HIS)

with a broad overview of systems applications in a hospital setting (it can be further adapted and extended to other health service delivery organizations). It is hoped that the reader will be able to integrate this knowledge with other aspects of HMIS theories, methodologies, technologies, and applications, in a real-world setting, in a way that will help health organizations to cope with rapid changes and challenges encountered in today's health service industry.

CHAPTER QUESTIONS

1. Can "data" and "information" be used as interchangeable terms? Why or why not? How is the user important in this distinction?

2. What qualities in data and information will be crucial to obtaining the best information possible? What effect would there be within the organization if some of these qualities, or even one, were missing? Give examples from the mini cases provided.

3. What are the elements of information theory? Provide an illustration of the theory as it applies to information transfer among patients, physicians, and providers in HMOs. What is the weakest link? The strongest?

4. Can you explain "leveling" in data flow diagrams? What is its purpose? How does leveling differ from "system" and "detailed" flow charts?

5. Can statistics lie? What types of health statistics are collected today? Why are they useful? What aspects must we consider in order to be cautious about their interpretations?

6. How do you identify whether a health service organization is not collecting, transforming, or managing information properly? Use the example of a hospital information system (HIS) to illustrate your answer.

MINI CASE 4
STREAMLINING PATIENT CARE AT ST. VINCENT'S,
BRITISH COLUMBIA

In the afternoon of April 29, 1994, 26-year-old Stephen Elderhorst experienced intense abdominal pain and discomfort (especially on the right side) at a social gathering with his friends. It lasted for a few hours and did not dissipate. Stephen then asked his friends to drive him to St. Vincent's Hospital in Vancouver, British Columbia.

Shortly after being registered into the ADT system at the emergency department, Stephen was examined by a physician on duty. After eliminating several other possibilities including food poisoning, the doctor suspected appendicitis. He then informed the relevant departments and personnel that exploratory surgery was needed. The examination confirmed the doctor's suspicion.

Three hours later, the surgeons and nurses started performing a laparoscopic procedure on Stephen. In the meantime a bed in the acute care unit was made available for the 2 days after surgery, and the intravenous glucose solution and other medications were prepared. In particular, the dietetics department was informed not to give Stephen any food or drinks except water until more than 24 hours after the operation.

After examining Stephen the day after the procedure, another physician-on-duty determined that Stephen was fit to be discharged. Other departments concerned were notified and Stephen left the hospital in the late afternoon on the day following his operation.

MINI CASE QUESTIONS

1. In Stephen's case, a significant amount of "right" information was needed by various departments in the hospital. Explain what characteristics should be evident in the right information here and why.

2. What could have gone wrong in the delivery of "right" information to the responsible personnel in Stephen's case? (Relate your answer to information theory.)

3. Assuming that the structure and operations of both University Hospital, University of British Columbia, and St. Vincent's Hospital, Vancouver, are completely identical, with the help of Figure 4–4, develop a DFD from the hospital administrator's perspective for all information on Stephen's condition, from the moment he was admitted into the emergency department until he was discharged. Try to number the data flows accordingly (e.g., first, second, last).

4. What kind of health data on Stephen would probably have been collected during his stay in the hospital?

5. Develop, possibly with the help of a student or medical resident, a flow chart showing all the procedures followed and decisions made regarding Stephen's condition, from the moment he was first seen by the physician on duty until he was discharged. Try to think of what would have happened otherwise (e.g., what if Stephen's recovery were below expectation on the day following the operation?).

6. Assume that the model of HIS discussed in the text was fully in place at St. Vincent's Hospital. Imagine you were a nurse on duty during Stephen's entire stay in the hospital (at a nursing station near his ward); discuss what modules of the proposed integrated HIS you probably would have inter-

acted with (concerning Stephen's condition). Relate your answers to those for Questions 3 and 5.

CHAPTER REVIEW

In many organizations or systems in our society, most interactions among various components or subsystems use information as a common link. This chapter explored the nature of data, information, and information flow; identified sources of health statistics; and also described the various components of a model of a health management information system in a hospital environment.

Data are the collection of unstructured, raw facts that arise through the observation of physical phenomena, whereas information is the data that have been processed into a form both meaningful and useful to the decision maker. Once the raw data are collected, they can then be processed into the required form of information. Characteristics of good and useful information include accuracy, verifiability, relevance, intelligent processing, timeliness, comprehensiveness, action orientation, sensitivity, objectivity, cost-effectiveness, simplicity, and uniformity.

Information theory is a collection of mathematical theories that are concerned with the methods of coding, decoding, sorting, and retrieving information, and with the likelihood of a given degree of accuracy in the transmission of a message through a channel. Within any (information) communication system, five major components can be identified: source, transmitter, channel, receiver, and destination. In particular, noise and distortion in the communication channel can greatly reduce the purity of the signals and hence the fidelity of the messages transmitted.

Diagrammatic representations are convenient tools and techniques to help understand the flow of information in an institution. One of the most popular techniques is the data flow diagram (DFD), which may also be called a node diagram, block diagram, data flow graph, or bubble chart. A data flow diagram is essentially a network representation of a system. The main purpose of these diagrams is to break down a system into manageable levels of detail that can be visualized, first at a very general level, then gradually in greater and greater detail, in a process termed "leveling" or "top-down analysis." The basic elements of a DFD are data stores, data sources, movement of data, and transformation processes.

Another frequently used technique for graphically representing a process is the flow chart or flow diagram. It is similar to the DFD but has evolved in both the public and private sectors to become a versatile tool for defining pictorially the steps taken in a process. The "system" and "detailed" flow charts are comparable to the DFD's leveling, which produces multiple levels of complexity in a form that can be understood at both the general and the specific level. Although the symbols of the flow chart are often modified to adapt to the needs of specific groups or contexts, they are built from seven basic elements. These elements are referred to as the activity, decision, terminal, document, and database symbols plus the connector and flow lines.

Certain types of health statistics are commonly used by virtually all health service organizations. They generally fall into three categories: health status statistics, health resource statistics, and environmental health statistics. Health status statistics include population statistics, vital statistics, and morbidity statistics. Health resource statistics include statistics on health personnel, facilities, and services. Formerly called public health statistics, environmental health statistics provide data on health hazards, including noise, pollution, and deficient sanitation.

An information system is a set of elements working interactively to gather and process input data and to disseminate and distribute output information. An HMIS can be defined as a set of interrelated components working together to gather, retrieve, process, store, and disseminate information to support the activities of health systems planning, control, coordination, and decision making. As shown in this chapter in a model network of a hospital information system (HIS), the state-of-the-art system consists mainly of a centralized computer-based patient record database linked to different modules within which are several subsystem application programs. The centralized database is essentially the primary repository for all the data amassed from patient care and related areas (operations of the hospital). The four major modules include administration, patient management, facilities management, and medical applications, all of which routinely feed data into and retrieve information from the central database. This model can also be readily modified and adapted to suit the needs of other health service delivery institutions.

NOTES

1. S.L. Alter, How Effective Managers Use Information Systems, *Harvard Business Review* (November–December 1976): 97–104.

2. J.R. Galbraith, Organizational Design: An Information Processing View, *TIMS Interfaces* 4, no. 3 (May 1974): 28–36.

3. M.C. Yovits, Information and Data, *Encyclopedia of Computer Science and Engineering*, 2nd ed. (New York: Van Nostrand Reinhold, 1983): 715–717.

4. G.B. Davis and M.H. Olson, *Management Information Systems: Conceptual Foundations, Structure, and Development*, 2nd ed. (New York: McGraw-Hill Publishing Co., 1985).

5. H.C. Lucas, Jr., *Information Systems Concepts for Management*. (New York: McGraw-Hill Publishing Co., 1978).

6. R.L. Ackoff, Management Misinformation Systems, *Management Science* 14, no. 4 (1967): 147–156.

7. N. Weiner, *Cybernetics of Control and Communication in the Animal and the Machine* (New York: John Wiley & Sons, Inc., 1948).

8. Ibid.

9. G. Thompson and I. Handelman, *Health Data and Information Management* (London: Butterworth Publishers, 1978).

10. M. Zviran, Defining the Application Portfolio for an Integrated Hospital Integrated System: A Tutorial, *Journal of Medical Systems* 14, no. 1/2 (1990): 31–41.

11. Ibid.

Chapter 5

Essentials of Management Functions and Roles: Management Performance As the Basis for HMIS Designs

LEARNING OBJECTIVES

1. Define basic managerial roles and functions.
2. Relate health managerial performance measures to HMIS designs.
3. Identify subcomponents of a management information technology infrastructure.
4. Match health managerial roles to HMIS designs.
5. Identify new perspectives of health management.
6. Delineate practical steps to realizing HMIS benefits.

INTRODUCTION

We are entering a period of change—a shift *from the command and control organization,* to the information-based organization—*the organization of knowledge specialists…it is the management challenge of the future!*[1]

Although much has been written about the basic functions and changing roles of health services managers, planners, and administrators, little if any discussion in the literature has focused on how health managerial roles and functions relate to various facets and components of HMIS. Perhaps one reason for this lack of attention is the relatively low priority that HMIS applications have had over the years in the managerial cultures of many health organizations. Health executives are not necessarily technologically oriented, and many have not been brought up to the traditions of HMIS thinking. With the rapid diffusion of advanced organization technologies into every aspect of health service management, the need to under-

132

stand management and managerial performance as a basis for HMIS design is a challenge for health executives and senior management today. The goal of this chapter is to review the essence of management functions and roles and to relate managerial performance to the field of HMIS. Drawing briefly from the discussions of previous chapters on systems thinking and information processing for analyzing and solving health managerial problems, this chapter concentrates on the evolution of health management functions and roles and discusses how these roles and functions can be applied to integrating various components of a management information technology infrastructure (MITI) for achieving the specific goals and objectives of health service organizations and, more generally, the higher-level goals and visions of the health service industry.

The discussion begins with defining health management from a systems perspective; in particular, HMIS components are defined as inputs to the system, managerial performance measures as outputs of the system, and management roles as the processes needed to bridge inputs to outputs. Attention is given to three key health managerial performance criteria as the basis for HMIS designs: service efficiency, service effectiveness, and service excellence. After this, the key subcomponents of MITI are separately discussed and the management of these components is shown to be an important part of health service management. Health managerial roles are then examined more fully and related to information management and HMIS solutions. Lastly, new perspectives that health managers need to further the impacts of HMIS on the future of the health service industry are also discussed.

MANAGEMENT: WHAT AND HOW?

The science of management, unlike the physical sciences, is relatively poorly structured because of the unpredictable nature of managerial roles and decision making. In addition, many variables are involved in the interactions between management and workers (or human resources) and between management and other parts and resources of health organizations such as financial resources, health facilities and equipment, health technologies, health information resources, and health programs, services, and task activities. Therefore, apart from overall management functions and decision making, health managers are also responsible and accountable for many administrative duties inside and outside the organization. Resolving conflicts among different groups of people advocating different viewpoints; taking charge of emergencies when there is, for example, a disruption of work arising from a strike of union workers; dealing with changes in the external environment so as to adapt to new governmental regulations and policies; and charting the future of the organizations or agencies by bringing about innovative and creative changes are among the duties managers must perform in supervising their subordinates.

From a health organizational behavior perspective, Longest defined "management" as "a process with both interpersonal and technical aspects, through which the objectives of the health service organization are specified and accomplished by utilizing human and physical resources and technology."[2] This view fits our previous discussion on systems theory and the dynamics of systems behavior (Chapter 3). Using the language of systems theory, the traditional process of health management may be conceived as the art of planning, organizing, directing, and controlling resources such as people, plant and equipment, money, materials, and information to accomplish some predetermined objectives.[3-5] For health service organizations in particular, these objectives include the production of efficient, effective, and excellent (top-quality) health services.

Figure 5–1 shows a systemic view of the health managerial roles and functions as the closing of gaps between HMIS resources on the one hand and organizational goals and objectives on the other hand. The failure to achieve some or all of these organizational objectives is a failure in management functions, and hence there may be a need to review or reengineer the management process. This indicates the need to define and clarify the various basic functions of a health service manager.

The PODC Model

Accordingly, Henri Fayol has been credited as the chief contributor to the concept of the four key managerial functions commonly identified as the PODC model:[6]

1. Planning
2. Organizing
3. Directing
4. Controlling

Figure 5–2 shows the ordering and relationships among the various functions identified in the PODC model. Several other functions, such as decision making, and human resource responsibilities, such as staffing and coordinating, have since been added to this list through the works of numerous others,[7,8] particularly those of Chester Barnard;[9] these various perspectives will be incorporated into our discussion as we move along. In general, the management of a health service organization is thought to begin with most planning activities being carried out by a senior executive team. This process entails the formulation of formal statements of vision, mission, strategic goals, and objectives of the organization by involving

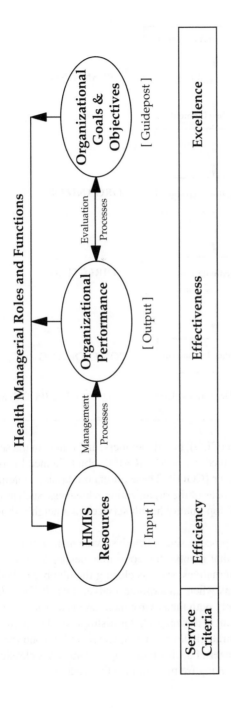

Figure 5–1 A Systemic View of the Health Management Process

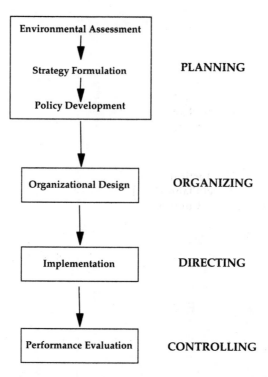

Figure 5–2 The Planning, Organizing, Directing, and Controlling (PODC) Model

the chief executive officer (CEO), board members, and others in the senior executive team (e.g., the chief medical officer [CMO], chief financial officer [CFO], and chief operational officer [COO]). These all-encompassing statements essentially define the strategic focus of the organization's business, such as the delivery of efficient, effective, and top-quality health services to a neighborhood community.

As part of the planning process, senior health service managers also make many other strategic decisions that involve the conscious design of strategies and the development of viable alternatives, such as closing the number of beds allocated to various health programs when undergoing budget cuts. In fact, the planning function interfaces intensely with the environment and is considered a high-order function of the organization; in this respect, it is distinguished from the other functions by its focus on the strategic level, that is, above and beyond the operational and tactical levels of managerial decision making in Anthony's classic three-level organizational decision-making framework (see Figure 5–3).

Environmental
Factors

Strategic
Level Planning
and Control

Feedback Loop
(Goal-Setting)

Tactical
Level Planning
and Control

Feedback Loop
(Goal-Seeking)

Operational
Level
Activities

Organizational
Resources

Figure 5–3 The Hierarchical Nature of the Management Control Feedback Loop

After planning, health managers must marshal and organize necessary and sufficient resources to accomplish the vision, mission, and predetermined goals and objectives of the organization. This activity ranges from establishing formal structures and designing a pattern of roles and relationships among subordinates to designing work systems, specifying procedures and flows, and structuring people-task relationships.[10] Personnel planning, or the determination of middle management positions and the selecting, orienting, training, and evaluating of health professionals and clinicians either directly or indirectly, as through delegated authority or representation, are also critical organizational functions for senior health managers. This is especially true since these activities are concerned with delivering health services rather than manufacturing commercial goods and services. Many people can easily place a dollar value on goods such as a video camera or services such as a haircut but would find it difficult to assess the cost of a heart transplantation operation. The value of the operative procedure depends in large measure on the nature and organization of professional services rendered, in particular, the quality of health provider–patient interactions.

Apart from the need to organize health service personnel and other resources efficiently and effectively, health managers must also direct (or actuate) by supervising and motivating their subordinates to fit individual goals and objectives with the planned vision, mission, goals, and objectives of the organization. This means that they must attempt to integrate the individual workers into an organized system of work. In this regard, the commitment shown by the workers to get their jobs done in a professional and timely fashion is a reflection of the success of management. Directions in a health service organization need not come only from daily supervision but can also arise informally from the organization's culture. The use of directives, policies, and established procedures exerts and extends the directing functions of management in different ways. In the end, the roles played by the CEO, the CMO, the COO, and other members of the senior management team (e.g., the board members) will shape the actual directions and activities taken by various other players in the organization.

Moreover, health managers need to control and evaluate the performance of the organization by establishing standards and ensuring the efficient and effective accomplishment of stated goals and planned activities. This is where the feedback mechanism of the system that is described in Chapter 3 is put to work. This control is hierarchical in nature and may be instituted at various levels of the organization; for example, middle management will exercise control over operational and tactical activities of subordinates, whereas senior management will exercise control over the professional and managerial activities of middle management. Behaviors not conforming to expected standards may be corrected (changed) by means of enforcing an effective feedback mechanism (e.g., a written warning, retraining or providing further professional development for a worker). Figure 5–3 shows the hierarchical nature of this control-feedback loop in health organization management.

The sequence underlying the PODC model—planning, organizing, directing, and controlling—although appearing cyclical in nature, is, however, iterative in practice. These various functions are interwoven and health service managers perform them simultaneously, often in no particular order but as a part of a continuum. Interestingly, the traditional PODC model dictates a strong formal line-staff reporting relationship and implies a top-down organizational chain of command. First, changes in the environment are assessed as threats and opportunities. These are further analyzed to provide inputs to top management in ongoing and future planning exercises. Second, the formal authority structure is used to carry out plans. Finally, performance is based on how well operating results conform to planned results and how well corrective actions are achieved by means of exercising control over exceptions (i.e., substandard performers). The paradigm of organizational change in this classical perspective is one of reacting to internal pressures, usually through intense managerial control, and assumes a more or less stable environment.

As the job of a health service manager becomes more complex as a result of increasing turbulence in the health care environment, there is a need to adopt new perspectives, create innovative mechanisms, and provide new tools and techniques to support managerial tasks. We will discuss these new perspectives later in the chapter; for now, we will focus on three managerial performance criteria as forming the basis for HMIS designs.

MANAGERIAL PERFORMANCE AS THE BASIS FOR HMIS DESIGNS

In this section, we will concentrate on three key performance indicators that determine the success of HMIS solutions within the context of the health service delivery industry. In a later section, we will discuss the components of HMIS to clarify the role that HMIS can play in health service organizations. Finally, we will relate the roles of health service managers to HMIS components in order to complete the discussion on how management can redesign HMIS in order to get the "value" out of HMIS investments. On the basis of our understanding that the ultimate goal of all managerial functions and activities is to accomplish some purposeful and meaningful outcome, our question then focuses on the outcome of health service management and the role that HMIS plays in assisting health management in this endeavor: What key performance criteria should be considered when applying HMIS design within the health service industry?

In reviewing the literature on health managerial performance relative to HMIS designs,[11–13] it appears that there are essentially three basic categories of systems-related measures of health service managerial performance when thinking about HMIS.

1. Service efficiency
2. Service effectiveness
3. Service excellence

Service efficiency implies doing things the right way: that is, it involves how best to perform a given service with regard to predetermined organizational performance criteria, for example, the expectation that HMIS designs will lead to timeliness and greater accessibility of clinical services.

Service effectiveness implies doing the right thing: that is, it involves what should be done in a given setting to ensure that the correct organizational performance criteria are chosen, for example, the expectation that HMIS designs will lead to better-quality patient care services and provision of more appropriate services.

Service excellence implies being at the leading edge in terms of quality service delivery; in essence, this involves strategic positioning of the organization within the industry marketplace and achievement of customer (i.e., both internal and external "customers") satisfaction, for example, the expectation that HMIS designs will lead to service differentiation and a recognized professional image.

Service Efficiency

Service efficiency assumes that HMIS designs will provide for the financial viability of the organization and enhance the administrative ability of the organization to gather, update, and maintain an appropriate database that can support the delivery of health services in a cost-effective and timely manner. Examples of benefits in this category are reduced operational costs such as unproductive labor and excessive inventories, increased revenue due to a greater number of patients serviced by each health service provider, improved cash flow optimization, improved allocation and use of financial and human resources, reduced delays (i.e., waiting time), and increased work productivity and information processing capabilities in the organization. Stated simply, it is the fulfillment of the promises of automation to make information resource handling more efficient and thus eliminate costly administrative financial errors and unnecessary human resource problems.

From a health management perspective, the traditional focus of information technologies, in the form of basic financial accounting and transaction processing system (TPS) applications, has been chiefly concerned with service efficiency. Zerrenner observed that these systems are typically characterized by large centralized databases and are thus justified largely on the basis of cost savings resulting from the automation of clerical and accounting functions.[14]

Admittedly, large data systems such as the TPS are designed primarily to improve organizational efficiency rather than organizational effectiveness; that is, from a process and subsystem point of view, these applications can be expected to produce cost-effective reports, but those reports may not necessarily meet management needs in achieving the system's vision, mission, goals, and objectives. In the past, these systems have almost always been large-scale systems that are also batch processed rather than processed on a real-time basis: that is, the transactions in these systems are collected (or batched) and processed periodically, and that is why they are so cost-effective. Missing transactions are detected through counting the number of transactions or through the use of some other totals such as financial totals. Today, real-time processing (i.e., data updates made to files as soon as the transaction takes place) even for large-scale systems is becoming a reality through rapid cost reduction in computer hardware, software, and communication technology.

One of the major criticisms that have been aimed at traditional TPS-based systems (e.g., stand-alone medical records and registry systems, pharmacy and food service inventory systems, nurse scheduling systems, and cost accounting systems) is that of data overloading, that is, the production of a full house of reports that are of virtually no "managerial" use, creating a so-called data rich, information poor organizational environment. As Zerrenner pointed out, "What most information systems do not do is search for the relevant data and then turn them into meaningful information. Presentation of the data is equally important. It can include ratios, historical perspectives, comparisons, and other internal or external data and can be presented in meaningful form, for example, in tables, bar graphs, or scatter graphs."[15]

In sum, although TPS-based applications in hospitals and other health service organizations (see Chapter 7) produce reports in an efficient and cost-effective manner (i.e., compared to manual production of reports), these reports may not necessarily be wanted or needed by management. These systems fall short of accomplishing higher organizational goals and objectives such as service effectiveness and excellence.

Service Effectiveness

Indeed, we may become so absorbed with increasing service efficiency that we overlook the need for service effectiveness. This implies that the services performed on patients should not just be "band-aid" solutions resulting in patients' being readmitted within a short period for the same problems. Such a system is ineffective although it may provide efficient care. Service effectiveness, therefore, is the concern of higher administrative and clinical decision-making levels as opposed to the more operational decision-making level of service efficiency.

At this higher level, HMIS designs that may be of interest are those that will call attention to benefits such as better allocation or more appropriate utilization of health service resources, improved quality of patient care, and more effective use of clinical services, for instance, the integration of fragmentary services, the elimination of data registry duplication, and the reduction of irrelevant data reporting that does not ultimately contribute to patient care. Tan et al. discussed the benefits of automated utilization care plans (UCP) for effective clinical and patient care data management.[16]

Unlike service efficiency, which is normally measurable by the amount of time taken to complete a service from beginning to end, the difficulty of focusing on effectiveness in applying HMIS designs is embedded within the broader issue of measurement. That is, from whose standpoint is service effectiveness to be defined (i.e., the patient, the physician, or the provider)? For instance, service effectiveness from a patient's viewpoint may just be the caring attitude of the service provider and the extra effort and time taken by the clinical staff to ensure that the patient is fully comfortable about the care process; service effectiveness from a provider's viewpoint may instead be the determination of what is an appropriate length of stay (to reduce the chance of the patient's being readmitted for the same illness after discharge). Generally speaking, service effectiveness may be improved if health service managers empower themselves and their subordinates with decision support, executive support, and knowledge capturing or knowledge transferring technologies.[17] These and similar types of technologies are discussed in Parts III and V (Chapters 7 through 9 and Chapter 14).

Decision and executive support technologies use automated databases and decision models to enhance health service executive, managerial, and clinical decision-making processes. Expert technology, in essence, is the automation of knowledge transfer and managerial learning processes (Chapter 8). One of the key benefits of using advanced technologies is to allow novice and less experienced workers to have access to expert opinions without paying the high consultation price of a human expert. Advanced technologies are intended to empower the users to make informed choices in an effective and intelligent manner. Moreover, these technologies retain expertise, skills, and knowledge among company workers. Also, they preserve what might have been lost through the retirement, resignation, or death of an acknowledged company expert.

Since advancing HMIS technologies is now in a stage of rapid diffusion among health service organizations, it is believed that it will begin to have dramatic and significant impacts on managerial and clinical practices over the next few years.

Service Excellence

The move to apply HMIS designs to transforming the practice of medicine is perhaps a consequence of the "corporatization" of health services in the United States and more recently in Canada.[18] According to Fried et al., "Corporatization is an organizational restructuring in the direction of an organizational form typically found in industrial corporations, characterized by clearly articulated corporate objectives and a division between corporate and operational levels."[19] Corporatization in health services in North America has occurred mainly through multiinstitutional arrangements such as the sudden exponential growth of health maintenance organizations (HMOs) or preferred provider organizations (PPOs) in the United States, and the trend of hospital mergers or the introduction of comprehensive health organizations (CHOs) in Canada. These multiinstitutional arrangements, with their corporate structures and their business orientation (i.e., having cost minimization and increased productivity as their corporate objectives), have forced other hospitals and facilities to become increasingly competitive in the new health care environment.

Service excellence implies being at the cutting edge. It involves enhancing both the internal and the external professional image and perceptions of the staff through heightened customer loyalty and satisfaction. Medical and nonmedical staff, for example, can be imbued with the ability to implement high-quality programs and services successfully by supplying them with the automated support and communication infrastructure that will enable them to leave more time for patient care and services. Ultimately, designing of HMIS to gain strategic and tactical advantages for the organization through quality differentiation from services offered by other organizations can enhance the image of the organization to its customers (i.e., patients, payers, and physicians) and thus position the organization at the forefront of the health service industry. Kropf noted that this can be accomplished, for example, through generating first-class, real-time, accurate, and more relevant information systems for strategic planning and decision making, marketing, and locking-in of customer (i.e., employees, associated clinicians and physicians, suppliers and patients) loyalty.[20]

Apart from the decision support and expert technologies, another class of HMIS applications that is particularly useful to health service managers and clinical professionals in being at the leading edge is the integrated telecommunication systems (Chapter 9). Integrated telecommunication systems have the capabilities to enhance current decision support and information sharing technologies such as group decision support systems, teleconferencing systems, teleradiology, and telemarketing systems. Other examples include the use of decentralized and distributed processing to support end-user computing[21] and the application of local area networking (LAN) and wide area networking (WAN) to interpret databases or to share data files and applications between groups and individuals.

Case management systems (CMS), which purport to integrate financial and clinical information, will allow hospital managers to promote "standardization" of clinical decision making and to encourage physicians who do not practice according to standards to do so. Such a system will in turn create a shift in the corporate power equilibrium from the physicians to the corporate managers. Physicians, who were "the captains" of the team, are now simply players.[22]

Exhibit 5–1 summarizes the various HMIS designs that may be appropriate for service efficiency, service effectiveness, and service excellence.

A major obstacle to the adoption and diffusion of these advancing information technologies, however, is the lack of communication standards for resolving intraorganizational and interorganizational systems incompatibilities (Chapter 9). Past experience has shown us the need to integrate the various isolated technological islands of data processing (DP), office automation (OA), and teleprocessing (TP) to realize the benefits of service excellence. We will discuss HMIS benefit realization more fully at the end of this chapter. Our focus now will be on the various subcomponents of a management information technology infrastructure (MITI) as inputs to be managed in the larger context of the health service management system.

Exhibit 5–1 A Classification of Health Management Information Systems (HMIS) Designs for Achieving Service Efficiency, Effectiveness, and Excellence

CRITERION	KEY EMPHASIS	HMIS SOLUTIONS
Service Efficiency	Doing Things Right	• Nurse Scheduling Systems • Pharmacy & Food Service Inventory Systems • Medical Record Systems • Utilization Management Reporting Systems • Cost Accounting Systems
Service Effectiveness	Doing the Right Things	• Electronic Billing Systems • Utilization Forecasting Systems • Responsibility Reporting • Performance Tracking Systems • Integrated Database Systems • Information Center for End-User Computing (EUC)
Service Excellence	Being at the Leading Edge	• Teleradiology • Nursing Expert Systems • Other Medical (e.g., Laboratory) Expert Systems • Real-Time Systems • Local Area Network (LAN) and Wide Area Network (WAN) Linking Databases

THE MANAGEMENT OF MITI SUBCOMPONENTS

A health management information system has been defined as a set of interrelated components working together to retrieve, gather, process, store, and disseminate information to support the activities of health systems planning, directing, organizing, controlling, coordinating, and decision making. The primary purpose of an HMIS is to provide managers of health service organizations with insight into the regular or irregular, satisfactory or unsatisfactory operations of the organizations so that they can exercise their management skills more productively, efficiently, effectively, and appropriately.

As a direct consequence of the general trend in the corporate restructuring of the health service delivery industry today, ideal HMIS designs should provide not only a convenient tool for administrative and decision-making processes within a health service organization but a continuous information backbone throughout the entire system to facilitate case management (CM) and strategic planning. Very likely, this would entail the establishment of a management information technology infrastructure (MITI). To this end, we will focus on the key components of a leading edge MITI, data, technology, end-users, and tasks, as well as on how these key components should be managed.

Figure 5–4 shows the subcomponents of MITI. The management of each of these components is critical to the successful management of HMIS as a whole, which in turn affects the total management of the health service delivery system.

Data Management

In Chapter 4, we said that data are the basic building blocks of an HMIS. They are the raw materials from which information can be generated. From our discussion on health managerial performance, we know that although it is important to increase overall system service efficiency by improving data processing time, the more critical role of HMIS designs is to improve service effectiveness and excellence by providing correctly formatted data to the right person at the right time. This aspect of HMIS management is sometimes overlooked by health administrators in their zeal to improve system efficiencies merely through acquiring larger and more powerful computers.

In general, all data inputs of an information system can be classified as being either external or internal. External data originate in the health service environment, such as the government, consumers, and third-party payers; internal data originate in sources within the organization such as the finance department, health records, and laboratories. As we shift our focus from service efficiency to service effectiveness and excellence, it becomes apparent that health managerial data processing must shift from internal data inputs to include and integrate more and

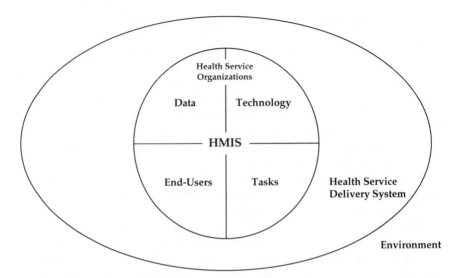

Figure 5–4 The Subcomponents of Management Information Technology Infrastructure (MITI)

more external data inputs. As well, the future HMIS should combine formerly distinct databases such as financial systems, clinical systems, dietetic systems, and laboratory systems through networking or building of data linkages; the same data can then be used for a variety of purposes. The design of integrated case-mix applications for multihospital arrangements is an example of the need to combine various sources of internal and external data.

Moreover, data captured in an HMIS should have both quantitative and qualitative components to be relevant, timely, and meaningful. Financial data such as the cost of supplies or volume in stock are mostly represented quantitatively by discrete numbers that are easily manipulated and automated, whereas clinical data must have both quantitative and qualitative elements; for example, the level of calcium or oxygen in serum is quantitative, but a description of a patient's symptoms is qualitative.[23] The automation of qualitative data has always been a challenge, although we are seeing more and more technical breakthroughs in this regard, such as the automation of large bibliographic systems and the application of imaging technologies.

Lastly, changes in the strategic or tactical direction in the management of a health service organization should be reflected in corresponding changes in the types and details of data entered into the system to ensure that the system has the "right" data to be processed into useful information. This requires regular review and auditing of various aspects of the entire system.

Technology Management

As data from different sources are combined to generate useful information for decision making, several questions arise as to how the outcomes (i.e., results of these decisions) should be incorporated continually into the system (i.e., through the use of a feedback mechanism). The purpose this would serve is to provide a follow-up of changes needed to improve future managerial decision making and performance. Questions also arise about managing the growth of automation and managerial information processing as the organization grows (see Chapters 1 and 2). To address these concerns, there must be a melding of computing technology and managerial knowledge. It is this combination of managerial and computing technology that gives rise to terms like "technology management," "management of technology," and "management technology." This last term refers to new and innovative techniques and perspectives for health service managers and is discussed later on in the chapter.

Management of technology is complex since it combines the fields of science and technology with organization and management. Familiarity with technical jargon is a prerequisite for health service managers to participate actively in decisions being made concerning technology management (Parts I and II). But knowledge of only the fundamentals of technology concerning hardware, software, communications, and networking is inadequate (Part III); there must be a corresponding understanding of management techniques and methods available to control and evaluate the use and diffusion of these technologies (Part IV). Health managers need to plan the growth, direct the use, and control the misuse of technology to achieve health service efficiency, effectiveness, and excellence.

Previously, we noted the need to plan an integration of isolated technological islands (i.e., islands of DP, OA, and TP technologies) to realize the benefits of service excellence. It is apparent that each of these separate technological islands is managed very differently from the others. For example, the management of OA technology, which includes word processing, desktop publishing, computer-based interactive media technology, and optical scanning equipment, has been placed in the hands of clerical and office workers from the beginning. As a result, there will be growing contention among the information system, telecommunication, and office administration groups regarding the direction in which OA should develop in order to move to greater integration. Perhaps each group sees itself as having a major stake in promoting its views of office systems.

As a result of conflicts among subsystem goals and objectives, a total systems perspective is advocated for technology management. Apart from careful planning and directing of the technology, it should also be controlled. In practice, it is often the case that after a technology has been installed, savings that were anticipated did not materialize and benefits that were expected were never realized.

Where reduced flow of paper within the organization was expected, more voluminous reports and memos were generated. Worse still, rising power struggles often emerged among systems people who were in charge of the technology and end-user groups who saw themselves as having an increasing, significant role in the design and application of the technology. In addition, rising expenditures of these separate departmental groups tended to have, sometimes beyond management control, a detrimental effect on the total budget for organizational automation projects.

Taken together, technology management in the context of MITI means managing the planning, utilization, and operation of all information technology of a health service organization; the stages-of-growth (SOG) theory, which was introduced in Chapter 2, provides a useful framework for managing technology for health managers.

End-User Computing (EUC) Management

Computing technology has in recent decades become more powerful and easier to handle. At the same time, its accessibility has also shifted the organizational focus from the technology itself to the user of the technology. In HMIS, this phenomenon is known as end-user computing (EUC). EUC is the design, development, and use of application programs and information systems by people who are not system professionals; it is described more fully in Chapter 6. Here, our discussion concentrates on the management of EUC.

When EUC began, most projects were simple applications. Today, EUC spans the whole health service organization and has significant impacts on the functioning of the whole organization system infrastructure. It is therefore imperative that management recognize the need to coordinate the efforts of multifaceted end-user applications. It is far more advantageous to coordinate EUC than to let it proceed fragmented or to impede its development. Application systems developed by end-users (i.e., system nonprofessionals, such as physicians, nurses, middle managers, and clerical workers) can in fact upset existing organizational stability and may become a source of organizational conflicts if inappropriately managed. The literature on the management of EUC agrees that there are several important benefits to be gained by successfully including end-users in organizational HMIS planning.

- End-users will receive optimal support for applying HMIS solutions to organizational problem solving and thereby developing a good communication link between end-users and systems personnel.
- End-users will become more sophisticated in their use of HMIS technologies and applications over time and thereby begin to appreciate the services of systems professionals and the significance of the HMIS functions.

- End-users will also begin to recognize the potential of these technologies and applications for supporting organizational tasks and thereby gain a better feel for ways HMIS technologies may be applied to improve service efficiency, effectiveness, and excellence.

Several areas of EUC management will only be highlighted in this discussion because of space limitations. First, policies and procedures to maximize the benefits of EUC should be implemented. A health service organization should have strategies for promoting, managing, and controlling the evolution of EUC.[24] At a minimum, management should request the documentation of individual user applications. Organizations should also limit the set of hardware, software, and vendor options available to end-users. Using a wide variety of microcomputers and applications can result in difficulties and inefficiencies in training and maintenance as well as incompatibilities among systems.

Second, EUC support services should also be made available. The development of end-user applications does not negate the need for guidance and assistance with difficult problems. To ensure service efficiency, effectiveness, and excellence, the development of an information support center[25] that is staffed by information system experts is advocated. Such centers can provides end-users with hardware, software, training, consulting, and problem solving resources. One issue that will become increasingly important in the consideration of providing support services for EUC is the appropriate mix of centralization (to achieve service efficiency), decentralization (to achieve service effectiveness), and distribution (to achieve service excellence) of computing resources and HMIS functions within the health "corporation."

Also, many end-users want to have access to the maximum amount of data stored on a database as possible, but some of the data in an HMIS may be sensitive. Examples of such sensitive data include the salaries of health professionals and detailed patient records and laboratory test results, as well as addresses and phone numbers. A policy for data access, privacy, and security (Chapter 11) must therefore be in place. Among the issues that have to be addressed are (1) the types of data to which users have direct or limited access, (2) the circumstances under which data can be uploaded (transferred from a personal computer or small computer system to a large mainframe system), (3) the circumstances under which data can be downloaded (transferred from the large mainframe system to personal computers or small computer systems), and (4) the procedures needed to guarantee prosper database access and use.

Lastly, other factors that contribute to successful EUC management are (1) encouraging positive user attitudes toward EUC, (2) augmenting the perception of user-friendliness of software tools and interfaces provided to EUC, (3) moderating the influence of computer background on EUC perceptions and attitudes, and (4) creating EUC independence from the data processing environment to enhance user satisfaction.[26]

Functional Task Management

From an information management perspective, the HMIS should be able to convert raw data into useful information to aid health administrators at all levels of organizational decision making: operational, tactical, and strategic. In addition, the provision of such computer-based management must penetrate all key task functions of the health service delivery organization: personnel (e.g., nursing), finance (e.g., accounting), plant and equipment (e.g., laboratory), and programs and services (e.g., emergency care).

Figure 5–5 shows an integrated model of the various functional task components that are supported by MITI, how these various task components may be integrated into the different levels of organizational decision making in a health service organization, and the respective HMIS applications for the different decision-making levels as conceptualized by the familiar pyramidal task structure.

Operational level decision making in a health service organization relates mostly to the line-staff or departmental tasks directed at improving service efficiency, accuracy, timeliness, and completion of services. Tactical level decision making involves the aggregation of data to provide a wider perspective related to planning and control decisions for middle managers such as department heads and program directors. At this level, the emphasis will be shifted more to organizational service effectiveness such as assessing the appropriateness of services rendered. Strategic decision making involves the use of information as a strategic resource in long-range planning for top management in the organization and therefore entails higher-level goals beyond efficiency and effectiveness, for example, achievement of service excellence (i.e., the ultimatum of a service organization).

To illustrate the role of HMIS in supporting the decision making of these various functional tasks, we will focus on the personnel subsystem, which is concerned with the hiring (input), employment (process), and termination (output) of personnel required to support the health service delivery of a patient care facility.[27] Exhibit 5–2 shows the input, process, and output functions that relate to the various levels of organizational decision making for this subsystem. At the operational level, the engagement of personnel begins with enlisting an appropriate mix of clinical and nonclinical personnel (operational input: enlistment). The capacity and skills of these people are then applied to support the delivery of health services (operational process: employment), and the workers are ultimately discharged or released from the subsystem (operational output: exit). HMIS applications at this level will therefore consist of personnel records that maintain personal data of individual workers from their enlistment through employment to exit. The entry,

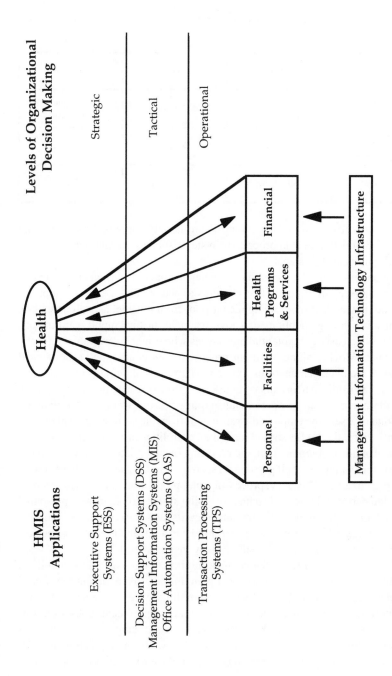

Figure 5–5 An Integrated Model of Functional Task Components, Organizational Decision-Making Levels, and HMIS Applications

Exhibit 5–2   The Input, Process, and Output Functions of the Personnel Subsystem of a Health Service Organization

Levels of Decision Making	Input	Process	Output
Strategic (Goal-Setting)	Personnel Requirements	Job Design	Personnel Reduction
Tactical (Goal-Seeking)	Recruitment	Review	Retirement
Operational	Enlistment	Employment	Exit

processing, and production of these reports are largely supported by traditional large-scale administrative data processing systems such as the automated personnel records and payroll systems.

Moving one notch up the hierarchy of management control (i.e., at the tactical level), the goal-seeking function that attempts to actuate the operational input of "enlistment" is the creation of an applicant pool from outside, as well as within, the organization through publicity and advertisement (tactical input: recruitment). This pool will consist of all potential employees who might be available to fill the required roles. Moving along the input-process-output continuum at the tactical control level, the management of the operational process of workers already "employed" is a periodic performance review function (tactical process: review), whereas the management of operational output of "exit" workers is a planning function that oversees the employee's retirement from the system (tactical output: retirement). Here, the HMIS should have the capabilities of gathering of data for evaluating candidate potential, periodic reporting of supervisory reviews of workers, and eventual archival of all personnel records for individuals who have retired from the organization. The entry, processing, and production of these reports may be supported partly by large-scale data processing systems (e.g., using a personnel records system for the archival of personnel records) and partly by microcomputer applications (e.g., using a decision support model to assist in the employee performance reviews to be completed by supervisory management).

At the strategic control level, the goal-setting function to control tactical input of "recruitment" will consist of personnel planning, that is, planning the mix of personnel resources required for delivering all of the services of the health service organization in question (strategic input: personnel requirements). As well, this higher-order control and feedback function has corresponding management roles and responsibilities for the tactical process of "review" through planning and designing jobs for employees (strategic process: job design). Similarly, the personnel planning function of determining when and for how long each type of worker is required may be used to control for tactical output of "retirement" (strategic output: personnel reduction). Types of HMIS applications that may support these kinds of analysis and that would allow senior management to have access to aggregate data generated at operational and tactical levels to produce new kinds of information at the strategic level include health executive information systems (HEIS) and health strategic information systems (HSIS). The matching of HMIS technologies and applications to the different interpersonal, informational, and decisional roles of the health managers is discussed next.

SUPPORTING HEALTH MANAGERIAL ROLES WITH HMIS TECHNOLOGIES AND APPLICATIONS

Henry Mintzberg, who intensively studied how managers spend their time, revealed that chief executive officers (CEOs) act as the nerve centers of their organizations.[28] Of the countless daily activities that the managers perform such as scheduled and unscheduled meetings, desk work, telephone calls, tours of facilities, and outside contacts, Mintzberg argued that these various activities may be classified essentially into one or more of three sets of interrelated roles as shown in Figure 5–6.

1. Interpersonal roles—These roles center on interacting with others.
2. Informational roles—These roles relate to information gathering, processing, and dissemination.
3. Decisional roles—These roles reflect managerial decision-making activities.

According to this view, health managers interact dynamically with their network of contacts both inside and outside the organization. From among these contacts, information of all types is gathered by these executives and managers for the primary purposes of decision making, information dissemination, and distribution. This view therefore advocates the importance of information as a resource and the need to manage its use for decision making and communications (see Chapter 11).

Interpersonal Roles and HMIS

On the basis of their formal authority and status, health managers and CEOs perform three interpersonal roles. First, as figureheads, they are often regarded as important and meaningful symbols in organizational rituals and ceremonies. For example, many hospital and health service CEOs are asked to represent their

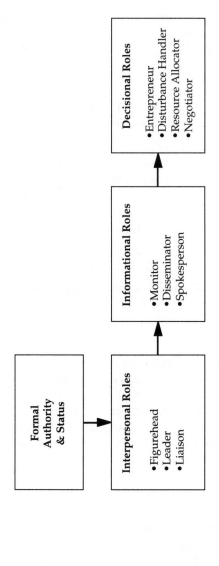

Figure 5-6 Mintzberg's Model of Managerial Roles

organization in board meetings and are expected to sit on various commissions, national task forces, and international committees. Second, as leaders, health managers often maintain formal reporting relations with their subordinates. One of the most difficult aspects of staying in the lead for health service CEOs and managers is the ability to cope with and adapt to changes in the health care environment. With "corporatization" of medicine and health organizations becoming a trend, many good leaders of community hospitals may find that their knowledge and skills are both limited and inadequate for overseeing large multihospital corporations. Perhaps this is due to their limited exposure to an environment fostering national competition. Third, as liaisons, health service CEOs and managers have to interact with and relate to stakeholders who are external to their organization. These managers, for example, must project and maintain a high professional image among stakeholders. To this end, they are expected to build good rapport with the government that regulates the system, third-party payers who fund it, and consumers of health services who use it.

In terms of interpersonal roles, therefore, it has been observed that a combination of advancing office and telecommunication technologies has provided management with new ways of keeping in close contact with and exerting an "electronic presence" on others. For example, Parker and Case cited office information systems (OIS), including electronic mail, facsimile, voice mail, audio conferencing, computer conferencing, desktop publishing, groupware, presentation graphics, and video teleconferencing, as providing effective mechanisms for managers to plan, organize, direct, control, and coordinate even when they are unable to be physically and interpersonally present.[29]

Apart from reducing intraorganizational and extraorganizational communication costs, OIS can greatly enhance managerial capabilities in capturing and transferring large volumes of information quickly through telecommuting. In effect, these technologies allow health service managers to continue their work outside the normal organizational confines of time and space, thus increasing their productivity. In practical terms, having a portable state-of-the-art computer in hand is like having a second office desktop whenever and wherever the need arises for a health service executive.

Informational Roles and HMIS

The three interpersonal roles just described define three informational roles for health service CEOs and managers. First, as monitors, health service executives and managers are expected continually to seek information from all sources and in all forms to inform them dynamically of what goes on in the environment, both inside and outside the organization. Second, as disseminators, health service managers and CEOs must interpret the information they have gathered and transmit relevant and privileged information to their subordinates to maintain loyalty and respect. In this regard, they must have a keen sense of current trends and knowledge of contemporary issues in health service administration so as to interpret available information correctly and quickly in context. Aside from information needing interpretation, some of the information transmitted by the managers in this role will be just plain facts and figures, and some will require the integration of diverse viewpoints of organizational key actors. Last, as spokespersons, health service managers and CEOs must selectively send information on the organization's plans, policies, actions, results, and decisions outside the organization to project a positive image of the institution in the public's eye and to ensure goodwill among institutional stakeholders (i.e., payers, physicians, and patients); in this sense, health service managers are regarded as experts on all aspects of their functioning.

As offshoots of earlier HMIS solutions, middle and higher management in many health service organizations have over the years shifted their attention gradually from traditional data processing systems (DPS) to management reporting systems (MRS) and more recently to strategic information systems (SIS). Therefore, systems that will help serve and fulfill their informational roles include utilization management reporting systems (UMRS), forecasting support systems (FSS), case-mix information systems (C-MIS), and other telecommunication systems (e.g., electronic mailing and networking).

UMRS will provide managers with insights as to the appropriate or inappropriate use of health resources and assist them to stimulate continuous quality improvements throughout the organization. Case-mix applications are capable of identifying, segregating, and describing the organizational product, service, and patient characteristics. SIS applications can assist the managers to solve a range of ad hoc managerial and policy decision-making problems such as the need to plan strategically, to monitor environmental trends, to scan market opportunities, and to simulate various what-if scenarios.[30] Today, health service executives and managers can also take advantage of these technologies to fulfill their interpersonal roles as figureheads, leaders, and liaisons discussed earlier.

Decisional Roles and HMIS

Out of these various interpersonal and informational roles, Mintzberg derived four decisional roles for health service executives and managers. First, as entrepreneurs, these executives and managers are perceived as constantly scanning their environment for critical information that can signal valuable opportunities or potential threats. In this role, health executives and managers are expected to initiate innovations or assign "improvement" projects to bring about significant organizational changes. Second, as disturbance handlers/troubleshooters, these managers are responsible for any organizational crises that arise. In this role they are expected to resolve conflicts among subordinates and to perform investigations of any disturbing allegations about them, their delegates, or any other agents of the organization. Third, as resource allocators, health service executives and managers will oversee the allocation of all organizational resources. In this role, they are often pressured into endorsing subordinates' decisions and activities. Finally, as negotiators, these managers must fight for their visions and secure meaningful and worthwhile contracts.

Several HMIS applications exist to aid health service executives and managers in their decisional roles. These systems range from simple management reporting systems (MRS) to those systems with advanced capabilities for structuring and analyzing relevant data and transforming them into timely and meaningful information for managerial decision making.[31] Examples include MRS and OIS (Chapter 7); KBS (Knowledge Based Systems) and ES (Chapter 8); and telecommunication and networking applications (Chapter 9).

Altogether, the general goal of HMIS technologies and applications is to assist health service managers in the fulfillment of their roles. These automated systems not only facilitate more efficient and cost-effective managerial performance but, more importantly, provide more effective means of information gathering, information interpretation, and information dissemination, thus enhancing health managerial service excellence. One observation that distinguishes Mintzberg's managerial roles from Fayol's PODC model described earlier in the chapter is the shift in focus from internal managerial functions, which tend to follow a traditional top-down approach, to a recognition that seeks to expand managerial networking relationships in all directions: inward, outward, upward, downward, and laterally. This explains why in this perspective, health service managers are regarded as the nerve centers of the organization, as shown in Figure 5–7.

In summary, the roles of health service CEOs and managers have expanded over the years, moving from primarily an internal to a dual internal-external focus. Moreover, another major shift in the organizational role perspective over the years is the move away from strictly formal structural reporting relationships to a greater emphasis on informal structural relationships. These two types of relationships coexist and are inseparable in today's organizations. As Blau and Scott observed; "It is impossible to understand the nature of a formal organization without investigating the networks of informal relations and the unofficial norms as well as the formal hierarchy of authority and the official body of rules, since the formally instituted and the informally emerging patterns are inextricably intertwined."[32]

Accordingly, Longest argues that these two aspects of organizational life are totally intertwined.[33] The distinction between the formal and the informal is only an analytical one and does not exist in practice; there is only one actual organization. Recognition of the informal organization is therefore critical for designing an

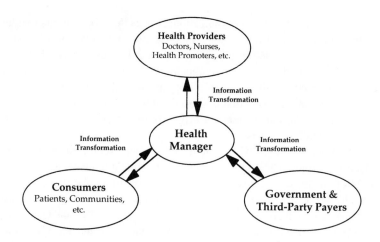

Figure 5–7 The Health Service Manager As the Nerve Center of the Organizational Information Processing System

organizational HMIS since it reflects the need to pay special attention to the potential power struggles among the various groups (i.e., end-users, systems professionals, and communications people). This brings us to the realization that there is a need for new perspectives of health service management to help us understand how the goals of service efficiency, service effectiveness, and service excellence may be achieved in today's changing health care environment, as well as to extend our understanding of potential HMIS impacts on the future of the health service delivery industry.

NEW PERSPECTIVES OF HEALTH MANAGEMENT AND IMPACTS OF HMIS ON TOMORROW'S HEALTH SERVICE INDUSTRY

The new perspectives of health service management to be discussed in this section are a synthesis of the earlier perspectives that will further enhance and expand the traditional PODC model and may be considered as a natural evolution of the Mintzberg model. Accordingly, the modern health service CEO focuses managerial attention on two fronts: (1) corporate culture and (2) organizational environment.

Overall, our intent here is to show that by focusing attention on corporate culture and organizational environment through a continuous quality improvement (CQI) approach, the modern health service CEO can bring about organizational changes (innovations) that will redirect the emphasis of HMIS technologies from service efficiency toward service effectiveness and excellence (see Chapter 13).

Notably, other structural elements and processes such as formal organizational arrangements (i.e., structure and operating systems), resources (i.e., people, finance, plant, and equipment), technology (i.e., tools, techniques, and methodologies), key actors (i.e., personal characteristics, goals, and strategies of dominant coalitions), and key organizational processes (i.e., information gathering, communications, decision making, and material/information flow), which have been largely covered in earlier discussions on managerial roles, functions, and activities, are still important parts of the organization.[34] Figure 5–8 shows the significance of corporate culture and environment in the context of a traditional model of health organizational structural elements and processes.

Managing Corporate Culture

Today, there are unprecedented pressures from all sectors of the health service industry to reduce waste (service efficiency), to justify cost allocation (service effectiveness), and to improve quality (service excellence). This is the inevitable result of the escalating health service costs of the last several decades and, as reflected, especially recently, in the need for changes in payment incentives and schemes for reforming the health service delivery system in North America. Since it is extremely difficult, if not impossible, for health service executives and man-

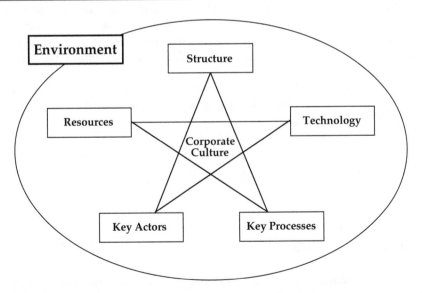

Figure 5–8 The Significance of Corporate Culture and Environment for Health Service Management

agers to control external changes fully, these executives must adopt organizational cultures that will allow their organizations to successfully adapt to outside turbulence. The question is, How?

For the purposes of our discussion, the concept of organizational culture refers to the goals, values, beliefs, management style, and power of individuals, or groups of individuals, associated with an organization. Whether the organization is a group practice, a hospital, or an HMO, successful achievement of organizational goals and objectives (e.g., the application of HMIS resources to achieve service excellence) cannot be realized without a culture that fosters commitment to these goals and objectives.

Cultures of organizations, as well as those of organizational subgroups, can differ substantially. For example, the nursing department of a health service organization may have a culture that puts a high value on quality of patient care whereas the IS department may have one that endorses technological growth and skill development. Nurses in such an organization will be expected to spend more time on patient care, but they will also be pressured to learn the technologies; therefore, conflicts sometimes arise because of competing values. Those who do not respect either culture will have difficulty surviving in the hospital. In such a case, it may be wise for management to pursue a culture of value alignment that encourages the application and use of leading edge technology for service excellence (e.g., computerized patient care services). Such a culture will explicitly emphasize the value of applying HMIS technologies for improving end-user commitments. Thus, nurses will be encouraged to key in clinical observations of patients at bedside terminals, and patients (together with their immediate families) can receive computer generated progress reports of their treatment programs and their response to treatment.

According to Ziegenfuss, there are six target "windows" in which the health service administrator or clinical leader can take actions to create different levels of culture within an organization:[35]

1. Observed behaviors
2. Announced values
3. Rules of the game
4. Norms
5. Philosophy
6. Feeling or climate

Observed behaviors and announced values are the artifacts and creations of culture. As a case in point, when promoting the application and use of HMIS for service quality as the organizational culture, the health service managers, by serving as role models, can demonstrate commitment to such a view. They can secure adequate technology and space to support service quality through computerization, perform frequent CQI exercises, encourage demonstrations of patient care software, and institute new standards and criteria for ensuring application of leading edge technologies for service quality throughout the organizational processes. HMIS services must be seen as a vehicle for achieving value alignment rather than a vehicle for promoting one value over another.

Rules of the game (written or unwritten) and norms (behavioral standards) are the values and beliefs shared among organizational participants. These include decision-making processes that are used to govern and regulate the behaviors and decisions of group members. At this level, promoting service quality through HMIS designs by the health service manager would necessarily involve the establishment of a "high tech and high touch" orientation as the corporate value and the encouragement of group responsibility for using HMIS to ensure service quality. Through their actions, health service managers can introduce a so-called bandwagon effect on computerized service quality throughout the organization, so that individuals in the organization who ignore "automated quality service" may be asked to change their behaviors or be pressured to alter their relations with the organization.

At the highest level of culture, which is mostly "intangible," lie the assumptions, feelings, ideologies, and philosophies of the organization. By promoting service quality improvement through technology at this level, the health service CEO can create a positive feeling, for example, among middle managers who commit to using HMIS for high-quality service. In addition, the organization's CEO can also direct relationships toward provider-client collaboration to support such a vision.

Ultimately, the implication of focusing on culture is to create changes in the internal behavioral patterns of the organization's participants. When this is translated into managerial roles and functions, the health service managers must oversee internal operations and processes to maintain high-quality programs and services, as well as provide overall technical leadership. In addition, these managers should structure the organizational design to increase commitment through flexible reporting relationships and encourage broader participation of key stakeholders, for example, medical staff, board members, third parties (e.g., government, insurers and consumers). A structure such as the matrix organization or the use of ad hoc committees provides flexibility that may be appropriate at one time or another. Conceivably, the introduction of flexible structures is one way of paying more attention to the importance of informal relationships within the formal organization. In addition, health service managers must be aware of what goes on in the organizational environment. This brings us to the topic of managing corporate innovations.

Managing Corporate Innovations

It is important to foster an organizational climate that is supportive of innovations: that is, an organizational structure and culture that are appropriate to accommodate the anticipated changes. This part of the process has been discussed in the previous section. In the following section, we focus on how health service managers can examine the available resources of the organization (physical, financial, skills, technology, and information) and tactically seek to direct planning and use of resources (i.e., resource planning, acquisition, and deployment) to achieve the organization's new mission, goals, and objectives. This essentially is the process of organizational change or innovation. For example, corporate HMIS planning may see a need for acquiring state-of-the-art technologies and the institution of a program for personnel training and skill development to ensure that the organization is prepared and ready to use advanced information technologies for the production and delivery of high-quality patient care, thereby setting in motion the process of organizational change or innovation.

Longest observed that in health service settings, organizational changes or innovations often fit into one of two broad categories: (1) changes in the organization's level of adaptation to its environment and (2) changes in the internal behavioral patterns of the participants.[36] As we have discussed managing changes in the internal behavioral patterns of organizational participants in the previous section, our concern here is on changes in health service organizations as they try to adapt themselves to changing external environments; that is, we will focus on how today's health service managers can manage changes driven by external forces.

Organizational innovation, according to Rowe and Boise, refers to an organization's success in the introduction and implementation of "new" processes, programs, products, or services as a result of management decisions in the organization.[37] It is a very complex and difficult process, and one that the modern health service executive or manager has to struggle with constantly because of changes occurring in the external environment (including economic, social, legal, technological, and competitive aspects of the health service delivery industry) and their effects on the organization.

The process of any organizational change is complex because of resistance and the uncertainty surrounding change. It is also a very difficult process because every manager who has attempted to introduce or implement a particular innovation or change within an organization will know the pressure to succeed in the face of such a challenge and the consequences of failing. Accordingly, the failure of an innovation may be disastrous for the manager if the organization's survival in an increasingly hostile environment is dependent upon innovation and change.

Most organizational changes or innovations in health service settings can be precipitated by the ongoing review of its mission, goals, and objectives. For example, the health service CEO may perceive that the need for more efficient performance, the need for reduced turnover, greater job satisfaction, and higher productivity among workers, is now less of a priority than the need to emphasize the use of information technologies for more effective reporting or for higher quality service, or any other matter concerning organizational effectiveness. Like their business counterparts, health service managers today must begin to identify market niches, monitor competition, sustain competitive advantages, and keep abreast of trends in the environment. Examples of emerging trends are changes in consumer life-styles and new demands for health promotion services, new governmental regulations and fiscal policies, new health informational and medical technologies, alternative modes of health service delivery, and alternative medicine. Having gained an understanding of industry trends, health service executives and managers will then be able to formulate their visions, missions, goals, and objectives more effectively.

The next step in the management of change process has to do with strategic alignment. In this respect, the goals and objectives of various departments within the organization must be aligned with corporate goals and objectives. For example, in aligning the strategies of the IS department to support the goal of service excellence for a health service organization, the use of information technologies must be directed to achieve service excellence; in short, the information strategy is molded according to the business strategy of the organization. The steps that follow have to do with strategically moving the organizational resources to accomplish the newly established corporate-IS linked strategies. The practical steps are discussed next.

Practical Steps to Benefits Realization

To complete the discussion of this chapter, we will attempt to answer a question that follows from the previous section regarding how to reallocate corporate and HMIS resources strategically to satisfy corporate goals and objectives: What practical steps should management take in order to actualize the benefits of HMIS in today's information era?

To answer this question, one useful framework, which is based on a combination of research in the planning and implementation of emerging and advancing technologies,[38,39] stresses the following:

- Visions
- Policies and standards

- Architectures
- Project management

First, an understanding of the new environment for the health service delivery industry as well as the technology marketplace is needed before management can proceed to articulate a "vision" for the organization. A key question to be asked by management is, Where is our organization heading in the next 5 to 10 years within the present and future context of the industry? This is the vision that will guide new directions in corporate culture and innovations for HMIS developments.

A strategic plan for HMIS development and a systems architecture is also needed to accomplish that "vision." This plan includes the systems, people, policies, and procedures that are needed to create the electronic organization. The strategic plan refers to the organization's management information technology infrastructure (MITI) discussed earlier; the architecture refers to the data models or high-level designs of the data elements to be captured in the system (Chapter 10).

To provide the bridge between the vision and the systems architecture to support that "vision," a set of policies and standards should be recommended to address and emphasize future "connectivity" and "compatibility." This will allow users to communicate up, down, across, and out of an organization. For example, the policies should spell out the use of international standards such as IBM's systems network architecture (SNA) and the open systems interconnection (OSI) reference model, to ease linking to the outside world (Chapter 9). There should also be standards for hardware acquisition (e.g., IBM, Macintosh, or a combination) and for software adoption (e.g., Microsoft Word 5.0, Excel 4.0, or Lotus 1-2-3). Further, apart from identifying the overall management needs for the use of the various technologies, there is also the need to provide the necessary expertise (resources), which in most cases will entail a range of skilled managers, technologists, analysts, and clerical staff.

Managers of health service organizations who have participated actively in the initial steps discussed will then be ready to capitalize on the benefits of new technological implementations. The next major step is systems implementation (Chapter 12). Here, project management comprises a series of the following substeps:

1. Identify and prioritize projects
2. Develop a cost-benefit evaluation plan
3. Set benchmarks and deliverables
4. Impose standards and pilot-test technologies
5. Monitor project progress
6. Evaluate project achievements

The first step involves the identification of projects and the breaking up of a series of major technological improvement projects into a longer list of short but prioritized projects. The priority scheme must explicitly differentiate efficiency from effectiveness projects to prevent effectiveness projects faced with high levels of uncertainty from being confused with HMIS designs offered only for efficiency problems. The timeline for each such project should be restricted to no longer than 9 months to a year.

For each project, a specific cost-benefit evaluation plan should be constructed. These values will be a measure of all relative end-user preferences and will pertain to perceived end-user acceptance, relevance, and empowerment. Exhibit 5–3 illustrates how end-user preferences may be weighted and scored for a project.

In assigning projects, management should ensure adequate resources and include staff such as a project supervisor, a project coordinator, user representatives, technologists, analysts, and programmers. Altogether, the series of short projects to be completed should be assigned under the guidance of a strategic 5- to 10-year plan, and there should only be as many short projects as there are resources to support them. At the beginning of the project, and sometimes during the project, tangible benchmarks and deliverables should be identified and set so as to control the development of the project. The total timeline should then be divided to cover the various phases of the project's development.

In the next step, the project supervisor should be asked to impose hardware, software, communications, and other installation standards and pilot test the technologies to ensure that the resulting pieces will interconnect and will function as expected. Each project will initially result in only small changes in operating procedures to ease the personnel problems associated with changing the way people work. However, inspections should be carried out at the end of each benchmark period to ensure that the quality of deliverables is acceptable. In some cases, there may be a need to redelegate, add, or remove team personnel. Once a project is completed, there should be built-in mechanisms to collect baseline data for the purpose of evaluation. Management should devote energy and time to evaluate the benefits that have been realized from the different projects.

The implementation of all these steps is difficult because of the division of responsibilities between the end-users (i.e., organizational unit that operates and benefits from the implementation of HMIS technologies) and the systems professionals (i.e., the information systems personnel). On the one hand, senior managers who represent the users often have little knowledge of technologies and systems; on the other hand, information specialists often feel frustrated in making decisions about information provisions without a complete knowledge of future organizational strategies because they are not involved in high-level management meetings. Neither party is therefore happy. Over the years, this situation has given rise to the creation of a new executive position in the HMIS area—the chief infor-

Exhibit 5–3 A Cost-Benefit Evaluation Plan for a Specific Project

Benefits			Costs		
Tangible Benefits	Rate	Weight	**Tangible Costs**	Rate	Weight
•Productivity	___	___	•Initial cost	___	___
•Reduced paper usage	___	___	(hardware & software)		
•Reduced document	___	___	•Setup cost	___	___
backing			•Equipment maintenance cost	___	___
•Sooner completion	___	___			
Intangible Benefits	Rate	Weight	**Intangible Costs**	Rate	Weight
•User satisfaction	___	___	•Location	___	___
•Ease of use	___	___	•User resistance	___	___
•Ease of training others	___	___	•Staff morale	___	___
•Corporate image	___	___	•Time for training/adjustment	___	___

Notes:

•Rating may be represented by a scale of, say, 1 to 5, with 1 denoting the highest priority and
  5 the lowest.
•Weight here refers to the relative emphasis each criterion is to be given.

mation officer (CIO). The CIO is a manager who participates in the formation of organizational strategies and then assures that the information strategies fit into, complement, and influence the overall strategies of the organization (Chapter 11).

CONCLUSION

Today's health service managers must develop corporate values, provide strategic directions and visions, define product mix and market, determine new ventures, and ensure realization of corporate goals. The emerging role of the health service manager is therefore to champion and propagate the corporate vision and build the desired corporate culture, apart from retaining the usual planning and control functions. The key to good management, therefore, is to maintain a dynamic balance among various stakeholders and to take on different roles at different times as the situation dictates. In terms of HMIS planning, health service managers in the past have focused on limited technological exploitation (i.e., very few HMIS developments actually go beyond hospital accounting and financial sys-

tems) and localized benefits (e.g., departmental information processing efficiency). In the context of new perspectives for health service management, HMIS
planning must begin to concentrate on new problems and strategic directions and
share in the benefits of automation throughout the organization, with customers
and suppliers and even with competitors through appropriate strategic alliance.[40]

CHAPTER QUESTIONS

1. Why is "management" often considered both a science and an art?
2. Distinguish between "process efficiency" and "system efficiency" and between "process effectiveness" and "system effectiveness" and provide the
   rationale for the need to reengineer the health management information
   system design, development, and management process.
3. What is meant by the "corporatization of medicine," and what are its implications for the design, development, and use of HMIS?
4. What are the basic components of an HMIS and how should each of these
   components be managed? Why might EUC become dangerous to a health
   organization?
5. Devise a scheme to match HMIS applications to various roles, functions,
   and activities of the health service CEO or manager.
6. Can HMIS applications be used to alter corporate cultures? If so, how?
7. Design a strategic framework to guide the implementation of a
   corporatewide plan to move from a DOS/OS platform to a UNIX platform.

MINI CASE 5
USING LEADING-EDGE TECHNOLOGIES AT THE NEW WORLD
MEDICAL CENTER

In the last 2 years, corporate management of the New World Medical Center
(NWMC) has decided to take a leading role in the application of information technologies for managerial decision support and patient services. The president and
CEO of NWMC received his MD from Harvard Medical School and has a PhD in
management information systems (MIS) from the University of Minnesota and an
MHA from the University of British Columbia. The center also has a CIO who
was a graduate of the Stanford Business School. Together, they conceived, developed, and implemented two innovative systems. One is Thinktank, an experimental management group decision support system that runs on an AT&T 3B2-4000
minicomputer under the UNIX operating system.[41] Several private terminals were

networked into the system together with a separate public terminal that was attached to a special projector for transmitting all messages appearing on the public terminal onto a large public screen. The other system is Commute, an electronic data interchange (EDI) and networking system that connects NWMC with those physicians and specialists contracted by the center for its ambulatory services. These physicians and specialists also have attending and practicing privileges at the center. The design and development of yet another major HMIS project to coordinate medical services provided within the center were still under active consideration.

The main use of Thinktank at this time was for internal electronic communications among the senior management team and for support of group meetings that follow a new weekly agenda. Group participants have the option to interact with the system at any time during the week to input their decision into the system. The final outcomes of these decisions are collated and summarized automatically by the system at the end of each week on the basis of majority votes and other statistical rules built into the system. These results are then revealed to all company staff by displaying them on the public screen. The president and CEO then act accordingly.

Thinktank was useful for several group tasks. For example, in one experimental meeting agenda, the exercise was to identify a set of five critical success factors (CSFs) for the center that could be used to direct corporate strategies in the next 10 years. In this regard, Thinktank used anonymity to mask the status differentials of the participants and thus lessen the fear of retaliation. Thinktank could also be used to perform other more structured tasks, for example, selecting from among a pool of physicians and specialists who applied to practice at the center or deciding from among a list of potentially promising and viable HMIS projects how funds from the NWMC Foundation were to be allocated.

The main uses of Commute at this time were external communications and electronic networking between NWMC and its referring physicians. Physicians who are contracted by the center are automatically provided with terminals that are linked to the Commute system. Commute has the capabilities of exchanging and receiving information on patient referrals on a real-time basis. Customers of NWMC requiring only ambulatory care attend at the offices of NWMC's referring physicians. At the end of each visit by one of NWMC's clients, the referring physicians are required to complete a profile of the patient services and an electronic form for recording billing. These are instantly dispatched to the center. Commute then summarizes the information from the physicians and uses a case-mix classification scheme to generate utilization and billing reports comparing all NWMC referrals for each quarter. These quarterly reports are then used by management to assess issues regarding whether to extend or terminate contractual relationships of NWMC with individual physicians on the basis of their practice patterns.

MINI CASE QUESTIONS

Picture yourself as the CIO of the center who is being asked by the president and CEO to brief the other managers inside the center, as well as the physicians outside the center, on the benefits to be realized from the implementation of Thinktank and Commute. A joint meeting was scheduled for you to meet the two groups to discuss benefits realization; this resulted in the following questions:

1. How would management decisions have been made differently if the Thinktank system had not been operational?
2. How would referral patterns of NWMC and physician practice patterns differ with and without the Commute system?
3. What benefits do these systems have on the center for enhancing service efficiency, effectiveness, and excellence?
4. What are the issues in the management of various components of these systems, in particular, the end-user computing (EUC) and technology management components?
5. How do these systems affect the interpersonal, informational, and decisional roles of the CEO, other managers, and physicians associated with the center?
6. What impacts do these systems have on corporate culture and innovation of NWMC?

Discuss briefly how you would have addressed each of the preceding questions, remembering that one group of your audience were managers and the other group were physicians, none of whom is a systems specialist.

CHAPTER REVIEW

This chapter has brought to focus many of the key management concepts relevant to HMIS solutions. We have presented the roles and functions of the health service executive from the classical, functional, and emergent role perspectives. Management, as defined, is a process with both interpersonal and technical aspects, through which the goals and objectives of the health service organization are specified and accomplished. In this regard, HMIS is introduced to enhance organizational service efficiency, effectiveness, and excellence. Management of the key subcomponents of the HMIS is shown to be an important part of health management. Attention has been called to the coexistence of both formal and informal organizational perspectives in health managerial roles. In addition, the effects of HMIS on the future of the health service industry will depend largely on the evolution of new perspectives of health managerial roles and functions.

In essence, managerial roles, functions, and activities are efforts to plan, direct, and control the organization and its coordination of resources toward achieving organizational goals and objectives. Unless health service CEOs and managers are able to internalize the necessity of the outcomes and determine just how essential HMIS components are, and how they can contribute to achieving these outcomes, the truly strategic benefits of HMIS will not be realized and the development of the health service delivery industry will be limited in scope.

Managers who can overcome these roadblocks may expect to see a more positive scenario for organizational automation and enjoy a series of well-planned and well-managed HMIS projects. This will in turn call attention to the significance of the HMIS functions and the need for top management involvement in information technology implementation. A new perspective on the role of information as a corporate resource will then surface and there will be a struggle of power within the organization for a top executive to manage the health information resources.

NOTES

1. P.F. Drucker, Coming of the New Organization, *Harvard Business Review* 66, no. 1 (1988): 40.

2. B.B. Longest, Jr., *Management Practices for the Health Professional,* 4th ed. (Norwalk, Conn: Appleton & Lange, 1990), 35.

3. F.C. Munson and H. Zuckerman, The Managerial Roles, in *Health Care Management: A Text in Organizational Theory and Behavior,* ed. S.M. Shortell and A.D. Kaluzny (New York: John Wiley & Sons, 1985): 38–76.

4. J.G. Liebler, et al. *Management Principles for Health Professionals* (Gaithersburg, Md: Aspen Publishers, Inc., 1984).

5. H. Mintzberg, *The Nature of Managerial Work* (New York: Harper & Row, 1972).

6. H. Fayol, *General and Industrial Administration,* trans. C. Storrs (London: Sir Isaac Pitman and Sons, Ltd., 1949).

7. L. Gulick and L.F. Urwick, eds., *Papers on the Science of Administration* (New York: Institute of Public Administration, 1937).

8. O. Tead, *Administration: Its Purpose and Performance* (New York: Harper and Brothers, 1959).

9. C. Barnard, *The Functions of the Executive* (Cambridge, Mass: Harvard University Press, 1968).

10. O.J. Kralovec, Achieving Information Systems Benefits, in *Information Systems for Ambulatory Care,* ed. T.A. Matson and M.D. McDougall (Chicago: American Hospital Association: American Hospital Publishing, Inc., 1990), 79–96.

11. J.K.H. Tan, Innovative Management: A Framework for Understanding and Evaluating Health Executive Roles and Performance in the 1990's, in *Proceedings of the 8th Annual Health Pacific Forum* (British Columbia: UBC Health Care and Epidemiology Alumni Association, 1990).

12. J.K.H. Tan, Information Technology Planning and Management for the Hospital of the Future, in *Proceedings of the 9th Annual Health Pacific Forum* (British Columbia: UBC Health Care and Epidemiology Alumni Association, 1991).

13. R. Kropf, *Service Excellence in Health Care through the Use of Computers* (Ann Arbor, Mich: Health Administration Press, 1990).

14. W.C. Zerrenner, Improved Management through Automation, in *Information Systems for Ambulatory Care,* ed. T.A. Matson and M.D. McDougall (Chicago: American Hospital Association: American Hospital Publishing, Inc., 1990); 45–54.

15. Ibid.

16. J.K.H. Tan, et al., Utilization Care Plan and Effective Patient Data Management, *Hospital and Health Services Administration* 38, no. 1 (1993): 81–99.

17. J.K.H. Tan, et al., The Application of Expert System Technology to Community Health Program Planning and Evaluation, *Canadian Medical Informatics* (in press).

18. D. Smitton, Corporatization of Medicine: The Use of Medical Management Information Systems to Increase the Clinical Productivity of Physicians: A Commentary, unpublished essay supervised by J.K.H. Tan, Faculty of Medicine, University of British Columbia (1991).

19. B.J. Fried, et al., Corporatization and Deprivatization of Health Services in Canada, in *The Corporate Transformation of Health Care. Issues & Directions,* ed. J.W. Salmon (Amityville, NY: Baywood Publishing Company, Inc., 1990), 167.

20. R. Kropf, *Service Excellence in Health Care through the Use of Computers.*

21. M.D. McDonald and H.L. Blum, *Health in the Information Age: The Emergence of Health Oriented Telecommunication Applications* (Berkeley, Calif: Environmental Science and Policy Institute, 1992).

22. J.B. McKinlay and J. Stoeckle, Corporatization and the Social Transformation of Doctoring, *International Journal of Health Services* 18, no. 2 (1988): 191–205.

23. J.A. Worthley and P.S. DiSalvio, *Managing Computers in Health Care* (Ann Arbor, Mich: Health Administration Press Perspective, 1989).

24. R.R. Panko, *End User Computing: Management, Applications and Technology* (New York: John Wiley & Sons, Inc., 1988).

25. J. Day, et al., *Microcomputers and Applications* (Glenview, Ill: Scott, Foresman & Co., 1988).

26. S. Rivard and S.L. Huff, An Empirical Study of Users As Application Developers, *Information and Management* 8 (1985): 89–102.

27. B.C. McNurlin and R.H. Sprague, Jr., *Information Systems Management in Practice,* 2nd ed. (Englewood Cliffs, NJ: Prentice Hall, 1989).

28. Mintzberg, *Managerial Work.*

29. C.S. Parker and T. Case, *Management Information System: Strategy and Action* (New York: McGraw-Hill Publishing Co., 1993).

30. Zerrenner, *Improved Management.*

31. Parker and Case, *Management Information System.*

32. P.M. Blau and W.R. Scott, *Formal Organizations* (San Francisco: Chandler Publishing Co., 1962).

33. B.B. Longest, Jr., *Management Practices.*

34. J.P. Kotter, *Organizational Dynamics Diagnosis and Intervention* (Reading, Mass: Addison-Wesley, 1978).

35. J.T. Ziegenfuss, Jr., *The Organizational Path to Health Care Quality,* Management Series, American College of Healthcare Executives (Ann Arbor, Mich: Health Administration Press, 1993).

36. Longest, *Management Practices.*

37. L.A. Rowe and W.B. Boise, *Organizational and Managerial Innovation: A Reader.* (Pacific Palisades, Calif: The Goodyear Publishing Co., 1973).

38. P. Griffiths, Using Information Systems and Technology To Gain Competitive Advantage, in *Information Resources and Corporate Growth,* ed. E. Punset and G. Sweeney (London: Printer Publishers, 1989).

39. P. Keen, *Shaping the Future: Business Design through Information Technology* (Boston: Harvard Business School Press, 1991).

40. R.J. Thierauf, *User-Oriented Decision Support Systems: Accent on Problem Finding* (Englewood Cliffs, NJ: Prentice Hall, 1988).

41. G.V. DeSantics, et al., Computer-Supported Meetings: Building a Research Environment, *Large-Scale Systems: Theory and Applications* 13 (1987): 43–59.

Chapter 6

The Evolution of Systems Development Methodologies: Life-Cycle, Prototyping, and Contemporary Models

1. Define systems development methodology.
2. Chart the evolution of systems development life-cycle methodologies.
3. Rationalize prototyping as an alternative to life-cycle methodologies.
4. Identify components and uses of the multiview framework.
5. Identify components and uses of object-oriented design and analysis.
6. Identify components and uses of CASE methodology.
7. Relate end-user computing to systems designs and development.

INTRODUCTION

When individual colleagues or students came to me with problems, I found that the best stance was to keep asking questions that would clarify how the person was seeing the problem and, more important, to ask what the person had already tried to do about it.[1]

The basic idea conveyed previously and in this chapter is that efficient, effective, and state-of-the-art health management information systems (HMIS) can be developed for health service organizations by the application of a well-defined managerial process, in spite of all the technicalities involved. Chapters 3 through 5 discuss the more theoretical aspects of HMIS designs and development; this chapter discusses the practical side of HMIS designs and development. Its primary purpose is to provide a historical survey of the field of system development methodologies (SDMs). This aspect of HMIS knowledge is fundamental and critical because of its methodological and practical value: that is, it deals with the tools, techniques, and methodologies available to HMIS analysts in managing the process of systems analysis, design, and development.

The discussion of this chapter follows an evolutionary perspective, leading the reader from early computer applications developed by specialist programming teams to the current reality of HMIS applications developed by end-users. Over the years, systems development has been driven by changes in management expectations of HMIS capabilities. Human dissatisfaction in concert with technical limitations has led to advancements in SDM at all fronts.

A multitude of SDMs have been designed to help minimize the problems of uncoordinated developmental efforts. Each methodology is based on a philosophical view, which can range from a complete focus on the humanistic side to the technical aspects of development of HMIS. A growing number of methodologies have emphasized systems analysis (SA) because of a past tendency to neglect the front-end stages of HMIS development. More specifically, when user and management needs are clearly identified in the SA stage, satisfaction with the completed system is more likely. Other methodologies have focused on systems design (SD) because it is the most creative stage of HMIS development. An adequate balance between the human and technical aspects in SD is requisite of an effective methodology. Present consensus calls for choosing a methodology that considers the context, that is, the health service organization itself, as well as the end-users and analysts who are developing the HMIS. Today among the most commonly used SDMs are the fourth-generation (4G) models, also termed "contemporary" models. In this chapter, we will discuss three of these models: multiview, object-oriented analysis and design (OOAD), and computer-aided software engineering (CASE).

Multiview is a contingency approach methodology that provides a framework for managing SA and SD phases contingent on changes in the organizational environment. The framework consists of five stages that progress from a needs assessment, to the blending of human and technical objectives, and finally, to the actual design specifications. It is a useful planning method because of its flexibility in mixing existing tools, techniques, and methodologies and because of its emphasis on integrating human and technical components.

OOAD is another flexible methodology that advocates a system approach to HMIS development. This methodology focuses not only on how a task is carried out, but on what is being acted upon. Software is developed in a layered fashion that builds upon what already exists. This minimizes the time required for refinement and revision and encourages rapid prototyping.

Our final approach to flexible systems development is the CASE tools. CASE tools automate one or all aspects of the software development life cycle. The purpose of these tools is to develop better software more quickly. The philosophy behind CASE is to embody a systems approach to development and enhance the interactions between users and developers. CASE tools seek to solve the correct problem. CASE tools can assist with programming and productivity, SDMs, and other development support tools; however, choosing the appropriate CASE tools is a nontrivial task and requires careful consideration of multiple criteria.

The need to balance human and technical aspects is the driving force behind the end-user computing (EUC) movement. In the context of health computing, EUC comprises the development and operation of HMIS applications at the individual level by users who are not systems professionals (see Chapter 5). There are advantages and disadvantages to EUC, but with careful planning and understanding of the process, the advantages can be maximized for successful incorporation of end-user application (EUA) into health organizational HMIS infrastructure.

SYSTEM DEVELOPMENT METHODOLOGIES

Early computer applications were typically designed without adequate planning. As computer technology evolved, the need for a systematic developmental approach or "methodology" became increasingly necessary. As a result, numerous SDMs have emerged to address the needs of users, programmers, and systems analysts.

Without the use of a framework or planning guidelines, the development of an HMIS will lack overall coordination and relevant system requirements might be neglected. The system developed under these conditions will tend to be "crisis-oriented" and will typically fail to meet the long-term goals and objectives of the health service organization or the system's users. It is therefore important to gain an adequate knowledge of SDMs to help select the most appropriate one for systems planning and implementation.

An SDM is a systematic approach to health information systems planning, analysis, and design.[2] A methodology is a collection of procedures, techniques, tools, and documentation aids that will help health systems developers and analysts in their efforts to implement a new information system. A methodology therefore provides a framework that guides HMIS designs and development. It consists of phases and subphases that guide systems analysts and developers in their choice of techniques that might be appropriate at each stage of a project. The phases and subphases also help systems developers to plan, manage, control, and evaluate their HMIS projects.

A technique is a way of performing a particular activity in the system development process. Examples of techniques include rich pictures, entity modeling, normalization, data flow diagramming, decision trees, decision tables, structured English, action diagrams, and the entity life cycle (a few of which have already been discussed in Chapters 2 and 4). Each technique may involve using one or more tools.[3] Examples of tools include database management systems, query languages, data dictionaries, fourth-generation languages (4GLs), methodology work-benches, project management tools, and expert systems. As an example to illustrate these concepts, imagine running a general business election meeting. To do this, one can follow an agenda (methodology) to guide the progress of the meeting. One "technique" used in making decisions during the meeting may be "voting," which might entail the use of a certain "tool" such as the use of a ballot card for each member to ensure equitable representation based on the principle of "one member one vote."

SDMs differ in their philosophical techniques and tools, as well as their recommended approaches. Some methodologies focus on the human aspects of developing HMIS: that is, they include user participation as part of their development. In addition, some methodologies are scientific in nature, whereas others are more pragmatic in their approach. Most recent methodologies attempt to automate as much of the work of developing a project as possible.

Methodologies naturally imply careful organization and planning throughout the entire development process. Methodologies attempting to include the end-user in the development process have been found to increase user satisfaction and acceptance of the final product. The primary advantages of employing a well-tested SDM include user satisfaction, the meeting of management needs, timely development, the avoidance of systems implementation deficiencies, and the appropriate provision of maintenance and support activities. This includes evaluation and ongoing support.

Making use of a methodology will lessen the risk of wasting resources during the course of system development. Holloway notes that methodologies increase the productivity of the development staff by[4]

- Providing a standard framework—to avoid reinventing the wheel for each HMIS project
- Providing the right tools—to assist successful completion of each stage of development task
- Providing effective review procedures—to identify errors and inconsistencies early
- Providing a productivity aid—to reduce the amount of development documentation

A good SDM allows health management to review the progress of an HMIS project. It also allows the HMIS developer or analyst to identify accurately the needs of the users. Lastly, a strong methodology makes HMIS project planning easier by allowing both designers and users to plan, correct, and replan the project as it progresses. The methodologies described in this chapter can be compared to these requirements or standards.

SYSTEMS DEVELOPMENT LIFE-CYCLE (SDLC) MODELS

The 1950s were characterized by computer applications that were oriented to the basic operational level of the organization. These applications included the production of voluminous reports and documents and the large-scale maintenance of files. An example of an early application would be the production of the company payroll.

During this early period, formalized methodologies to develop information systems were typically absent. These early computer applications involved replacement of manual systems by "data" processing systems and were implemented without the aid of an explicit methodology. In these early days, the emphasis of computer applications was on programming, and the people who implemented the systems were therefore computer scientists and programmers who had technical training but lacked planning and communication skills. In addition, few university courses that offered the education and training necessary for the SA and SD work related to developing data processing systems were available.

Systems analysts and designers relied on their personal experience when developing these early information systems. Projects were typically seen as short-term exercises or "one-off" solutions to sort out problems rather than as long-term, well-planned implementation strategies for new applications. The needs of users in the application area were not well articulated or were simply ignored. Consequently, HMIS designs were frequently inappropriate for the end-users. Often, the development of applications was costly and arrived later than expected. Users were frequently dissatisfied with the operational systems since their needs were not clearly identified. Documentation was scarce and out of date; also, documentation standards were resisted because they restricted creativity and increased work loads and the time needed to develop systems. Most health service organizations became very dependent on the few people who knew the system really well.

As computers became popular and both management and users had greater demands, changes began to evolve. Figure 6–1 shows how the evolution of SA and SD processes has affected the various people involved in the development process. The diagram shows that the development of EUC and modern SDMs has eliminated the need for many intermediary computer specialists, thereby allowing the users to create many of their own applications directly. Three main changes have been noted in the evolution of SDM for health service organizations.

1. A move away from "one-off" solutions to particular problems and more integrated HMIS designs as health organizations grew in size and complexity

2. The need for a standard or an accepted methodology for developing HMIS with more emphasis on the SA and SD phases of the HMIS development process

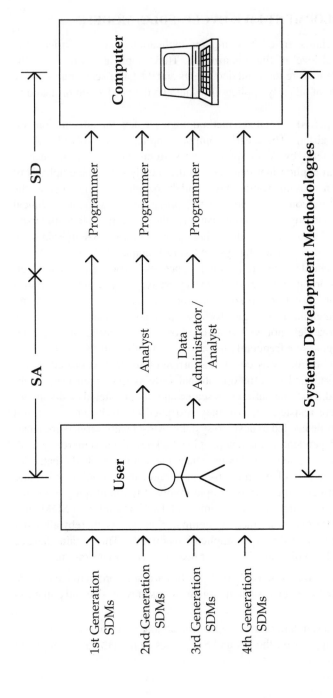

Figure 6–1 The Evolution of Systems Analysis and Design (SA/SD) Processes

3. The gradual shifting of the roles of systems analysts, designers, and programmers to the end-users

Accordingly, new and competing methodologies have been devised to guide the
development of HMIS applications from one generation to another (see Figure 6–
1). The first "formal" methodology, the Waterfall model, was developed in the
late 1960s and widely dominated the field until others were introduced.

The Waterfall Model

The Waterfall model, a first-generation SDM, embodies the systems development life-cycle (SDLC) concept. The SDLC concept was highly regarded among
health systems analysts throughout the 1970s and early 1980s. This model consists of six steps: (1) feasibility study, (2) systems investigation, (3) systems
analysis, (4) systems design, (5) systems implementation, and (6) systems maintenance and review. Essentially, the life-cycle concept dictates that whenever a systems review indicates that the current system is no longer adequate, a new feasibility study is then initiated for the new system. Figure 6–2 illustrates the Waterfall
model embodying the life-cycle concept.

This first formal approach provided much more control over SA and SD processes than was possible before. It represented a methodology that was a significant improvement in this field. It included all the attributes expected of a methodology: a philosophy (automated solutions will lead to reduced costs and gains in
processing speed), a series of steps (from the feasibility study to system maintenance), a series of techniques (e.g., ways to evaluate the costs and benefits solutions), and a series of tools.

Even though the conventional methodology was a definite improvement, it was
frequently criticized. For example, it failed to meet the needs and expectations of
end-users because they were not involved in the development process. The SA
process was literally ignored. Inflexible and unambitious systems designs resulted
because revisions were not provided for in the SD process. In addition, incomplete
systems and large application backlogs resulted from the lack of emphasis on
front-end planning. Finally, this traditional methodology involved heavy maintenance work load and was laden with problems of documentation.

Traditional (SDLC-Based) Methodologies

The next generation (second-generation SDMs) integrated basic techniques and
tools to create more complete specifications for the systems designer. Exhibit 6–1
provides a summary of these SDMs, which are often classified as traditional
(SDLC-based) methodologies. Many of these early methodologies focus on the

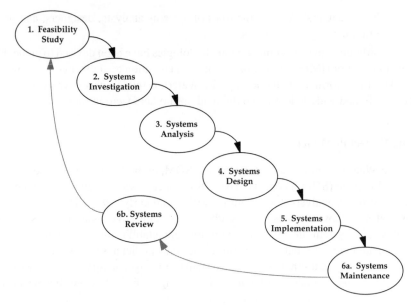

Figure 6–2 The Waterfall Model

---

planning involved in developing HMIS that will meet the objectives of the health organization. Key examples are

- Accurately defined systems (ADS)
- Business information analysis and integration technique (BIAIT)
- Business systems plan (BSP)

ADS comprises an integrated systems representation of systems inputs, outputs, processes, procedures, and files.[5,6] The analysis package also includes cross-referencing structures, which ensure consistency across the sets of documents produced. Some aspects of ADS may now be automated to assist in the development process.

BIAIT addresses top management requirements by using a set of seven close-ended binary questions to generate a model that aids the analyst in determining an organization's information requirements.[7] The resulting model or profile is a grid or matrix of possible responses classifying existing relations between "orders" and "suppliers." This grid or matrix also defines who the data owners and data users should be. This information-handling activity profile of the organization is then used for effective systems planning and future analysis.

BSP addresses the requirements of top management and aligns systems planning with the organization's strategic plan.[8,9] Three principles are observed in BSP: (1) the need for an organizationwide perspective, (2) top-down analysis but

Exhibit 6–1   Traditional Methodologies Based on System Development Life Cycle (Second-Generation Development Models)

METHODS	MAJOR CONCEPTS
Accurately Defined Systems (ADS)	Represents system inputs, outputs, processes, procedures, and files; also includes cross-referencing structures to ensure consistency.
Business Information Analysis and Integration Technique (BIAIT)	Creates a grid based on seven closed-ended binary questions to aid analysts in systems planning and future analysis.
Business Systems Planning (BSP)	Similar to SDLC model except that it has a two-level design stage theme and a new emphasis on strategic planning.

bottom-up design and implementation, and (3) the need for independence of the business plan from computer application systems (i.e., changes in the business plan may take place without effecting changes in computer application systems). Except for the emphasis on strategic planning in the analysis stage and the subdivision of the design stage into general design and detailed design phases, the stages in the BSP methodology are fundamentally similar to those discussed in the classical SDLC model. BSP is further elaborated in Chapter 10.

Structured Methodologies

These third-generation SDMs represent a new level of SA and SD approaches that address multiple structural issues.[10] The lack of attention to structural issues in SDLC-based methodologies has slowed the progress of software design stages and given rise to the need for greater structural detailing in SDM. This brings a whole new approach to systems development—the structured methodologies. Exhibit 6–2 provides a summary of these models. Among the numerous structured methodologies that have earned wide popularity and acceptance are

- System analysis and design technique (SADT)
- Structured analysis and structured designs (SA/SD)
- Structured system analysis and design methodology (SSADM)

SADT is a proprietary methodology, although a public version has now been released.[11,12] In addition to depicting data flows between functions, SADT diagrams portray the control under which each function operates and the

Exhibit 6–2   Structured Methodologies (Third-Generation Systems Development Models)

METHODS	MAJOR CONCEPTS
System Analysis and Design Technique (SADT)	Both data- and process-oriented; provides analytical detail at all levels and is easy for nontechnical personnel to use.
Structured Analysis/Structured Design (SA/SD)	Supports analysis and design stages; uses transformational and transactional analysis; generates hierarchical structure charts for defining the various functions.
Structured System Analysis and Design Methodology (SSADM)	Supports both analysis and design stages; used by the British government.

mechanism(s) responsible for the implementation of the function. This is not unlike the information structural diagrams (ISD) that are discussed later in this chapter. Moreover, the SADT diagramming technique is supported by function descriptions and a complete data dictionary (DD) package. A DD is a catalog of data types that includes their names, structures, and usages. A function that reports on cross-references between the components of a data or business model is provided. The methodology therefore combines basic elements of traditional approaches with structured methods; Olle et al. describe SADT as both a data-oriented and a process-oriented methodology.[13] Colter claims that it provides analytical detail at both high and low levels and is reasonably usable for nontechnical personnel.[14] However, SADT has been criticized as focusing primarily on the analysis stage of the SDLC model. Other competing methodologies have since been developed to provide more comprehensive support for the different stages of the SDLC model.

Unlike SADT, the SA/SD methodology clearly supports both the SA and SD stages.[15,16] To make the transition from SA to SD, two techniques are used: (1) transformational analysis and (2) transactional analysis. Essentially, these are design strategies for deriving modular structures from different parts of the data flow diagram (DFD), which has been discussed in Chapter 4. It is claimed that continuous applications of these strategies will ultimately result in the generation of hierarchical structure charts[17] (another variant of the data structure diagram [DSD] technique, which is documented later) for defining the various functions to be performed by the separate modules. SA/SD is also closely related to certain other structured methodologies, such as structured analysis, design, and implementation of information systems (STRADIS), structured analysis and system specification (SASS), and Yourdon. The spectrum of these methodologies ranges from a traditionally process-oriented perspective to a data- and behavior-oriented perspective (for details and examples, see Olle et al.).[18]

SSADM is a powerful methodology sponsored by the United Kingdom government and extends soft system methodology (SSM), which was introduced in Chapter 2. It has been successfully promoted as a standard in all central government computer projects in Great Britain since 1983.[19] Like SA/SD, SSADM strongly supports the analysis and design stages of the SDLC model. The major stages in the SSADM methodology represent an extension of those of the classical SDLC model. These include (1) analysis of the current system, (2) specification of the required system, (3) user selection of service levels, (4) detailed data design, (5) detailed procedure design, and (6) physical design control.

Both SDLC-based and structured methodologies required the user to know precisely what information will be required in the system weeks, months, or even years in advance. Yet, users often find it difficult to specify what they want, and even if they can, their wants often may not match their real needs. This is evidenced by the number of revisions that systems go through after implementation before users get all the information they really need. Prototyping, a fourth-generation SDM, deals with this problem.

PROTOTYPING

Over the past few years much controversy has been generated around prototyping, concerning how it may best be applied to achieve the productivity gains in software development claimed by vendors. Tan and Hanna identify two different views or prototyping approaches emerging from this debate, (1) the evolutionary approach and (2) the revolutionary approach.[20] Exhibit 6–3 provides a summary of these two types of prototyping development models.

Revolutionary Approach

Advocates of the revolutionary approach argue that the only way productivity gains in software development can be realized from prototyping is by applying them in a new and revolutionary way. Here, it is argued that the traditional methodological "mind-set" (for example, the emphasis on precise specifications of application systems before they are built, the abstraction of a static set of user requirements, and the concern about code details and exactness) prevents the effective use and application of prototyping tools and techniques. Rather, these tools and techniques are meant for people who can adapt to an environment supportive of a creative trial-and-error process using nontraditional programmers and including interactive editing and updating, until the right system is developed. The framework of the applications is the major concern and details are ignored until

Exhibit 6–3 Prototyping (Fourth-Generation System Development Models)

METHODS	MAJOR CONCEPTS
Revolutionary Approach	Applies programming tools and techniques in a new and revolutionary way; argues against traditonal methodological mind-sets.
Evolutionary Approach	Merges prototyping techniques and produces an evolution of traditional and structured programming.

later. SDLC-based methodologies address the problem of analyzing and designing a system "right;" however, there is also the problem of designing the "right system." The revolutionary approach addresses this problem.

Evolutionary Approach

Advocates of the evolutionary approach want to see prototype techniques incorporated into the "proven" SDLC methodology, which in essence will produce a merging of traditional and structured programming approaches. They argue that fourth-generation languages (4GLs) and prototyping provide only marginal benefits since they primarily affect the coding phase of application development. They also argue that prototyping using 4GLs does not encourage a structured approach, so that there may be difficulties in interfacing such a system with existing applications, which were developed by using SDLC-based tools, techniques, and methodologies. Thus, it appears reasonable to incorporate 4GLs and prototyping into classical SDLC models in order to achieve fine-tuning of the development process in the same way that structured methodologies were incorporated to fine-tune earlier methods and approaches. McNurlin and Sprague believe that many companies will likely adopt this "safer" approach when introducing these new methods of programming.[21]

CONTEMPORARY MODELS

The proliferation of SDMs over the years has caused HMIS practitioners to become confused about which methodology is "best." Many argue that it is unreasonable to rely on any one approach alone. Each methodology has its strengths and weaknesses; tools and techniques that are appropriate for one set of circumstances may not be appropriate for others. Choosing an appropriate methodology will therefore depend on the context, the organization, and the users and analysts who are developing the HMIS. The best compromise is to choose an approach in which the choice of techniques and tools can be made within a loose methodology or framework. Therefore, contemporary models that emphasize a flexible systems approach, rather than the traditional software approach, are preferable in many cases. These fourth-generation SDMs are a synthesis of many earlier approaches and include the modification of techniques and tools. Multiview is one such option. Other alternatives are object-oriented analysis and design (OOAD) and computer-assisted software engineering (CASE) tools. OOAD focuses on the objects that are acted upon in the development process; CASE tools automate different parts of software or systems development. All of these approaches support flexibility in SA and SD processes.

Multiview

The central theme of the contingency approach when applied to HMIS designs and development purports that each health service organization or situation is unique and that this uniqueness should be considered in choosing any systems development tools, techniques, and guidelines.[22,23] In other words, the mix of guidelines, tools, and techniques used to design an HMIS should be customized to the situation. The flexibility offered by a contingency approach does not obviate the need to use a comprehensive methodology; such a methodology is still required to guide the coordination of efforts of users, programmers, and analysts.

Multiview is an example of such a comprehensive methodology and is described in considerable detail by Wood-Harper, Antill, and Avison in *Information Systems Definition: The Multiview Approach.*[24] The authors saw it as a blending of the previous methodological approaches but especially emphasized the influence of SSM (see Chapter 2) and effective technical and human implementation of computer-based systems (ETHICS),[25] both of which strive to incorporate the human aspects of systems development. Indeed, Multiview is based on the systems paradigm (Chapter 3) and emphasizes the relationship between the organization and its environment. In this aspect, the ultimate objective of Multiview is to amalgamate the human and technical subsystems for the enhancement of HMIS development as a whole.

Multiview is a nonprescriptive methodology that strives to be flexible. As a result, it continues to evolve as an SDM. Multiview is continually refined by using "action research," whereby knowledge gained from real applications in the field is incorporated into the methodology. Multiview was originally designed to aid development of information systems for small business and small-scale HMIS projects, but it is no longer limited to this scope. To date, the methodology has been used successfully in small, medium, and large businesses and health service organizations alike on micro-, mini-, and mainframe computers.[26]

Multiview contains five major steps: (1) analysis of human activity, (2) analysis of information (information modeling), (3) analysis and design of sociotechnical aspects, (4) design of human computer interface, and (5) design of technical aspects. Figure 6–3 illustrates the Multiview framework and the relationships among the five stages. Exhibit 6–4 provides a summary of activities entailed within each of the five components of the Multiview framework.

Stage 1: The Analysis of Human Activity

For a health service delivery organization, the objective of Stage 1 is to identify the purpose and problem related to HMIS within the context of the organization. This stage attempts to answer the question of how the HMIS is supposed to further the aims of the organization.

Rich pictures (as discussed previously in Chapter 2) are frequently used to accomplish this stage of development. A rich picture is a tool used for communication by the analysts and users of the system that concentrates on understanding the problem situation. Its ultimate objective is to identify problems, and avenues to relieve these problems, related to HMIS design and development.

In summary, the first stage of Multiview provides the information necessary to conceptualize the human activities within the health service organization and helps to understand what HMIS can do for the organization. It also provides the inputs for the subsequent stage(s).

Stage 2: Analysis of Information

The objective of Stage 2 is to analyze the information collected in Stage 1 according to data flow and data relationships. This stage attempts to answer the question of what information processing functions the HMIS is to perform. There are two primary steps: the development of a functional model and the development of an entity model. The functional model begins by identifying the main functions of the system. This model is then progressively broken down into subsystems until they can no longer be subdivided (usually four to five levels). This may be accomplished by using a DFD (Chapter 4).

The development of an entity model serves a slightly different function. The entity model defines all entities within the system. An entity is anything that is relevant to records keeping; for example, in a bed allocation system, care providers, patients, and hospital beds are entities perceived to be useful for generating information about the system. It is also important to describe the relationship between entities and any other relevant attributes for designing an effective HMIS. The entity-relationship (ER) model has been discussed in Chapter 2.

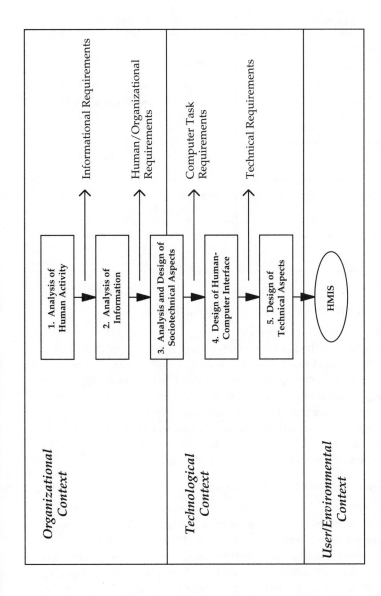

Figure 6–3 A Layered Multiview Framework for HMIS Design and Development

Exhibit 6–4 The Stages of the Multiview Framework

STAGE	MAJOR CONCEPT
1. Analysis of Human Activity	Identifies problem within an organization and suggests HMIS solutions to solve problems.
2. Analysis of Information	Uses information modeling techniques to analyze the problems of Stage 1.
3. Analysis and Design of Sociotechnical Aspects	Balances the social objectives with the technical objectives and ranks and chooses among these alternatives.
4. Design of Human-Computer Interface	Gathers user input to create the technical design of the HMIS.
5. Design of Technical Aspects	Formulates the technical specifications of the HMIS.

Stage 3: Analysis and Design of the Sociotechnical aspects

The objective of Stage 3 is to produce a design that incorporates the needs of individual users, as identified in the preceding stages, while balancing them with the technical objectives of the system. The sociotechnical analysis follows a logical sequence of events that begins with the identification of separate objectives for both the social and technical aspects and then goes on to develop alternatives that blend the objectives. Alternatives are ranked according to their ability to meet both sets of objectives, and a final selection is made of the best sociotechnical option. Unlike other stages, this stage addresses the question of how the HMIS can be incorporated into the working lives of the people in the organization.

Stage 4: Design of Human-Computer Interface

The objective of Stage 4 is to define the technical aspects of the system, including, for example, whether it will be menu driven or have an icon or mouse interface. The users are major contributors to these decisions, but this stage relies heavily on the systems analyst to guide the process and detail the final technical requirements. Equally important is the ability to incorporate the multiplicity of hardware and software already in existence within the overall HMIS design. Users should express their concerns to the analyst, who must in turn find the most appropriate human-computer interface to address these concerns. This stage attempts to answer the question of how individuals (i.e., users) can best relate to the HMIS in terms of operating it and using the system.

Stage 5: Design of the Technical Components

The objective of Stage 5 is to formulate the technical requirements of the system. At this point in the development, the human needs should already be integrated into the HMIS design. Therefore, this stage is only technical as the analyst(s) concentrates on detailing the full specifications of the HMIS design for efficient operations. This stage attempts to answer the question of what technical specifications are required for the HMIS to satisfy the needs identified in the four preceding stages.

Altogether, the Multiview methodology is characterized by several underlying assumptions. First, it provides a framework for resolving a problem. Multiview is not intended as a development prescription; but rather, it offers guidelines within which to assemble a set of tools and techniques for developing an HMIS. Second, it is situation-dependent, and the people who employ Multiview must be knowledgeable about the methodology as well as the problem situation, the users, and the organization. The practical approach produces knowledge for subsequent applications within similar contexts (i.e., action research). Third, it strives to integrate the human and technical subsystems, whereas past practices tended to focus on just one domain while ignoring the other.

Object-Oriented Analysis and Design

Another recently popularized option that addresses the limitations of earlier approaches to SDM is object-oriented analysis and design. Although many SA and SD techniques remain primarily process-oriented, OOAD goes further by defining the objects that are acted upon in the process. In other words, early SDMs address the "hows" of the process; OOAD defines the "whats" of the process.[27] Object-oriented technology is based on the premise that all software should be developed out of standard, reusable components whenever possible.

Taylor identifies three mechanisms that are key to understanding object technology. Exhibit 6–5 summarizes these mechanisms.[28] All software is constructed out of basic elements or objects, which combine related data and processes. Usually, these objects correspond to real-world objects, but they may be tangible things (bed, computer); roles played by an individual (patients, nurses); incidents (recovery, heart attack); interactions, such as object relations (membership, assignment); and specifications (patient type, physician specialty). Messages are the vehicles through which objects communicate in order to carry out real-world operations. Objects, depending on their function, are of many different types, but they share common characteristics and responses, called classes. One class, for

Exhibit 6–5 Three Key Mechanisms in Object-Oriented Analysis and Design (OOAD)

MECHANISMS	MAJOR CONCEPTS
1. Object	Objects correspond to real-world objects; they may be tangible things, roles played by an individual, incidents, interactions, or specifications.
2. Message	The vehicles through which objects communicate with each other in order to carry out real-world operations.
3. Class	Objects share common characteristics and responses; classes may have multiple levels arranged in a hierarchical fashion; embodied in the definition of "class" is the concept of "inheritance."

example, might be outpatient records. All outpatient objects, such as admission and discharge records and test results, would constitute the outpatient record class. Classes may consist of multiple levels in a hierarchical fashion or in a network schema. Embodied in the definition of "class" is the concept of "inheritance." For example, if a new object is introduced into a given hierarchy, it automatically inherits all the attributes of its predecessors and may in fact generate new characteristics for the objects that come after it in the hierarchy.

There are two types of tools that are used in the OOAD process: (1) the information structure diagram (ISD) and (2) the state transition diagram (STD). The ISD outlines how the objects within a class are related to each other. In the ISD, a block represents an object with attributes, and a line with arrows shows the relationship between objects and the inheritance properties. Figure 6–4 illustrates the use of an ISD to show patient-physician interactions in a hospital setting.

Whereas the ISD describes the object in relation to other objects, the STD describes the possible states that a single object can take. In the STD, a block represents one state of the object, with each block indicating actions that the object can perform, and arrows show the transition events triggered by an action. Figure 6–5 provides an example of an STD.

Object-oriented software is developed in layers.[29] Usually, the bottom layer consists of standard classes that are the standard, reusable components. The middle layer comprises the working, reusable models of the organization that can be utilized by numerous applications. These business models may include inventory control, billing, and admission/discharge records. The advantage to having

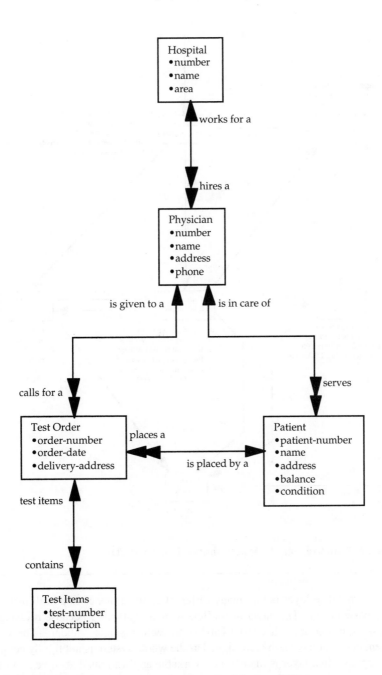

Figure 6–4 An Example of an Information Structure Diagram (ISD)

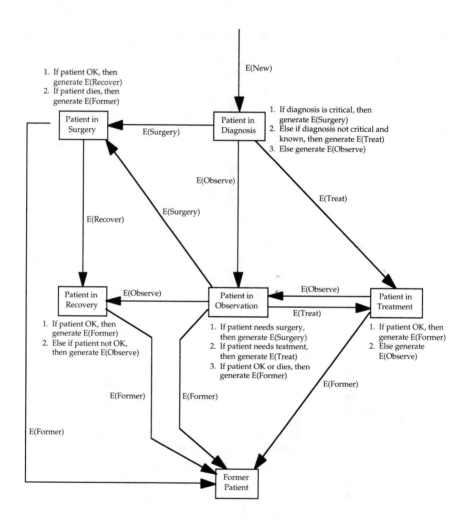

Figure 6–5 An Example of a State Transition Diagram (STD)

this intermediate layer is that many different applications can be built using the same basic design. This layer also offers increased stability because if change is necessary in one area, it can be carried out with a single "model." The whole system does not have to be redesigned as the whole system is not tightly coupled. The top and final layer is made up of workable applications that solve real problems. Thus, object applications are simply generated by using existing working models.

The overall advantage of this layered approach to development is the relatively fast assembly of new applications, a process known as "rapid" prototyping. In this context the term has a slightly different meaning than it has in the prototyping methodology. Here, the prototype is the program. A working version of the program is quickly developed by using existing classes and models. That working form is then revised and refined until it meets the desired requirements. Hence, rapid prototyping has the advantage of being fast, since the necessary classes and models are already available. OOAD is more flexible than traditional SDMs because users and programmers are already familiar with existing parts (or codes) reused in the applications. Furthermore, these applications can be further modified easily because the object-oriented prototypes often require only a relatively small amount of coding.

OOAD offers benefits that reflect other flexible approaches to systems development. It increases productivity and reduces cost in a number of ways: for example, the apparent advantages of reusability, flexibility, and reliability. Furthermore, since objects possess the characteristics of inheritance, maintenance requirements are also reduced. Changes that need to be made in the entire system are only carried out once, because inheritance affects the total system. These advantages to system development make OOAD a very attractive choice for HMIS designs and development.

CASE Tools

The last approach to be discussed among our contemporary models that challenges traditional development methodologies is computer-aided software (or systems) engineering (CASE). CASE tools can assist with any or all aspects of the SA and SD processes. The CASE tool customer usually wants a tool that will help organize, structure, and simplify the development process. The goal is to develop better software more quickly. It has been shown that close to 80 percent of the problems in a given application system stem from SA and SD stages.[30] Hence, automating the SA and SD functions, rather than only those of physical development, should make development effort more efficient and productive.

The CASE concept includes tools for building systems, platforms for integrating tools, methods for developing applications, and techniques for managing the SA and SD processes. CASE encourages an environment for interactive development and automation of repetitive HMIS developmental tasks. It has been called "a philosophy of application development which embraces a systems approach"[31] in which better connections between end-users (health professionals) and HMIS developers are supported. Traditional software approaches focus on technical aspects of applications and the best way to solve a given problem; the CASE approach looks at the broader health organizational context and searches to identify the right problems to solve, as well as how to solve those problems.

CASE can provide automated support for the following: HMIS application development; health systems verification, validation, and testing; SA and SD tool support; HMIS project management; and health organization office automation and communications. In the past, CASE tools have provided some of these functions, but not all of them together as one truly integrated tool-set that covers the entire SDLC process. IBM's Application Development/Cycle (AD/Cycle) is one proprietary example of an open platform or framework within which any CASE tool can participate.[32] It can support HMIS application developers with everything CASE currently offers, as well as the ability to adapt and incorporate future technologies.

An individual CASE tool automates one small, specific part of the development process. There are several categories of tools. For example, diagramming tools pictorially depict systems specifications. Screen and report painters create systems specifications and may be used for basic prototyping. Dictionaries are information management tools and facilitate storing, reporting, and querying of technical and project-management information. Specification tools detect incomplete, syntactically incorrect, and inconsistent system specifications. Code generators can generate executable codes from the pictorial system specifications. Lastly, documentation generators can produce technical and user documentation that is necessary in using structured approaches. Brathwaite has described three types of CASE tools, which are summarized in Exhibit 6–6.[33]

1. Systems development methodology (SDM) tools
2. Systems development support (SDS) tools
3. Programmer/project productivity (PP) tools

SDM tools combine to minimize effort and maximize coordination. These tools give support for an SDM at any (or all) of the stages of the SDLC process. They can include any of the tools appropriate to the methodology being used, while enforcing methodological rules and providing expertise to the users. SDS tools provide support for SA and SD techniques used at any stages of the SDLC process, but they do not necessarily enforce a methodology. PP tools provide support for programmers/designers of software mostly at the back end of the development life cycle. Examples include project management and documentation tools.

More broadly, CASE tools may also be classified according to the following taxonomy. CASE "toolkits" are integrated tools that automate only one part of the SDLC process. CASE "workbenches" provide integrated tools to automate the entire SDLC. CASE tools that are integrated and linked with non-CASE systems developmental tools are known as CASE "frameworks." Finally, CASE "methodology companions" sustain a specific methodology by automating the entire SDLC process.

Exhibit 6–6 Three Types of CASE Tools

TOOLS	CONCEPTS
Systems Development Methodology Tools	Combine to minimize effort and maximize coordination; enforce methodology rules and provide expertise to users.
Systems Development Support Tools	Support systems development tools and techniques at any stage in the life cycle; do not necessarily enforce a methodology.
Programmer/Project Productivity Tools	Provide support for software programmers and designers at the back end of the development life cycle.

It can be difficult to decide which of the many CASE tools available is most appropriate for a given situation or environment. Brathwaite proposes asking several of the following simple questions:[34]

- What are the future direction and functionality of the tools?
- Does the tool's manufacturer have a philosophy of "open architecture"?
- Does the tool interface with other CASE tools that have been purchased or are being considered?
- Does the tool provide a detailed means of prototyping?
- Does the CASE design provide analysis support for design documentation?
- Does the tool enhance project management?

Although CASE has been in existence for many years, it is still in its infancy in terms of its potential for use. For many years, technical aspects of SDMs predominated over human aspects. Only recently has there been a shift to a more humanistic perspective. This shift has resulted in the emergence of a whole new field of SDMs that extends from contemporary models to end-user computing (EUC), which is the final topic of discussion in this chapter.

END-USER COMPUTING

The need to balance the human and technical aspects in the evolution of SDMs was fueled by the predominance of the technical components and the subsequent user dissatisfaction. The shift to a more humanistic perspective and the infiltration of the microcomputer at the worksite have led to the emergence of EUC.[35] The microcomputer explosion, along with increased knowledge of its potential, resulted in more requests for HMIS projects. EUC emerged to meet the growing demand for numerous end-user applications that do not rely on traditional programmers or processing centers.[36]

EUC is not personal computing; personal computing is a subcategory of EUC. An end-user is anyone who uses information generated by a computer, and hence EUC is any direct use of the computer by an individual whose primary interest is something other than just that use.[37] Stated simply, EUC is the capability of users to have direct control of their own computing needs. For example, a student (the end-user) who is primarily interested in writing a paper may access a database at a university library, submit a set of requests to the computer to conduct a literature search (EUC), and use that information for the purposes of writing the paper.

End-User Applications

Nowadays, end-user applications (EUA) encompass a wide spectrum, including personal computing, communications, data retrieval/analysis, activity management, office automation, decision support, and expert systems. These applications are the result of very high level computer languages (i.e., fourth- or fifth-generation languages) that have been incorporated into end-user tools. There are two types of EUAs: prewritten software packages and flexible software.[38]

The most common prewritten software packages in use today are:[39]

- Word processors
- Spreadsheets
- Databases
- Graphics
- Communications programs

Word processing software provides an electronic notepad for the creation of business or personal documents (i.e., letters). These programs also provide formatting, spell-check, and storage options. A spreadsheet is an electronic table of rows and columns that provides a quick method for performing mathematical calculations and tabulations. Database software creates an electronic card index for secondary storage of information. Its purpose is to make the organization, storage, and retrieval of information easier and more accurate. Graphics programs can provide the user with a number of options, ranging from the selection of predesigned graphics to insert within a text to the creation of presentation graphics, including tables, charts, and graphs. Communication programs are software that electronically links one computer to other computers, thereby providing an avenue to communicate information without the need for direct physical contact.

Among the flexible software are 4GLs and application generators (AGs). These very high level languages (VHLL), as end-user tools, allow health professionals who have only limited knowledge of computers to develop their own HMIS applications. In this sense, end-user technology can be employed in conjunction with any of the SDMs discussed earlier. For example, hospital administrators who decide to develop a rough budget forecast for the coming year may do so by using an end-user tool such as a spreadsheet and the prototyping method; that is, they begin by designing a rough spreadsheet resembling a budget and continue to upgrade the spreadsheet until all the relevant variables for their budgets have been included.

Because of the sophistication of some tools available in the health computing marketplace (e.g., OOAD and CASE tools), end-users are now able to develop some of the more elaborate HMIS applications on their own. The range of options for HMIS development has expanded substantially over the years.

Advantages and Disadvantages

The evolution from a centralized control mechanism to individual user control has both advantages and disadvantages. There are five main advantages to EUC: (1) users retain control; (2) users are more committed to change; (3) users are more knowledgeable and therefore better trained; (4) users derive a better solution of information systems problems; and (5) users reduce their dependence on the information service department.[40] Generally, these advantages translate into cheaper and faster HMIS application development and the greater acceptability of the products to the user.

There are, however, several disadvantages as well: (1) the loss of the analyst in the development process, which may result in the loss of expertise, completeness, and an organizational viewpoint in the system's development; (2) the ability of users to identify systems requirements correctly; (3) the neglect of quality assurance procedures, including documentation; (4) the difficulties in training new personnel and ensuring communications among subsystems when private information systems are predominant in an organization; (5) the saturation of computer time and resources by multiple indiscriminate end-user applications.

There is, of course, also increased concern regarding the organizational data sharing and data consistency. The evolution of computer capabilities has resolved some of these disadvantages, especially regarding the integrity of the data and the concerns about efficiency. However, to reap the majority of the advantages while minimizing the disadvantages, EUC must be coordinated within an organization.

Planning for Success

The emergence of the personal computers (PCs) has provided for more freedom and flexibility but has also added to the complexity of designing HMIS. As health organizations become increasingly dependent on computerized systems, the ability of end-users to use the systems effectively becomes critical. The PC revolution has placed EUC on the top ten list of concerns for management, and EUC ranks second as a concern of overall information systems planning.[41]

When EUC began, most projects were simple applications. Today, EUC spans the whole organization and has significant impact on the functioning of the entire information system. Studies have shown that EUC may account for 25 to 40 percent of an organization's information system.[42] It is therefore imperative that management recognize the need to coordinate the efforts of multifaceted EUAs. It is far more advantageous to coordinate EUC than to impede its development or let it proceed fragmented.

The literature on EUC agrees on two primary guidelines for the successful inclusion of EUC within the organizational HMIS planning process.

1. Policies and procedures for the use of system quality control: To maximize the benefits of EUC, an organization should have strategies for promoting, managing, and controlling the evolution of EUC.[43] At a minimum, management should request the documentation of individual user applications. Organizations should also limit the set of hardware, software, and vendor options available to end-users. Having a wide variety of microcomputers and applications can result in training difficulties and inefficiencies, maintenance difficulties, and system incompatibilities.

2. Support services: The development of end-user applications does not obviate the need for guidance and assistance with difficult problems. The development of an information support center is encouraged by information systems experts to ensure the effectiveness and efficiency of EUAs. Such centers can provide hardware, software, training, consulting, and problem-solving resources.

CONCLUSION

To a health service administrator in today's environment, it is crucial to incorporate SDM as a key instrument in the effective and efficient development of an HMIS. To this end, administrators should be informed HMIS consumers. They must have a broad perspective of HMIS theoretical concepts (Chapters 3 through 5) and know the practical applications of tools and techniques for the development of an HMIS. Successful HMIS development is a building block process that begins with an understanding of general systems theory (Chapter 3). Knowledge of individual system components and subsystems leads to a better understanding of data and information (Chapter 4). It is also important to have a general understanding of effective management and the technology available on the market to maximize the potential of these applications (Chapter 5).

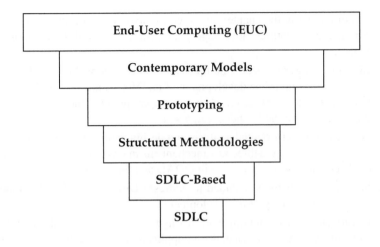

Figure 6–6 The Evolution of Systems Development Methodologies

SDMs have evolved from rigid step-by-step formulas for success to contemporary models, such as Multiview, OOAD, and CASE, which offer guidelines for high-quality HMIS development. Figure 6–6 is a summary of the evolution of the SDMs. The diagram shows how each methodology has built on its predecessor to produce greater effectiveness. The advent of EUC has created awareness and consideration of end-user needs in the development of information systems.

In the end, the problem of choosing among alternative SDMs is one of recognizing the broader environmental, organizational, and technological contexts in which the need for health information systems designs and development is embedded. Part II, which ends with this chapter, has provided a solid introductory foundation of the first two contexts (i.e., the environment and the organization). Part III (Chapters 7 through 9) will continue this discussion with an in-depth analysis of the technological context of HMIS designs and development.

CHAPTER QUESTIONS

1. Define the following and describe a health-related example that incorporates all these terms: (a) methodology, (b) technique, (c) tool, (d) phases and subphases.

2. List the steps of the Waterfall model, and discuss this methodology's strengths and advantages over early systems development strategies.

3. Provide a list of the second-, third-, and fourth-generation methodologies as well as the flexible and integrated methodologies (i.e., contemporary mod-

els) discussed in the chapter and devise a taxonomy to contrast and compare the main features, advantages, and disadvantages of these alternative SDMs.

4. List at least three tools or techniques that can be used within the Multiview framework to aid in the development of an information system. Identify at what stage each tool/technique is most appropriate, which inputs are required, and what the intended outputs are.

5. Define the object-oriented analysis and design approach to systems development. What are the three key mechanisms in OOAD? Describe the "layered" development of software in OOAD and the advantages of its use.

6. What are CASE tools intended to address? Discuss how CASE supports various aspects of systems development.

7. Define end-user computing and distinguish it from personal computing. Describe an example of an end-user application in the health care industry.

MINI CASE 6
A COMPUTER-BASED MODEL FOR COMMUNITY HEALTH
PROGRAM MONITORING

The federal government, through the Science Council, Canada, recently funded a number of sites to develop community health programs for neighborhood residents. Each of these sites was first equipped with a computer and a small office run by a full-time hired program coordinator. The council also requires that the site coordinators report to the community supervisor and the medical health officer (MHO) of the region for which the community was funded. Residents of these communities interact with their program coordinators as volunteers as well as participants in community health awareness programs. The council also funds a team of evaluators, who are affiliated with certain university research groups, to provide technical assistance to the various community sites and to conduct independent reviews of the various community health demonstration programs.

Apart from setting up various community health programs and managing the daily chores of tracking levels of community participation in various programs, the site coordinators must also try to mobilize community support and delegate responsibilities to task forces for the different programs. In one of the communities, a number of health programs were suggested and initiated by the collaborative efforts of the site coordinator, the community supervisor, the MHO, and most importantly, the task forces, whose memberships mainly comprise volunteers drawn from various community groups. The coordinator is expected to report the latest developments on each of these programs during scheduled meetings and to perform his or her role efficiently and effectively.

Realizing the power of automation in achieving greater efficiency and effectiveness, a particular community coordinator decided to get help from the evaluation team by asking for the design and implementation of a Macintosh-based (as this site was given a Macintosh for the project) software that would track, on a real-time basis, the various pieces of information from each of the three programs currently being conducted at that community: (1) the walking program, (2) the restaurant program, and (3) the worsksite program. Since these are new programs and the coordinator is still uncertain about the response of the community at large to them, she has never been able to give a very accurate description of the process when asked to do so. To make matters worse, the coordinator has never used computer software even though she knows that it will greatly assist her in reducing her heavy work load and thus provide her more time to carry out her various responsibilities.

MINI CASE QUESTIONS

Imagine yourself to be the analyst from one of the evaluation teams being asked to assist this program coordinator in designing and developing a community information system (CIS) product. You decided to analyze the situation encountered by this program coordinator by using a rich picture (see Figure 2–3). You then proceeded to design a prototype of the system envisioned by the program coordinator by working on several possible screen layouts (Figures 6–7 to 6–9). Your meeting with the program coordinator to discuss the rich picture as well as the screen layouts resulted in the following questions:

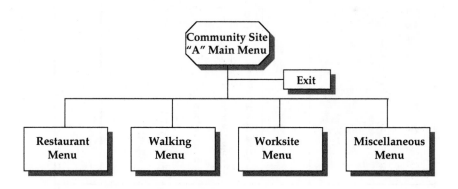

Figure 6–7 Main Menu Subsystem for Multicommunity Health Promotion Project (MCHPP): Community Site "A"

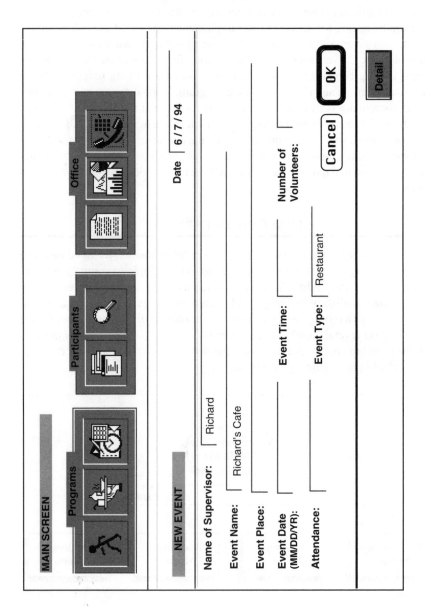

Figure 6-8 The Main and New Event Screens for Community Site "A." Courtesy of Microsoft Corporation, Redmond, Washington.

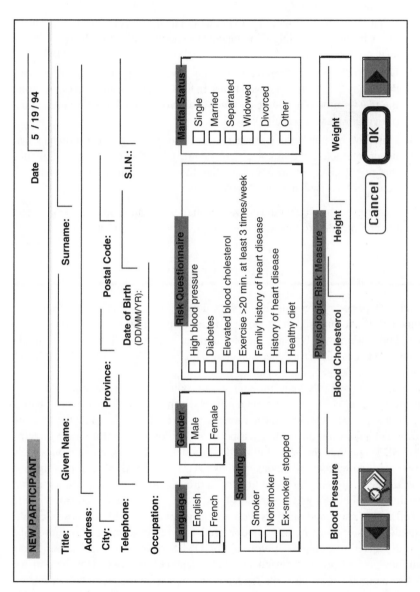

Figure 6–9 The New Participant Screen for Community Site "A." Courtesy of Microsoft Corporation, Redmond, Washington.

1. Did you think using a rich picture might be a worthwhile approach for you to begin the system development process? Why and why not?

2. What types of information do you, as the analyst, feel you might want to know before proceeding with the development of the CIS? Relate your answers to Question 1.

3. Distinguish between "rapid prototyping" and "prototyping." Which do you think may be a better approach to use in the CIS modeling process? Assuming that "prototyping" were chosen, would you then advise a revolutionary or evolutionary approach? Why?

4. How do you plan to overcome the fact that the program coordinator has never interacted with a computer system? Choose a contemporary model that might give you the assurance that the system you will design and develop will be used and justify your choice.

Discuss briefly how you would address each of these questions, supposing your responses are intended for an audience with little or no computing experience.

CHAPTER REVIEW

The early period of computer technology development was characterized by the absence of any formalized methodology or development framework. Developing HMIS applications was typically the programmer's responsibility. As the technology and the needs of the users became increasingly complex, the need for a formal development process became evident.

A multitude of SDMs were subsequently introduced to help minimize the problems of uncoordinated developmental efforts. Each methodology has been based on a philosophical view, which can range from an exclusive focus on the humanistic side to a focus on the technical aspects of developing an information system. These SDMs include the Waterfall (SDLC) model, SDLC-based techniques such as BSP, structured methodologies such as SADT and SSADM, and prototyping using the revolutionary or evolutionary approach. Present consensus calls for choosing a methodology that considers the context, that is, the organization itself, as well as the users and analysts who are developing the HMIS. These flexible methodologies or contemporary models are based on the systems paradigms that currently offer the greatest potential for HMIS development. They include Multiview, object-oriented design and analysis, and CASE tools. However, many of these methodologies have the tendency to emphasize the technical aspects of SDM at the expense of the human aspects. The recent shift toward EUC and EUA is likely to reverse that emphasis, putting the human perspective in a more important position.

NOTES

1. E. Schein, *Process Consulting,* Vol. 2. (Reading, Mass: Addison-Wesley Publishing Co., Inc., 1987).

2. J. Rowley, *The Basics of Systems Analysis and Design for Information Managers* (London: Clive Bingley, 1990).

3. D. Avison and G. Fitzgerald, *Information Systems Development—Methodology, Techniques and Tools* (Boston: Blackwell Scientific Publications, Inc., 1988).

4. S. Holloway, *Methodology Handbook for Information Managers* (Aldershot, England: Gower Technical, 1989).

5. J. Cougar, et al., eds, *Advanced System Development/Feasibility Techniques* (New York: John Wiley & Sons, Inc., 1982).

6. M. Colter, A Comparative Examination of Systems Analysis Techniques, *MIS Quarterly* 8, no. 1 (1984): 51–66.

7. D. Burnstine, *BIAIT: An Emerging Management Discipline* (New York: BIAIT International, 1980). Read this reference for a detailed discussion of the seven questions used in the BIAIT method.

8. IBM, *Business Systems Planning* (1975).

9. Cougar, *Advanced System Development.*

10. Colter, *A Comparative Examination.*

11. D. Ross and K. Schoman, Structured Analysis for Requirements Definition, *IEEE Transactions on Software Engineering* SE-3, no. 1 (1977): 6–15.

12. D. Ross, Structured Analysis (SA): A Language for Communicating Ideas, *IEEE Transactions on Software Engineering* SE-3, no. 1 (1977): 16–34.

13. T. Olle, et al., *Information Systems Methodologies: A Framework for Understanding* (Reading, Mass: Addison-Wesley Publishing Co., Inc., 1988).

14. Colter, *A Comparative Examination.*

15. T. DeMarco, *Structured Analysis and System Specification* (Englewood Cliffs, NJ: Prentice Hall, 1979).

16. E. Yourdon and L. Constantine, *Structured Design* (Englewood Cliffs, NJ: Prentice Hall, 1979).

17. C. Floyd, *Information Systems Design Methodologies: Improving the Practice* (Amsterdam: North-Holland, 1986).

18. T. W. Olle, et al., eds. *Information System Design Methodologies: A Comparative Review* (Amsterdam: North-Holland, 1982).

19. E. Downs, et al., *Structured Systems Analysis and Design Method: Application and Context* (Englewood Cliffs, NJ: Prentice Hall, 1988).

20. J.K.H. Tan and J. Hanna, Integrating Health Care: Knitting Patient Care with Technology through Networking, *Health Care Management Review* 19, no. 2 (1994): 72–80.

21. B. McNurlin and R. Sprague, *Information Systems Management in Practice,* 2nd ed. (Englewood Cliffs, NJ: Prentice Hall, 1989).

22. D. Benyon and S. Skidmore, Towards a Tool Kit for the Systems Analyst, *Computer Journal* 30, no. 1 (1987): 2.

23. Avison and Fitzgerald, *Information Systems Development.*

24. A. Wood-Harper, et al., *Information Systems Definition: The Multiview Approach* (Oxford: Blackwell Scientific Publications, Inc., 1985).

25. E. Mumford and M. Weir, *Computer Systems in Work Design: The ETHICS Method* (London: Associated Business Press, 1979).

26. D. Avison and A. Wood-Harper, Information Systems Development Research: An Exploration of Ideas in Practice, *Computer Journal* 34, no. 2 (1991): 98–112.

27. L. Garceau, et al., Object-Oriented Analysis and Design: A New Approach to Systems Development, *Journal of Systems Management* 44 (1993): 25–32.

28. D. Taylor, *Object-Oriented Information Systems: Planning and Implementation* (New York: John Wiley & Sons, Inc., 1992).

29. Ibid.

30. L. Towner, *CASE Concepts and Implementation* (New York: McGraw-Hill Publishing Co., 1989): 2. This is a technical book that is part of an IBM series.

31. S. Montgomery, *AD/Cycle: IBM's Framework for Application Development and CASE* (New York: IBM, 1991): 9.

32. Ibid.

33. K. Brathwaite, *Applications Development Using CASE Tools* (New York: Academic Press, Inc., 1990): 108.

34. Ibid.

35. R. Panko, *End User Computing: Management, Applications and Technology* (New York: John Wiley & Sons, Inc., 1988).

36. J. Day, et al., *Microcomputers and Applications* (Glenview, Ill: Scott, Foresman & Co., 1988).

37. G. Weinberger and A. Tenebaum, End-User Computing, *Computers in Healthcare* (July 1986): 39–41.

38. E. Turban, Decision Support Systems in Hospitals, *Health Care Management Review* 7, no. 3 (1982): 35.

39. T. Athey, et al., *Computers and End-User Software* (Glenview, Ill: Scott, Foresman & Co., 1989).

40. H. Lucas, *The Analysis, Design and Implementation of Information Systems* (New York: McGraw-Hill Publishing Co., 1992).

41. Panko, *End User Computing.*

42. Ibid.

43. G.B. Davis and M.H. Olson, *Management Information Systems: Conceptual Foundations, Structure and Development,* 2nd ed. (New York: McGraw-Hill Publishing Co., 1985).

Part III

Setting the Bricks and Mortar of Health Management Information Systems: HMIS Technologies and Applications

Chapter 7

A Survey of HMIS Technologies: State-of-the-Art Applications for the Health Service Delivery Industry

LEARNING OBJECTIVES

1. Identify types of hardware technologies in HMIS applications.
2. Identify types of software technologies in HMIS applications.
3. Classify the range of user-computer interface designs.
4. Specify the components of a telecommunication and network system.
5. Characterize state-of-the-art HMIS applications for the health service industry.
6. Chart the significance of HMIS technologies for the future.

INTRODUCTION

For all its power, the computer is still merely a tool.[1]

The growing importance and acceptance of computing technology as a component of health service management are reflective of the many organizational benefits expected of computer based information systems (CBIS) support. CBIS in the health service field improve health service management decision making and are beginning to play an increasingly important role in organizational control, clinical decision making, and strategic planning.

There are three primary reasons for developing CBIS. First, they improve operational efficiency so that inadequacies in the operation of administrative systems (e.g., medical record processing, patient administration, and financial accounting management) can be detected and analyzed. Second, they promote organizational innovations by allowing new ways of doing old things. Finally, they build strategic resources that will give broad access to timely and relevant information for effective decision making. The application of CBIS in health management areas is known as health management information systems (HMIS). HMIS applications are developed by blending organizational, technological, and human resources. In this chapter our focus is on the technological resources. These include hardware, software, user-computer interface, and telecommunication components. To understand the role and capabilities of IS in the health care environment, it is necessary to have a working knowledge of the various technologies available in the IS marketplace. The chapter will look at how various facets of HMIS technologies can be applied and how new information technologies will affect the future of the health service industry.

HARDWARE TECHNOLOGIES

Hardware includes all physical devices (machines, storage devices, and input/output devices) that constitute a computer system. A computer system is a subsystem of an organization's overall information system and is an integrated assembly of physical devices centered around at least one processing mechanism—the central processing unit (CPU). Figure 7–1 provides an overview of how various parts of a computer system are related operationally, the CPU, the primary and secondary storage, and the input/output devices.

The Central Processing Unit

Often referred to as the "brain" or "heart" of the computer, the CPU is at the primary core of a computer system. The CPU consists of three associated elements.

1. The control unit (CU), accesses program instructions, decodes and interprets these instructions, and then issues to the other parts of the computer system the necessary orders to carry out the functions. It is the responsibility of the CU to coordinate the flow of data in and out of the arithmetic/logic unit, registers, primary storage, secondary storage, and various input and output devices.

2. The arithmetic/logic unit (ALU) receives instructions from the CU and then performs the necessary mathematical calculations and logical comparisons.

3. The registers, also called temporary storage, are used in the CU or the ALU. Registers are high-speed storage areas used to hold small units of program instructions and data temporarily, immediately before, during, and after execution by the CPU. They are designed so that data can be placed into or removed from a register faster than from a location in the main storage.

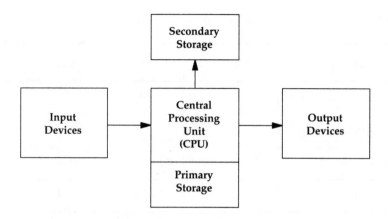

Figure 7–1 A Schematic Representation of Major Components of a Computer System

---

The CPU has the ability to process raw data into information and execute directions and instructions in a program. The execution of an instruction is known as a machine cycle. The machine cycles of modern computers are measured in nanoseconds (one-billionth of a second) and picoseconds (one-trillionth of a second), which determine the speed of the computer processing.

As shown in Table 7–1, each personal computer (PC) has a variety of components, such as clock speed, performance, address bus, and data bus. Each CPU is driven by a series of electronic pulses at a predetermined rate, called the clock speed. Clock speed is the speed at which the CPU executes an instruction, and it is usually measured in megahertz. Megahertz ratings can be misleading indicators of the overall effective processing speed of microprocessors as measured in millions of instructions per second (mips). This is because processing speed also depends on factors such as the circuitry paths or buses between microprocessor components. Table 7–1 compares the clock speed, performance, addresses, and data buses of various popular PC models.

Data are transferred from the CPU to other system components by way of bus lines, which are the physical wires connecting the various computer system components. The number of bits that a bus line can transfer at any one moment is known as the bus line width. Bus line width should be matched with CPU word length. Word length is the number of bits a CPU can process at any one time.

Multiprogramming involves executing more than one program at a time. The memory is divided into segments known as partitions, each of which holds a program. Virtual storage is an extension of multiprogramming, in which, instead of storing a complete program in memory, the computer will store in memory only a small part of the program at a time while the rest is stored on disk. Thus, the entire

Table 7-1 Performance Characteristics of Various Personal Computer (PC) Models

Computer Type	386SX	386DX	486
Clock Speed (MHz)	16	16, 20, 25, 33	25, 33, 50, 66
Performance (mips)*	2.5-3.0	4-8	15-40
Address Bus**	24 bits	32 bits	32 bits
Data Bus***	16 bits	32 bits	32 bits

* Performance: the number (millions) of instructions a computer can execute in 1 second.
** Address bus: the path that carries memory addresses to all devices connected to the data bus.
*** Data bus: the wires that connect the CPU with the random access memory (RAM).

program is not needed because the computer is executing only a few instructions at a time. The CPU is therefore less likely to be waiting for programs to be transferred from disk to memory. This reduces idle CPU time and increases the number of jobs that can be done within a given time span.

Primary and Secondary Storage

Primary storage, also called main memory, is closely associated with the CPU. Primary storage holds program instructions and data immediately before or after the registers and provides the CPU with a working storage area for program instructions and data. All programs and data must be transferred to primary storage by way of an input device or secondary storage before programs can be executed or data can be processed.

Types of primary storage include

- Random access memory (RAM)
- Read only memory (ROM)
- Programmable ROM (PROM)
- Erasable PROM (EPROM)

RAM is used for short-term storage of data or program instructions. It is the memory where a program is stored when it is presently active in the computer. One major disadvantage of RAM is that is volatile: that is, it requires a continuous application of power to retain data and programs. If the power is turned off, everything in RAM is lost, unless it is first saved or stored. There are two types of RAM chips: dynamic RAM (DRAM) and static RAM (SRAM). The main difference between them lies in how often each needs to be refreshed or recharged per second. DRAM needs to be refreshed thousands of times per second, whereas SRAM needs to be refreshed less often.

ROM is used for the permanent storage of program instruction. All of the computer's standard instructions are kept here. ROM can only be read, not changed or erased. Furthermore, ROM is nonvolatile. The information it stores is not lost when the power to the computer is interrupted.

PROM is a memory device in which the memory chips can be programmed only once and are used to store instructions entered by the purchaser. Once a program is written into PROM, it is permanent. EPROM is a device whose memory chips can be erased and reprogrammed with new instructions.[2]

The memory capacity of primary storage is commonly measured by access time and storage capacity. As shown in Table 7–2 storage capacity is measured by bytes (a group, usually 8, of adjacent bits [binary digits] configured to represent one character). Prefixes such as kilo (10^3), mega (10^6), and giga (10^9) are used to denote increasingly larger memory storage capacities. Table 7–2 compares the processing performance, RAM size, physical size, and approximate current prices of various computer configurations.

Secondary storage, also known as external storage, supplements main memory by holding data and instruction in machine readable form outside the computer. Secondary storage offers the advantages of nonvolatility, greater economy, and greater capacity then primary storage. Common forms of secondary storage are

* Floppy disk
* Magnetic tape
* Optical disk storage

Table 7–2 A Classification of Various Computer Types

Computer Type	Processor Speed	RAM Size	Physical Size	Cost
PC	8-16 MHz	0.64-16 MB	Desktop	< $5K*
Workstation	16-32 MHz	16-64 MB	Desktop	$5K–$20K
Mini	1-12 mips	32-128 MB	Closet-sized	$20K–$100K
Mainframe	10-60 mips	32-256 MB	Car-sized	$50K –$1M**
Super	1-10 gigaflops	> 256 MB	Room-sized	$5M–$20M

* K = Thousands
** M = Millions

Small areas or spots of magnetized particles are used to represent bits on magnetic tapes or disks. Two types of access to the information stored on the magnetic media are available. Direct access allows the computer to go directly to any desired piece of data, regardless of its location on the magnetic medium, such as a floppy disk, which is a flexible disk inside a plastic sleeve. Sequential access, on the other hand, can only read and write data in sequence, one data item after another (i.e., a cassette tape).[3]

Operating like a compact disk player, an optical disk device uses laser beams to store and retrieve data. One advantage of optical disk storage is its ability to withstand wear, fingerprints, and dust. Two of the most common optical disk storage systems are compact disk–read only memory (CD-ROM) and write once, read many (WORM).

Data are stored onto CD-ROM by burning small crevices into their coatings. This allows another laser device to read the CD-ROM by measuring the difference in the reflected light caused by the crevices on the disk. Each crevice represents the binary digit 0, and the smooth surface area represents the binary digit 1. A compact disk is capable of storing 500 to 700 megabytes of information, which includes text, sound, and pictures, and it has the ability to hold a large amount of information (e.g., an encyclopedia). However, one of the disadvantages of optical disk storage is that it is slower and more expensive than magnetic disk storage.[4,5] WORM format allows users to record data only once on a customized basis and then access it whenever needed. WORM disks are nonerasable and are often used to store original versions of valuable documents or data (e.g., archives). Figure 7–2 shows the storage capacity of different forms of primary and secondary storage with respect to both cost and speed.

Input/Output Devices

A number of devices can be used to input or enter data into a computer system. For larger computer systems, key-to-tape and key-to-disk devices, in which data are keyed directly onto a secondary storage device, are widely used. PCs are often used for initial entry, editing, or correction of data before they are downloaded to a larger system for processing.

Keyboards are inexpensive and easy-to-use devices that enter alphanumeric data. Some keyboards allow special character data input at the same time. On-line data entry and data input devices are connected directly to the computer system by phone lines or cables. The mouse is another example of an input device. Track balls, which evolved from the "mouse" concept, are becoming popular for use with portables. Voice recognition systems are still at an experimental stage but will eventually allow computers to capture and respond to human speech. Direct magnetic ink character recognition (MICR) systems allow data printed in a special

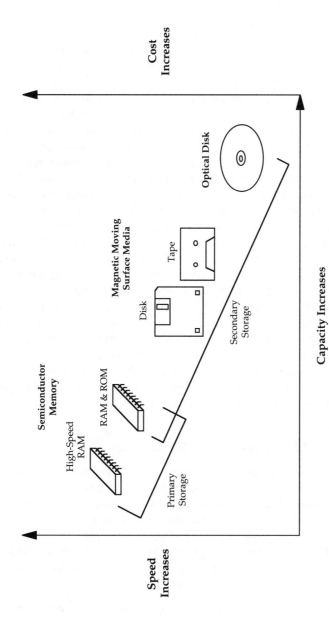

Figure 7–2 Cost, Speed, and Capacity Trade-Offs of Storage Media

magnetic ink to be read by both humans and computers; the bottom part of a check is an example.

Optical data readers can read characters directly from a page without using special ink. Optical character recognition (OCR) equipment can read alphabetic, numeric, and special characters (i.e., bar codes). Image processing systems use scanners (much like miniature photocopiers) to input an image into memory. Scanned images can then be manipulated by using graphic programs and reprinted as desired. Other input devices include light pens, data tables, and touch screens. Like voice recognition systems, these technologies are still to be perfected before they can gain wider user acceptance. We turn now to discussing output devices.

There are many forms of computer output media. The most common types are printers. Printers are classified as impact or nonimpact printers. Impact printers strike the paper during the process and include dot-matrix and daisy-wheel types. By striking the paper several times while printing, near-letter quality output can often be achieved. Nonimpact printers include ink-jet and laser printers.

Other output devices are video display terminals (VDT), plotters that draw graphics on paper, computer output microfilm (COM) devices that can place data directly from the computer onto microfilm for future use, and voice output devices that range from audio-response units to speech synthesizer microprocessors.

As we move into the future, there will be an increasing reduction in hardware size, resulting in increased processing capabilities and reduced costs.[6] Hardware will be able to perform a greater number of functions at an increasingly quicker speed. This will generate faster and more accurate information for the user.[7] Furthermore, the miniaturization trend of hardware technology will reduce the size of peripheral equipment, CPUs, storage, and other computer components. In addition, it will simultaneously give users increased access to a greater amount of data.[8]

SOFTWARE AND USER INTERFACE TECHNOLOGIES

Over the last few decades, software and user interface technologies[9] have constituted a larger share of total system costs. Advances in hardware technology have dramatically reduced hardware costs; however, prices in software and user interface technology have increased to offset these reductions. Currently, software encompasses 75 percent or more of the cost of an organization's computer system.[10] Increasingly complex software requires more time and money to develop, and, in turn, increases the demand for the product and the salaries of developers. There are two basic types of computer software.

1. Systems software: machine executable programs designed to supervise and support the overall functioning of the computer system
2. Applications software: programs written to solve specific domain problems

Systems Software and Operating Systems

Systems software is independent of any specific application area. It manages computer resources such as the CPU, printers, terminals, communication links, and peripheral equipment. There are three main types of systems software used to manage instructions for computer hardware.

1. Operating systems (OS)
2. Language translations programs (LTPs)
3. Utility programs (UPs)

An OS is a set of computer programs that run or control the computer hardware and act as an interface with application programs. OS are written for specific computers, and most are limited to use with specific computers. OS are usually stored on disk and transferred to memory when a computer is "booted" (i.e., turned on). Examples of OS are Systems 7.5 (Macintosh), MS-DOS, OS/2, and UNIX.[11]

LTPs convert statements from high-level programming languages into machine code. The high-level program code is referred to as the source code, and the machine language code as the object code. In order to perform such a conversion, a compiler is used. A system software interpreter executes each machine language statement, discards it, and then continues on to translate the next statement.

UPs perform specialized functions directly related to the actual computer operation. They are considered part of the systems software and are used to prepare documents, merge and sort files, keep track of computer jobs being run, manage printers and disk drives, recover lost programs, and lock confidential files.

A mainframe is a large computer that has access to extremely large amounts of data and is capable of processing these data very quickly. Mainframes use one of two types of processing approaches, which were discussed previously (Chapter 1). Batch processing is one of the oldest ways of running programs: a batch of programs is collected and run on the computer system one at a time. On-line processing involves the running of a program whenever data are collected and entered into the computer system. On-line processing is possible because terminals and other devices are directly connected (on-line) to the main computer; as a result, data files are kept as current as possible.

Application Software and Programming Languages

Application software cannot be used without the system software. Application software are programs designed to handle the processing for particular computer applications. Application software translates the user's instructions for the systems software, which, in turn, forwards the instructions to the hardware. A company can either develop application software itself (in-house) or use an existing software program (off-the-shelf). Popular application software includes software packages such as Word Perfect, Microsoft Word, Lotus 1-2-3, Excel, and DBASE IV.

A programming language is a set of symbols and rules used to write program code. Programming languages, like computers, have evolved over time. Today, we have gone through five different "generations" of programming languages (as depicted in Figure 7–3).

1. First-generation (1GL) or machine language

2. Second-generation (2GL) or assembly language

3. Third-generation (3GL) or procedure-oriented language

4. Fourth-generation (4GL) or very high level language (VHLL)

5. Fifth-generation (5GL) or artificial intelligence

1GL is the most basic level of computer operation. It is a machine-level language that uses binary coding and addresses to execute instructions. First-generation language is difficult to write because of its binary representation of information as 1's and 0's corresponding to "on" and "off" electrical states of the computer.

2GL is a low-level symbolic language, unique to a specific computer. 2GL replaces binary digits with understandable symbols to ease programming; for example, one assembly language instruction equals one machine language instruction.

3GL is a high-level language that uses English-like statements in the coding of program instructions. Each instruction is thus equivalent to multiple machine-level instructions. Some common examples of 3GLs are Cobol, Fortran, Pascal, and C.

4GLs are nonprocedural and are more English-like than 3GLs. Their distinctive features include high-level query language for direct access to database; interactive dialog; simple-to-learn, helpful error messages; and use of defaults and relational database management. However, they are often less efficient in terms of computer running time than 3GL. Examples include Excel, Mantis, Ramis II, and Oracle.[12,13]

5GLs include expert systems and natural language interfaces, which will be discussed in more detail in the next chapter. Research in 5GLs has also advanced our knowledge of user-computer interface.

User-Computer Interface

When the concept of interface began to emerge, it was commonly understood as "the hardware and software through which a human and computer could communicate."[14] As it evolved, the concept has widened to include "the cognitive and

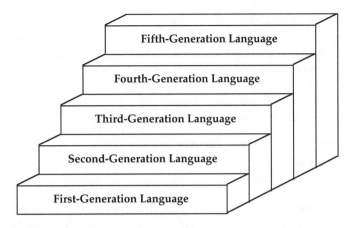

Figure 7–3 Levels of Programming Languages

---

emotional aspects of the user's experience as well."[15] From a user's perspective, an interface is therefore defined as a discrete and tangible thing that can map, draw, design, implement, and attach items to an existing bundle of functions. Interfacing allows users to interact with the computer to perform various interactive functions.

There are two main types of user-computer interfaces: action language and presentation language.[16] In action language the user instructs the computer to take a series of actions; it is the way in which the user's intentions are translated into syntax that the machine understands. A simple example is the use of a touch screen or an icon. Presentation language is the way in which the computer communicates with the user, for example, by the use of color and graphics.[17] Four main designs for user-computer interface are described in this section.

1. Graphical interfaces
2. Iconic interfaces
3. Direct manipulation
4. Group interfaces

A graphical interface is associated with presentation languages. It allows tables and numbers to be converted and represented graphically. Common examples are line graphs, scatter plots, bar graphs, and pictorial graphs. Graphical interfacing enables the computer system to display graphical representations of taxonomies, trends, summarization of data, comparison of points and patterns, problem finding, forecasting, reporting, and planning.[18] In general, graphical interfacing gives the user an increased understanding of data patterns and trends.[19]

An iconic interface relates to action language. It uses pictures or images to represent commands and objects that can be invoked by a user.[20] Iconic interfacing allows for improved performance and learning and helps to eliminate unnecessary errors. Icons allow for easy recognition and categorization and are usually faster to absorb than words. A key disadvantage of iconic interfaces is that it is often difficult to convey the desired meaning to the user without sometimes invoking other undesirable properties and connotations. There are three different classes of icons.

1. Representational icons (or metaphor graphics)
2. Abstract icons
3. Arbitrary icons

Representational icons or metaphor graphics[21] are images that are prototypical of a specific class of physical objects. These types of icons correspond to "real-world" objects, thereby enabling the user to recognize the icons and make some inferences based on them. Examples of representational icons are file folds, trash cans, and document images.[22] Abstracts icons convey a specific concept through the use of a visual image. Examples of abstract icons are warning labels that are used on household products. Arbitrary icons have a meaning assigned to them; however, they are often uninterpretable. In order for these types of icons to be meaningful and useful, there needs to be some standard definition.

Direct manipulation involves communication between a system and a user through the physical manipulation of object representations using a device such as a mouse. The general characteristics of direct manipulation interfaces are:[23]

1. A continuous representation of the object of interest
2. Physical actions instead of complex syntax
3. Rapid incremental reversible operations whose impact on the object of interest is immediately visible

In general, direct manipulation incorporates the concept of an analogy between the system and a problem domain. Through direct manipulation, the users will feel as if they are working on the actual problem of interest rather than interacting with an abstract, computer-based model.

As HMIS become more complex and there is a need for communication and collaboration between several individuals, the complexity of the user interface increases. Malone defines a group interface as an organization interface, that is the parts of a computer system that connect human users to each other and to the computing capabilities provided by systems.[24] A group interface provides a flexible interface that allows different individuals to communicate with one another effectively and efficiently, which brings us to the topic of telecommunications and network technologies.

TELECOMMUNICATIONS AND NETWORK TECHNOLOGIES

The long-term goal of communication technology is for more people to be able to communicate more information over greater distances at a faster rate. Numerous types of telecommunications available today are designed to increase speed and accuracy of communications among systems users and to allow users to share views and decisions efficiently and effectively. These differing telecommunications also have a variety of costs and levels of reliability. In this section, we will discuss (1) transmission of signals, (2) communication media, and (3) networks and telecommunication applications.

Transmission of Signals

Communication is the transmission of a signal, by way of a medium, from a sender to a receiver. It allows for a signal to go through some sort of medium, resulting in a communication link between two hardware devices. It is necessary for hardware devices to speak a compatible language; otherwise, an interpreter program is needed to translate the message.

Telecommunication is the electronic transmission of signals for communication between remote devices. A telecommunication medium is anything that carries an electronic signal and intervenes between a sending device and a receiving device. Important factors to be considered in communications and telecommunications include

- Types of signals
- Transmission capacities
- Transmission modes

Analog signals involve continuous waves that fluctuate over time within a certain frequency range. These fluctuations can be measured by the change in voltage over a given frequency. Digital signals involve two states of discrete voltages: "on" pulse coded as a 0 bit and "off" pulse coded as a 1 bit. Digital media are subjected to less distortion and have the potential to be faster than analog media.

Most common carriers are capable of carrying only analog signals. However, since most computer systems are digital, special devices are often needed to convert the digital signal from a sending computer to an analog signal for the common carrier, and another device is needed to convert the analog signal back to digital for the receiving computer. This is what a modem (modulator-demodulator) does. A modem prepares computer signals for transmission. In doing so, the modem changes the computer's digital signal ("on" and "off") into analog signals. The analog signals are then carried over the telephone line to another computer. The receiving computer must have a modem so that the analog signals can be changed back to digital signals. Translating data from digital to analog is known as modulation, and translating from analog to digital is called demodulation. Figure 7–4 depicts this modulation/demodulation process as the functioning of a modem.

There are two types of modems: external and internal. An external modem is one that is attached externally to the computer. Early models of external modems were acoustic couplers that made the connection to the telephone by placing the receiver on rubber cups in the modem. Signals were then audibly sent and received through the coupler. The acoustic coupler modem has been replaced by a direct-connect modem. This is an external modem that plugs into the telephone jack and is connected to the computer via a cable. The internal modem is becoming more popular as technology progresses. This type of modem resides on an expansion board that plugs into a slot inside the computer. Many microcomputers now have an internal modem as part of the standard equipment. Smart modems contain microprocessors that allow them to operate and function under a variety of circumstances. Cellular modems are being placed in portable computers to allow people on the move to communicate with other computer systems.

A telecommunication system includes various hardware devices that either allow the communication to occur or allow the communication to occur more efficiently. Modems often use communication software designed to facilitate the transmission of data and information. Modem transmission rates are measured by baud rates, that is, the number of signal changes per second transmitted through a communication medium, where each signal change represents a certain number of bits. The more data that can be transmitted per second, the faster the medium. If data are sent over long distances, the analog signal may become weak and distorted. To prevent this, communication amplifiers are used. When the digital mode is used over long distances, a communication repeater receives and retransmits the signal in order to strengthen it.

A multiplexer is a device that allows several signals to use the same channel. There are two main types of multiplexers. A time division multiplexer (TDM) slices multiple incoming signals into small time intervals. Then the multiple incoming lines are merged into time slices that go over a communication line. At the receiving end, another TDM splits the time signals into separate signals again. Figure 7–5 illustrates this merging and splitting of signals by TDMs.

With a frequency division multiplexer (FDM) the incoming signals are placed on different frequency ranges and sent across the telecommunication medium at the same time. At the recieving end, another FDM splits the frequencies into multiple signals again.

The speed of transmission media is measured by bits per second (bps), which is the number of bits that get transferred in 1 second. The number of signal cycles per second (hertz) is called the signal frequency. The range of signal frequencies that can be sent over a given medium at the same time is known as the bandwidth. Bandwidth therefore is a measure of transmission capacity. Transmission media

Figure 7-4 The Functioning of a Modem (Modulation/Demodulation)

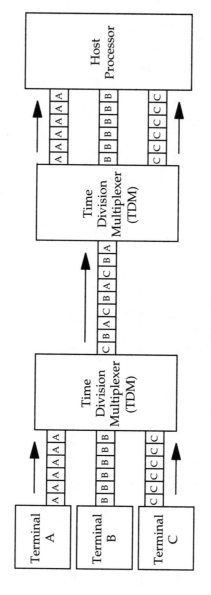

Figure 7–5 Signal Transmission with Time Division Multiplexing

that permit transmission of only one signal frequency at a time are known as baseband media. Those media that permit numerous signal frequencies to be transmitted simultaneously are called broadband or wideband media.

The arrangement of data for transmission purposes and flow direction are two important considerations about signal transmission modes in telecommunications. Data transmission may be arranged or classified as asynchronous or synchronous data. Asynchronous data are sent in packages of characters, one character or byte at a time. Each character set includes a parity bit (used for error checking) and is surrounded by start and stop bits (this is also called the start/stop method). Synchronous data are sent in packages of more than one character at a time with each block sandwiched between a header byte and a trailer byte, called flags. The flags are used to synchronize the sender and the receiver.

Data can flow between communication lines in three forms of transmission.

1. Simplex—data flow in only one direction at all times (e.g., television, radio)
2. Half-duplex—data flow in both directions but in only one direction at a time (e.g., telegraph, two-way radio)
3. Full-duplex—data flow in both directions at the same time (e.g., telephone, computer-to-computer links)

This ends our discussion of signal transmissions. We now turn to the topic of communication media, which is also fundamental to understanding communication and network technologies.

Communication Media

Among the major types of communication media are

- Physical cables
- Microwave and satellite transmission
- Cellular technology

Physical cables are the least expensive and most common type of communication medium; however, they have limited ranges. The three most common types of cables are

1. Twisted wire pairs
2. Coaxial cables
3. Fiber optic cables

Twisted wire pairs can be either shielded or unshielded. Shielded cables have a special conducting layer within the normal insulation. This conducting layer makes the cables less prone to electrical interference or noise. The primary advantage of twisted pair cables is that they are inexpensive to purchase and install. Coaxial cables consist of an inner conducting wire surrounded by insulation (called the dielectric). The dielectric is, in turn, surrounded by a conductive shield (usually a layer of foil or metal braiding) that is covered by a layer of nonconductive insulation called a jacket. More expensive coaxial cable offers higher transmission rates and cleaner and more crisp data transmission with less noise and interference than twisted pair cables. Fiber optic cables consist of thousands of extremely thin strands of glass or plastic bound together in a sheathing that transmits electric signals by using light beams. The light is generated by lasers and conducted along the transparent fibers. These fibers have a thin coating called cladding that works as a mirror preventing the light from leaking the fiber. Fiber optic cable is very expensive but has the potential to transmit enormous amounts of information. Fiber optic cables have the greatest transmission capacity of any communication medium.

Microwave transmission consists of high-frequency radio signals sent through the air up to distances of 30 miles. These types of transmission must be in "line of sight," meaning that the straight line between the transmitter and the receiver must be unobstructed. A satellite transmitter is a microwave station placed in outer space. Transmissions are received and then rebroadcast back to earth at a frequency compatible to that of the receiver. Microwave systems using communication satellites overcome the distance limits of other types of systems. With cellular radio technology a local area, such as a city, is divided into cells. As a car or vehicle with a cellular device moves from one cell to another, the cellular system passes the phone connection from one cell to another.

Organizations providing communication services are called data communication carriers. They are classified as either common carriers or special purpose carriers. Common carriers are primarily telephone companies. These companies have two forms of lines—a standard telephone line and a dedicated line. The standard telephone line, also called a switched line, uses switching equipment to allow one transmission device to be connected to another. A dedicated line provides a constant connection between two points. WATS is a billing method for heavy users of voiceband media. For companies with a high volume of calls, WATS can be substantially less expensive than normal billing.

Networks and Telecommunication Applications

An important function of any telecommunications system is to enhance overall system integration. System integration refers to the relating and tying together of various subsystems. A computer network consists of communication media, devices, and software for connecting two or more computer systems and/or devices.

The procedures embedded in software that instruct computer systems and devices how to transfer data from one place to another are commonly called protocols. Protocols are rules and procedures governing the use of data communication media. Typically, a network control program (NCP) handles the software and protocol needs of a network communication system. Communication software provides a number of functions.

- Micro-to-mainframe linkage
- Control and coordination that prevents several devices from attempting to use the same communication line at the same time
- Security procedures that allow only certain users to access a network
- Automatic backup of programs/data
- Software protection to prevent illegal copying or downloading of hardware
- Virus protection
- Error control

Using common protocols is important because it allows communication among computers of different types and from different manufacturers. Many protocols have several layers of standards or procedures. Open systems connection (OSC) is a protocol that is endorsed by the International Standards Committee (ISC) and has the following layers:

- Physical—the way physical connections are to be made
- Data link—the way data are to be transformed for sending over communication lines
- Network—the way data are to flow through a network from one location to another
- Transport—the way data flow or are transported through several networks
- Session—the coordination of the use of resources and equipment
- Presentation—the handling of the display, formatting, and appearance of information
- Application—the specification of the programs and applications available on the network

Ideally, when widespread standards are established the ultimate open system will allow access to any data, from any computer. This will facilitate the flow of complete information with much less effort. To use an open system, one must first access an existing network.[25] A network operating system (NOS) uses systems software that controls the operations of the network. The NOS performs the same types of functions for the network as the operating system for a computer does.

Networks can be classified by their maximum communicating distances. Three main classifications are (1) local area network (LAN), which uses communication channels to connect computers in the same general physical area; (2) wide area network (WAN), which covers large geographic areas; and (3) international network. Figure 7–6 illustrates an example of WAN in North America, which includes all the previously discussed telecommunication technologies.

To prevent communication breakdowns, several companies are developing fault-tolerant networks that will not break down when one part of the network malfunctions. A value-added network (VAN) is a network with additional services that supplement those offered by a traditional network, for example, advanced switching that allows faster and more economical communications.[26] Typically, these networks use packets of data of approximately 128 bytes, sent at high speeds over telecommunication lines. Value-added carriers are companies that provide the services of a VAN.

When there are hundreds of thousands of computer devices linked to a network, it becomes important to coordinate data communication. Polling is a procedure by which the main computer checks each device to see whether there are any messages coming from that device at a given time. In choosing a network, factors to consider include reliability, security, response time, vendor support, and cost.

At this point, we will attempt to synthesize all the previously discussed concepts to illustrate practical applications for using telecommunication technologies.

- Connecting or networking computers of different sizes in automated offices, for example, allows PCs to be connected to large mainframe computer systems.

- Electronic mail (E-mail) allows users to send messages to other users who are using the same system. This technology helps to eliminate "telephone tag" and reduces charges for long-distance calls.

- Telecommuting allows employees to work at home using a PC or terminal that is connected to the office via a modem.

- Telecommunication is increasingly redefining traditional work-at-home arrangements. With teleconferencing, managers can have conferences with individual participants who are at distant locations by going to a local teleconferencing center that has voice, video, and audio systems. Pictures, sound, and computer printouts can then be sent from one center to another.

- Facsimile, or fax, allows the remote transmission of text and graphics, eliminating the need for courier service.

- With voice storage forwarding systems (voice-mail), users can leave, receive, and store verbal messages for or from other people around the world.

- Electronic data interchange (EDI) connects computers in separate organizations. EDI uses network systems and follows standards and procedures that allow output from one system to be processed directly, without human inter-

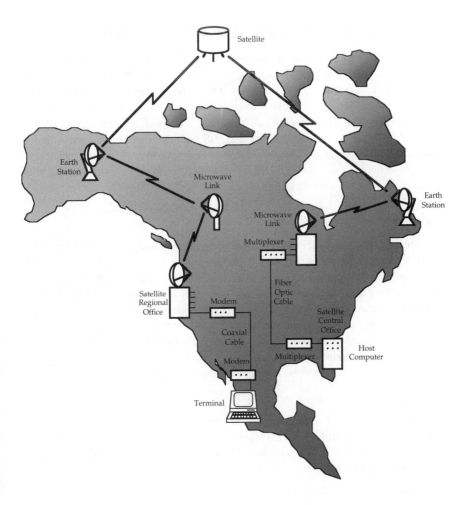

Figure 7–6 An Example of the Telecommunications Media in a North American Wide Area Network (WAN)

vention, as input to other systems. With EDI, the computers of customers, manufacturers, and suppliers can be linked. This technology eliminates the need for paper documents and substantially cuts down on costly errors.

In recent years, advancing technologies have evolved to provide health service workers with more efficient, but also more complex information systems. The next two sections will show how the health service industry has benefited from HMIS technologies and will describe some of the emerging trends in the industry as these technologies continue to evolve.

HMIS TECHNOLOGIES AND HEALTH SERVICE APPLICATIONS

Advancing computing technologies have contributed significantly to all industries, including the health service industry. Although the health service sector has
been a little slow in adopting some of the newer technologies in its delivery system, there is a general awareness among all health service professionals that the
role that HMIS technologies play will have increasingly significant impact on the
future of health services. Not only will HMIS technologies play a part in traditional administrative areas such as patient administration and financial systems;
more importantly, they will also be more widely used to support clinical and
higher-order management functions and activities.

Administrative-Type Applications

In the 1920s, management information technology mainly consisted of a type-
writer, a file cabinet, and a secretary. Data processing technology was introduced
into hospitals in the early 1960s and was focused largely on high-volume transaction processing and administrative tasks. The process of mechanization, automation, and computerization has been dramatic, and numerous administrative HMIS
subsystems have evolved: financial, personnel, accounting, inventory management, materials and facility management, office automation, scheduling and communication, equipment systems, and facility utilization systems. Our approach
here is to discuss a few of these applications in greater detail.

Business and Financial Systems

Today, business and financial applications are still the most common HMIS
applications used in hospitals. The applications are mostly designed to support
well-defined operational task activities. These applications may be independent or
integrated and may include

- Accounts/receivable and billing
- Payroll preparation and accounting linked to a personnel data system
- Processing of accounts payable linked to purchasing and inventory control
  systems
- General ledger accounting
- Budgeting and budget control

By the mid-1980s there were many accounting and financial systems on the
market. General accounting systems may assist with the general ledger, accounts
receivable and payable, fixed assets, and payroll. Financial reporting and analysis
software can help with budgeting, forecasting, financial modeling, worker productivity, contributions (charitable or in-kind), and investment analysis.

Medical-Record Systems

Medical-record systems (M-RS) can be used to measure the efficiency of clinical resource use and currently are a priority in many organizational HMIS portfolios. For example, in the United States, the legislated Medicare prepayment plan was an impetus for the implementation of utilization review systems (URS). In fact, there are both implicit and explicit legal and financial incentives to implement URS and other similar M-RS to monitor incoming patient occupancy rates, service volume, resource utilization, and costs. Often, the demands on services, beds, and resources; high consumer expectations; accountability for a global hospital budget; and accreditation standards pressure hospitals to use resources efficiently and effectively, thereby increasing the need for M-RS.

According to Austin, to improve efficiency, computerized monitoring and scheduling systems can be used for advanced bed booking, preadmissions, outpatient clinic appointments, and operating rooms.[27] A computerized operating room management system (ORMS) can provide information on case-mix analysis, supply and equipment usage, operating room (OR) utilization, daily room utilization, and infection control.

Administrative Core and ADT Systems

Martin describes core systems that combine common, centralized functions and associated databases.[28] These systems include registration systems (demographics); patient census databases that use the master patient index (MPI) for indexing patient records; admission-discharge-transfer (ADT); order entry/results reporting (OE/RR) systems; and coding systems. The efficiency and effectiveness of these systems depend on how well they have been or may be standardized for all departmental health service professionals and workers in order to reduce redundancies and confusion among system users.

As indicated in Chapter 5, personnel systems can assist with human resource planning and analysis by maintaining and updating employee records and analyzing turnover and absenteeism or other performance indicators (e..g, costs). Other commonly used management systems in health service organizations include computerized purchasing, inventory control, menu planning, materials and food service management programs, equipment location, maintenance management, depreciation, and utilization analysis.

Clinical Support Applications

Apart from accounting and financial applications to support most administrative and operational aspects of the health service facility, there has been a gradual realization of the potential of HMIS for clinical support. Today, as a result of the growing complexity of the modern health care environment, many separate but specialized clinical information systems have evolved, especially in the areas of nursing, patient care, radiology, the clinical laboratory, and the pharmacy.

Nursing and Patient Care

Clinical (or medical) support systems involve the organized processing, storage, and retrieval of information to support patient care activities. Patient management systems (PMS) are the chief source of personal and clinical information on a patient. Although many computerized clinical support systems have become operational in the last two decades, patient medical records are still predominantly kept on paper. An example of a medical abstract that is implementable on a microcomputer was discussed in Chapter 1. Several authors have also pointed out the benefits to be gained from the automation of patient medical records.[29,30] Apart from the patient medical record, there are still many clinical areas that need attention; unfortunately, after more than two decades of computer use, the hospital industry has still been unable to tap the full potential of computerization.[31]

Tan et al. discussed the use of the computer-based utilization care plan (UCP), which follows protocol-based nursing care guidelines to assist in the planning and administration of patient care.[32] The use of a UCP-based system in nursing is expected to result in a reduction of documentation time that will lead to an improvement in the quality of patient care, as well as increased efficiency in the time spent on the wards. The UCP and other similar systems are defined as standardized patient guidelines that reside in a computer database to support comprehensive and high-quality patient care. They provide health practitioners with reminders, alerts and clinical decision support and can be linked to bodies of medical literature and other medical aids.[33]

A number of computer-based technologies are emerging in radiology. Computed tomography (CT) scanning, gamma cameras, ultrasound scanners, digital subtraction angiography, and magnetic resonance imaging (MRI) have appeared in the last decade. Medical imaging has become an extremely important component of modern medical technology. Image management vendors are working to develop products that are tailored to a broad range of imaging modalities. Recent advances in image management systems allow for image modality equipment to be connected to large patient record databases.[34]

The equipment vendors for CT and MRI have endorsed standards to develop interoperability among systems. Also, changes in diagnostic management systems have resulted in a new generation of picture archiving and communications systems (PACS). PACS[35] are composed of several subsystems; images in one or more modalities are read in digital form. This allows medical images to be transmitted over a film distribution system or teleradiology system, using a standard telephone line or network, to one or more sites, where they are displayed and/or converted into hard copy. As a result, two or more physicians or other medical practitioners can examine duplicated images from different locations and formulate plans for optimum patient management.

Patient monitoring systems use computer technology to monitor vital signs continuously and physiological data periodically. Most modern medical devices are used in critical care units; they include vital sign monitors, ventilators, and infusion pumps. These machines are designed to allow digital communication of information. Some monitoring systems use microcomputers built into individual patient bedside monitoring units. Results are displayed on monitors at the bedside and at a central monitor display unit at the nursing station.

Computer systems have been designed to process and interpret data from various diagnostic devices. Much of the work in signal processing has been done in the interpretation of electrocardiograms and the analysis of electroencephalograms. Pulmonary function testing also makes use of computerized analysis. To improve the decision-making abilities of all health professionals, point-of-care access allows patient data to be entered at the bedside as care is being provided. The technology for entering data at the bedside is just emerging and its usefulness will still have to be evaluated.

Two general classes of bedside workstations are seen as likely to prevail. "Smart" terminals will use a graphical user interface (GUI) and will communicate through client/server architecture in a LAN setup. Hand-held terminals or other portable devices will facilitate manual or voice entry of data. For example, CliniView RF is a hand-held wireless terminal that communicates interactively with a network through high-speed radio frequency.[36] Chapter 14 further discusses and illustrates these future-oriented clinical support systems.

Clinical Laboratory and Pharmacy

The clinical laboratory is well suited to the study, analysis, and implementation of computerized systems. As a result, laboratories are among the most common clinical service departments to apply computer technology. Clinical laboratory systems (CLS) are used in both data processing and laboratory management. More specifically, computers are integrated into many medical instruments and are used to analyze primary data, store and distribute test results, monitor testing quality, document laboratory procedures, and provide information used by managers in controlling inventory, monitoring work flow, and assessing laboratory productivity. This collected information must be accurate, timely, and easily accessible in order to be useful.[37]

Pharmacy information systems (PIS) have had a strong impact on the four traditional pharmacy settings: inpatient, community, clinical, and drug-information services. Complete, accurate, and up-to-date records are a prerequisite for high-quality patient care. Cost control strategies are needed to manage the acquisition, storage, and distribution of drugs. Computers are also used to search for and re-

view drug related literature. The future will see computers performing drug-distri-
bution, record-keeping, and routine monitoring functions to simplify time-consuming tasks so that pharmacists can concentrate more on patient services.

Management Support Applications

Management support functions are those that facilitate the management of
hospitalwide data flow, general management information needs, staffing, staff
scheduling, resource management, and strategic planning.

Strategic Management

Strategic information technology (SIT) is an innovative management tool for
health service managers. Henderson has developed a framework called the "Strategic Alignment Model" that can be used to guide SIT development.[38] Chapter 10
discusses strategic information systems planning that is consistent with the principle underlying development of SIT or similar systems.

Decision and Executive Support

HMIS are also used by senior management for decision support and organization of resource management. Such systems are mostly graphic-oriented and provide generalized computing and telecommunication facilities. Health decision
support system (HDSS) and executive information systems (EIS) are discussed
widely in current literature.[39] EIS differs from HDSS in that the system should be
easier to use and geared more toward upper-level management. An EIS allows an
executive to access and review key financial and clinical statistics at any level of
the organization quickly. An example of an EIS is described by Werner,[40] the
president and CEO of a 1,200-bed hospital in Florida that is part of a multihospital
corporation with 17 hospitals in seven states. Each night, data for all of the 17
hospitals are collected and transferred to the host. Nine set of statistics are available with graphs, data tables, and three levels of reporting—corporate, cluster, and
hospital—for a total of 81 graphs that can be used by the CEO or other senior
management in analysis and decision making.

HMIS TECHNOLOGIES AND THE FUTURE

Morris believes that in the future, we will see an increase in the use of advanced
HMIS techniques in supporting the role of hospital and health service management. He believes that technologies such as neural network, optical disk storage,
voice interaction, and local area networks will be integrated, resulting in an automation revolution in the early twenty-first century. According to Morris, neural
network computers hold the promise of unlimited flexibility because of their abil-

ity to mimic the architecture of the human brain.[41] When they are combined with instructional, reference, and raw data held on optical disks, the potential for problem solving through a "trial-and-error" process is limitless.

In designing the hospital of the future, Rychman and Rushing developed several modules that ideally will assist various hospital managers.[42] For example, patient admitting technologies will speed up patient identification and verify financial data and insurance information. Plastic "SMART" cards, used by each patient, will store current health data and communicate the data to the patient admitting system through automated card readers. The business office will contain an integrated network that communicates charges to the patient accounting system from many diverse systems and will provide for the electronic editing and billing of hospital claims. A network link to the material management system will help automate the supply process, including inventory control and purchasing. The executive office will have an executive workstation to give the executive up-to-the-minute information on institutional activity and performance. Glimpses of these and similar technological breakthroughs for the health service industry are also given in Chapter 14.

CONCLUSION

Until recently, very little attention has been devoted to applying information beyond entry-level applications in the health service delivery industry. However, as this chapter has illustrated, technology is going to become the essential tool for all health service professionals.

Spending on information technology has increased manyfold in the past decade, making it one of the economy's fastest growing capital expenditure industries. Yet, productivity growth has been steadily dropping over the last 25 years. Information technology must be part of an organization's overall competitive strategy. Health service organizations must change the way they operate in order to take full advantage of emerging technologies. Implementing new technology in conjunction with traditional work systems rarely works. Information systems need to be reengineered or overhauled if real productivity gains are to be achieved. It is, therefore, critical that today's health service managers familiarize themselves with the range of HMIS technologies and applications that are available so that they can rise to or remain on the "leading edge" of this information-intensive industry.

CHAPTER QUESTIONS

1. Describe what is meant by information technology. How does it differ from an information system?

2. What is the definition of a computer system? What are the four fundamental components? Describe two units of the CPU and how they interact with main memory.

3. Explain the advantages and disadvantages of telecommunications. Provide examples of applications in telecommunications for health care.

4. What is meant by the term "modem"? Discuss why the modem is an essential part of communication.

5. What do you think are the major contributions of information technology to the health care industry?

6. In your opinion, what is the future of information technology in health care?

MINI CASE 7
MERGING OF TWO HOSPITAL INFORMATION SYSTEMS

As a result of a recent merger between two hospitals, a multihospital organization was created. You have been newly appointed as the director of finance of the new organization. With the merger, a moderate sum of money was allocated to the finance department, and as a well-trained administrator, you want to use this money to implement some sort of link between the two existing systems.

With a quick survey of the information technology marketplace, you discover that there are literally hundreds of packages and systems available. Not a computer expert, you seek the advice of colleagues within the hospitals, but their opinions are as diverse as the choices of systems. The different systems offer different features in terms of overall characteristics (e.g., user friendliness and modes of linkage), processing speed, memory capacity, hardware and software options, and vendor reputations.

You want to make a good impression with your first project in the new organization; therefore, you want to implement an effective, efficient, and high-value system that will be usable for the next 10 to 15 years.

MINI CASE QUESTIONS

1. What is the danger of making a decision about technological choices without first recognizing the information needs of the merger? What do you perceive as your role in relation to the existing IS personnel? Why would you not delegate this project to them?

2. Prepare an evaluation plan to narrow down your choice of hardware, software, and communication vendors whom you might invite to submit a request for proposal (RFP). Provide some features and characteristics of systems support that you would expect from these vendors. How would you justify your plan of actions taken for this project to your board members?

3. Do you think that skills of an HMIS consultant may be useful? If so, what qualities and skills will be required of this person?
4. What are the types of HMIS applications you think should result from the linkage of the two existing systems?

CHAPTER REVIEW

A health management information system blends organizational, technological, and human resources. This chapter has focused on the technological features of an HMIS. Hardware consists of the physical components that are needed in an IS. These include machines, storage devices, input/output devices, and communication devices that are linked to a central processing unit (CPU) that is made up of an arithmetic/logic unit, a control unit, and registers. Primary storage stores information in RAM; secondary storage is used to store and transfer large amounts of data by using either magnetic or optical media. Input devices are used to enter information into an IS, whereas output devices are used to display the results of processed data. Both systems and applications software are needed to run an IS. Applications software is designed to solve specific problems. Applications software translates instructions to the systems software, which in turn translates the instructions to the hardware. Telecommunication devices allow for the transmission of information between separate computers or information systems. Several communication devices with varying capacities, transmission modes, ranges, and costs are available. Networks are used to exchange information between ISs.

Information technology is used widely in the health service industry. Business and financial systems, medical record systems, and core systems are used to ease daily administrative tasks. Nursing, laboratory, pharmacy, and patient care systems support clinical functions. Management support systems, including health decision support and executive information systems, are available to assist with strategic planning and decision making of senior management. Support systems will also become available for physicians and other health professionals in the form of expert systems that will distribute knowledge widely. User-interface technology attempts to make ISs easier to use, and system integration aims to provide standards so that separate hospital information systems can be integrated into a whole.

NOTES

1. H.L. Capron, *Computers: Tools for an Information Age,* 2nd ed. (Redwood City, Calif: Benjamin/ Cummings Publishing Company, 1990).
2. K.C. Laudon and J.P. Laudon, *Business Information Systems: A Problem-Solving Approach* (Hinsdale, Ill: Dryden Press, 1991).

3. J. O'Brien, *Introduction to Information Systems in Business Management,* 6th ed. (Homewood, Ill: Richard D. Irwin, Inc., 1991).

4. J.S. Berstein, *Computer System Fundamentals* (Hinsdale, Ill: Dryden Press, 1990).

5. D. Cassel, *Understanding Computers* (Englewood Cliffs, NJ: Prentice Hall, 1990).

6. T.K. Zinn, HIS Technology Trends, *Computers in Healthcare* (February 1991): 46–50.

7. C. Dunbar, It Comes Down to Managing Minutes, *Computers in Healthcare* (March 1992): 6.

8. S.L. Mandell, *Dr. Mandell's Ultimate Personal Computer Desk Reference* (Toledo, Ohio: Rawhide Press, 1993).

9. P.J. Hills, *Information Management Systems: Implications for the Human-Computer Interface* (Toronto: Ellis Horwood, Ltd., 1990).

10. J. Burn and E. Caldwell, *Management of Information Systems Technology* (Orchard, Oxfordshire: Alfred Waller Ltd., 1990).

11. L. Long and N. Long, *Computers,* 2nd ed. (Englewood Cliffs, NJ: Prentice Hall, 1990).

12. A.M. Jenkins, Surveying the Software Generator Market, *Datamation* 31, no. 17 (1985): 105–120.

13. J. Karat, ed. *Taking Software Design Seriously* (New York: Academic Press, Inc., 1991).

14. I. Benbasat, et al., *The User-Computer Interface in Systems Design* (British Columbia: Faculty of Commerce and Business Administration, University of British Columbia, 1993).

15. B. Laurel, ed. *The Art of Human-Computer Interface* (Reading, Mass: Addison-Wesley Publishing Co., Inc., 1992).

16. J. Bennett, Analysis and Design of the User Interface for Decision Support Systems, *Building Decision Support Systems* (1983): 41–64.

17. J.K.H. Tan, Graphics: Theories and Experiments, *Computer Graphics Forum* 11, no. 4. (1992): 261.

18. S.L. Jarvenpaa and G.W. Dickson, Graphics and Managerial Decision Making: Research Based Guidelines, *Communications of the ACM* 31, no. 6 (June 1988): 764–774.

19. J.K.H. Tan and I. Benbasat, Processing of Graphical Information: A Decomposition Taxonomy to Match Data Extraction Tasks and Graphical Representations, *Information Systems Research* 1, no. 4 (December 1990): 416–439.

20. D. Gittens, Icon-Based Human-Computer Interaction, *International Journal of Man-Machine Studies* 24 (1989): 519–543.

21. W.G. Cole, Metaphor Graphics and Visual Analogy for Medical Data, Section on Medical Information Science. (San Francisco: University of California at San Francisco, 1988).

22. Benbasat, et al., *The User-Computer Interface.*

23. Ibid.

24. T.W. Malone, Designing Organizational Interfaces, *Proceedings of CHI'85* (1985): 66–71.

25. W. Mougayar, Open Systems in Healthcare, *Healthcare Computing & Communications* (August 1991): 18–20.

26. M.A. Hax, Toward Enterprise-Wide Networking, *Computers in Healthcare* (November 1990): 53–54.

27. C. Austin, *Information Systems for Health Services Administration,* 4th ed. (Ann Arbor, Mich: Health Administration Press, 1992).

28. J.B. Martin, The Environmental and Future of Health Information Systems, *Journal of Health Administration Education* 8, no. 1 (1990): 11–24.

29. R.S. Dick and E.B. Steene, eds. *The Computer-Based Patient Record: An Essential Technology for Health Care* (Washington, DC: National Academy Press, 1991).

30. A.M. Thompson, An Evaluation of the Selection Process of Hospital Information Systems, *Journal of Medical Systems* 14, no. 5 (October 1990): 245–282.

31. R.L. Nolan et al., Computers and Hospital Management: Prescription for Survival, *Journal of Medical Systems* 1, no. 2 (1977): 187–203.

32. J.K.H. Tan, et al., Utilization Care Plan and Effective Patient Data Management, *Hospital & Health Services Administration* 38, no. 1 (1993): 81–99.

33. R.S. Dick and E.B. Steene, eds., *The Computer-Based Patient Record: An Essential Technology for Health Care* (Washington, DC: National Academy Press, 1991).

34. D. Kohn, Computer-Based Record Emerges in Radiology, *Computers in Healthcare* (February 1992): 40–43.

35. W. Schneider, Computers in a Human Perspective—an Alternative Way of Teaching Informatics to Health Professional, *Methods of Information in Medicine* 28, no. 4 (November 1989): 313–320.

36. C. Dunbar, Nurses Want I/S Selection Power, but Do They Have It? *Computers in Healthcare* (March 1992): 20–24.

37. E.H. Shortliffe and L.E. Perreault, eds., *Medical Informatics: Computer Applications in Health Care* (Reading, Mass: Addison-Wesley Publishing Co., Inc., 1990).

38. J.C. Henderson, Aligning Business and Information Technology Domains: Strategic Planning in Hospital, *Hospital and Health Services Administration* 37, no. 1 (1992): 71–86.

39. J.K.H. Tan, The Design of Effective Health Decision Support Systems: Towards Automating the Health Administrator's Decision Process, *Health Services Management Research* (in press).

40. Thomas L. Werner, A New Approach to Decision Support at Adventist Health Systems/Sunbelt, *Computers in Healthcare* (March 1990): 49–50.

41. D.C. Morris, The Future for Information Systems, *Computers in Healthcare* (September 1987): 39–40.

42. D. Ryckman and S. Rushing, Hospitals of the Future—Not Just Technology Talk, *Journal of Medical Systems* 14, no. 4 (1990): 183–189.

Chapter 8

The Emergence of Artificial Intelligence and Expert Systems: Their Diffusion in the Health Service Delivery Industry

LEARNING OBJECTIVES

1. Define artificial intelligence (AI).
2. Identify major subdisciplines of AI.
3. Define expert systems (ES).
4. Identify components of ES.
5. Assess potentials of fifth-generation technologies.
6. Illustrate ES technology as applied to the health service delivery industry.

INTRODUCTION

A situation where the construction of an ES [expert system] would be appropriate is when the knowledge of many experts needs to be fused, e.g., an epidemiologist, an infection control nurse, and an infection control doctor. In medicine their most useful role has been in knowledge-based systems where they work as Intelligent Assistants or Intelligent Alarms.[1]

In the late 1960s and early 1970s, the emphasis of health management information systems (HMIS) functions in health services was on improving operational efficiency. As noted previously, this inception of automated health data processing may be classified as "operational control."[2] Simply defined, operational control implies actively monitoring routine task performance, with emphasis on doing highly structured tasks better, faster, and cheaper (Chapter 7). From a health service management perspective, the scope and type of automated activities that fall into this realm are limited to the processing of large volumes of data to support administration of patient care and financing operations. At present, management reporting systems (MRS) and health database management systems (HDBMS) are widely used to fulfill these purposes. For example, epidemiological surveillance, population surveys, and vital statistics monitoring have been made more efficient by the application of HDBMS in public health.

The next era of HMIS applications, which followed in the late 1970s and early 1980s, shifted attention toward functional effectiveness. This stage of automation was termed "management control." Functionally effective management control helps health service managers make improved decisions. The scope and type of automated activities that fall into this realm are those that better contribute to the achievement of managerial goals and objectives beyond those of efficient task performance. In practice, this is often accomplished through the structuring of management data, including data aggregation, analysis, interpretation, and presentation (e.g., the use of graphical representational methods). It is also accomplished through the generation of computer models and the automation of semistructured decision-making tasks such as the forecasting of drug expenditures. In this regard, health model-based management systems (HMBMS), health statistical/simulation systems (HSS), and health decision support systems (HDSS) are examples of computerized support tools that have been used successfully to assist health service executives and managers in their creative problem-solving strategies.

The diffusion of computerized support in the late 1980s and early 1990s has led to new levels of automated assistance for health professionals and managers. Today we are aware of advances in artificial intelligence (AI) and expert system (ES) technology as the result of work in "fifth-generation" computing applications. This latest era of progress in health computing may be referred to as the era of "transferred control," or the empowering of end-users to apply expert methods in clinical and health service managerial problem solving. Abilities such as capturing, storing, and transferring expertise have been achieved with these new computer-based systems. In short, this fifth-generation technology is expected to be much more "intelligent" than any or all of those HMIS software available in earlier generations. The key feature of this work therefore is the creation of knowledge bases such as a health knowledge-based management system (HKBMS). Figure 8–1 depicts the evolution of these various eras of computing leading to AI/ES technology.

This chapter discusses artificial intelligence and ES technology as they relate to the health service delivery industry. Examples from various health service domains will be used to illustrate the application of this technology. Accordingly, we will first focus on the evolution of AI and its various subdisciplines, including computer vision, robotics, natural language processing, neural networks, and expert systems. The focus will then shift to ES because this technology appears to have greater potential impact on health service managerial decision making as compared to other AI subdisciplines. In addition, issues relating to the potentials

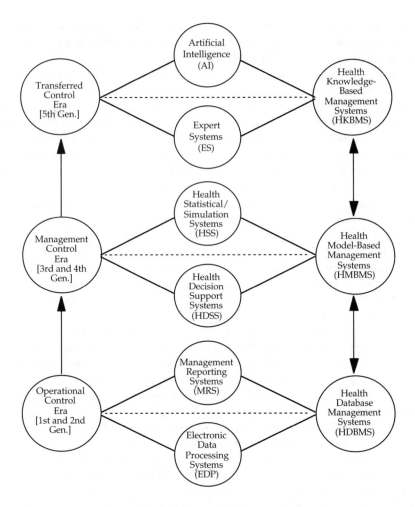

Figure 8–1 The Evolution of Knowledge-Based Systems (KBS) to Support AI/ES Technology

---

and advantages of fifth-generation applications in health service management will be highlighted.

THE COMING OF ARTIFICIAL INTELLIGENCE (AI)

The creation of "intelligent" electronic machines started after World War II. Their evolution may be traced to the design and development of fast calculating machines in North America. The manufacture of these machines, which used numerical operators, marked the beginning of computers and the discipline of computer science. An important shift occurred in 1950, when a British scientist named Alan Turing wrote a landmark paper entitled "Can Machines Think?"[3] This paper advocated research into the possible use of symbolic or logical operators (e.g., "and," "or"), as opposed to numerical operators (e.g., "+," "×") in computer programs and software instructional codes. It was this idea that sparked interest in AI, a branch of computer science that has blossomed into a variety of subdisciplines today, one of which is expert systems.

What Is Artificial Intelligence?

Many definitions of AI exist in the literature as a result of the interdisciplinary nature of the field.[4–6] For the health service delivery industry, the field of AI may be defined as the science of developing computer-based systems that simulate various facets of health service professional and managerial behavior, most notably health managers' and professionals' problem-solving behavior.[7–10] An important characteristic of this artificial simulation is the exhibition of humanlike "intelligence" which reflects a repertoire of clever behaviors like perception, pattern recognition, knowledge acquisition, learning, discerning, and decision making. Therefore, we should not consider computer programs that perform purely numeric analysis such as payroll calculations or statistics to be AI applications. One of the new purposes of AI applications is to transfer knowledge and expertise to the end-user.

AI application in health service organizations are therefore best understood by studying health professional (expert) problem-solving behaviors. Simply defined, "problem solving" may be perceived as finding ways to get from an initial situation to a desired state. More definitively, good problem solving demands cognitive activities involving memory processes, pattern recognition, logical thinking about the problem, and ascertaining of the knowledge or expertise required to reach a solution. In short, the problem-solving process involves recognizing the problem, generating alternative solutions, and choosing among appropriate responses.[11]

In solving problems, several approaches may be used. Newell and Simon discuss two alternatives.[12] First, the simpler is the "algorithmic" method, which comprises a sequence of actions with possible decision and branching points that need to be learned or discovered to solve the problem. It is most appropriately used when the problem to be solved is well formulated and its goal or endpoint has been explicitly stated. A second method, the "generate and test" method, is used when there are no ready-made solutions. In this case, trial-and-error is often used to find solutions that satisfy the objectives or goals of a given problem. Stored experience or knowledge of the situation provides a way of limiting the number of trials needed to reach an acceptable solution. Therefore, problem solving and the development of human skills require sophisticated utilization of real-world knowledge.

Identifying objects in a visual scene, for example, requires prior knowledge or sight of the object in question. Since humans tend to use the "generate and test" method in real-world problem solving, the simulation of such human problem solving behaviors using advancing computing technology constitutes the dominant form of AI programming.

In practice, however, AI programs resemble games (which are formalized and constrained by a set of rules) more closely than they resemble manual, everyday processes in which all the rules are never known, and in which normalization is resisted. AI programs utilize symbols and rules of thumb (or, heuristics) for solving problems. The first AI program, the "General Problem Solver" (GPS), was developed by Newell and Simon in 1961.[13] Since the development of the GPS, AI concepts have expanded into several related subdisciplines. Today, AI applications in the health service industry have advanced beyond systems that initially focused on tools that assisted physicians in diagnosing illnesses. AI applications are now viewed as having a greater payoff than earlier-generation software or manual paper-based applications. For example, it has been noted that "with knowledge-based systems, a user can define medical procedures and personnel, facilities and equipment required for each procedure, as well as certain constraints. If conditions change—a larger than usual number of people is out sick or called away for emergencies, for example—the system can incorporate this information and produce new schedules in minutes, not the hours required with manual procedures."[14]

In summary, AI technologies are those applications capable of providing intelligent assistance to end-users. AI programs simulate human problem-solving methods, acquire and verify knowledge, and use powerful software development techniques that will allow the end-users to perform their work more efficiently, effectively, competitively, and appropriately (Chapter 5).

Functions of Artificial Intelligence

AI research can be described as computing, storing, transferring, and manipulating huge amounts of specialized knowledge, not just information. More specifically, the goal of using AI applications for health service planners, managers, and administrators is to achieve high-quality decision making through the availability of accurate, timely, and relevant knowledge and expertise. Success in achieving this level of automation is contingent upon advances in AI work. An important question that arises from this line of thinking is therefore, What purposes will AI research serve and how will it contribute to advancing our knowledge and practice of health service planning or managerial decision making? Such a discussion might provide health planners and administrators with insights as to the rationale and significance of AI work and place AI research into the broader spectrum of health service managerial decision-making methods and technologies.

Three primary purposes or functions of AI research that are relevant to the domains of health service management and decision-making may be identified.

1. Theory testing
2. Interface design
3. Knowledge propagation

AI systems design is concerned with simulating human problem-solving behaviors. These systems provide a vehicle for testing and validating cognitive science theories as they pertain to health services planning, management, and other related activities. One of the major challenges facing AI development is to design more intelligent human-computer interfaces. By improving the computing capabilities and the user-friendliness of computers, AI promises to assist the end-users (i.e., health professionals and managers) in making better-quality health service decisions. Expert systems (ES) are the branch or subfield of AI research concerned with gathering, storing, transferring, and disseminating knowledge and expertise. The knowledge and expertise propagated by ES offer much potential for reshaping the future of the health service industry.

Consequently, research in AI is critical to our understanding of health professional and management decision making by integrating various approaches to studying human problem-solving behaviors. More precisely, AI research can contribute to our knowledge of how experts will go about making complex decisions, and this will enable us to transfer that expertise to novices. The knowledge that is captured through AI research can then serve as feedback for us through "smart" machines.

Subfields of Artificial Intelligence

Figure 8–2 shows five major subdisciplines of AI.

1. Computer vision
2. Robotics
3. Natural language processing
4. Neural networks
5. Expert systems

Because of space limitations, each of these topics will only be briefly discussed. Apart from these various subfields, there have been new attempts to integrate AI techniques into advanced computing technologies such as electronic data interchange (EDI) and group decision support system (GDSS) (see Chapter 14).[15,16]

Computer vision focuses on computer simulation of human perception and vision. This field integrates many disciplines, such as physics (optics), mathematics (especially geometry and statistics), electrical and electronic engineering, com-

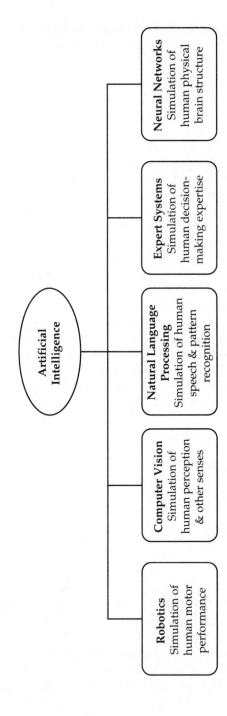

Figure 8–2 Subdisciplines of Artificial Intelligence

puter science, and manufacturing.[17] The integration of these multiple disciplines has led to many advances in medicine and other health service areas. For example, devices such as the computed axial tomograph (CT) scanner have used computer vision techniques to identify and detect the exact location of a lesion or an emerging tumor in a human brain.[18]

Robotics is the domain of AI that is concerned with the design, manufacture, and implementation of robots: that is, the physical simulation of human motor activities.[19,20] Intelligent robots are capable of "sensing" their environment and changing the style and level of their performance on the basis of external conditions. They are usually aided by other AI procedures such as vision and natural languages to accomplish their tasks.[21] In terms of application, robots have been used to perform "repetitive" and "dangerous" tasks in the health service industry. For example, they can be used to load or reload environmentally hazardous chemicals, such as radioactive and other toxic industrial wastes.

Natural language (NL) processing is the AI domain that is concerned with computer speech understanding and generation, as well as tasks such as multilingual translation.[22] To date, progress in speech recognition and generation has been slow, even though many products on the market allow the end-user to invoke commands using natural languages such as English, French, Spanish, German, Chinese, and Japanese. Nevertheless, speech recognition prototypes like NETtalk and MRBtalk are still being tested for their ability to simulate human learning by performing word pronunciation tasks. In terms of patient care, an important breakthrough in this technology may be the creation of a culturally friendly environment for health services in which communications between primary health service providers and consumers is improved, particularly in those cases where they do not speak or understand each other's language.

Neural Networks (NN) represent the domain of AI that uses knowledge-based systems to imitate human physical brain structure. These systems are not preprogrammed to give anticipated responses like traditional algorithms (that process information in a serial manner); rather, they are designed to "memorize" and "learn" through observations and repetitions. As an example related to health service planning and patient care management, Gelernter mentions the use of a "Trellis" machine for monitoring a hospital patient's condition through sensors that track measures such as blood pressure and heart rate and sending this information upward or downward through the "Trellis" to computers that compile and evaluate the data.[23] The learning component might be the accumulation of a range of normal readings so that unusual readings outside the range would be recognized and signaled.

As a subdiscipline of AI, ES are designed to replicate the problem-solving behavior of human experts.[24,25] At present, ES researchers are focusing on automating decision-making expertise in a clever manner to offer vital information and guidance regarding decision-making strategies to health service professionals. The need to understand, apply, and synthesize complex health-related processes when making critical care decisions has further stimulated the application of ES. Numerous applications in ES technology have been developed for medicine, such as MYCIN,[26] ONCOCIN,[27] INTERNIST-1,[28] and CASNET.[29,30] ES have also been developed in pharmacy, such as HEADMED,[31] MENTOR,[32] and RXPERT,[33] in nursing, such as COMMES;[34,35] and in health promotion, such as EMPOWER/ Canadian Health.[36] Because this particular branch of AI knowledge and research has the greatest relevance to health professional decision making, ES technology will be the major focus of the rest of this chapter.

COMPONENTS OF EXPERT SYSTEMS (ES)

The field of ES is emerging and proliferating. As with AI, a definition of ES has not yet been accepted universally. An ES may be defined as a computer-based consultation program that uses both knowledge-based and inference-ruled procedures to simulate the decision-making process of an expert. In this context, an expert is a highly skilled individual who has advanced training, knowledge, and experience in a particular field (e.g., physicians, nurses, administrators, technical personnel). Experts support their colleagues in solving difficult problems requiring specific areas of knowledge. Experts have the ability to interact positively, the technical skills to perform their roles, the aptitudes to acquire and use knowledge, the competence to organize and synthesize information, and the abilities to judge and make sound decisions in the absence of complete information. In this sense, an ES is an automated "expert."

In terms of application, ES provide health service managers and professionals with the intelligence to make sound decisions requiring specific knowledge domains, without the need for physically contacting a human expert. This is crucially advantageous to all health service institutions because expertise is generally both scarce and expensive. The relevance of ES to health administration and management becomes even clearer when one considers the need for intelligent managerial decision-making support in an era of increasing accountability within the health service industry and growing scarcity of resources in the public sector.

Figure 8–3 shows the architecture of an ES. It consists of four basic parts:

1. The knowledge base (KB)
2. The knowledge acquisition (KA) process
3. The ES shell
4. The user interface

KB contains the knowledge (specific facts and relevant data) about the expert domain. The KA process enables relevant portions of the knowledge base to be

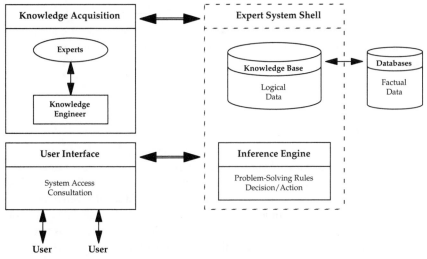

Figure 8–3 Architecture of Expert Systems

built and updated. The ES shell provides computational facilities for applying the knowledge base to user decisions, and the UI allows interactions between the users and the system. Each of these ES components will now be discussed separately.

The Knowledge Base

To develop an ES one must accumulate and codify expertise to construct a knowledge base (KB). The main components of a KB are (1) symbolic descriptions for defining and characterizing the empirical relationships of a domain and (2) procedures for manipulating these relationships to provide information in an organized fashion and for computing inferences to permit rapid access and classifications. In this way, new knowledge or information can be generated.

The distinction between a database (DB) and a KB is often emphasized in ES work. Computer databases are collections of individual observations or data points that are organized only for providing information, and not for creating new knowledge. A database, for example, might record an observation such as "Mr. John Doe had a blood pressure of 180/110 millimeters of mercury 24 hours ago, and a heart attack today." A KB makes both the previous observation and a new observation, derived from analyzing the initial observation: "Hypertension is associated with increased risk of myocardial infarction." Thus, KB incorporate both "facts" and "rules" for manipulating assimilated data, in order to create new knowledge, whereas databases contain only facts.

The KB of an ES requires enormous amounts of information (knowledge). It is, therefore, essential to organize information in an efficient way so it can be manipulated conveniently. Three major AI techniques encode and organize knowledge in a KB.

1. Production rules
2. Semantic networks
3. Frames

Production rules are the first technique for representing knowledge, a process that is achieved through a series of rule-based strategies. These rules or guidelines are expressed in the form of IF-THEN statements in the ES. Basically, production rules are statements for handling procedural information (a set of given or derived facts) that are designed to outline the critical steps in producing a desired course of action. Therefore, each IF-THEN rule within an expert system contains two elements: the premise (IF statement) and the conclusion (THEN statement).

These rules may be

1. Definitional: *"If* a patient is male, *then* the patient is not menstruating."*
2. Cause-to-effect: *"If* a patient has chronic high blood pressure, *then* expect a heart attack, a stroke, or kidney damage."*
3. Effect-to-cause: *"If* a patient cannot see far objects, *then* he or she has shortsightedness or myopia."*
4. Associational: *"If* a patient has a severe pain in the chest and has been actively exercising, *then* the condition may be angina pectoris."*

Production rules were used in developing a variety of clinical ES prototypes.[37] This method is relatively straightforward, but one could easily end up with an intricate set of thousands of interconnected rules. Such a condition will not only make the software difficult to maintain but will also degrade the performance efficiency of the system. Furthermore, not all concepts may be represented in the form of IF-THEN rules. Production rules are therefore most appropriate for situations in which the domain of knowledge is highly restricted.

A semantic network formulates knowledge as objects or nodes that are connected with labeled arcs. Nodes are used to represent physical objects or conceptual entities such as events or abstract categories. In general, the semantic network scheme is flexible in nature. New nodes and links can be added or defined as the need arises or a node can inherit the characteristics of other nodes related to it. For example, the symptom "dizziness" can be the result of three or more diseases (hypertension, diabetes mellitus, and ischemic heart disease), which are also represented as nodes in this scheme. Unfortunately, one major disadvantage of semantic networks is their inability to handle situations in which many exceptions exist.

Frames are treelike structures that are linked via nodes. They have several slots that contain lists of the typical attributes of an object. Each attribute is stored in a separate slot. These slots have structure or scheme attributes (or they represent instance variables of an object) that contain properties or values to which procedures can be attached. The major advantage of slots is their use as pointers to relate frames and procedures for computing values. In this way, knowledge about an object is stored together in one slot.[38] An example of a medical frame scheme is provided in Figure 8–4.

The Knowledge Acquisition Process

ES acquire knowledge through a process known as knowledge acquisition (KA). KA can be defined as those activities or methods involved in the extraction of data, information, and experience. This acquired knowledge serves as an operational template to problem solve and is built on a foundation of formal study and heuristics (rules of thumb). Formal study involves the grouping of facts, prin-

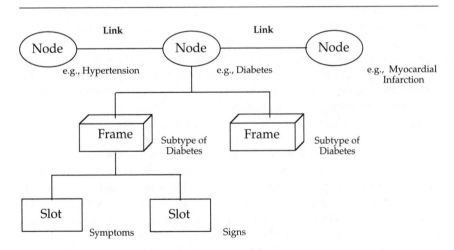

Nodes: domain entities such as particular disease, e.g. thyroid carcinoma
Links: relationships between the diseases
Frames: subtypes of domain entities, e.g. follicular, medullary, anaplastic carcinoma
Slots: features of disease subtypes, e.g. symptoms, signs, complications

Figure 8–4 An Example of a Medical Frame Scheme

ciples, axioms, and laws, derived from an exhaustive review of the literature, that are useful in explaining and justifying why a solution succeeds or fails. Heuristics is a rule of thumb, a compilation of knowledge that is extracted from the practice, judgment, and experience of an expert. Thus, from a health service perspective, an ES needs to incorporate factual knowledge, for example, about diseases or drug therapy with judgment and knowledge based on human experience and so-called heuristic or rule of thumb knowledge.[39]

KA is a time-consuming process that is undertaken by a knowledge engineer whose task is to mine the necessary information from the expert and construct a KB. "The method of representation of this knowledge in the computer is decided upon by the engineer. Computer representation is a set of syntactic and semantic conventions, making it possible to describe knowledge. It is therefore a systematic codification of an expert's domain knowledge."[40] Thus, KA is the key to developing a useful and successful ES. The acquisition of such a base of health-related information provides a unique glimpse into the logic and understanding possessed by health service experts about the domains of the problem to be solved.

The Expert System Shell

The ES shell is the programming environment of the ES. Expert systems can be programmed by using either AI languages such as LISP and PROLOG or advanced software tools, known as ES shells. "LISP" stands for List Processing Language and is used mainly in the United States and Canada, whereas "PROLOG" refers to Programming Language for Logic and is used mainly in European countries. AI languages have the disadvantage of requiring one to build the ES from scratch, thus requiring extensive amounts of programming expertise and time.

ES shells or building tools are user-friendly, providing the advantage of a rapid development environment capable of quickly generating user-interface screens, capturing knowledge bases, and managing strategies for searching the rule base.[41] Thus, the ES shells provide not only a substantial amount of the computer codes that would otherwise need to be written, tested, debugged, and maintained but the tools and specific techniques for handling knowledge representation, reasoning, and explanation.[42] One well-known example of an ES shell is EMYCIN (which stands for Empty MYCIN), derived from MYCIN, a program designed to assist with the diagnosis and therapy of bacteremia and meningitis.[43]

The inference engine is one component of the ES shell. It stands between the KB and the user and controls the use of the KB in solving problems. Basically, the inference engine performs three functions that correspond closely to the human problem-solving process: (1) identification of applicable rules (i.e., examining existing facts and identifying relevant rules); (2) conflict resolution or selection of the best rule for next step processing (and, where necessary, addition of new facts to the KB); and (3) rule execution and solution updating (i.e., deciding when an acceptable solution has been found). To determine which rule to apply next, these functions are continuously iterated by a rule-chaining mechanism that is part of the inference engine.

The search span for finding solutions could be so extensive as to make some exhaustive searches impractical. Therefore, the inference engine requires some means of limiting searches. There are three basic ways in which the inference engine controls the flow, searching, and reasoning strategies for solving a given problem.

1. Goal-directed (backward chaining)

2. Data-directed (forward chaining)

3. Hypothesis-directed

The goal-directed (or backward chaining) strategy starts with a goal or hypothesis and works backward through subgoals (e.g., the ES tries to find the patient's disease and works backward from there by posting questions regarding symptoms to confirm or refute a diagnosis). This approach is very efficient when only a few possible outcomes are known.

The data-directed (forward chaining) strategy is used when the solution to a problem still needs to be assembled or structured. Premises of the rules are examined to evaluate whether they are true, using the given information; those conclusions that are true are added to the list of known facts, and the system examines the rules again until it arrives at a suitable solution. For instance, a medical ES that examines a patient's symptoms and provides a diagnosis based on the symptoms might locate several possible disorders, then ask for further symptom information to differentiate among the several possible diagnoses.

The hypothesis-directed strategy mimics the deductive reasoning behavior of human problem solving much more closely than the backward and forward chaining strategies. It starts with the data-directed invocation of an initial hypothesis, and then selects additional rules based on the set of active hypotheses for consideration. It is similar to letting a differential diagnosis, for a given case, guide the direction of subsequent data collection, which in turn allows the diagnostic hypothesis list to be refined. Some ES, like ONCOCIN, use a combination of these three strategies to enhance their problem-solving capabilities.

Essentially, the inference engine classifies the outcome and recommends a line of action along with explanations for the suggested solution. These explanations may include rankings and specific probabilities of the alternatives, together with the probability of the recommended solution. The rules used to arrive at the given solution are normally made available through the ES user interface, either automatically or at the user's request.

User Interface

The user interface (UI) allows effective communications between users and the ES. It is through the UI component that the interviewer and inference engine communicate their questions, solutions, and explanations. As the component with which the user has immediate contact, the interface determines the acceptability and "ease of use" of the system through its quality. One aspect of the "ease of use" in AI research is concerned with the design of high-level user interface features, such as mouse-cursor-control in window environments, computer vision, and natural language processing. It is expected that the next generation of technology for designing ES interface will come from an integration of the various facets of AI research (see Chapter 14).

An important determinant of the success of ES applications in the health service delivery industry will be the acceptance of this new technology by health professionals. Consequently, to overcome the problem of acceptance, one must develop truly "user-friendly" ES interfaces. Of course, this does not imply that less attention should be paid to the other components of ES. Some ES, like ONCOCIN, have incorporated graphic screen displays to enhance user acceptability. Currently, most interfaces consist of a video display and keyboard; others have incorporated number pads, touch screens, mouse pointing devices, light pens, and speech recognition to reach greater user acceptance.[44]

ASSESSMENT OF FIFTH-GENERATION TECHNOLOGIES

AI and ES techniques fall under the class of "fifth-generation" technology. This term refers to computers that use parallel and vector processing as opposed to traditional serial processing. Serial processing is the processing of one instruction at a time, whereas vector processing can process many parts of a problem at the same time. These processors function as the human brain does, in that they can carry out multiple streams of activities at once. In terms of speed, vector processors work about 10 to 100 times faster than conventional serial processors.[45]

There are four major potential uses of fifth-generation technologies for enhancing health service delivery.

1. To improve efficiency and effectiveness of end-user decision making
2. To achieve a competitive advantage
3. To produce greater user satisfaction and confidence
4. To learn to explain its reasoning process

The first benefit of fifth-generation software is that it can contribute significantly to improving the efficiency and effectiveness of end-user decision making. This is especially true for semi-structured and ill-structured tasks that require the intervention of expert knowledge. While traditional technologies provided personal, group, and institutional decision support in areas of general knowledge, the single most important objective of an ES application is to automate available expertise in particular problem areas. It has been observed that gaining access to expertise that is captured in a computer system is much easier (i.e., more convenient, faster, and less expensive) than consulting a human expert.[46] Moreover, the specialized knowledge stored in the system can be shared electronically by all those interested or working in the area, with the knowledge that is captured being preserved permanently. Ideally, making such technology available to experts (e.g., experienced planners) could improve their productivity to the extent that they would be able to verify the quality and rationality of their decisions quickly.

The second major advantage of fifth-generation applications is that health service institutions can achieve a competitive advantage over other institutions that operate with only conventional programs. In fact, the technology that is available to a health service organization is a major factor in projecting that organization's image; this in turn will influence the levels of interest and support that can be expected from existing and potential clients. Kropf provides an excellent discussion of how the use of advanced technologies can benefit physicians, patients, and health service administrators.[47]

The third major advantage is that end-user interaction with fifth-generation technology can result in greater user satisfaction and confidence with the system's final outputs than those achieved with conventional programs. Some of the benefits associated with an improved computer-user interface design include greater user satisfaction and perceived usefulness and lesser need for user training and dependence on computer intermediaries (i.e., systems analysts and programmers).

A final positive characteristic of fifth-generation technology is the simulation of human reasoning and learning behaviors; for example, the ability of the system to explain its reasoning process just as a human "expert" does.[48,49] In many instances, users are interested not only in the final output of a system (i.e., the recommended solution), but in the line of reasoning that was used by the system to draw its conclusions.[50,51] This is crucial because if the line of reasoning appears faulty to the users, then the conclusion reached by the system may be unacceptable.

APPLICATIONS OF EXPERT SYSTEMS IN THE HEALTH SERVICE DELIVERY INDUSTRY

The use of ES in health service delivery has undergone a fairly long historical development. The following sections will present some examples of ES in the medical, pharmacy, nursing, and health promotion fields.

ES in Medicine: Management of Illness

Attempts have been made to develop ES in a wide range of fields of medicine, including thyroid diseases, breast diseases, drug poisoning, electrolyte disorders, abdominal pains, neurology, interpretation of electroencephalograms (EEG), liver diseases, ventilator management, pulmonary function test interpretation, infectious diseases, digitalis therapy, rheumatology, hematology, chest pains, ophthalmology, and oncology. Quite a number of these attempts have been successful (e.g., PUFF in pulmonary function test interpretation and ONCOCIN in cancer therapy). Other examples are provided in Exhibit 8–1 together with their pertinent features.

Most of the research involving ES in medicine deals traditionally with diagnosis. The reason for this is that the knowledge-based rule and rules of diagnosis change less frequently than therapeutic information. Clinical decision making, a dynamic process that is often poorly structured, usually involves tentative guesses and the use of rules-of-thumb knowledge. In this respect, computers using a strictly numerical problem-solving approach would not be suited to support this domain of expertise. In contrast, ES applications using symbolic reasoning and knowledge representation promise to provide fast and reliable advice to clinical professionals.

Since 1960, Professor Shortliffe and his affiliates at Stanford University have sought to develop "intelligent" systems to assist physicians in medical diagnoses. To date, most systems have been applied to specialized areas of medicine that are consistent with the way physicians collect and process data. There are four experimental systems that are regarded as having set the research directions of AI in medicine.

1. MYCIN, a program to advise physicians on antimicrobial selection for patients with bacteremia or meningitis
2. Present Illness Program (PIP), a system to gather data and generate hypotheses in patients with renal disease
3. INTERNIST-1, to assist with diagnosing problems in internal medicine
4. CASNET, an ophthalmology adviser to assess glaucoma states and to make recommendations for their management

Each of the following systems was built by using general problem-solving (GPS) techniques developed earlier. INTERNIST-1 is a diagnosis-oriented medical ES designed at the University of Pittsburgh that contains information on approximately 500 diseases. Unfortunately, INTERNIST-1 has some deficiencies, including an inability to reason anatomically, which has resulted in the generation of inappropriate conclusions. An expanded version of this system, called the Quick Medical Reference (QMR), which incorporates over 4500 possible manifestations of diseases including symptoms, signs, and laboratory tests of nearly

Exhibit 8–1 Applications of Expert Systems Technology in Medicine

Name of ES Product	Functional Areas/Capabilities
Pathfinder	Interprets findings in surgical pathology
Intellipath	Facilitates pathological diagnosis, integrated with a videodisk library of historical slides
RED	Interprets results from antibody identification tests in blood banks
MENTOR	Monitors drug therapies of hospitalized patients and warns of potential side effects and drug-drug interactions
GUIDON	Uses knowledge base of MYCIN in teaching
NEOMYCIN	Assists in clinical medical diagnosis, addresses many limitations in MYCIN
HELP	Generates alerts when abnormalities in patient record are noted because of its ability to provide an integrated hospital information system
QMR (Quick Medical Reference)	Provides expert consultation and general medical diagnosis; can be used as electronic textbook and medical spreadsheets

600 internal medicine diseases, is currently available on microcomputer. It provides a ranked list of plausible diseases based on signs and symptoms.[52] Prototypes for other ES have been developed in areas such as pulmonary function testing, ventilator management, digitalis therapy, psychiatric disorders, rheumatology, pathology, hematology, and hepatic and renal diseases.[53]

ATTENDING represents another form of a medical ES. This expert method is a program that critiques or evaluates the proposed treatment plan selected by the user. Apart from the capability of generating the diagnosis or treatment recommendations, ATTENDING provides "an assessment of the therapeutic scheme designed by the clinician. This type of program does not impose a particular plan of therapy on the user but provides acceptable alternatives for consideration."[54] The medical domains encompassed by ATTENDING include anesthesiology, hypertension therapy, ventilator management, and workup therapy for patients.

A third kind of "true" medical ES is an on-line system called ONCOCIN, which advises oncology physicians treating cancer patients participating in clinical trials. ONCOCIN uses a graphic interface and has the capability of integrating a temporal record of a patient's treatment with an underlying knowledge base of treatment protocols.[55] In short, ONCOCIN is intended to eliminate the paper trail generated in the treatment of cancer patients by providing rules for adjustment of doses of chemotherapeutic agents, ordering of tests, treatment protocols, and other diagnostic and patient care management activities.

ES in Pharmacy: Drug Therapy Management

Pharmacy is a complex and challenging discipline; its knowledge base is huge and often not completely understood. For instance, patients often have coexisting diseases and, as a result, accuracy in drug therapy is vital since knowledge changes constantly. In this sense, statistical or probabilistic methods are generally insufficient for the administration and management of pharmaceutical therapy. Even so, ES in pharmacy can be developed to increase the efficiency of these administrative and management components of pharmacy. In order to do so, an ES needs to incorporate factual knowledge of diseases and drug therapies with deductive knowledge based on human experience and heuristics (or rules of thumb). The most critical component such an ES provides would be the ability to make judgment under uncertainty.

At present, manipulation, storage, and preparation of drug products for dispensing can be automated. With over 125,000 drug products available in Canada, a great deal of effort is required to maintain current information on these products. As an immediate application, an ES program can be developed to handle routine tablet identification, provide literature or evaluate large volumes of information from the patients' records, and provide recommendations on proper drug therapy.

There are several systems currently under development, including a robotics system for preparing cancer chemotherapy admixtures.[56] In fact, several programs focusing on drug therapy have also been developed. For example, one microcomputer-based ES is discussed solely for detecting potential drug interactions.[57] Drug names entered into the system are matched against a list of the main functions, assisting in drug literature retrieval, drug use evaluation, pharmacy dosing, drug interaction screening, parenteral nutrient solution preparation and monitoring, and financial analysis.

One prototype ES, MENTOR, interfaces with an existing hospital IS (HIS) to monitor the prescribed drug therapy and to provide appropriate advisory messages when it detects previously defined problems. MENTOR's knowledge base includes topics associated with amino glycosides, surgical prophylaxis, digoxin, and blood culture results. PK, an on-line MENTOR module, takes information on drug dosage, drug concentration results, and desired therapeutic range to monitor drug dosing and make recommendations for future dosage adjustments. The system is capable of generating a pharmacokinetic model of the drug using Bayesian forecasting techniques to calculate changes in pharmacokinetics over time. As the information base increases, the system "learns" more about the patient, thereby enabling it to supply patient-specific advice.

The use of computing technology as educational tools for clinical pharmacy students is not new to pharmacy. Case-based interactive expert software has been developed to guide a student through a patient's response to drug therapy.[58] Such an ES will not only challenge the student to assess drug response but assist in making decisions on future drug therapy. Moreover, computer-based instruction can be extended to involve the use of AI techniques to develop pharmacy tutor programs. These programs can be designed to build models of filling prescription and generate feedback to the student on the basis of an approach that would be used by a clinical expert.[59] Tutorial programs like these could then be integrated into pharmacy school curricula to aid in clinical instruction and the development of problem-solving techniques.

ES in Nursing: Patient Care Management

There has been little progress in the development of ES in the nursing domain. The lack of agreement on the boundaries of nursing knowledge and the nature of nursing decisions is one critical reason for this. To establish the role of nursing in decision making, the boundaries of nursing action and the levels of nursing decisions must be defined. There is no concise description of what nurses must know and use in making decisions in promoting a patient's well-being. There is only one area of agreement among nurses about their role: that nursing is concerned with the person as a whole entity.[60] This is a broad and very vague delineation of nursing knowledge. Knowledge must be specific, concrete, and operational if it is to be used in the development of an ES. Despite these constraints, three groups have been working separately to develop ES in nursing.

Bloom et al. developed a prototype to assess the feasibility of ES used in analyzing nursing assessment data and the generation of nursing diagnosis and other nursing related interventions.[61] This prototype is currently being evaluated in a clinical setting. The Ozbolt group developed a prototype ES using various conceptual models of nursing.[62] Because of inherent limitations of nursing models, Ryan and Evans at the Creighton University School of Nursing developed a practical ES known as COMMES (Creighton On-line Multiple Modular Expert Systems), which appears to overcome the difficulties faced by the Ozbolt group.[63] COMMES was designed to assist and support clinical decision making about patient conditions and has since been evaluated in 10 clinical sites across North America.

COMMES's goal is to train an entry-level professional nurse. The COMMES system contains a hierarchically organized network of instructional goals that eventually constitute an entire educational program. The goal tree is broken down into "cognitive fundamentals" that are in turn separated into three areas: clinical problem solving, professional knowledge (and humanistic needs), and "clinical integration."[64,65]

As its components COMMES includes a protocol consultant and an educational consultant. The protocol consultant assists the nurses in the development of individual care plans for their patients.[66] A patient care plan is prepared by the nurse from the data gathered when a patient is admitted and is revised and updated as the patient's condition changes. The nurse enters the medical diagnosis, signs and symptoms, or nursing diagnosis of the patient, and the system responds with a list of possible nursing goals for a patient with that diagnosis or symptom. Nurses then review the goals and select the one (or several) that describes what they want; then the system dramatically constructs a protocol of care from its knowledge base. The educational consultant is used as a self-learning tool. Nurses are asked to enter the patient condition they wish to learn more about and the system presents a list of goals that can be selected to meet the learning objectives. COMMES outlines the relevant subgoals for learning and provides a reference KB that is included in an extensive database.

ES in Health Promotion: Health Program Management

Technology related to artificial intelligence and expert systems can provide opportunities to extend expertise the same way consultation of human experts does. Essentially, health program planning and evaluation are complex and sophisticated processes. They require recognition of the role of distinct elements of the planning process and an understanding of their interrelationships. Community organization, administration, and evaluation skills are used by health professionals in the planning of effective programs and in the identification and allocation of resources. One major problem faced by these professionals, in utilizing such a broad science base, is the difficulty in applying knowledge from different disciplines.

One system capable of meeting this need is Expert Methods for Planning and Organizing Within Everyone's Reach (EMPOWER/Canadian Health), which is viewed as a tool that will add to the planner's ability to plan from a global perspective. It involves community leaders' assessing their own visions, needs, perspectives, circumstances, and preferences, or cultural values and norms. The system is designed to provide expert guidance and technical assistance in the planning and evaluation of community-based health prevention and health promotion programs. Inputs to the system come from multiple sources, including data entered by users responding to a set of questions as well as external sources such as data pertaining to community health care needs assessment or priorities (Figure 8–5).

EMPOWER/Canadian Health knowledge base follows the planning approach of the PRECEDE-PROCEED framework.[67] PRECEDE is an acronym for Predisposing, Reinforcing, and Enabling Constructs in Educational Diagnosis and Evaluation; PROCEED refers to Policy, Regulatory and Organizational Constructs in Educational and Environmental Development. Figure 8–6 summarizes the various phases of planning in the PRECEDE model, which include sequential assessments and cumulative diagnoses of the social, epidemiological, behavioral and environmental, educational, organizational, administrative, and policy targets of change. The PROCEED model then applies these diagnostic results in the implementation and evaluation of programs.

In terms of structure, EMPOWER/Canadian Health has six modules designed to link global, national, and provincial goals, policies, and standards for evaluation. These modules guide health professional managers through a series of steps to address pertinent questions regarding the design and conduct of process, impact, and outcome evaluations. For example, Module 1 provides community health planners with a situational analysis that identifies which of the federal-provincial health objectives would be most relevant to planning in the particular community, and what resources for planning are available. It guides in identifying and ordering priorities that play roles in local program planning.

Although Modules 2 through 6 are often seen as sequential, the benefit of the proposed system is that there is the opportunity to conduct continuous "What-IF" analyses by moving dynamically back and forth among the modules. Module 6 (Guidance on Evaluation Planning) is meant to provide continuous feedback during all phases of program planning and implementation using process, impact, and outcome statements. The last module (i.e., Module 7) corresponds to the PROCEED portion of the model that provides guidance on developing the community health evaluation. Exhibit 8–2 provides some sample questions that one of the modules (Module 5) of EMPOWER/Canadian Health used to capture internal data from program leaders.

The knowledge engineer for EMPOWER (Gold) collected and assembled the expert knowledge base (KB) systematically with the help of the two authors of PRECEDE-PROCEED (Green and Kreuter) and other experts on health promotion, planning, and evaluation.[68] The EMPOWER/Canadian Health KB has the additional advantage of several hundred development and evaluation efforts in the fields of cardiovascular disease prevention and health promotion programs that have applied and tested the PRECEDE-PROCEED model in hypertension; smoking prevention and cessation; dietary fat reduction and related nutrition programs;

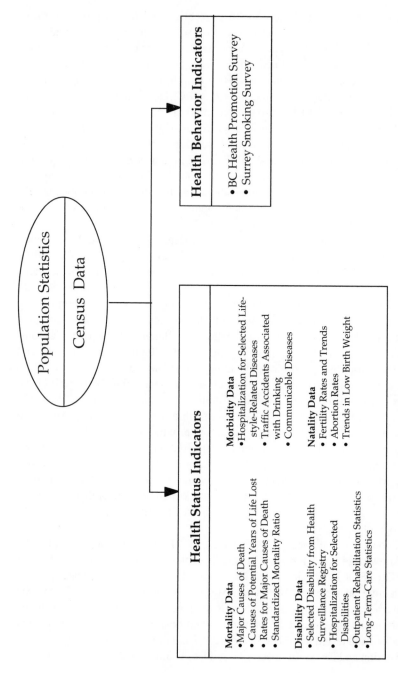

Figure 8–5 Information Sources for Community Health Care Needs Assessment

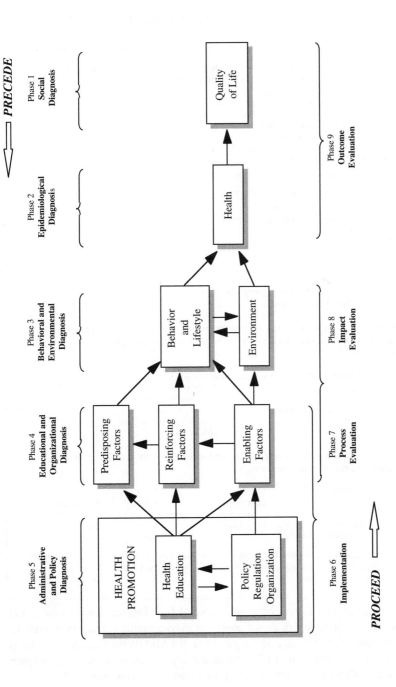

Figure 8-6 The PRECEDE-PROCEED Model. *Source:* Reprinted with permission of Green, L.W. and Kreuter, M.W., *Health Promotion Planning: An Educational and Environmental Approach*, 2nd Edition, Mountain View: Mayfield Publishing Co., p. 24, © 1991.

Exhibit 8–2 Sample Questions from EMPOWER/Canadian Health (M5—Social Diagnosis)

I. Which of the following steps do we want to add to the action agenda to verify our vision statement and establish it as a shared vision?
- Convene your planning team
- Explain the importance and rationale for a vision statement
- Utilize working groups to draft a vision statement
- Gather feedback on the draft vision statement
- Redraft vision as a shared vision
- Communicate this shared visions statement with appropriate groups
- Revise the vision statement

--> Click to add to steps to your action agenda

I I. Ensuring participatory planning in the social diagnosis
1. Community Participation
2. Channels to Community Involvement
3. Examine Planning Team

I I.1 Community Participation

A. Preferred size of the planning group
How large a planning group do you wish to work with?
--> Select the group size

B. As a step toward ensuring appropriate representation of the target population in our planning effort, please verify or modify the population profile for which we are planning.

Delimiting Factors/Project Limitations (i.e.)
Age   25–29 years
Ethnicity   Hispanic/Latino
Socioeconomic Status   Poverty Level
Settings   Clinical/Primary Care
Geography   Urban/Rural

C. Please specify who can help in planning, developing, implementing, or evaluating the eventual program.

Contact Category	Contact Last Name	Contact Priority	Contacted
Stakeholder	John Doe	High	Yes
Community Leader	Peter Nolan	Low	No

Source: Adapted with permission from Gold, R.S., and Green, L.W., Computer Modeling of Community Organization, *2nd National Conference on Health Promotion Research,* Vancouver, British Columbia, March 1993.

physical activity and fitness programs; several broad-based, school-based, and worksite-based multiple risk-factor programs in communities; and cancer prevention programs. More recently, the application of EMPOWER/Canadian Health is considered a dissemination of ES work in the larger context of using information technology (IT) for community health promotion and development.[69,70]

CONCLUSION

Although research in AI/ES technology as applied to health service delivery has been conducted for about two decades, a few systems have been implemented and are truly "operational." By the early 1990s, AI/ES technology had still not grown out of its experimental state. What, then, does AI/ES technology really offer that its predecessors (EDP, MIS, HDSS, DBMS) do not? Are these fifth-generation applications worth investing in? Health service planners, managers, and professionals who are able to answer these questions will be better able to assess the value of investing in fifth-generation technology.

Human experts respond to requests in a more flexible and individualized manner than automated ES. In simulating human cognitive processes, ES ignore most of the information processing that animates and occurs naturally in human behaviors. Therefore, ES programs cannot even closely resemble human behavior (no matter how narrowly constrained the domain is). In addition, ES domains use areas of expertise that work with one problem at a time, asking questions of their users and proceeding from these inputs to a conclusion. Consequently, there are still a number of breakthroughs in AI research that need to be pursued in the near future. Among the most important ones are (1) investigation into the nature of intelligence, including the imitation of cognitive processes of humans; (2) simulation of "common sense" (i.e., aiming to make computers less rigid and more understanding); and (3) use of metaphor graphics, icons, animations, and dynamic graphics to redesign ES-HMIS applications as natural human-computer interfaces. Accordingly, the slow growth of ES in the medical field has been due to unnatural user interfaces. Earlier ES models were slow and could only run on large computers. This limitation is now being addressed, with new ES being designed to run on high-performance personal workstations. Ultimately, the design of simpler human-computer interfaces will contribute to greater acceptance of ES applications.

The perception that ES are not cost-effective has unfortunately reduced the spread of these systems among physicians' offices. Several studies indicate that physicians view ES as being "threats" rather than "intelligent" assistants. Their perception is that ES may one day replace them, and this creates a state of anxiety, fear, and uneasiness that can only be due to ignorance about technology. For instance, many health professionals, especially nurses and physicians, have resisted change whenever automation has been perceived to threaten their status. This perception generates uncertainties and negative attitudes toward computer systems. Such perception is accentuated by a lack of exposure to computers during formal training. To change these attitudes, the design of user-friendly interfaces must be undertaken, and health professionals must be thoroughly educated in the use of computers.

Furthermore, the difficulty of dividing the health fields into more concrete operational domains is another key factor that has slowed progress in the field of ES consultation in medical care; for example, internal medicine has identified more than 500 diseases. It has been equally difficult to delineate the knowledge required for nursing—with the result that few attempts have been made to develop ES in this field.

The acceptance of ES and AI technologies in the health service industry has also been hindered because of technical problems arising during implementation. These technical problems result from a lack of trained personnel and an inability to define concrete and operational domains in which to develop expert consultation systems. Today, most of the ES in use have been developed by computer scientists and knowledge engineers who have little or no background in health management information systems (HMIS). In addition, few health professionals have considered HMIS as a career. As a result, little progress has been made in the HMIS field, and incentives to encourage health professionals to specialize in AI/ES areas have been lacking.

Finally, we are in an era when the costs of computer hardware have fallen dramatically, although software costs have not. That is to say that the need for a new technology like artificial intelligence or expert system can only expand since the high costs of software production can now be easily shared among a growing number of users who already own computer hardware.

CHAPTER QUESTIONS

1. Distinguish fifth-generation technologies from those of earlier generations. Why do you think fifth-generation technologies will be widely accepted? If not, why not?

2. What are the subdisciplines of AI? Why is ES considered the most relevant to health administration and management?

3. Can you think of real-life ES implementations in the areas of financial accounting and other managerial functions? How would these ES contribute to user knowledge and ability to carry out a task requiring specialized expertise?

4. Provide some examples of human cognitive processes that are currently not found in ES. Which do you think need to be investigated to move the field forward?

MINI CASE 8
DESIGNING A DECISION TREE

Within expert systems, the inference engine creates a set of rules derived from its knowledge base. These rules are designed to assist the system in reasoning with the data presented and ultimately arriving at correct clinical decisions. This process of searching through the knowledge base to find the "best" solution to an identified problem occurs via a structure known as a decision tree. A decision tree, through hierarchical organization of information, has the unique advantage of offering alternative solutions to a given problem. The following exercise is designed to give the reader an appreciation of the complexities associated with decision tree design.

Imagine, for the moment, you are a vascular surgeon at a teaching hospital in the bustling community of Transylvania. You have been approached by a radical young medical resident, Dr. C. Dracu, to assist in the design of a decision tree. The goal of the decision tree is to reduce the chance of a patient's dying from pulmonary embolisms (clots in the blood vessels leading to the lungs) after general surgery. Although death is relatively rare, the incidence of patients' dying while under the care of Dr. C. Dracu has become increasingly alarming.

The current approach is to treat postoperatively when venous thromboembolism becomes clinically evident. The clinical signs may include pleuritic chest pain, shortness of breath or coughing up of blood, or pain and tenderness in the thigh or calf (deep-vein thrombosis). Once the signs appear, the diagnosis is confirmed by lung scanning (for pulmonary embolism) or by venography (for deep-vein thrombosis). The treatment for both types of venous thromboembolism is the same—full-dose anticoagulant therapy consisting of intravenous heparin followed by outpatient treatment with sodium warfarin.

Being the astute vascular surgeon that you are, you recognize immediately that Dr. C. Dracu's appreciation for primary prophylaxis is severely lacking. In designing a decision tree for high-risk pulmonary embolism surgical patients you make the following suggestions:

1. Administer subcutaneous low-dose heparin—in this approach all patients would be given heparin therapy. If you suspect deep-vein thrombosis (DVT) or pulmonary embolism (PE), then venography or lung scanning, respectively, is performed. If this confirms the diagnosis, then full-dose anticoagulant therapy would be given.

2. Administer intravenous dextrin—in this approach all patients would be given dextrin intravenously (postoperatively). If you suspect DVT or PE, then venography or lung scanning, respectively, is performed. If this confirms the diagnosis, then full-dose anticoagulant therapy is undertaken.

3. Administer intermittent pneumatic compression of legs—in this approach all patients are given an inflatable cuff strapped to their leg which gently applies a regular cycle of pressure. If you suspect deep-vein thrombosis or pulmonary embolism, venography or lung scanning, respectively, is performed. If this confirms the diagnosis, the full-dose anticoagulant therapy is undertaken.

MINI CASE QUESTIONS

Set out the three primary prophylaxis alternatives in the form of a decision tree for Dr. C. Dracu, showing the sequence of diagnostic and therapeutic actions. Remember, this decision tree starts with "high-risk surgical patients"!

CHAPTER REVIEW

Significant progress has occurred in the application of artificial intelligence and expert system technology in the health service delivery industry during the last few years. This trend will continue as long as specific and operational areas in health service are continually defined. More expert systems will also be upgraded from experimental to real-life settings. However, successful implementation of these systems will depend upon the design of simpler and friendlier computer interfaces as well as the provision of courses on health management information systems to future health professionals aimed at changing negative attitudes about computers. The knowledge-based expert systems, referred to here as expert systems (ES), are considered a subarea of artificial intelligence (AI); other subareas include robotics, natural language processing, neural networks, and computer vision.

Expert systems consist of four components: the knowledge base, knowledge acquisition process, expert system shell, and user interface. These components must be examined in detail when real-life expert systems are designed. Four main advantages of expert systems and other fifth-generation technologies are (1) significant improvements in the efficiency and effectiveness of end-user decision making, (2) competitive advantages over other health institutions with lesser technologies, (3) greater user satisfaction and confidence in a system's output due to improved end-user interfaces, and (4) simulation of human reasoning and learning behaviors. Many prototypes of ES in medicine, pharmacy, nursing, and health promotion now exist and many more are expected to become operational in the coming years. It is expected that cheaper hardware and the growing acceptance of computers by health professionals will result in even more applications of expert systems in these and other health-related fields.

NOTES

1. M.C. Kelsey, Intelligent Systems: How Can They Help?, *Journal of Hospital Infection* 18, Supplement A (1991): 418–423.
2. N.R. Anthony, *Planning and Control Systems: A Framework for Analysis* (Boston: Division of Research, Harvard Business School, 1965).

3. A.M. Turing, Can a Machine Think?, in *Computers and Thought,* ed. E.A. Feigenbaum and J. Feldman (New York: McGraw-Hill Publishing Co., 1963).

4. E.H. Shortliffe, *Computer-Based Medical Consultations: MYCIN* (New York: Elsevier Science Publishing Co., Inc., 1976).

5. S.M. Blois, Expert Systems: More Than a Book, Less Than a Human, *MD Computing* 4, no. 4 (1987): 53–56.

6. P. Szolovits, *Artificial Intelligence in Medicine* (Boulder, Colo: Westview Press, Inc., 1982).

7. B. Shell, Thinking about Artificial Intelligence, *Harvard Business Review* (July–August 1987): 91–97.

8. A. Newell and H. Simon, *Human Problem Solving* (Englewood Cliffs, NJ: Prentice Hall, 1972).

9. E. Turban, *Decision Support and Expert Systems: Management Support Systems,* 3rd ed. (New York: Macmillan Publishing Co., Inc., 1992).

10. L.A. Zadeh, The Calculus of Fuzzy If/Then Rules, *AI Expert* (March 1991): 23–27.

11. H. Simon, *Science of Management Decision* (New York: Harper & Row, 1960).

12. Newell and Simon, *Human Problem Solving.*

13. A. Newell and H. Simon, GPS: A Program That Simulates Human Thought, in *Computers and Thought,* ed. E.A. Feigenbaum and J. Feldman (New York: McGraw-Hill Publishing Co., 1963).

14. D. Palmer, Artificial Intelligence in Healthcare Management, *Healthcare Informatics* (March 1990): 54.

15. E. Turban and P. R. Watkins, Integrating Expert Systems and Decision Support Systems, *MIS Quarterly* (June 1986): 121–136.

16. M.W. Aiken, et al., Integrating Expert Systems with Group Decision Support Systems, *ACM Transition on Information Systems* 9, no. 1 (January 1991): 75–95.

17. B.C. Jiang, Development of Machine Vision System for Education, *Computers and Industrial Engineering* 18, no. 1 (1990): 23–28.

18. L. Cherry and R. Cherry, Another Way of Looking at the Brain, *New York Times Magazine* (June 1985): 56–118.

19. M. Brady, Artificial Intelligence and Robotics, *Artificial Intelligence* 26, no. 1 (1985): 79–121.

20. E. Rich and K. Knight, *Artificial Intelligence,* 2nd ed. (New York: McGraw-Hill Publishing Co., 1981).

21. G.W. Pearson, Robotics: A Future View of Workplace Safety, *Risk Management* (October 1990): 42–46.

22. Rich and Knight, Workplace Safety, 42–46.

23. D. Gelernter, The Metamorphosis of Information Management, *Scientific American* (August 1989): 66–73.

24. J.H.K. Tan and D. Amoko, Expert Systems in Health Care: A Review, Working Paper (Vancouver Department of Health Care and Epidemiology, University of British Columbia, 1990).

25. L.W. Green, et al., EMPOWER/Canadian Health: The Application of Expert System Technology to Community Health Program Planning and Evaluation, *Canadian Medical Informatics* November/December (1994) 20–23.

26. Shortliffe, *Medical Consultations.*

27. E.H. Shortliffe, et al., ONCOCIN: An Expert System for Oncology Protocol Management, *Proceedings of the 7th International Joint Conference on Artificial Intelligence,* Menlo Park, Calif (1981): 876–881.

28. R.A. Miller, et al., INTERNIST-1: An Experimental Computer Based Diagnostic Consultant for General Internal Medicine, *New England Journal of Medicine* (December 1986): 468–476.

29. S.M. Weiss, et al., A Model Based Consultation System for the Long-Term Management of Glaucoma, *International Joint Conference on Artificial Intelligence* 5 (1977): 1030–1037.

30. C.A. Kulikowski, Representation of Expert Knowledge for Consultation: The CASNET and EXPERT Projects, in *Medicine* ed., P. Szolovits, AAAS Selected Symposium 51 (Boulder, Colo: Westview Press, 1982).

31. J.J. Heiser, et al., Progress Report: A Computerized Psychopharmacology Advisor, in *Proceedings International Neuro-Psychopharmacological,* Vienna, Austria, 1978.

32. S.M. Speedie, et al., MENTOR: Integration of an Expert System with a Hospital Information System, in *Proceedings of the 11th Annual Symposium of Computer Applications in Medical Care,* ed. L. Kingsland (Washington, DC: IEEE Computer Society Press, 1987): 220–224.

33. M. Greer, RXPERT: A Prototype Expert System for Formulary Decision Making, *Annals of Pharmacotherapy* 26 (1992): 244–250.

34. S.A. Ryan, An Expert System for Nursing Practice: Clinical Decision Support Systems in Nursing, *Proceedings of the IFIP-IMIA International Symposium on Nursing Uses of Computers and Information in Science* (1985): 85–91.

35. J.G. Ozbolt, Developing Decision Support Systems for Nursing: Issues of Knowledge Representation, *Proceedings of the 5th Conference on Medical Informatics* (1986): 186–189.

36. Green, et al., EMPOWER/Canadian Health.

37. E.H. Shortliffe, Medical Expert Systems: Knowledge Tools for Physicians, *Western Journal of Medicine* 145, no. 6 (1986): 830–830.

38. B.T. Williams, *Computer Aids to Clinical Decision.* Vol. 2. (Boca Raton, Fla: CRC Press, 1982).

39. J.F. Dasta, Application of Artificial Intelligence to Pharmacy and Medicine, *Hospital Pharmacy* 27 (April 1992): 312–322.

40. Kelsey, Intelligent Systems, 420.

41. P. Harmon and D. King, *Expert Systems: Artificial Intelligence in Business* (New York: John Wiley & Sons, Inc., 1985).

42. Rich and Knight, *Artificial Intelligence,* 7.

43. B. Buchanan and E.H. Shortliffe, *Rule Based Expert Programs: The MYCIN Experiments of the Stanford Heuristic Program Project* (Reading, Mass: Addison-Wesley Publishing Co., Inc., 1984).

44. C.D. Lane, et al., Graphical Access to a Medical Expert System. II. Design of an Interface for Physicians, *Methods of Information in Medicine* 25 (1986): 143–150.

45. K.C. Laudon and J.P. Laudon, *Business Information Systems: A Problem Solving Approach* (Hinsdale, Ill: Dryden Press, 1991).

46. V.C. Yen and R. Boissoneau, Artificial Intelligence and Expert Systems: Implications for Health Care Delivery, *Hospital Topics* 66, no. 5 (September/October 1988): 16–19.

47. R. Kropf, *Service Excellence in Health Care through the Use of Computers* (Ann Arbor, Mich: Health Administration Press, 1990), 15. A review of this work appears in J.K.H. Tan, *Hospital and Health Services Administration* 38, no. 1 (1993): 159–161.

48. D.A. Waterman, *A Guide to Expert Systems* (Reading, Mass: Addison-Wesley Publishing Co., Inc., 1986).

49. A. Juma, Artificial Intelligence in Medicine, *Management Guide to Health Care Information Systems* (Gaithersburg, Md.: Aspen Publishers, Inc., 1987): 171–199.

50. C. Parker and T. Case, *Management Information Systems: Strategy and Action,* 2nd ed. (New York: McGraw-Hill Publishing Co., 1993).

51. N.R. Anthony, *Planning and Control Systems: A Framework for Analysis* (Boston, Mass: Division of Research, Harvard Business School, 1965).

52. Dasta, Application of Artificial Intelligence, 314.

53. E.H. Shortliffe, Computer Programs To Support Clinical Decision Making, *Journal of American Medical Association* 258, no. 1 (1987): 61–66.

54. Dasta, Application of Artificial Intelligence, 314.

55. Ibid., 315.

56. D.D. Cote and M.G. Tochia, Robotic System for I.V. Antineoplastic Drug Preparation: Description and Preliminary Evaluation under Simulated conditions, *American Journal of Pharmacy* 46 (1989): 2286–2293.

57. E.L. Kinney, ES Detection of Drug Interactions: Results in Consecutive Inpatients, *Computer Biomedical Research* 19 (1986): 462–467.

58. Dasta, Application of Artificial Intelligence, 318.

59. Ibid., 319.

60. D.E. Orem, *Nursing: Concepts of Practice,* 3rd ed. (New York: McGraw-Hill Publishing Co., 1985).

61. K.C. Bloom, et al., Development of an Expert System Prototype to Generate Nursing Care Plans Based on Nursing Diagnosis, *Computers in Nursing* 5, no. 4 (1987): 140–145.

62. Ozbolt, Developing Decision Support Systems.

63. S.A. Ryan, An Expert System for Nursing Practice, *Journal of Medical Systems* 9 (1985): 29.

64. S. Evans, A Computer Based Nursing Diagnosis Consultant, *Proceedings of the Eighth Annual Symposium on Computer Applications in Medical Care* (1984): 651–658.

65. S. Evans, Clinical and Academic Uses of COMMES System: An Implemented AI System, *Proceedings of the Ninth Annual Symposium on Computer Application in Medical Care* (1985): 658–661.

66. Green et al., EMPOWER/Canadian Health.

67. L.W. Green and M.W. Kreuter, *Health Promotion Planning: An Educational and Environmental Approach* (Mountain View, Calif: Mayfield Publishing Co., 1991).

68. R.S. Gold and L.W. Green, Computer Modeling of Community Organization (Paper presented at 2nd National Conference on Health Promotion Research, Vancouver, March 1993).

69. N. Milio, New Tools for Community Involvement in Health, *Health Promotion International* 7, no. 3 (1992): 209–217.

70. L.W. Green, et al., Community Information Technology Infrastructure and Support Systems, in *The Theoretical and Evaluation Plan for the BC Heart Health Demonstration Project (BCHHDP),* Vol. 2. (Vancouver: Institute of Health Promotion Research, Faculty of Graduate Studies and Department of Health Care and Epidemiology, Faculty of Medicine, University of British Columbia, 1993).

Chapter 9

Advances in Health Informatics and Telematics: Toward an Integrated Health Information System

LEARNING OBJECTIVES

1. Define systems integration.
2. State the need to integrate information systems in health service organizations.
3. Provide examples of the capabilities of advanced communications and networking technology.
4. Identify how case-mix management information systems and clinical management information systems have begun to integrate HMIS technologies and applications.
5. Identify the functions and roles of management in systems integration development.

INTRODUCTION

If the health care industry develops a unified, proactive stance regarding telecommunication, transformative clinical and administrative advances (such as remote clinical viewing, automatic claims processing, the interactive lifetime health record and advanced imaging) could be universally accessible.[1]

As mentioned in earlier chapters, the duplication of services and procedures has been a problem in the North American health service delivery system (NAHSDS). For each occurrence of service duplication, the amount of time and other resources required can be saved if the services and procedures are streamlined through better interdepartmental and crossinstitutional coordination. As a consequence, health services can then be available to more individuals in the community at large. This is where integrated health management information systems (HMIS) come into play.

This chapter will describe the need to integrate HMIS technologies and applications in health service delivery organizations to facilitate the evolution of the hospital of the future and to encourage the development of systems integration. The progress of integration from data/horizontal integration of the 1970s, to clinical/vertical integration of the 1980s, to the dawn of systemswide integration in the 1990s will be discussed. The focus of the discussion will be on the evolution of and advances in health informatics and telematics. Specific examples of applications in health informatics and advancing telecommunications and networking technology will also be given. Lastly, the development of case-mix information systems (C-MIS) and clinical management information systems (CMIS) and their significance to and impact on the eventual establishment of total systems integration will be highlighted. To tie all of this discussion together, we propose a pyramidal framework for understanding the evolution of health telematics and systems integration.

SYSTEMS INTEGRATION: A PYRAMID MODEL

In view of today's soaring health care costs, health service managers and planners are increasingly charged with the task of providing more for less. Throughout the United States and Canada, a variety of solutions have been proposed to change the ways health services have been provided and to reduce the costs of health services while maintaining quality, accessibility, comprehensiveness, and universality of care. Some examples that have been suggested as possible solutions include the capping of physicians' salaries; the institution of user fees; the redesigning of health service organizations, such as arranging multihospital mergers, regionalizing, and corporatizing health service delivery; and the rationing or prioritizing of health services. Most, if not all, of these solutions rely largely on the concept of systems integration (Chapter 3).

The idea and concept of systems integration as a solution to many of the problems in health service delivery have been around for at least two decades, but as the health reform in North America gathers momentum, there has been increased and renewed interest in systems integration and the development of a total HMIS to coordinate patient services.[2] Today, the concept of HMIS integration goes beyond concepts of horizontal and vertical integration of health service organizations: it encompasses a new concept of systems integration in the organization and management support of health services. A framework for understanding systems integration in the context of evolving health informatics and telematics is illustrated in Figure 9–1.

The pyramid model of Figure 9–1 illustrates the development of systems integration and HMIS as two sides of the same coin. It provides a logical framework for our discussion on the frontiers of knowledge in HMIS technologies and appli-

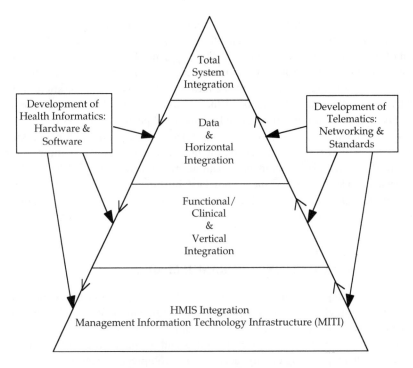

Figure 9–1 A Pyramid Framework for Systems Integration

cations. Systems integration refers to the relating and tying together of various subsystems in the health service delivery industry. Its ultimate goal is to eliminate redundancy, fragmentation, and duplication of services and thereby reduce the overall costs of health care substantially. Achieving systems integration may require a completely new management culture that constantly translates the needs of the population in a community (e.g., increased demand in certain health services) into inputs to the integrated HMIS and the outputs of the HMIS (e.g., better integration of administrative and clinical data) into inputs to the community. Figure 9–2 illustrates the key variables involved in systems integration. The establishment of systems integration is often referred to as an organized delivery system (ODS).[3]

The central component to systems integration is clearly the development of a management information technology infrastructure (MITI) that encompasses all of the players in the specific population's health services. The components constituting MITI have been discussed previously in Chapter 5 (see Figure 5–4). Figure 9–3 illustrates the potential of an MITI to support the HMIS of the future. For

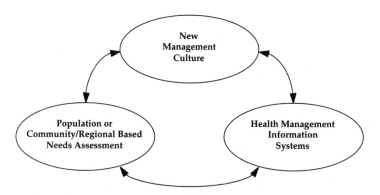

Figure 9–2 Major Components Involved in Systems Integration

example, the new HMIS structure will allow such subsystems as laboratories and drug companies to provide inputs (e.g., lab test results and new drug information) into the HMIS and receive outputs (e.g., additional lab tests and orders for new drugs) from the HMIS upon the compilation of these inputs and the subsequent decision making. In this fashion, the integrated HMIS of the health service delivery system resembles the brain in the central nervous system in terms of information gathering, decision making, and controlled information dissemination.

Health Informatics and the Evolution of Systems Integration

Shortliffe and Perreault described in some detail the evolution of three waves of integration in health informatics (HI) during the last few decades: (1) the centralized model of hospital information systems (HIS) in the early fifties and sixties, (2) the modular HIS of the seventies, and (3) the distributed systems of the late eighties.[4] In the past, emphasis on data and functional integration for transaction planning and management control may have contributed partly to the lack of progress in HI applications. Overall, the lack of an initial clear vision with regard to changing technology and planning of an integrated HMIS has clearly resulted in obstacles to the efficient and effective functioning of health service organizations. The narrow confinement of HMIS to specific operational as well as specialized clinical tasks has contributed to soaring costs in health services. In addition, it has precluded the use of advancing information technology (IT) in organizationwide data sharing and strategic decision-making applications. In the end, although most health service organizations that subscribe to traditional views of HI applications have achieved certain levels of data and functional integration, their potential to achieve more extensive and greater levels of systems integration is still far from being realized.

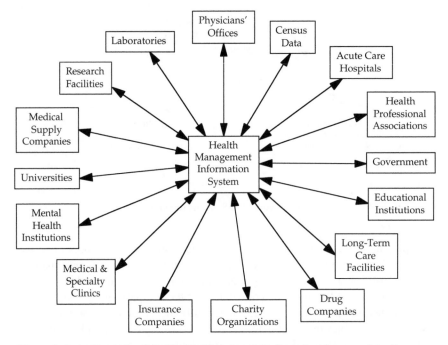

Figure 9–3 An Example of the Health Management Information System of the Future

Early Applications of Health Informatics: The Shortfalls

During most of the previous two decades, HI applications were mainly in the form of "islands" of computerized data processing applications such as accounting, payroll, drug inventory, computer-assisted medical instrumentation, and laboratory systems. Implemented in the health service setting, these applications were meant to reduce costs of health service delivery. Instead, costs steadily rose in many instances after the introduction of computerized solutions. Possible explanations for this disappointing outcome include the following:

- The lack of a futuristic approach to IT planning among health service delivery organizations
- The lack of both physical and systems integration among existing HI technologies and applications used in hospitals and other health agencies
- The lack of accepted standards in the HMIS software industry
- The lack of a theoretic framework for understanding the role that information technologies should actually play in the management of health service delivery and in the growth of the industry

Thus, although automation should prove itself to be an effective means of cost containment and quality improvement, there needs to be a follow-up analysis on how innovative planning, reassessment of rapid changes using available technologies, and better management of technology can optimize and realize the potential benefits of IT (see Chapter 5).

Over the past few years, many health institutions have simply ignored the need to eliminate data redundancies by implementing systems that focus only on the needs of departmental users. Cavanaugh comments that although these systems were beneficial to their specific users, many "islands of automation" resulted.[5] Figure 9–4 depicts the traditional structure of piecemeal HMIS development often resulting in systems fragmentation and duplication.

Stories about the shortsightedness of early IT solutions abound in almost every health organization. One example is a case involving a 448-bed acute-care hospital in Ontario that serves a community of 250,000 citizens.[6] In this hospital, approximately 198 personal computers (PCs) and 114 terminals in the hospitalwide information systems were found to operate basically on a "stand-alone" basis:

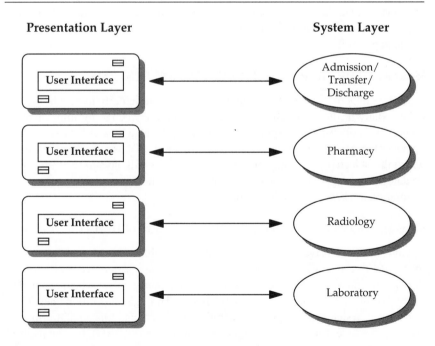

Figure 9–4 Islands of Automation. *Source:* Reprinted from Tan, J.K.H., and Hanna, J., Integrating Health Care with Information Technology, *Health Care Management Review*, Vol. 19, No. 2, p. 74, Aspen Publishers, Inc., © 1994.

instances of data sharing occurred infrequently and when they did, it was only among a few users who were connected to each other. Although senior management recognized the importance of better systems integration, the problem persisted. There was no policy for the adoption of software standards among various departmental end-users; specifically, there were four versions of Lotus being used, three different versions of WordPerfect, two versions of DBase, and a range of similar but noncompatible specialty software such as desktop publishing, form generators, and schedulers.

Another case involves a health care facility in British Columbia (BC), where an assortment of computer equipment had been acquired over the years but was largely unused. Despite the availability of computers, the internal tracking of patients in this facility was done entirely on paper to avoid the costly maintenance of the aging machines and the hiring of experts to handle them. As a further consequence, vital patient information could only be in one place at a time, and the attempt to integrate this paper-based tracking system into a larger network became an extremely frustrating, if not impossible, endeavor. From such a confined view and without any visionary recognition of IT potentials, it is not surprising to see that HMIS technologies and applications either stagnate in the hands of dissatisfied and sometimes unmotivated users or become an unmanageable and undirected paper mill.

RESTRUCTURING HEALTH INFORMATION SYSTEMS

As noted, there is a need to "do more with less," particularly in health services today. Many health organizations have risen to the challenge by implementing higher levels of systems integration. After having taken a look at the early development of systems integration, we will, in this section, discuss a few ways through which the objective of "doing more with less" can or will have to be met. In particular, the concepts of case management (CM), vertical integration, and clinical integration are key to achieving IS integration for health services.

Case-Mix Information Systems (C-MIS): The Dawn of HMIS Integration

More comprehensive integration started to be visible in health institutions as a more effective information sharing environment was encouraged and nurtured through the introduction in the 1980s of case-mix management, which resulted in a new HI integration in health service delivery. Through case-mix management information systems (C-MIS), the integration of clinical and financial information becomes possible. Case-mix, or diagnostic related groups (DRG), frequently used in the United States, refers to a hospital output expressed in terms of specific groups of patients who are considered to be relatively homogeneous in their consumption of resources. C-MIS integrate clinical and financial data because inpatient stays are categorized and grouped according to similar clinical characteristics and costs. Thus, by identifying bundles of goods and services delivered to each patient, it is possible to predict and control the use of resources. Overall, using the case-mix concept, major health administrative and managerial issues of access, quality, and cost can be addressed in a unified and more comprehensive manner because the integrated nature of data is captured in the system. Lichtig describes it as follows:

> Based on these groups of patients, utilization patterns among physicians in the hospital can be compared to identify patterns that are atypical. These atypical patterns can then be further evaluated through detailed case analyses to see whether there is really a problem with the quality of care or with proper utilization of hospital resources. . . . With such information hospital administrative and clinical managers can evaluate how their resources are being consumed, how they might better direct those resources, and, generally, how they can continue to provide high-quality care for the lowest possible cost.[7]

The key to a successful C-MIS is therefore the effective integration of clinical and financial information. Clinical information from the medical records department, billing information from the patient accounting department, and cost information from the finance department need to be merged into a single source.

Figure 9–5 provides a simple illustration of the integration of clinical and financial data that may be achieved with a single or multiple C-MIS. Note that in the figure, horizontal integration, which is characterized by the channeling of information between two or more health organizations, is also accomplished (interorganizational C-MIS). Various departments of the hospital provide raw data to the medical records department and the business office. Here the data are combined for use and made available to the C-MIS. From here, data may also be periodically forwarded from individual hospital systems to a multihospital system.

To examine the C-MIS data structure more closely, Figure 9–6 illustrates the merging of information from the various sources in a hospital. With C-MIS becoming a trend, some form of systems integration is already visible in many hospitals throughout the United States. The value of the information and analysis reports provided through such a system must still be evaluated in the long run. At this point, we turn to two concepts of integration: vertical and clinical integration.

Vertical Integration (VI): A Redesign of Health Service Organizations

In the late 1980s the concept of vertical integration (VI) was popularized.[8] Understanding the concept of a vertically integrated health service organization and the incentives involved in integration is important for understanding the transition to total systems integration. A vertically integrated health service organization

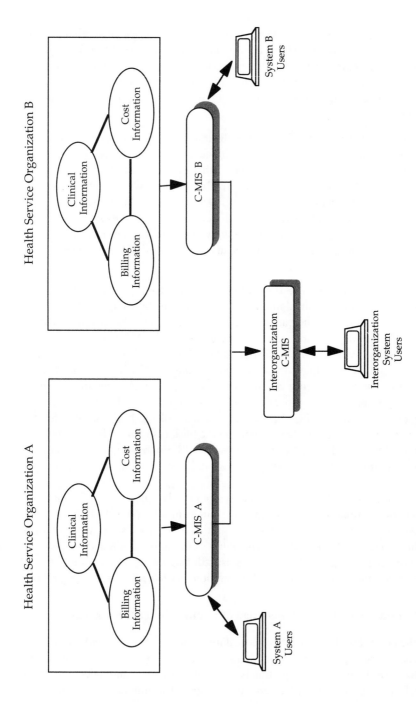

Figure 9–5 Overview of Information Flow into Case-Mix Information Systems (C-MIS). *Source:* Adapted with permission from Lichtig, L.K., *Hospital Information Systems for Case Mix Management*, John Wiley & Sons, Inc., © 1986.

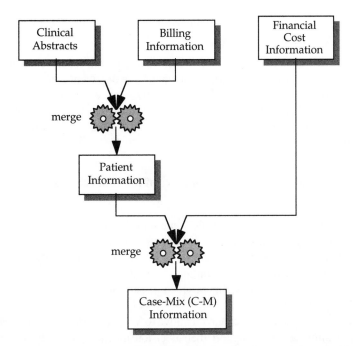

Figure 9–6 Ingredients of a Case-Mix Information System. *Source:* Adapted with permission from Lichtig, L.K., *Hospital Information Systems for Case Mix Management,* John Wiley & Sons, Inc., © 1986.

offers, directly or indirectly, through other health service facilities or agencies, a broad range of patient care services and support services in a comprehensive and functionally organized manner. The idea is similar to the idea of a value-added chain. For instance, a CM team of a health service delivery organization, consisting of a physician, a registered nurse, a physiotherapist, and an occupational therapist, may be put in place to take charge of the well-being of an inpatient. This is a result of VI. (In contrast, the fast channeling of information among the physicians or physiotherapists in different institutions concerning that patient is an example of horizontal integration.) Ideally, both production and transaction costs should be lowered as the time interval between consumption of various services is shortened in the vertically integrated chain.[9] The American Hospital Association has argued for three major gains to be accrued in the vertically integrated hospital:[10]

1. The forestalling of competitive physician activities
2. The admission of more qualified patients into inpatient units (enhanced referral of patients to appropriate care units)

3. The attraction of more ambulatory business to offset declining inpatient revenue

These gains can also be applicable to Canada. In the end, the principal aim of VI is to enhance the comprehensiveness and continuity of patient care while controlling the sources of patients and other users of the services. It has also marked the dawn of the development of a systems approach to health service delivery and the establishment of an organized delivery system (ODS) that is capable of offering a continuum of care.

Clinical Integration (CI): The Emergence of the Clinical Management Information System

More recently, the concept of clinical integration (CI) has been recognized as a necessary part of achieving VI.[11] The CI of patient care provides for the coordination of care for individual persons and for populations. This logically corresponds with VI and the development of a continuum of care. The implementation of more sophisticated systems such as clinical management information systems (CMIS) is now being studied.[12]

McMahon et al. note that despite the move to VI, administrators and physicians have little information to support their decision making.[13] In addition, the "islands" of information systems still exist and what is really needed is an information system that uses language that both administrators and physicians can understand. McMahon et al. further note, "Important data in a clinical management information system must be translated easily into cost center–based information for administration, and this same cost center–based financial information must be easily translated into specific clinically relevant descriptions for practicing physicians."[14]

Ultimately, the CMIS will have a merged database in which resource utilization and physician practice patterns can be recorded. Changes in resource utilization and practice over time can also be monitored. It is hoped that through identification, qualification, and comprehension of underlying clinical practices, clinical practice and the health service delivery system can be better managed. Thus, with the advent of new CMIS, clinical and administrative/financial data can be more closely integrated, and the development of systems integration and the health networks envisioned in the future should also be closer to reality.[15]

Telematics and Networking

As retail prices of hardware continue to drop and advances in telecommunications software (telematics) and networking continue, systems integration among health service organizations will become a reality. The importance of connectivity among hardware devices is of significance in the trend to move away from mainframe systems toward decentralized, integrated systems. The declining cost of microcomputers has enabled individual departments to operate independently and yet share data to reduce information redundancies. Recently, a fourth wave of technology, the communications software (telematics) and networking infrastructure, has arrived. Telematics is the use of computer-based information processing in telecommunications and the use of computer networks in the transfer of programs and data. "Networking" refers to the actual connections between the computer systems and their attached communication devices and computers. That is, it consists of the communication media, devices, and software (Chapter 7) needed to connect two or more computer systems. Telematics and networking are vital to the enhancement of overall systems integration.

DEVELOPMENT OF INTEGRATED SYSTEMS

Today, an important concern among HMIS analysts and hospital executives is the appropriate direction in which hospital information systems planning should be led. In a recent survey of hospital IS executives, Zinn indicated a trend toward the integration of hospital information systems.[16] Figure 9–7 shows that hospital networking by 1987 was already very prevalent in the United States.[17]

Faced with increasing competition, government regulations, and a strong need to have justifiable outcome measures or quality improvements, hospitals have been forced to rely on more complex information systems to keep them viable in the 1990s. As a result, most executives see systems integration as the key to developing successful health service delivery organizations of the future. Today, HMIS applications go beyond basic data processing and capitalize on advances in health telematics (telecommunications software and networking) to achieve systems integration and to enhance the quality of patient care beyond the limited benefits available from existing systems. The move toward integration of department and organizational data will have the widespread effect of making health services more accessible by eliminating various existing forms of communication barriers, including financial, functional, geographical, and technological barriers.

With continued advances and applications of IT in health service delivery, opportunities abound for health planners to apply concepts of systems integration and systems thinking to combining administrative and clinical patient care services to achieve a comprehensive continuum of care. New integrated HMIS will provide administrative and clinical decision support to both health service administrators and physicians. It is hoped that achieving systems integration through HMIS applications such as C-MIS and CMIS will connect the various subsystems in health service delivery in such a way as to reduce service redundancy and pro-

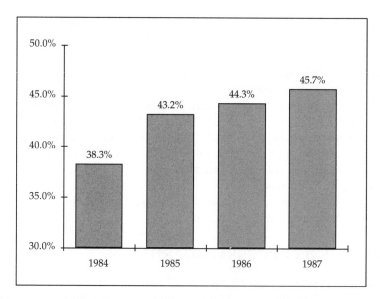

Figure 9–7 Percentage of U.S. Hospitals Belonging to Multihospital Information Systems. *Source:* American Hospital Association, *1989 Annual Report of the Section for Health Care Systems*, 1989.

vide for more coordinated, cost-effective care. Ultimately, systems integration will provide an ODS that will accomplish increased service efficiency and effectiveness while increasing quality and excellence of care (see Chapter 5).

Steps To Initiate Systems Integration

Hale predicted that automation of health service systems in the future will have to be both standards-based and distributed.[18] Being distributed means that the different systems, often on different platforms, will have to be able to communicate with each other. Our foregoing analysis (based on our experience with health service organizations) suggests the following four steps as being necessary to integrate health care systems and to achieve an effective information sharing environment that will allow systems integration:[19]

1. Physical networking of existing systems
2. Evolution to an "open system" platform
3. Adoption of software standards
4. Establishment of a management information technology infrastructure (MITI)

In the next few sections, we will discuss in some detail each of these aspects of systems integration and what health service executives, planners, and managers should know about the process of achieving total systems integration. In this era of rapid technological diffusion, the idea of total systems integration is truly becoming a reality.[20]

Networking Existing Systems

The trend in telecommunications technology is for more people to be able to communicate more information, over greater distances, at a faster rate (Chapter 7). Rapid communication reduces the amount of time individuals have to wait to get information they need to make business decisions. Donovan sees the acquisition and deployment of telecommunications capabilities as a starting point to network among existing information systems and argues for a three-tier implementation of connectivity standards throughout the organization—physical, systems, and applications.[21]

Figure 9–8 shows that physical connectivity is achieved by, first, ensuring hardware compatibility, then applying teleprocessing (TP) technology to link users' hardware and enable it to share common information processing capabilities, and, finally, maintaining the linkage through routine network management. Numerous types of telecommunications with a variety of costs and reliability are available today. Chapter 7 provided a detailed discussion on the subject. Here, it is appropriate to note that reductions in telecommunications costs and the use of private branch exchanges (PBX) have made local area networks (LAN) and wide area networks (WAN) viable solutions for many health service organizations. The recent development of a broad-band technology, known as an integrated services digital network (ISDN), shown in Figure 9–9, has promised to lead to standardized digital communications.[22]

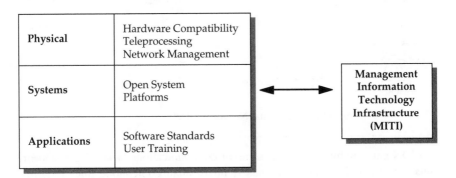

Figure 9–8 Key Elements Involved in Achieving Systems Connectivity. *Source:* Reprinted from Tan, J.K.H., and Hanna, J., Integrating Health Care with Information Technology, *Health Care Management Review*, Vol. 19, No. 2, p. 75, Aspen Publishers, Inc., © 1994.

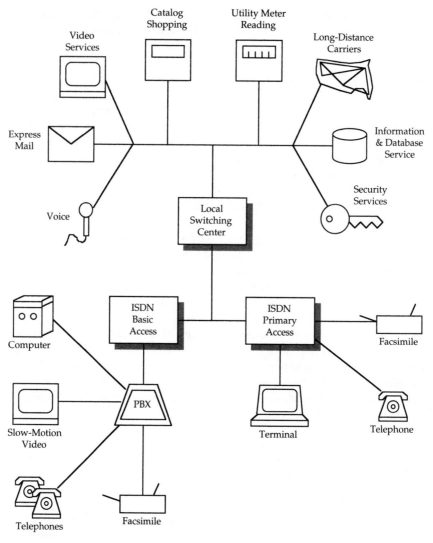

Figure 9–9 Integrated Services Digital Network (ISDN)

ISDN can combine different forms of communications (voice, data, and imaged) in the architecture. Whereas standard analog telephone lines require a modular-demodular (modem) to convert data from digital to analog, and vice versa, ISDN provides common carrier lines that are digital, and therefore conversion devices and procedures are not required. In addition, data can be transferred at significantly higher speeds. The main reason for merging voice and data is cost and management control. However, while maintenance costs may eventually be reduced, the initial costs of integrating voice and data are high. In addition, equipment incompatibilities and poor marketing by the carriers have limited the potential for ISDN's adoption.[23,24]

Parallel investment in the development and standardization of other high bandwidth switching technologies has also begun. Fiber distributed data interface (FDDI) is a shared connection LAN with a variable packet size. FDDI can transfer data at rates up to 100 million bits per second (mbps) compared to 56,000 bps for a standard business phone line. Asynchronous transfer mode (ATM) is the newest and fastest technology. ATM breaks data down into packets of uniform size (53 groups of 8 bits) that can be sent asynchronously (i.e., out of sequence); the packets are then reassembled in the proper sequence at the other end. This uniform cell size enables different platforms to talk. An ATM network can handle from 50 to 155 mbps. There is no definitive answer as to which technology is better. Currently, two advantages that the FDDI has over ATM are the lower prices and tested interoperability.[25] However, many FDDI users are intrigued by ATM's potential and plan to switch to ATM in the future.[26]

The Medical College of Georgia and SouthBell are using broad-band videoconferencing technology to enable specialists at the teaching hospital in Augusta, Georgia, to examine patients 130 miles away. Through sophisticated telemetry (e.g., electronic stethoscope, digitized X-rays, microscopy, and electrocardiography [ECG] and interactive video equipment, physicians at the Medical College of Georgia have actually heard heartbeats, studied X-rays and laboratory results, and peered down the throat of patients in rural hospitals without having actual physical contact with the patients. In its limited application to date, these video consultations have resulted in an 88 percent reduction of patient transfers from rural hospitals to the medical colleges.[27]

The telecommunications industry has invested heavily in digital switches and fiber optic transmission technology. Now that fiber optic transmission is becoming cost-competitive with copper wire transmission, it is being rushed into service. In 1992, the Science Council of Canada reported that 85 percent of Bell Canada's long-distance call trunks and 35 percent of its local lines are using digital technology all the way to the handset terminal.[28] Although many businesses already have the need for the bandwidth offered by ISDN, few residential subscribers would be willing to pay for such a service today. However, the future of ISDN depends on the fact that optical fiber not only allows present operations to be carried out faster, but also provides the opportunity for entirely new applications. These applications must be developed to take advantage of the power of high-speed networks for fulfilling business needs.

Paul Thiel, marketing manager at MPR Teltech, foresees the transfer of radiological images as an initial step in developing broad-band applications for the health sector.[29] He notes that the administration of radiological images is largely inefficient; for example, hospitals in the United States report that as many as 5 percent of X-ray images must be retaken as a result of being lost. Massachusetts General Hospital (MGH) has joined with NYNEX to offer a fiber optic network that transmits high-resolution patient images quickly (e.g., up to 45 mbps) for its main hospital in Boston and its various satellite centers. The savings have been considerable since MGH produces as many as 1,200 images a day.

Open Systems Architecture

Open systems architecture offers a solution to organizations that are sometimes locked into the technologies of the past. Instead of retaining systems that are poorly integrated, costly, difficult to maintain, and hard to change, open systems architecture provides flexibility that can lever investments to take advantage of both existing systems and new technologies. While an open systems solution may be difficult to obtain, it is critical that organizations understand the architecture and plans needed to advance to such a platform.

As there are two prototyping approaches discussed in Chapter 6, there are two basic approaches for adopting open systems: revolution and evolution. Not many organizations can afford to pull the plug on proprietary systems and build open systems from scratch. Often, there exists a large installed base of equipment that needs solutions varying from point-to-point connections to networking on an enterprisewide level.[30] Evolution appears to be the only logical and practical approach for existing systems in health services, especially those that have invested heavily in their current systems. However, for new systems, revolution—the selection of distributed client/server architecture that conforms to open systems protocols—would provide the most flexibility.

An example of the benefits of an open system has been demonstrated in Dallas, Texas. The Zale Lipsy University Hospital, a 160-bed private teaching hospital, selected a standards-based distributed architecture anchored by a fiber optic Ethernet backbone that interconnects a variety of multivendor departmental systems. The distributed architecture allows care providers and administrators, using one of 150 workstations, access to data and image networking on radiology (teleradiology), pharmacy, and patient records systems. Based on a Health Level 7 (HL 7) technology, the distributed architecture gives the hospital departments the flexibility to implement information systems that meet their needs and allow employees to access any type of information (see also Chapter 7). The fiber Ethernet backbone supports five Hewlett Packard (HP) file servers running 3+Open LAN Manager and a clinical management application from Quantitative Medicine Inc. (QMI). The QMI software compiles clinical data as well as data from other departmental systems, and presents them in a standard format to users working at HP Vectra workstations. The open systems architecture project took less than a year to complete and cost $3 million.[31] George Horne, a consultant with George Horne

Associates, noted that the success of this project can be attributed to the commitment of the CEO, who had a vision of an electronic medical record.

Keen notes that incompatibility is the bane of integration.[32] Eventually, when widespread standards are established, the ultimate "open system" will allow access to any data, on any computer, from any database. Obviously, this would facilitate the flow of more complete information with the least effort and expense necessary to provide the integration of networks that will work together. The result of such a system would be the availability of information through a common interface, thereby making all the heterogeneous systems act as one homogenous system for the end-user.[33] Figure 9–10 illustrates the structure of an integrated hospital information system that uses an open systems architecture. The connectivity of the different platforms implies a need for using organizationalwide standard software.

Software Standards

In light of rapid changes, new technological and organizational ground rules need to be set for health service organizations that aspire to be at the forefront of technology. For example, the need for enterprisewide distributed processing is becoming more important to support the flow of information horizontally, vertically, and between organizations. Horizontal (interdepartmental) flow of information in real time is prerequisite to providing quality care and is a basis for the measurement of that care. Conflicts in procedural scheduling and drug-to-drug interactions are two examples of ways that poor or inadequate interdepartmental

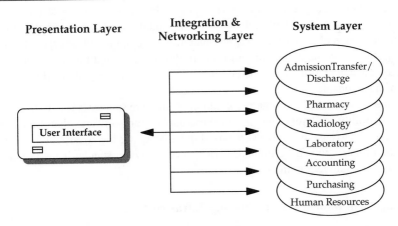

Figure 9–10 Integrated Hospital Information System. *Source:* Reprinted from Tan, J.K.H., and Hanna, J., Integrating Health Care with Information Technology, *Health Care Management Review*, Vol. 19, No. 2, p 74, Aspen Publishers, Inc., © 1994.

communication affect the quality of care. In addition, vertical flow of information is critical to satisfying institutional goals and providing timely, relevant information for decision making. For example, administrators require information from the admission-discharge-transfer (ADT) system in order to analyze utilization rates for strategic planning and resource allocation decision making. From a competitive advantage standpoint, information is being shared between organizations in the customer-supplier relationship in order to reduce costs. A classic example of this interorganizational information sharing is the line order-entry system developed by American Hospital Supply.[34] Such electronic data interchange (EDI) capabilities are beginning to appeal to the health service industry because of their ability to ensure the timeliness and integrity of information that is captured within the system.

Without standards, taking the path to any integrated approach to information systems has proved to be a costly venture; indeed, the absence of standards has slowed the adoption of IT in the health sector.[35] Most health care technology environments are made up of heterogeneous applications. Multihealth service organizations (i.e., corporations) face unique challenges in providing information services for all of their entities. For example, they must consider corporate philosophy, geography, and computing configurations and determine whether their HMIS approach capitalizes on centralized economies of scale or on regional flexibility and control.

Software standards facilitate the integration of resources and ensure compatibility. These standards promote communications and the sharing of data, thereby reducing data redundancy. Software standards have to be set for operating systems, database management systems, and user applications. In addition, standards must encompass programming issues such as the languages used, the structure of codes, the naming of variables, documentation, and the verification of data. With the proliferation of easy-to-use fourth-generation programming languages (Chapter 7), it has become easier for end-users to develop personal programs, but the lack of documentation and transferability makes the real benefits of these programs questionable.

In the short term, good strategy for adopting software standards is to reduce the incompatibility (different vendors) of these application softwares that are being run, and then to ensure that the versions of those programs are consistent throughout the organization. By eliminating variety of software, standards also reduce end-user training requirements.

Management Information Technology Infrastructure

The challenge in selecting a management information technology infrastructure (MITI) is in forming an overall plan to interconnect and reconcile the ever evolving perspectives of general management, the HMIS department, and user groups. Holloran notes that "this technical infrastructure design process for an organization is one of the most important activities IS departments can undertake in providing the enterprise with an enabling infrastructure."[36]

IT can provide opportunities for, and impose constraints on, the design of infrastructure. Opportunities exist in using technology in ways new to the organization. Constraints are those aspects of existing technology infrastructure that limit the possibilities for innovation that cannot be changed in the relevant time frame. It is no longer acceptable to take a laissez-faire attitude to establishing an organization's MITI. Organizational culture and the strategic role of IT should be explicitly considered. To prepare the organization for growth and maturation in HMIS for the future, management must clearly provide three primary functions.[37]

1. Direction
2. Support
3. Control

Direction focuses on discovering and evaluating cutting-edge technology to improve organizational competitiveness or service excellence. Support focuses on providing the necessary technical assistance to end-users to interconnect the various user groups with common technology and on empowering them with accessible information and knowledge. Control provides a means of standardization and integration toward universal compatibility and a means of control of wasteful replication of end-user programming efforts.

In the end, it is the user and the operational unit that ultimately decide on the need and appropriateness of IT. Thus, innovation lies not only in the domain of the HMIS staff but also in the domain of users. Conflicts often arise when users strive to fulfill short-term needs at the expense of orderly long-term HMIS development. In transferring technology between users who lack the vision of a unified purpose for the organization, a loss of competitive leverage and integration anticipated of that technological transfer will result. This brings us to the topic of barriers to integration.

Barriers to Systems Integration

If we are to ascertain that the path to total systems integration is a straight one, we then must identify, understand, and deal with the barriers that may be encountered in the process. System integration in health service is still a dream of many health service organizations and reformers. Despite rapid advances in networking capabilities and telecommunications, health informatics, and telematics, many obstacles still need to be overcome before systems integration can become a reality. Shortell et al. have identified eight major barriers that will have a profound influence on the adoption of IT that will facilitate the development of an ODS and its corresponding HMIS.[38]

1. Failure to understand the changes that are occurring in health care (i.e., the shift from acute care and the need to provide a continuum of care to patients)

2. Inability to look beyond the hospital setting (i.e., community and systemwide issues)

3. Inability to convince hospitals with their own money to accept systemwide strategies (i.e., hospitals with money will continue to invest in their own capital projects as long as they have the ability to fund them)

4. Inability of the hospital board to understand the new health care environment and their responsibilities

5. Ambiguous roles and responsibilities of health service managers throughout the system (i.e., operating unit managers often fail to understand their role in the overall evolving system)

6. Inability to "manage" managed care (i.e., operating units are confused about their respective roles in the strategy)

7. Inability to execute the integration strategy (i.e., there is a general unwillingness to focus on a core strategy because it might constrain a given unit's choices or autonomy)

8. Lack of strategic alignment (i.e., resources are misallocated and managers are confused about what the real strategy is)

The development of a new management culture will help to address many of these barriers. In addition, advances in telecommunication software and networking will facilitate the development of the integrated HMIS, which will in turn see the establishment of total systems integration in our health service delivery industry.

An HMIS is a tool and its value depends on how we plan for it and how we use it. Properly employed, an HMIS can play a strategic role in supporting staff and can make the difference between mediocre and excellent service. Walton, in *Up and Running: Integrating Information Technology and the Organization,* suggested that IT strategy must be compatible with both organizational strategy and business strategy.[39] That is to say, executives can no longer segregate the management of IT from the management of their hospitals.

CONCLUSION

There will be many challenges in the future when integrating HMIS. Keen notes that we will need more empirical research to measure the impact of telecommunications on organizational effectiveness.[40] We do not yet know how to measure the value of a telecommunications infrastructure. As in other industries, the movement in health services to adopting unified standards for communications and data exchange is progressing painstakingly because of what it takes to merge them into a unified whole. Fortunately, major progress in interconnecting heterogeneous computer systems and applications is being made.

Case-mix information systems (C-MIS) were among the first new "waves" in the integration of information systems in health care services. Today, new systems such as clinical management information systems (CMIS) that vertically integrate administrative and clinical information systems are being developed. Total systems integration and the health networks of the future will eventually be achieved when the complete range of subsystems in health services can be effectively integrated and linked (see Chapter 14). Ideally, the completely integrated system will be able to give health service providers access to information when and where they need it and to do so in a manner that minimizes training and expense, while maximizing efficiency, effectiveness, and quality of care.

CHAPTER QUESTIONS

1. What is systems integration in the health care setting? What is its significance?
2. Name some early examples of applications of information technology in systems integration.
3. What are case-mix information systems (C-MIS)? What are their functions? How do they differ from clinical management information systems (CMIS)?
4. What are other recent technological applications in systems integration? What are their advantages over those from earlier generations?
5. Describe in detail the steps that can be taken in implementing an integrated information system in the health service delivery industry.
6. State six barriers to systems integration in the health service settings and suggest solutions.

MINI CASE 9
THE NEED FOR AN INTEGRATED HMIS NORTH OF
THE ARCTIC CIRCLE

The town of Inuvik is located on the east channel of the Mackenzie River Delta, about 97 km south of the Beaufort Sea, in the Northwest Territories. The Inuvik Region covers a vast geographic area of approximately 118,000 square miles.

Eleven health centers located in the various communities of the Inuvik Region and a regional hospital situated in Inuvik form the region's total health organization.

The region's health organization serves a diverse population comprising Dene, Metis, Inuit, and nonnative peoples, which totals about 8,000. Access to the communities, with the exception of two that can be reached by roads, is possible only by air. During the winter months when temperatures plummet and the Mackenzie River freezes, an ice road is constructed to give road access to two other communities. The communities in the Inuvik Region range in size from Colville Lake, with a population of 50 people, to Inuvik, which is home to about 2,800 people.

The Inuvik Regional Hospital (IRH) serves as a general hospital for acute and chronic care patients for the town of Inuvik and as a referral center for the entire Inuvik Region. The hospital has an approved complement of 72 beds, with 52 beds currently staffed and in operation. Major services include general medicine, general surgery, obstetrics and maternity care, pediatrics, long-term care, radiology, laboratory, pharmacy, physiotherapy, occupational therapy, and community health promotion services.

All services are provided on an inpatient, outpatient, or emergency basis. Additional specialized services and procedures are undertaken by visiting specialists or referred to an appropriate center. The total staff complement includes approximately 200 people working at the hospital and another 30 working in the health center.

In the mid-1980s, with technology advancing and resources shrinking, the senior management of the IRH felt a strong need to streamline operations. Large amounts of paper flowing through the hospital and the constant scrambling of managers to assemble reports were indicative of an inability to collect and organize information in a manner necessary for staff to carry out their responsibilities effectively. The duplication of procedures in various departments lowered the level of efficiency and needed to be addressed.

Health management information systems could provide the solution by enabling staff members to gather, manipulate, and extract data in a more timely and efficient manner, and either reduce or eliminate duplication of procedures. Sixteen stand-alone (not linked) personal computers using mainly WordPerfect and Lotus were addressing some of the office automation needs but were not a solution for the major issues at hand.[41]

MINI CASE QUESTIONS

Given that you are an HMIS expert asked to develop a completely integrated health service information system for the Inuvik Region, your job is to see that the health organization is able to achieve its goal of an integrated health information system. Address the following questions, assuming that you are speaking with people who are unaware of information technology and the advantages of the latest telecommunications software.

1. Imagine that you are back in the mid-1980s and the Inuvik Regional Health Organization is granted full funding of the development of a modern management information system. Devise a framework for this health management information system. Justify your design by stating the system's ultimate goal and how it is to be achieved and by tailoring the design to the environment of the region.

2. What are some of the problems in communications in places like the Inuvik Region? How would an integrated HMIS be designed to overcome these problems?

3. What are some of the specific benefits of systems integration over the present paper-based system?

4. What support has to be in place in each facility to ensure that the total integration of all the systems is ensured?

5. What is the importance of case-mix management in the development of this new information system?

CHAPTER REVIEW

This chapter discussed the importance of integrating health care with information technology to improve the efficiency, effectiveness, quality of patient care, and innovativeness of health service institutions. The importance of planning for achieving technological integration in health service organizations is emphasized. It is argued that in addition to networking and selecting a distributed client/server architecture that conforms to open systems protocols, adopting standards and establishing a management information infrastructure would provide the necessary steps and mechanisms to allow for a smoother transition to greater sophistication in the development of total systems integration. Case-mix information systems are monitored as among the first "waves" of integration that have occurred in some hospitals through the integration of clinical and financial information, followed by clinical management information systems and the latest "wave" of technological advancements in health informatics, telematics, and networking.

NOTES

1. M.D. McDonald and H.L. Blum, *Health in the Information Age: The Emergence of Health Oriented Telecommunication Applications* (Berkeley, Calif: Environmental Science and Policy Institute, 1992): 25.

2. D.A. Conrad, Coordinating Patient Services in Regional Health Systems: The Challenge of Clinical Integration, *Hospital & Health Services Administration* 38, no. 4 (Winter 1993): 491–508.

3. L.F. McMahon, Jr., et al., The Integrated Inpatient Management Model's Clinical Management Information System, *Hospital and Health Services Administration* 39, no. 1 (Spring 1994): 81–92.

4. E.H. Shortliffe and L.E. Perreault, eds., *Medical Information Computer Applications in Health Care* (Reading, Mass: Addison-Wesley Publishing Co., Inc. 1990): 4–5.

5. F. Cavanaugh, Information Architecture: Bridging the Islands, *Computers in Healthcare* (November 1991): 41–42.

6. M. Hurwicz, FDDI: Not Fastest But Still Fit, *Datamation* 1 (April 1993): 31–36.

7. L.K. Lichtig, *Hospital Information Systems and Case Mix Management* (New York: John Wiley & Sons, Inc., 1986): 4–5.

8. C. Doremus, Can Telecommunications Help Solve America's Health Care Problems? *Arthur D. Little, Inc. Corporate Communication Report* (Cambridge, Mass: 1992).

9. Science Council of Canada, *Sectoral Technology Strategy Series: The Canadian Telecommunications Sector,* DSS cat. no. S525-1 (1992): 2–17.

10. J.K.H. Tan and J. Hanna, Integrating Health Care with Information Technology: Knitting Patient Information through Networking, *Health Care Management Review* 19, no. 2 (1994): 72–80.

11. Conrad, Coordinating Services, 491–508.

12. McMahon, Information System, 81–92.

13. L.F. McMahon, et al., The Integrated Inpatient Management Model: A New Approach to Clinical Practice, *Annals of Internal Medicine* 111 (August 1989): 318–326.

14. McMahon, et al., Information System, 82.

15. Ibid.

16. T.K. Zinn, Healthcare I/S Executives Look toward the Next Decade, *Computers in Health Care* (February 1992): 32–39.

17. American Hospital Association, 1989 Annual Report of Section for Health Care Systems (Chicago: 1989).

18. P. Hale, Tactical Considerations for HIS Strategy, *Computers in Healthcare* (October 1989): 39–40.

19. Tan and Hanna, Integrating Health Care with Information Technology.

20. J. Dearden, MIS Is a Mirage, *Harvard Business Review* 50, no. 1 (January/February 1972): 90–99.

21. J. Donovan, Beyond Chief Information Officer to Network Manager, *Harvard Business Review* (September/October 1988): 134–140.

22. W. Denzel, High-Speed ATM Switching, *IEEE Communications* (February 1993): 26.

23. T. Cross, ISDN: Under Construction, *Infoworld* 13 (January 1992): 64– 66.

24. V. Lai, et al., ISDN: Adoption and Diffusion Issues, *Information Systems Management* (Fall 1993): 46–52.

25. Hurwicz, FDDI: Not Fastest But Still Fit.

26. S. Kerr, ATM: Ultimate Network, or Ultimate Hype? *Datamation* 1 (April 1993): 30–34.

27. Doremus, Can Telecommunications Help?

28. Science Council of Canada, *Sectoral Technology,* 2–17.

29. Interview with Paul M. Thiel, Marketing Manager of MPR Teltech, Ltd. (Part of the British Columbia Tel Group) (Burnaby: March 10, 1973).

30. C. Dunbar, The Networking Standards Evolution: Toward a Real Electronic Medical Record, *Computers in Healthcare* (February 1990): 18–21.

31. W. Eckerson, Hospital Hopes HL7-Based Net Will Ensure Versatility, *Network World* 20 (August 1990): 19–20.

32. P. Keen, *Shaping the Future: Business Design through Information Technology* (Boston: Harvard Business School Press, 1991).

33. G. Wu, et al., Multilink—an Intermediary System for Multi-Database Access, *Methods of Information in Medicine* 32, no. 1 (1993): 82–87.

34. D. Moriarty, Strategic Information Systems Planning for Health Service Providers, *Health Care Management Review* (Winter 1992): 85–90.

35. W. Mougayar, Information Technology: Communications Standards in Healthcare, *Healthcare Computing and Communications* (April 1992): 38–42.

36. J. Holloran, Achieving World-Class End-User Computing, *Information Systems Management* (Fall 1993): 7–12.

37. M. Alavi, et al., Managing End-User Computing as a Value-Added Resource, *Journal of Information Systems Management* (Summer 1988): 26–35.

38. S.M. Shortell, et al., Creating Organized Delivery Systems: The Barriers and Facilitators, *Hospital and Health Services Administration* (Winter 1993): 447–466.

39. R. Walton, *Up and Running: Integrating Information Technology and the Organization* (Boston: Harvard Business School Press, 1989).

40. Keen, *Shaping the Future.*

41. Adapted from *Healthcare Computing & Communications* 6, no. 3 (April 1992): 30–35.

Part IV

Placing the Capstones on Health Management Information Systems: HMIS Administration and Impacts

Chapter 10

HMIS Strategic Planning: Facing the Challenges of a Turbulent Health Care Environment

LEARNING OBJECTIVES

1. Define strategic information systems planning (SISP).
2. Formulate a "framework" for HMIS strategic planning.
3. Realize the significance of aligning health service organizational goals and objectives with health management information systems goals and objectives strategically.
4. Relate SISP to information requirements.
5. Identify appropriate methodologies to elicit information requirements (IR) for HMIS prioritization and implementation.
6. Conceptualize a state-of-the-art management information technology infrastructure (MITI).

INTRODUCTION

Pitfall One, or, "You can't drive a car without a driver."
Pitfall Two, or, "You can't start unless everyone is in the car."
Pitfall Three, or, "The plan as an end in itself."
Pitfall Four, or, "The road without milestones."
Pitfall Five, or, "Allowing assumptions to become facts."
Pitfall Six, or, "You can't drive the car in five different directions at once."
Pitfall Seven, or, "Conflicting hopes with objectives."
Pitfall Eight, or, "You can't drive to San Francisco in one day and you can't drive to London at all."

301

Pitfall Nine, or, "When you give out the rewards, make sure you know what the rewards are for."
Pitfall Ten, or, "You can't drive the car all by yourself."[1]

Among the most perplexing challenges facing health service chief executive officers (CEOs) and managers in today's rapidly changing health care environment are the tasks of planning and achieving the long-term success of their hospitals or health service organizations. This challenge demands that the skills and ability of health service CEOs be intelligently used to recognize the new environmental threats and opportunities, to seize the competitive initiatives, and to manage the organizational change processes needed to counterbalance these environmental changes. Today, and more so in the future, health management information systems (HMIS) should no longer be viewed simply as tools to automate and assist an organization in achieving its efficiency and effectiveness goals and objectives, but should be regarded more as the engine for the long-term growth and strategic survival of the organization.

This chapter discusses the importance of developing a strategic information systems plan (SISP) for the deployment of an organization's HMIS strategies and the establishment of its HMIS infrastructure. Its primary goal is to demonstrate the need for aligning HMIS planning with the health service organization's overall goals and objectives strategically. As information is the key resource for supporting strategic management and decision making, various information elicitation techniques are also covered. However, before we turn our attention to formulating a general framework for corporate-HMIS strategic alignment, it is useful for us to revisit the concept of SISP and its evolution in the context of today's health service delivery industry.

WHAT IS STRATEGIC INFORMATION SYSTEMS PLANNING?

As with many other areas in the HMIS field, the concept of SISP and its evolution arise chiefly from theories and experiences in the private business sector. Organizations have increasingly been turning their attention to opportunities for achieving "competitive advantages" through information systems technology (IST). This new phenomenon may be attributed to several key forces.

- Economic conditions, which include factors such as long-term inflationary pressures and high interest rates
- Structural changes in the economy that are caused by global competition
- New information technology economics, for example, telecommunications and network cost performance[2]

Other environmental forces such as changes in population, demographics, and legal and social factors have already been discussed earlier (see Chapter 3 through 6).

In light of today's economic climate of fiscal restraints,[3,4] SISP may be considered one of the most fundamental tasks that a health service organization CEO and HMIS executive can perform together to achieve desired strategic positioning of the organization. The challenge for SISP is to demonstrate how IST and related technology can make the greatest contributions to the efficient and effective conduct of the business concerns of a health service organization. Although it mainly entails conceptual work that must inevitably be poorly defined as opposed to well-structured operational activities, SISP gives the HMIS manager the opportunity to recognize broad initiatives, prioritize commitments, and identify those hardware applications and software technologies that will help the health service organization carry out its current business strategy more successfully.[5,6] SISP also provides the organization with means to identify opportunities to use IST to create new business strategies and the chance to develop a vision of IST that has the highest potential to contribute to organizational success.

Before we go any further, we need to answer a fundamental question: What is SISP? Lederer and Gardiner define SISP as "the process of identifying a portfolio of computer-based applications that will assist an organization in executing its business plans and realizing its business goals."[7]

For health service organizations, HMIS strategic planning is therefore needed to guide the use of IST as a competitive "safeguard" for future organizational growth and survival.[8] As health service organizations have become increasingly vertically integrated in recent years (see Chapter 9), the need to develop cutting-edge, institutionwide information systems for strategic decision making has become paramount. The rapidly changing health care climate has fostered new incentives for the development of organizational strategies that reach far beyond the traditional service efficiency mission statements still relied upon by many hospital and other health service CEOs. Today, health service CEOs are paying more attention to developing innovative programs and making strategic decisions about future directions. This then requires a general conceptualization of the target areas of the HMIS strategic planning process.

In order to achieve effective HMIS administration and management, Earl notes that a well-designed SISP should target the following four areas:[9]

1. Aligning investments in IST with corporate goals
2. Exploiting various aspects of IST for service excellence
3. Achieving efficient and effective management of IST resources
4. Developing IST policies and procedures

Briefly, the first two areas are the topics of this chapter (HMIS strategic planning), the third is discussed in Chapter 11 (Health Information Resource Management), and the last in Chapter 12 (Health Management Information System Implementation).

A FRAMEWORK FOR HMIS STRATEGIC PLANNING AND ALIGNMENT

In terms of our foregoing discussion, CEOs and HMIS managers need to address several critical questions during the SISP process.[10,11]

- How can IST be used to generate new health services in response to new market demands?
- How can IST be used to distinguish among services provided by the organization from those of other organizations; for example, how can IST enhance the quality of services provided by one's organization?
- What is the emerging IST that will be critical to one's organizational strategy?
- What supporting HMIS applications and infrastructure are needed to make the new strategy work?
- How does one induce health service organizational end-users (e.g., physicians, nurses) who will directly benefit from IST to use it?

The underlying philosophy of HMIS strategic planning is that the type of management information technology infrastructure (MITI) in place will determine the organization's ability to support the type of business functions and processes encountered in health service delivery. In turn, the design of an organization's business functions and processes should determine the necessary information needed to support the business goals and strategies.

A number of techniques can be and have been used to facilitate the HMIS strategic planning process. However, one problem that frequently occurs is knowing which specific technique to use in the wide flow of activities for developing a long-range HMIS plan and for establishing a long-lasting management information technology infrastructure (MITI). Figure 10–1 shows a top-down (hierarchical) stages planning model that can be used as a general framework to guide HMIS strategic planning, design, and development. This framework is consistent with and extends that of Bowman, Davis, and Wetherbe.[12]

A fundamental concept of HMIS strategic planning is that the organization's strategic plan should be the basis for the HMIS strategic plan.[13] However, the alignment of HMIS strategies with corporate strategies is often overlooked in health service organizational HMIS strategic planning. In many cases, HMIS planning occurs in isolation from the organization's strategic plan; the result is that top management lacks appropriate information for making strategic decisions and solving problems effectively.[14] In a recent study, Dunbar and Schmidt observed that the majority of U.S. hospitals' current strategic plans applied only 5 to 10 percent to HMIS planning.[15] In order to ensure the survival of health service

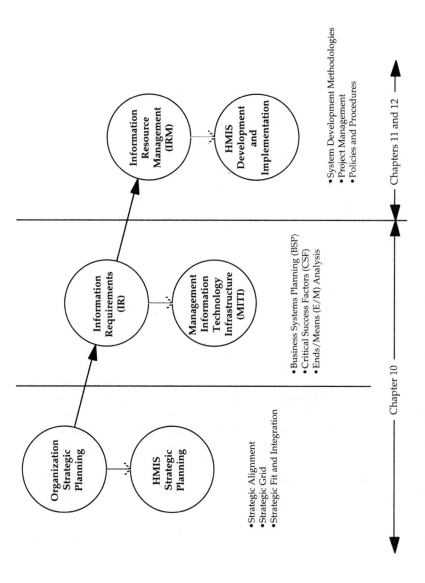

Figure 10–1 A Framework for HMIS Strategic Planning: A Top-Down Stages Planning Model

organizations in the 1990s, they recommend that at least 35 percent of the total strategic plan include tie-ins with information system plans.

The framework presented in Figure 10–1 helps to clarify the generic planning activities, the order of activities, and the alternative techniques, methodologies, and strategies that are applicable at each stage. It can be used to aid HMIS planners to recognize the nature of planning problems in a health service organization as well as to select the appropriate stage of planning to move the health organization forward in terms of HMIS strategic planning. In any case, it is important that strategic alignment exists between the organizational and HMIS goals and objectives and that such an alignment precedes the elicitation of information requirements, the design and development of MITI, and the implementation of actual HMIS applications.[16] In the following section we focus on strategic alignment, the first stage of this HMIS strategic planning framework.

As noted, one of the first and most critical steps in HMIS strategic planning is the strategic alignment of goals between senior management and information systems people within a health service organization or agency. Essentially, this has three implications.

1. The integration of IS group's mission with health service organization's core vision

2. A fitting of IS culture with organizational culture

3. The alignment of IS management philosophy with organizational philosophy

Henderson and Thomas suggested that strategic alignment means more than linking IS strategies to organizational strategies.[17] While they concur that such a linkage is necessary to achieve congruency between the HMIS and the organizational plans, they argue that it alone is inadequate to ensure success. Technology, structures, processes, and skills must also "be fitted to match this integration."

As shown in Figure 10–2, corporate-HMIS strategic planning and adjustment can be achieved through the use of the following techniques: (1) strategic grid, which is a diagnostic tool that will assist in positioning the health organization in the external marketplace and in clarifying the potential role of current and future HMIS in the internal workplace; (2) strategic fit, which refers to the requirement of aligning or integrating strategy formulation and implementation between top management and HMIS groups; and (3) strategic integration, which refers to the requirement of integrating HMIS strategy with organization strategy and integrating IST functions with other line and functional areas of the health service organization.

The McFarlan-McKenney Strategic Grid

One contingency approach that has been widely used in identifying the strategic impact of HMIS development in a health service organization is the McFarlan-

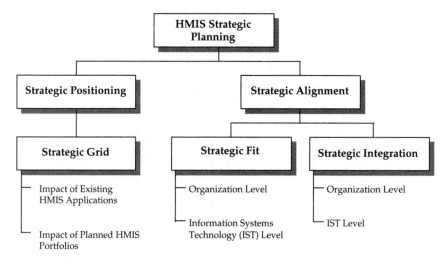

Figure 10–2 Corporate-HMIS Strategic Planning and Alignment

McKenney strategic grid.[18] This grid defines four types of HMIS planning situations that depend on the strategic impact of the existing information systems application portfolio and the strategic impact of the portfolio of applications planned for development. Table 10–1 illustrates the categorization of these four positions in terms of HMIS activities relative to the functioning of a health service organization.

1. HMIS support applications
2. HMIS factory applications
3. HMIS turnaround applications
4. HMIS strategic applications

HMIS support applications are those traditional applications that are useful in supporting the activities of the health service organization such as data processing systems (DPS). The IS activities for these systems are not "vital" to critical operations and are not included as part of future strategic directions. Traditional DPS applications such as stand-alone administrative and clinical systems, patient registry systems, clinical data storage, and retrieval systems are examples of a portfolio emphasizing the "support" category. These systems were discussed in Chapter 4.

HMIS factory applications are vital to the successful functioning of well-defined, well-accepted activities. However, IS activities are not part of future strategic operations. Examples of HMIS applications in this category will include many existing hospitalwide administrative and clinical systems that are still linked to traditional technologies such as the admission-discharge-transfer (ADT) systems,

Table 10–1 The McFarlan-McKenney Strategic Grid for HMIS Planning

SI-EOAP	SI-PADP	Position in Grid	Examples of HMIS Applications	Involvement of Top Management
Low	Low	Support HMIS	• Stand-Alone DPS • Class A HIS	Little involvement from top management but delegated authority to HMIS managers on priority of projects and daily supervision. Regular reporting is necessary.
High	Low	Factory HMIS	• Radiology System • ADT Pharmacy System	May delegate all supervisory responsibilities to the HMIS managers. Get periodic reporting.
Low	High	Turnaround HMIS	• C-MIS • CMIS	Leadership from top management is required.
High	High	Strategic HMIS	• EDI Applications	Top management assumes role of visionary and leadership.

ADT: admission discharge transfer
C-MIS: case-mix information system
CMIS: clinical management information system
DPS: data processing systems
EDI: electronic data interchange

HIS: hospital information system
HMIS: health management information system
SI-EOAP: strategic impact of existing operating applications portfolio
SI-PADP: strategic impact of planned application development portfolio (future-oriented)

facility equipment management systems, and materials management system (MMS) on the administrative side, and laboratory systems, health record management system (HRMS), pharmacy, and radiology systems on the clinical side. These systems were discussed in Chapters 3 through 7.

HMIS turnaround applications represent a transition state from "support" to "strategic." The organization has had support-type applications but is now planning for applications vital to the strategic success of the organization. These are HMIS implementations that are capable of integrating administrative and clinical information, for example, the case-mix information system (C-MIS) and the clinical management information systems (CMIS) discussed in Chapter 9. Another example is ES, which has been discussed in Chapter 8.

HMIS strategic applications are critical to the current competitive strategy and to future directions of the health service organization. HMIS applications falling in this category are part of new strategic directions. ES and robotics (Chapter 8) can be classified into this category. Other prime examples are group decision support systems (GDSS) and electronic data interchange (EDI) systems such as hospital-physician linkage systems and other future-oriented telecommunication systems discussed in Chapter 14.

Put together, the McFarlan-McKenney strategic grid argues that HMIS planners can analyze current and planned portfolios to change directions in HMIS strategy. Table 10–1 also shows how the position of IS in the grid can be used to explain the needed level of top management involvement and to highlight the relationship of the IS plan and the organizational plan.[19]

Henderson's Strategic Fit and Integration

"Strategy" refers to the positioning of the health service organization in the external marketplace (corporate strategy) or the IST marketplace (HMIS strategy). "Infrastructure" refers to internal arrangements of the organization (corporate infrastructure) or IST structure, processes, and skills (HMIS infrastructure) necessary to execute this strategic positioning. Figure 10–3 depicts two different levels of strategies and infrastructures. The top level reflects the corporate level strategy and infrastructure and the bottom level depicts the corresponding strategy and infrastructure for the IST level.

The HMIS strategy parallels the corporate strategy as it is defined in terms of the external marketplace. Thus just as top management strategy defines the position of the organization in the health service delivery (i.e., corporate business) marketplace, the HMIS strategy defines the position of the organization in the IST marketplace. Analogously, the IST infrastructure parallels the organization infrastructure in the sense that it is defined in terms of actions, events, and interactions that occur internally. For a health service organization, the IST infrastructure

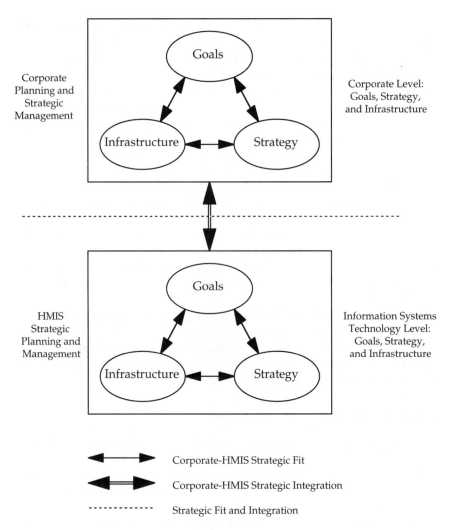

Figure 10–3 A Strategic Fit and Integration Model between Corporate and Information System Technology (IST) Levels

therefore reflects the internal arrangements of the IST functions necessary to execute the HMIS strategy, for example, how the architectures, processes, and skills are acquired and organized to attain the HMIS goals and objectives.

Figure 10–3 shows two types of strategic alignments: strategic fit and strategic integration. In the broader organization context, strategic fit involves the alignment of corporate goals, strategy, and infrastructure to position it in the health service marketplace. At the IST context, the corresponding strategic fit entails the alignment of HMIS goals, strategy, and infrastructure to position the organization in the external IT marketplace. Therefore, the questions to be asked at the corporate level include the following:

- What business niche do we want to occupy in the health service marketplace?
- Do our goals and objectives reflect this strategy?
- How do we set up the appropriate mechanisms (infrastructure) to execute this strategy?

The same questions can be asked in the context of the IST marketplace with regard to HMIS goals, strategy, and infrastructure. Altogether, strategic fit involves aligning health service organization and HMIS strategy formulation and implementation at either the corporate or IST level.

The other type of corporate-HMIS strategic alignment is strategic integration, which may again be conceptualized at two levels. The first level is between corporate strategy and HMIS strategy, and the second level is the corresponding integration between the corporate infrastructure and the IST infrastructure.

The corporate level of strategic integration is concerned with the integration between the positions of a health service organization in the health service marketplace and the IST arena. Henderson and Thomas argue that an appropriate alignment between these two strategies is a fundamental requirement for realizing the value of HMIS investments.[20] Realigning HMIS positioning in the IST marketplace strategically, such as adopting EDI technology to match the vision and positioning of the health service organization as a leader in automated patient care, exemplifies strategic integration at this level.

In general, if the organization has a strategic plan that concretely reflects the organization's goals, objectives, and strategies, the HMIS goals, objectives, and strategies can be directly derived from it. Each objective, goal, and strategy in the plan is analyzed for required information system support, which can then be organized into HMIS goals, objectives, and strategies. For example, if one goal of a hospital's strategic plan is to maintain information on and monitor the changes in the demographic profile of the neighboring communities, the derived goal for the HMIS plan may be to provide an automated geographic information system (GIS) that will supply specific information regarding the demographic trends in the communities, the ethnicity of communities, the current and potential services provided to the communities, and the profiles of other health service providers in the neighborhoods of the communities.

The second level of strategic integration is the alignment between the organization and the IST infrastructures. In this sense, the ability to design, implement, and operate HMIS technologies and applications (i.e., the IST infrastructure) is directly related to the organization structure, processes, and skills (i.e., the organization infrastructure). Conversely, the design of the corporate infrastructure should also determine the requirements for the IST infrastructure (i.e., architecture, processes, and skills). For example, the redesigning HMIS reporting systems to parallel the functional reorganization of the health service facility is a strategic integration at the infrastructure level.

Once strategic alignment has been achieved and the HMIS goals and strategy have been clearly delineated, the next step in HMIS strategic planning is to specify the necessary organizational information requirements for the development of the HMIS portfolio. Information requirements (IR) are needed to develop an appropriate management information technology infrastructure (MITI). In the following section, we concentrate on IR, the next stage of the HMIS strategic planning process.

INFORMATION REQUIREMENTS (IR)

Successful HMIS planning requires not only corporate-HMIS strategic alignment but also effective IT resource management.[21] Ideally, HMIS managers would want to ensure that technology and information resources are adapted to meet the needs of the organization's functions and activities best. More importantly, the trend in HMIS planning and management has emphasized the role of top management in the process because of the growing acceptance that information is a corporate resource and as such needs to be managed just like any other health organization resource, for example, labor and capital (see Chapter 11). The most critical as well as the most difficult tasks in information management for health service organizations are identifying and prioritizing information needs.

Information Needs

The problem of having data but not useful information in health service organization planning situations is usually a result of too much rather than too little information. This problem occurs because in an organization as complex as a hospital, for example, massive amounts of data are collected to serve many different purposes. In most cases, data collected for particular uses are not necessarily transferable to other uses. Consequently, it is critical that the right information needed by health service CEOs and managers is supplied by the HMIS; this requires that appropriate steps be taken to identify these needs.

Informational needs vary in terms of focus and volume according to the level of planning and decision making within an organization.[22] In general, the decisions that health service managers make may be classified into two broad categories: (1) strategic decisions that relate to the formation of organization policies and (2) operational decisions that relate to the day-to-day operations and the formation of the organization procedures. It is important that the information providers recognize this distinction because the different decisions require different types of information to be provided at different times (and probably in different formats).

Strategic decisions are business positioning decisions that influence the future direction and strategy of the organization. At this level, individuals address what are essentially value and identity considerations. They seek to determine the "business" of the health service organization and the philosophies and beliefs that underlie it, in essence, those "soft" concepts that are so difficult to translate into "hard" facts. Little quantitative or statistical information is needed at this level. However, individuals must be able to look at the organization as a whole and express its desired contributions to society and to various stakeholder groups. For example, one hospital may decide that its long-term goal is to offer specialized geriatric care to meet the growing needs of its area. Similarly, another hospital may decide to focus on providing ambulatory care services and concentrate on establishing linkages with community agencies as part of its strategic plan. As these are one-time decisions, it is very difficult to forecast the relevant categories of information needs. However, the types of decisions to be made will be known even if the precise decisions themselves are not. Thus it is possible to make a reasonable judgment as to what information may be required.

Operational decisions are short-term decisions that relate to the planning, coordinating, monitoring, and control of day-to-day activities of the health service organization. As these decisions involve repetitive decisions made on a regular basis, the accuracy, specificity, and volume of information required are easier to predict. For instance, the pharmacy department of a hospital will need information on the inventory of drugs, the number of prescriptions filled and repeated, the physician who prescribed the medication, and the patient who received the medication. Since this information is easy to predict, it will not be difficult to determine the data elements that would have to be included in an HMIS designed for the pharmacy manager.

In summary, lower level management generally makes more operational decision, whereas top management makes more strategic ones. However, this is not always true as the types of decisions made also depend largely on the type of business and the business situation. For example, in the event of a labor dispute (or a dismissal), top executives in hospitals are sometimes required to take the place of subordinates, thus the need then to make operational-type decisions. When developing an HMIS it is important to consider the needs of the end-user, in our case the health service manager, to ensure that information provided is accurate, timely, and relevant to the decision or problem at hand.

Sources of Information

Much of the critical information required for HMIS planning is already in our minds but needs to be elicited (directly or indirectly) through in-depth discussions and interviews. The techniques used in eliciting information requirements (IR) are numerous. Figure 10–4 shows three of the more commonly used approaches.

1. Business systems planning (BSP)
2. Critical success factors (CSF)
3. Ends/means (E/M) analysis

Each method reflects a different way of thinking about IR, and their use in combination can increase the probability of obtaining a more comprehensive set of information requirements. The following three sets of questions posed to managers are reflective of each of the three respective methodologies:

1. BSP: What decisions or problems do you face and what information do you need to deal with the situation(s)?
2. CSF: What factors (activities) are most critical to achieving business success for your organization and what information do you need or must you monitor to achieve successful progress?
3. E/M analysis: What are the outputs (ends) from your activities and what information (means) do you need to judge performance (efficiency and effectiveness) relative to outputs?

Health service CEOs and managers should be warned that during the interviews and fact finding, the fewest possible constraints should be imposed (i.e., asking open-ended questions and assuming that nothing that is currently in place will remain that way). Later, considerations of allocating limited resources may rule

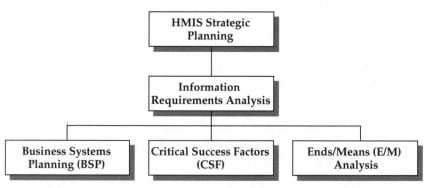

Figure 10–4 Three Approaches for Organizational Information Requirements (IR) Analysis

out some suggestions from the interviews, but creative solutions would not have been stifled.

In addition to various interview techniques, a useful source of information about the organization are job descriptions.[23] Most organizations today have job descriptions that outline the main activities and accountabilities of management level staff. Anyhow, it is quite appropriate to inventory the current HMIS portfolio and to catalog the hardware, software, and application functions performed by each application system that is operational. This provides the basic data for analyzing the current HMIS applications portfolio and the internal IST infrastructure.

The objective of analyzing the results from fact finding is to ensure that the most complete picture possible of the information needs of the organization can be defined with a relative priority for each. Once this has been established, the information needs can be grouped logically into an organization data model and implemented as databases. The business functions that access the information can then be assessed to identify potential application systems.

METHODS FOR THE DETERMINATION OF INFORMATION REQUIREMENTS

Almost all of the current IR approaches are model-based, requiring some form and combination of data, process, or object models to be produced. In other words, development of HMIS has historically been based on techniques that are independent of technology (i.e., data analysis, functional analysis, data flow analysis), as discussed in Chapter 6. The primary use of these models is to create an information road map that guides the coherent definition of the target applications and database portfolios needed to support the health organizational business in the future. These in turn are used to drive the required MITI along with some form of resource management plan to put HMIS strategic planning progressively in place.

Business Systems Planning

Business systems planning is an example of a process-based approach to determining IR.[24] BSP was originally developed by IBM and is used in many private sector businesses for IS planning (see Chapter 6). The concept underlying this approach is that business processes (groups of decisions and activities required to manage the resources of the organization) are the basis for information systems support. As processes remain relatively constant over time, the requirements derived from the processes will reflect the transactional and decisional support needs of the organization. In addition, if the process is "reengineered" the information requirements and system support are already part of the planning (see Chapter 13).

Figure 10–5 shows how a top-down analysis of the business goals and objectives of a health service organization can be used to drive the bottom-up design and implementation of an organization's HMIS portfolio using the BSP philoso-

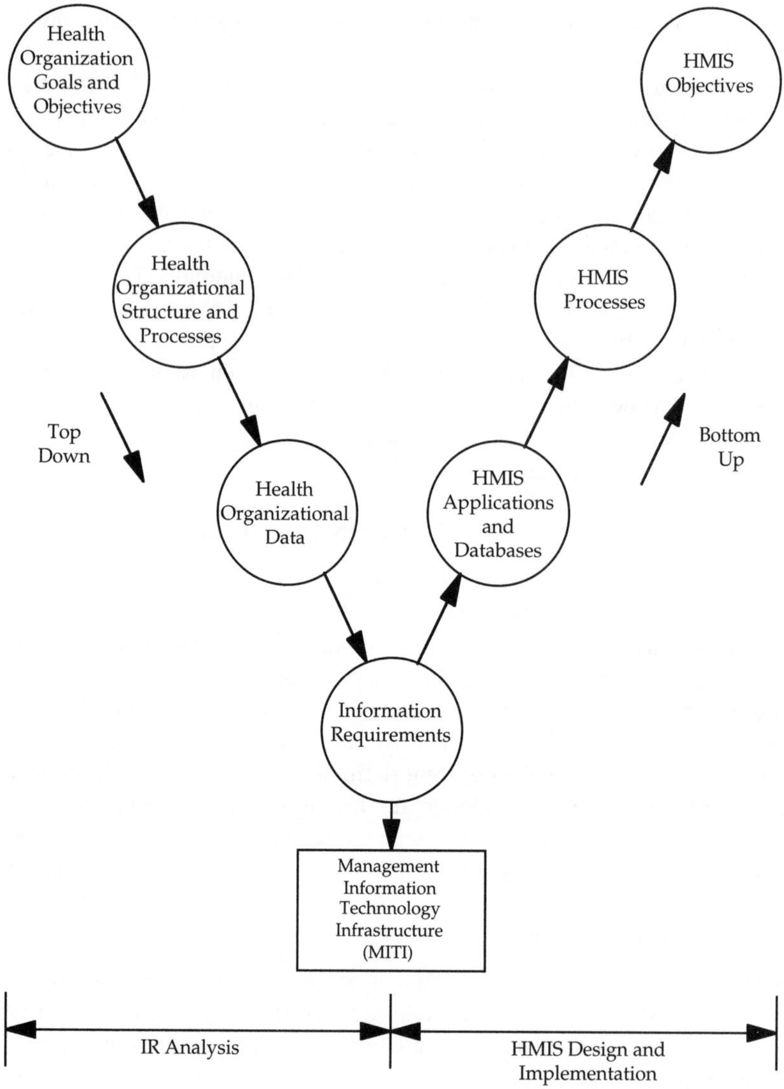

Figure 10–5 Business Systems Planning (BSP): Top-Down Information Requirements (IR) Analysis and Bottom-Up Health Management Information Systems (HMIS) Design and Implementation

phy. Essentially, the BSP approach relies on interviews with top management to define and plan the IR of the health service organization. In the interview process, managers are asked questions designed to specify key decisions and problems. These questions are related to their job responsibilities and objectives, their current information needs, and their perceived projection of information needs. For example, managers may be asked the following:

- What are the major decisions you must make that affect your specific objectives?
- What type of internally generated information do you use to meet your objectives?
- Within the next 5 to 10 years, do you anticipate emerging technologies or changing business practices to affect the nature of your responsibilities and managerial objectives? If so, how will these changes affect your informational needs?

The BSP approach begins with a top-down analysis of IR and ends with a bottom-up HMIS design and implementation strategy. The information requirements (processes) identified are consolidated into a statement of needs that can be used to identify logically related categories of data that are cross-referenced to the business goals, objectives, structure, and processes. In turn, this information is then used to engineer the proposed MITI, which will be used to drive or define corresponding databases and applications, HMIS processes, and HMIS goals and objectives. Put together, this methodology allows a critical reexamination of tasks within a process that do not serve a "purpose" or "add value" to the business solutions of the health service organization.

Critical Success Factors

The CSF concept, first introduced in business administration, has recently received considerable attention in the field of health service administration and planning.[25-27] CSF indicate the key areas of activity in which favorable performances are necessary to ensure the survival and success of an organization.[28] Therefore, CSF refer to prime informational factors that alert health service managers and planners to the positioning of critical components and task processes within an organization. Implicit in the CSF concept is the question, What key performance indicators (information) are needed to measure the attainment of a set of goals whether they are identified at the level of the individual, group, or organization?

CSF have been defined by Rockart as "the limited number of areas in which results, if they are satisfactory, will ensure successful competitive performance for the organization. They are the few areas where *things must go right* for the business to flourish."[29] The philosophy is derived from the same thinking as the 80/20 rule: that is, 80 percent of organization business needs can be met with 20 percent of the information currently available in the HMIS.[30] The key to CSF identification is therefore dependent on successfully eliciting the 20 percent critically needed information.

CSF have two main functions: (1) to encourage individual employees to focus on the issues that are most important and (2) to help them think through and sort out their information needs in these areas. CSF analysis often forces executives to make explicit the unconscious or implicit CSF that they have been using for some time. Past experience has shown that the identification of generic CSF is the most important step in the CSF process. Figure 10–6 illustrates the five Rockart-Bullen prime sources from which CSF can be derived.[31]

1. Industry factors
2. Market factors
3. Environmental factors
4. Managerial factors
5. Temporal factors

The first three sources are external, whereas the last two are internal sources. Examples of these factors, relating to the health service industry and health service organization setting, are also provided in the figure.

In using the CSF approach, the first step is to establish the objectives of the organization as a whole. From this point the organization's business strategy must be derived. The next step is to generate the CSF required to realize the strategy and thus achieve the stated objectives. This is accomplished by eliciting the critical information set from the staff through a series of interviews or brainstorming sessions. While there is no one standard procedure for the evolution of a CSF planning process, Figure 10–7 shows five phases and their respective benchmarks that are considered indicative of a "successful" application of the approach.[32–35]

- Phase 1—Understanding all externalities
- Phase 2—Winning executive support and championship
- Phase 3—Revisiting corporate mission and goals and reviewing managerial objectives
- Phase 4—Promoting staff education and participation
- Phase 5—Translating generic CSF to specific CSF and linking specific CSF to information requirements

Phase 1 involves achieving a better knowledge of, and reducing uncertainties about, potential threats and impacts of changes due to external forces acting on the organization: specifically, identifying the CSF associated with the three external

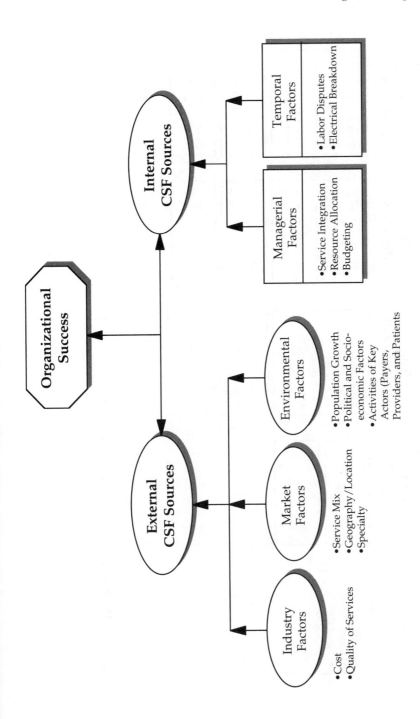

Figure 10–6 The Rockart-Bullen Five Prime Sources of Critical Success Factors (CSF)

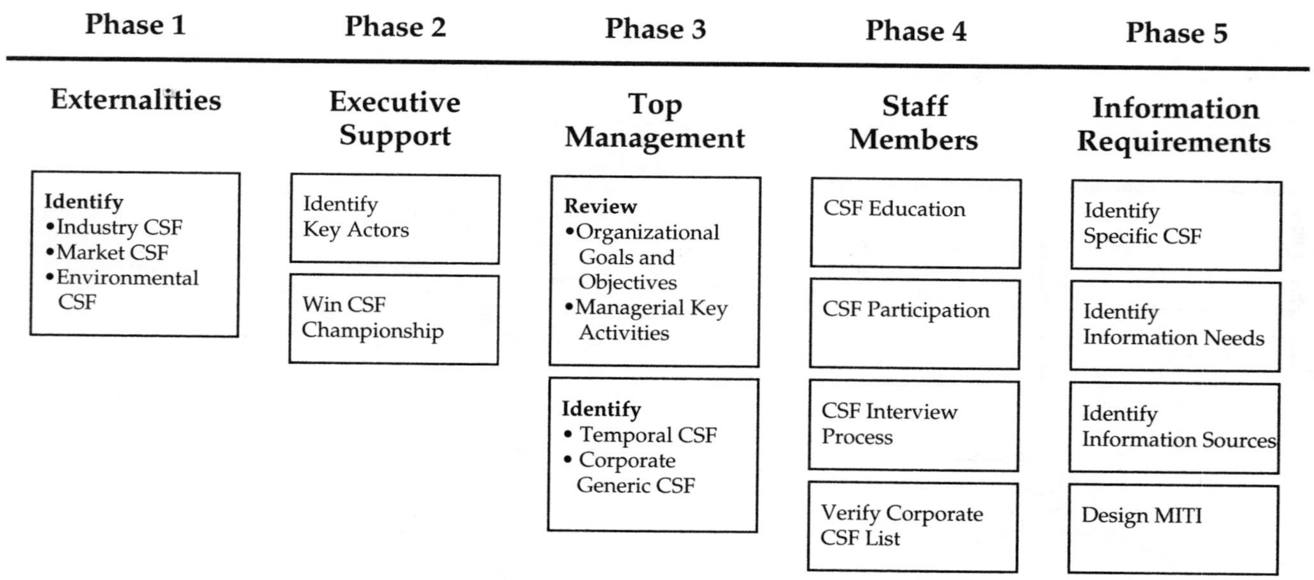

Phase 1	Phase 2	Phase 3	Phase 4	Phase 5
Externalities	**Executive Support**	**Top Management**	**Staff Members**	**Information Requirements**
Identify • Industry CSF • Market CSF • Environmental CSF	Identify Key Actors	**Review** • Organizational Goals and Objectives • Managerial Key Activities	CSF Education	Identify Specific CSF
	Win CSF Championship	**Identify** • Temporal CSF • Corporate Generic CSF	CSF Participation	Identify Information Needs
			CSF Interview Process	Identify Information Sources
			Verify Corporate CSF List	Design MITI

Figure 10–7 The Five Phases in the Critical Success Factor (CSF) Methodology

sources discussed earlier, industry, market, and environmental factors. Examples of CSF relevant to health services that can be identified from three external CSF sources might include "cost" and "quality of services" (industry factors); "service mix," "geography/location," and "specialty" (market factors); and "population growth," "political and socioeconomic factors," and "activities of key actors (payers, providers, and patients" (environmental factors).[36]

Phase 2 involves identifying the key actors and decision makers within the organization and gaining the active support of a CSF champion, in particular a member of the senior management team. The "activities of key actors" are an environmental CSF (see Figure 10–6), which thus implies that in carrying out Phase 1 and Phase 2 the actions in both are actually mixed rather than isolated. The support of senior management will increase the motivation of their subordinates in the organization to be receptive to the adoption of the CSF methodology, an important criterion for success if the methodology is to work.

Phase 3 involves reviewing the organizational mission statement(s) and clarifying managerial goals and objectives in order to specify a core set of issues. These issues are then redefined in terms of key activities that would "fit" these goals and objectives. In this way, a core set of generic CSF can first be identified and then specific activity sets can be determined at the individual managerial level at a later stage. The identification of internal CSF including managerial function and temporal factors also occurs at this point. Examples of CSF for these two categories would be "service integration," "resource allocation," and "budgeting" (managerial factors) and "labor disputes" and "electrical breakdown" (temporal factors).[37]

Phase 4 involves educating organization staff members on the CSF concept and encouraging their participation in the CSF interview process. Active involvement of the unit staff members in the CSF interview process prevents that threat of potential biases in CSF identification that may result from a limited participation.

The final phase involves aggregating and prioritizing generic corporate CSFs, refining them to specific level CSF and linking these specific level CSF to the information needs of management groups. The resulting CSF-generated information "map" is used to define the new management information technology infrastructure (MITI) for the organization. The MITI aims at closing performance gaps, addressing deficiencies, and replacing existing HMIS infrastructure. In essence, the fifth phase of the CSF planning process can be considered the point where technological or analytical solutions are finally applied by the organization to design a functional HMIS portfolio.

Ends/Means (E/M) Analysis

The IS technique of ends/means (E/M) analysis is based on systems theory (Chapter 3). As such, it can be used to determine IR at the level of the organization, the department, or the individual manager. The technique separates the definition of ends (or outputs), which are goods, services, and information generated by an organizational process, from the means (or inputs) used to accomplish them. The methodology begins with the ends and works back to the means related to achieving the ends.

Figure 10–8 illustrates how the ends from one process, whether it is viewed as organizational, departmental, or individual, is the input to the same or some other process. For example, the hospital accounting process provides budget information for other organizational processes. If the hospital has a deficit, the organization may respond by laying off employees or reducing expenditures in hospital services. Similarly, the deficit information may also be used to adjust the budgeting process for the future years.

In E/M analysis, health service managers are asked to define the outputs (ends) and the inputs (means) related to all their decision-making activities. In addition, they are asked to identify performance evaluation measures at two major levels, that is, the efficiency and effectiveness of performance. Efficiency criteria can include timeliness, accuracy, productiveness, responsiveness, and capacity of the reporting system, whereas effectiveness criteria can include appropriateness, reliability, flexibility, and acceptability of the HMIS generated reports. Another level of possible feedback is the productivity performance of individual workers. The information or feedback developed from E/M analysis is then used to determine IR for the new system. For example, the manager of a hospital pharmacy department may request information on drug inventory to evaluate the filling of an order that is requested (efficiency). Overall, the information could be used to determine if the drug inventory system in place is appropriate for the level of order-filling activities (effectiveness). Similarly, the pharmacy manager may want to compare the prescription patterns among physicians for different case loads to evaluate the drug utilization by a particular physician (productivity). E/M analysis has been used in various industrial settings with very positive results.

A problem with many current IR methods is, however, that their applications often result in the generation of a limited set of primarily efficiency-oriented information. As noted, most researchers now agree that it is important to use multiple IR methods[38] to bring out the efficiency and effectiveness dimensions of IR more fully to improve the definition of the type of supporting MITI needed to deliver an HMIS portfolio that supports total quality management in health service organization (Chapter 13).

MANAGEMENT INFORMATION TECHNOLOGY INFRASTRUCTURE

An overall management information technology infrastructure (MITI) is needed to deliver an HMIS portfolio that produces efficient and effective

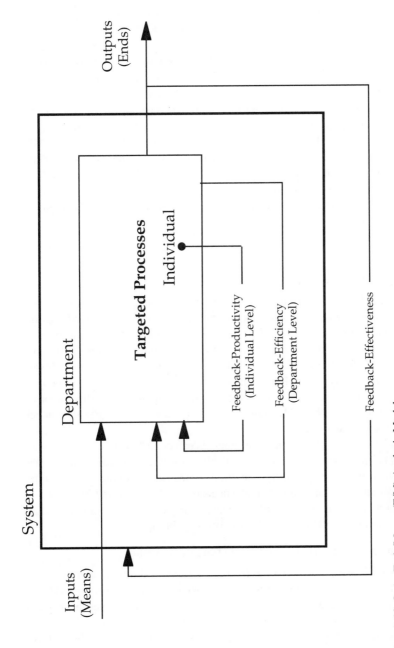

Figure 10–8 An Ends/Means (E/M) Analysis Model

corporatewide information and includes policies that optimize compatibility or minimize redundancy and system inconsistencies. An MITI plan has as its primary objective the establishment of an organization's long-term management information technology, which will allow HMIS to be designed and implemented in a progressive but efficient and effective way. Using the IR obtained in the second stage of HMIS strategic planning, MITI defines the goals toward which all future HMIS activities should be targeted.[39] It is used to delineate the organization's use and integration of IST and management components, functions, structures, and processes, including all hardware and software interfaces. In addition, an MITI puts into place policies and standards so that hardware purchases are compatible and software acquisitions allow access to organizationwide data sharing and consolidation. This is crucial because "if it isn't documented, it doesn't exist." Figure 10–9 illustrates the context in which an MITI model evolves for health organizational service delivery.

- Environmental context
- Organizational context
- Technological context

We have indicated that the health care environment context presents a challenge to health service CEOs and managers in terms of identifying and specifying their organizational business niches. The organization context defines the business strategy and infrastructure (i.e., structure, processes, culture, etc.) for HMIS strategic planning and alignment. In establishing the MITI for a health service organization, it is necessary to develop an information technology context that spells out the role of HMIS in the organization, the IST infrastructure (i.e., structure, operations, and activities), the HMIS policies, and the HMIS procedures or practices among the staff and end-users.

Figure 10–9 shows how each of the contexts can contribute to the development of the MITI; therefore, MITI constitutes the last stage of the HMIS strategic planning process. It defines potentially automated means for moving data and information around the organization to make decisions and to perform tasks. The various components of MITI are interdependent entities that have been integrated into a total structure upon which the HMIS portfolio is built.

Environmental Context: Formulation of Strategic Vision

In Chapter 3, we showed that the North American health service delivery system (NAHSDS) embraces the marketplace in which each health service delivery organization unit thrives. Likewise, the IST marketplace determines the available technologies that can be deployed by a health service organization.

A health service organization's strategic vision must therefore be derived from an understanding of the NAHSDS and an assessment of the available technologies

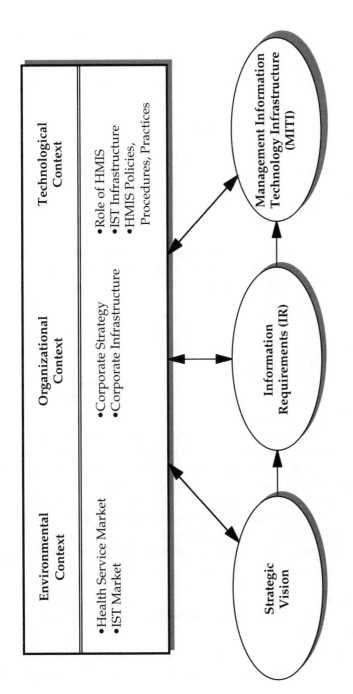

Figure 10–9 The Evolution of a Management Information Technology Infrastructure (MITI)

in the IST marketplace. It is this strategic vision that drives and defines corporate strategy as well as the HMIS strategy discussed earlier. In turn, the alignment of these two strategies spells out the conditions for putting in place the appropriate infrastructure support for HMIS portfolio development and future implementations.

Organizational Context: Determination of IR

Since HMIS applications should be an integral part of an organization and be critical to its overall effectiveness, it is essential that they support the organization's true business needs.[40] These needs are clearly expressed by the corporate strategy and infrastructure in the quest for information requirements. IR is therefore the fundamental concept underlying the whole purpose of corporate-HMIS strategic alignment exercise.

IR determination is dependent on organizational or business decisions, activities, and processes. In this sense, data required to support these decisions, activities, and processes are specified by IR. These processes or activities are in reality the means by which the data requirements are to be brought together as models for future decision processes or activities. For example, within the hospital environment, a modern hospital information system (HIS) data model may link the administration system, patient care services, and support services or even future expansion of a registry system (see Chapter 4).

Although the exact organizational context for IR determination will be unique to each organization, there are several important general considerations that are applicable across health service organizations.

1. IR determination should cover the complete range of systems that could be developed for an organization even though resources or justification may not be currently available. With a complete set of IR, it will be easier to set new priorities and meet changes in the business environment.

2. IR determination should be conducted independently of "bias in information technology context." Otherwise, the end-product may not be a true reflection of organizational decisions, processes, and activities but the mere attempt to implement cutting-edge technologies that may not be needed.

3. End-users (i.e., managers) must participate actively in IR determination. The resulting data sets should be evaluated for improvement or total replacement by the users. One major effort of information analysts should be to sort out key pieces of information needed so as to reduce information overloading on the users.

Although we have covered three important methods of IR determination, there are several that are often used but not studied as intensively as BSP, CSF, or E/M analysis. These include discussing the process with executives or their support personnel, attending or participating in group discussions and planning meetings, examining computer-generated and non–computer-generated information, examining other organizations' IR, examining strategic plans, tracking executive or managerial activity and software usage, and conducting workshops or focus group discussions.[41]

Technological Context: MITI Establishment

The technological context provides the means by which the strategic vision and IR are to be actualized. Without this context, it would be difficult and probably inefficient to provide the right information to the right person at the right time. The technology context develops the MITI, which includes the role of HMIS and IST infrastructure (i.e., interface considerations, hardware, software, communications, network and HMIS policies, procedures, and practices). MITI then provides the context that drives the subsequent determination of what goes or does not go into the organization HMIS portfolio. If structured effectively, MITI should not require updates of any significant components and interfaces, except when advancing technology becomes widely available.

In summary, an established MITI of a health service organization should include the ability to

- identify what and where appropriate data should be held
- identify the HMIS application portfolio and requirements
- select a database model that is independent of advancing technologies
- identify the scope of HMIS applications needed at each physical site or unit
- design a communications and network structure to serve and link the various sites or units

With a state-of-the-art MITI in place, the health service organization can feel confident that it will allow service efficiency, effectiveness, and excellence to surface (Chapter 5). Without a coherent MITI the organization may expect much of its HMIS capacity to shrink instead as technology will continue to advance and the health care environment will continue to change in the years ahead.

CONCLUSION

The potential use of information systems technology as a "competitive weapon" to achieve strategic advantage is one of the leading interests of academics and practitioners in the health management information systems area. However, more research is needed to investigate the role of information in strategy development and organizational adaptation in the health care sector. This will require both a better understanding of the strategic planning process in general and more studies of actual planning behavior in health service organizations.

As HMIS development in the past has been driven largely by environmental influences, there has been a corresponding lack of coherent policy for IST application in most organizations. This has resulted in HMIS systems' being developed in isolation with little capability for integration across functions. The development of an effective HMIS that contributes to the long-term success of health service organizations will require more than the merger of existing administrative systems. A proactive IS strategy that is based on the health care organization's strategic decision will be necessary to ensure that HMIS meet both current and emerging organizational needs.

CHAPTER QUESTIONS

1. What do you perceive as the possible reason(s) that have led to MIS development occurring at a slower pace in the health service sector than in the business sector?

2. Compare and contrast the value of using the BSP, CSF, and E/M methodologies in the health service field. Why is the use of a combination of these techniques advisable?

3. Imagine you are an IS consultant from the business sector and have been hired by the chief executive officer (CEO) of a small rural hospital to assist in the development of an HMIS. What could you say about the difference in environmental, organizational, and technological contexts between the two industrial sectors? How would your strategy be the same and how would it be different in comparison to planning and developing an MIS for a large health service organization versus a small one?

4. To illustrate the relationships among strategic alignment, information requirements, and MITI, draw a rich picture (refer to Chapter 2). Include the major steps and subsystems involved and the people and the entities that comprise these subsystems.

MINI CASE 10
"WE FIX IT" HOSPITAL

"We Fix It" Hospital was one of the first in its vicinity to adopt a managed care approach to providing health care services. This approach has been in place at the hospital for 3 years and has, according to staff and patients, improved both the delivery of health services and patient outcomes. However, "We Fix It" Hospital has been reluctant to employ computerized tools, for example, electronic records, that their competitors have eagerly adopted to support similar activities.

During a recent accreditation process, the accrediting body insisted the hospital adopt an electronic tracking system for documenting interventions and patient outcomes. Although somewhat resistant, "We Fix It" decided to employ bedside terminals for order entry, charting, and dissemination of test results. However, this project was implemented at the hospital without input from an HMIS professional to help identify the software and hardware necessary to support the hospital operations. As a result, radical hardware, software, and network changes had to be made in an attempt to piece together a system of electronic support. In addition, managed-care tasks had to be altered to compensate for the limitations imposed by the existing IST infrastructure.

MINI CASE QUESTIONS

You are a recent master of health administration (MHA) graduate who has been exposed to the concepts of managed care and HMIS. Imagine you have been hired to create an HMIS strategic plan for the development and implementation of electronic documentation at this facility.

1. How would you approach this problem? What key areas do you think need to be addressed before an appropriate electronic tracking system for the facility can be determined?
2. How would you go about identifying the information requirements for the development of the electronic tracking system? Envision the different types of data models that could result from this IR analysis.
3. How would you ensure end-user satisfaction with the choice of system? What key individuals would you need to consult and what would be their possible concerns about changing from a paper-based to a computerized environment for patient documentation?

Discuss briefly how you would address each of these questions, drawing from your training and experience in health administration.

CHAPTER REVIEW

The rapidly changing environmental influences that have accompanied the abundant introduction of IST make the health service sector an important arena for examining the strategic use of HMIS. Following the steps of private businesses, health service organizations are turning to the development of strategic HMIS as a means to realize their corporate strategy, achieve service excellence, and improve efficiency and effectiveness of health service delivery. In order to ensure that HMIS and related technology make the greatest contributions to realizing all of these benefits in health service organizations, HMIS strategic planning has emerged as a critical issue for health service managers today.

Altogether, there are three identifiable components in the HMIS strategic planning process leading to the development of an MITI: (1) achieving strategic alignments, (2) determining information requirements, and (3) developing a state-of-the-art management information technology infrastructure. All three areas must be addressed by HMIS planners to ensure the availability of key information to support organizational goals and objectives as well as effective management of this information. In developing an HMIS, the processes of planning and the implementation of plans should be viewed as equally important. Chapter 11 will discuss the management of information resources, whereas Chapter 12 will discuss the HMIS implementation process and provide details on how management can ensure that this process will be a meaningful experience for both end-users and systems personnel.

NOTES

1. M.R. Goodes, Seizing the Competitive Initiative: Strategic Planning in the Health Care Field, in *Strategic Management in the Health Care Sector: Towards the Year 2000*, ed. F. Simyar and J. Lloyd-Jones (Englewood Cliffs, NJ: Prentice Hall, 1988): 136–142.

2. R. Benjamin and M. Scott Morton, Information Technology, Integration and Organizational Change, *Interfaces* 18, no. 3 (May–June 1988): 86–98.

3. M.J. Earl, Experiences in Strategic Information Systems Planning, *MIS Quarterly* (March 1993): 1–10.

4. T. Moynihan, What Chief Executives and Senior Managers Want from Their IT Departments, *MIS Quarterly* 14, no. 1 (1990): 15–26.

5. R.A. Atkinson, The Real Meaning of Strategic Planning, *Information Systems Management* (Fall 1991): 57–59.

6. A.L. Lederer and V. Gardiner, Strategic Information Systems Planning: The Method/1 Approach, *Information Systems Management* (Summer 1992): 13–20.

7. Ibid., 13.

8. K.K. Kim and J.E. Michelman, An Examination of Factors for the Strategic Use of Information Systems in the Healthcare Industry, *MIS Quarterly* (June 1990): 201–214.

9. Earl, Experiences, 1–10.

10. A. Enthoven, Managed Competition of Alternative Delivery Systems, *Journal of Health Politics, Policy and Law* 13, no. 2 (1988): 305–331.

11. G. Harrell and M. Fors, Planning Evolution in Hospital Management, *Healthcare Management Review* 12, no. 1 (1987): 9–22.

12. B. Bowman, et al., Three Stage Model of MIS Planning, *Information and Management* 6, no. 1 (February 1983): 11–25.

13. P.J. Pyburn, Linking the MIS Plan with Corporate Strategy: An Exploratory Study, *MIS Quarterly* 7, no. 2 (1983): 1–14.

14. D.W. Conrath, et al., Strategic Planning for Information Systems: A Survey of Canadian Organizations, *INFOR* 30, no. 4 (1992): 364–378.

15. C. Dunbar and W.A. Schmnidt, Information Systems Must Represent 35 Percent of Total Strategic Plan, *Computers in Healthcare* 12, no. 7 (1991): 22–24.

16. Bowman, et al., Three Stage Model, 11–25.

17. J.C. Henderson and J.B. Thomas, Aligning Business and Information Technology Domains: Strategic Planning in Hospitals, *Hospital and Health Service Administration* 37, no. 1 (Spring 1992): 71–87.

18. F.W. McFarlan and J.L. McKenney, *Corporate Information Systems Management: The Issues Facing Senior Executives* (Homewood, Ill: Richard D. Irwin, Inc., 1983).

19. G.B. Davis and M.H. Olson, *MIS: Conceptual Foundations, Structure, and Development* (New York: McGraw-Hill Publishing Co., 1985).

20. Henderson and Thomas, Aligning Domains, 71–87.

21. Kim and Michelman, Examination of Factors, 201–214.

22. C. Cashmore and R. Lyall, *Business Information: Systems and Strategies* (Englewood Cliffs, NJ: Prentice Hall, 1991).

23. Ibid.

24. E.A. Van Schaik, *A Management System for the Information Business: Organizational Analysis* (Englewood Cliffs, NJ: Prentice Hall, 1985).

25. J.K.H. Tan, Critical Success Factors: A Model for Health Services Planning, Working Paper (Vancouver: Department of Health Care and Epidemiology, University of British Columbia, 1988).

26. C.R. Ferguson and R. Dickinson, Critical Success Factors for the Directors of the Eighties, *Business Horizons* 25, no. 3 (May/June, 1982): 14–18.

27. C.P. O'Connor, A Data Set for Hospital Planning, *Healthcare Management Review* (Fall 1979): 81–84.

28. C.V. Bullen and J.F. Rockart, A Primer on Critical Success Factors, in *Working Paper No. 69* (Cambridge, Mass: Center for Information Systems Research, Massachusetts Institute of Technology, 1981).

29. J.F. Rockart, Chief Executives Define Their Own Data Needs, *Harvard Business Review* 57, no. 2 (1979): 81–85.

30. W.C. Zerrenner, Improved Management through Automation, in *Information Systems for Ambulatory Care*, ed. T.A. Matson and M.D. McDougall (Chicago: American Hospital Publishing, Inc., 1990): 45–54.

31. Bullen and Rockart, A Primer.

32. E.W. Martin, Critical Success Factors of Chief MIS/DP Executives: An Appendum, *MIS Quarterly* (December 1982): 79–81.

33. A.C. Boynton and R.W. Zmud, An Assessment of Critical Success Factors, *Sloan Management Review* (Summer 1984): 17–27.

34. M.E. Shank, et al., Critical Success Factors Analysis As a Methodology for MIS Planning, *MIS Quarterly* (June 1985): 121–129.

35. M.C. Munro and B.R. Wheeler, Planning Critical Success Factors and Management Information Requirements, *MIS Quarterly* (December 1980): 27–38.

36. G.O. Eni and J.K.H. Tan, Going North on a Northbound Trail: A Model for Achieving Health Management Goals and Objectives, *Health Services Management Research* 2, no. 2 (1989): 146–154.

37. Ibid.

38. H.J. Watson and M.N. Frolick, Determining Information Requirements for an EIS, *MIS Quarterly* 17, no. 3 (September 1993): 255–269.

39. Van Schaik, *A Management System.*

40. D.S.J. Remenyi, *Introducing Strategic Information Systems Planning* (Oxford: NCC Blackwell Limited, 1991).

41. Kim and Michelman, Examination of Factors.

Chapter 11

Health Information Resource Management: Expanding the Roles of the CEO/CIO to Health Information Resource and Technology Management

LEARNING OBJECTIVES

1. Recognize health information as an essential corporate resource.
2. Characterize efficient and effective health data administration.
3. Identify organizational models of health databases.
4. Define health information resources management (HIRM).
5. Identify the components of HIRM.
6. Define the roles of the CEO/CIO in HIRM.
7. Conceptualize case management information systems as a model of HIRM.

INTRODUCTION

1. The information you have is not what you want.
2. The information you want is not what you need.
3. The information you need is not what you can obtain.[1]

The health service delivery industry is very information intensive. Health data, whether clinical or managerial, are required as inputs in decision making at virtually all levels of a health service organization. The management of health information resources in a health service organization and the management of the organization itself are very closely related. The most successful health service organizations are those that can make the best possible use of their health data from the external environment as well as from within the organization.[2]

Health information resource management (HIRM) is a concept that starts with viewing information resources including health data, health information flow, health information technology, health information personnel, and health information systems portfolio as major corporate resources that should be managed using the same basic principles applicable to managing other traditional economic assets. It is a mind-set designed to elevate the significance of effective and efficient management of health data within a health organization.

HIRM is not a new concept. It has existed as long as health organizations have kept patient records. However, over the last few decades, the health service industry has been somewhat behind other businesses in computer automation.[3] The reason for this is not only cost constraints, but also the management styles, thinking, and attitudes of administrators in health service organizations. In this respect, the main purpose of this chapter is to provide a new perspective on health service management, in particular, the significance of its role in health information resource management.

Generally, the topics covered in this chapter are intended to provide managers (both the CEO and CIO) of health service delivery organizations with a framework that will help them to do the following:

- Identify their health information resources
- Obtain accurate, timely, and relevant health data that are needed for effective decision making
- Organize health databases and generate required information in the most efficient way
- View management of health information resources as part of their managerial roles
- Exert controls to achieve health data security and privacy protection
- Relate to the emergence of case management information systems

A taxonomy of HIRM consisting of various aspects of health resource management within a health service organization is emphasized in these dimensions: health resource management (HRM), health strategic management (HSM), health technology management (HTM), health distributed management (HDM), and health functional management (HFM). Together, these five aspects of HIRM should be carried out with the purpose of producing timely and high-quality information useful for achieving specific health organizational goals and objectives. In practice, however, HIRM is realized through an iterative process that involves planning, organizing, directing, and controlling. It requires the recognition that the involvement of top management in health management information systems (HMIS) functions is as important as in any other organizational functions. The roles of CEO and CIO are therefore discussed here in terms of managing health databases, as well as managing the hardware, software, and financial and human resources required to gather, process, and manipulate these databases for generating useful management information.

HEALTH DATA AS CORPORATE RESOURCES

As we learned in Chapter 4, well-managed communication channels can help reduce uncertainties in the information transmitted, and this in turn reduces uncertainties in the functioning of a health service organization. In this perspective, information may be viewed as a vital resource for the survival, growth, and continuing development of a health service organization. The significance of viewing health data as corporate resources may be summarized as follows:

- Information is vital for the effective management and performance assessment of an organization.
- Effective planning, decision making, and operation of any health service facility are virtually impossible without proper access to and utilization of appropriate and meaningful information.
- The process of generating relevant and meaningful health data to assist decision making will by itself consume a significant amount of resources.
- As cost containment pressures grow and as new information technologies continue to advance, the need for information changes with time; this trend will intensify the urgency of managing the information resource in a health service organization more efficiently, effectively, and flexibly.

Inefficient and ineffective use of information is not only wasteful and dysfunctional to a health service organization, but severely limits the organization's ability to handle complex decision-making tasks that are necessary to thrive in a dynamically changing environment. Examples of inefficient use of information in a health service organization include collecting information that is not needed; storing information long after it is needed; disseminating information more widely than is necessary; employing poor and inadequate means for collecting, analyzing, storing, and retrieving information; duplicating collection and storage of the same basic information; and experiencing difficulty in assisting potential users to gain access to relevant and meaningful information.[4]

For a health service organization to be successful, the chief executive officer (CEO), chief information officer (CIO), and subordinates should be trained in the intelligent use of information and information systems. In particular, information systems in a health service delivery organization are often important for supporting decision making relating to

- Promoting wellness, preventing illness, and curing diseases
- Monitoring, evaluating, controlling, and planning health service resource allocation and utilization
- Formulating health and social service policies

• Advancing knowledge through research and disseminating knowledge through education

Evidently, then, information systems are important corporate resources in a health service organization. Since data are the raw materials or building blocks from which useful and meaningful information can be generated (in all information systems), there is a need to take a look at the fundamentals of data administration, including its availability, quality, independence, and control.

Health Data Administration

Efficient and effective data administration is critical for successful HIRM. Four areas of data administration that are applicable to health service delivery have been identified by Fry and Sibley.[5]

1. Health data availability
2. Health data quality
3. Health data independence
4. Management's control of health data

One of the primary goals of health data administration is to enhance the availability of health data. Specifically, this implies that the organization health data (i.e., databases, programs, models, and processes) should be available to be shared among a wide range of end-users, for example, everyone from executives to line staff in a health service organization. Such sharing of health data reduces average cost by having the community pay for the health data and the individual users pay only for their use. Under these circumstances, the health data do not belong to any individual, program, or department; rather, they belong to the community as a whole.

Therefore, to ensure a high degree of data availability and data sharing, the health data must be compatible with most (if not all) of the machines employed. The levels of system compatibility embrace (1) processor types, (2) operating systems, (3) databases, and (4) applications. HMIS managers should decide on data standards and ascertain the use of uniform software throughout the health service organization. For instance, if a department that uses Microsoft Word interacts heavily with another department that uses WordPerfect, then document transfers between the two departments may become inefficient. Furthermore, if the appropriate health data are not available for consultation in an important decision as a result of incompatibility between various departments of a health service organization (or if duplicate but irreconcilable health data exist across the organization), then a wrong decision may be made.

On the one hand, the availability of health data does not ensure that the correct or relevant decisions will be made; on the other hand, the quality of the available health data does. In other words, high-quality health data must be maintained to ensure that high-quality decisions will be made. Very often, poor quality health data may result when data are

- Undesirable
- Altered by human error on input or subsequent manipulations
- Altered by a computer program with a bug (erroneous with respect to the intended needs)
- Altered by a mechanical error
- Destroyed by a major catastrophe such as a mechanical failure of a disk

To maintain health data quality, errors must be detected and investigated to determine how they occurred. Corrective and preventive actions should also be taken to eliminate or prevent future errors. In general, the quality and integrity of health data depend on the validation of inputs and the recording of periodic up-dates by end-users. These operations must be carefully controlled or monitored in efficient and effective health data administration. This brings us to the concepts of health data independence and management control.

There are two aspects of health data independence: (1) physical health data in-dependence and (2) logical health data independence. Health data are physically independent if the program or ad hoc requests are relatively unaffected by the storage or access methods. Such systems provide a discrete number of choices for implementing the physical storage of health data. For example, physicians and nurses who are requesting data from a patient medical record database do not need to know how the data were physically stored or accessed: all that they see and interact with is the computer interface.

Logical health data independence refers to the ability to make logical changes to the health database without significantly affecting the programs that access it. This form of independence has the capability to support various system or user views of the health database and to allow for modification of these views without adversely impacting the integrity of total applications. By analogy, end-users (i.e., physicians and nurses) can request individual views of the patient records and make changes to the database without the need to know the software codes used to access and protect the integrity of the data.

Lastly, effective control of health data is necessary if the organization database is expected to support the proper functioning of a health service organization. The management of the health service organization must be able to control both the people who enter the health data and those who have access to the entered health data. Irresponsible use and unauthorized changes made to health databases can cripple the functioning of the health service organization. Data security can be accomplished easily by implementing controls at various levels. One level (sys-tem level) of controls seeks to protect the integrity and confidentiality of the stored health data by using, for example, passwords and antivirus programs. Another level (procedural level) of control is aimed at protecting the daily operations of the information systems, whereas physical facility controls are essential for the physical protection of the computer systems.

Health Databases

Following our discussion on the various aspects of health data administration, we now turn to the database models: that is, structures of organized health data resources captured and maintained in a health service organization. Traditionally, these structures fall into three categories.[6]

1. Hierarchical
2. Network
3. Relational

Object-orientation is the latest form of organized structure, which may not be diffused and implemented in the immediate future. A brief discussion on object-orientation has been provided in Chapter 6.

Hierarchical health databases are those in which the structures are organized in a top-down or inverted treelike structure. Health data are stored as nodes in a tree structure, with each node having one "parent" node and perhaps multiple "child" nodes, which may or may not contain health data. For instance, health data about a community health promotion project (CHPP) run by certain staff members from a community hospital may follow this hierarchical model, as shown in Figure 11–1. At the top of the tree of hierarchy is the root segment of an element of the tree that corresponds to the main record type, which in this case is the CHPP. Below the root element is a subordinate level of health data elements, possibly including the walking and restaurant programs (see Mini Case 6), each linked directly to the root. Health data elements at each subsequently subordinate level are linked to only one element above, but they may be linked to more than one element below: the various events of Programs 1 through N in our example. Accordingly, E1 and E2 may refer to the Walkathon event and the Walk-for-Life event of the Walking Program (Program 1).

The hierarchical organizational structure is best suited to situations in which the logical relationship between data can be properly represented with the one-to-many approach, that is, where subordinate levels of health data can sufficiently define all relevant attributes of the superior data element. In our case, the CHPP has several programs, which in turn are filled with numerous events. In a hierarchical health database, data are accessed logically by going through the appropriate levels of data elements to get to the desired data element. There is usually only one access path to any particular data element.

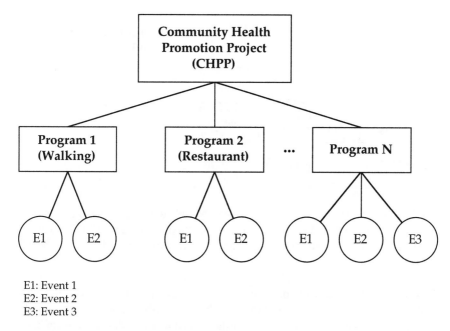

E1: Event 1
E2: Event 2
E3: Event 3

Figure 11–1 An Example of the Hierarchical Model

Network health databases are extensions of the hierarchical model used in organizations. Instead of having various levels of one-to-many relationships, the network structure represents a "many-to-many" relationship. As shown in Figure 11–2, the CHPP and the University "Health Outreach" (UHO) project, for example, may require work from three or more programs: walking, restaurant, smoking cessation, and so on. Although all three of the programs mentioned here are involved in the CHPP project, only the latter two are part of the UHO project. These relationships are indicated by the lines joining the responsible program(s) with the respective project(s). In a network health database, there is often more than one path through which a particular health data element can be accessed.

Unfortunately, health databases structured according to either the hierarchical or the network model suffer from the same deficiency: once the relationships are established between data elements, it is difficult to modify them or to create new relationships. For this reason, a third structure for health databases, the relational structure, has gained wide popularity in recent years.

Relational health databases are those in which all health data elements are placed in two-dimensional tables that are the logical equivalent of files. The purpose of the relational structure is to describe health data by using a standard tabular format. As long as the tables share at least one common health data element,

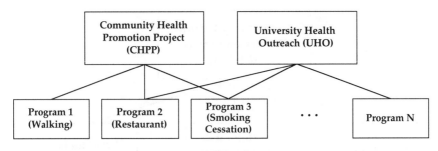

Figure 11–2 An Example of the Network Model

any health data elements in these tables can be linked and the desired health data elements generated in a usable fashion. The health data in the relational model, in most cases, can be linked according to the actual relationship of the various health data elements.

In the two-dimensional tables of relational models, each row, called a "tuple," normally represents a record or collection of related facts. The attributes are represented by the columns of these tables, with each attribute able to take on only certain values. The allowable values for these attributes or columns constitute the domain. The domain for a particular attribute indicates what values can be placed in each of the columns of the relationship role. The concept is analogous to a series of vectors.

Figure 11–3 provides an example of how a relational health database may be organized and accessed for the evaluation of the CHPP case. A health program evaluator may, for instance, want to find out the performance of the leader of a particular program (say, the walking program) under the CHPP mentioned previously and the number of events that have been held to date for that program by this supervisor. The evaluator would make an inquiry to the health database, perhaps via a desktop microcomputer. The computer would start with the project description and search the Project Table (Data Table 1) to find out the appropriate program number, then use the number to search Program Table (Data Table 2) for the project leader's employee identification number. The computer would then use this identification number to search Supervisor Table (Data Table 3) for the name and other attributes of this supervisor. From here, the evaluator can easily tell that there were 50 events held to date by this supervisor as a response to the inquiry.

MANAGING HEALTH INFORMATION RESOURCES FOR HEALTH SERVICE ORGANIZATIONS

The recognition of health information as a corporate resource leads us to various aspects of managing this important resource; for example, the processing of

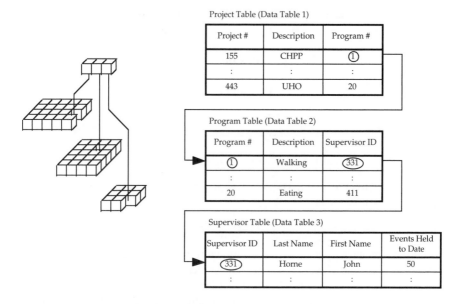

Project Table (Data Table 1)

Project #	Description	Program #
155	CHPP	①
:	:	:
443	UHO	20

Program Table (Data Table 2)

Program #	Description	Supervisor ID
①	Walking	331
:	:	:
20	Eating	411

Supervisor Table (Data Table 3)

Supervisor ID	Last Name	First Name	Events Held to Date
331	Horne	John	50
:	:	:	:

Figure 11–3 An Example of the Relational Model

health data into useful information requires both human and material resources. In particular, a health service organization will need both information technology capabilities and professional expertise to operate, maintain, upgrade, and plan for all of these health data processing activities. As shown in Figure 11–4, all these elements, including hardware, software, and personnel, are considered basic health resources, and as such, they will also need to be appropriately managed. This aspect of HIRM is known as the health resource management (HRM), which centers on the basic organizational components (e.g., personnel).

The health service organizations that will excel in the 1990s and beyond will likely be those that view their HIR as a corporate resource and manage it well. Apart from this fundamental health resource aspect of HIRM, there are other aspects as well, which center on various organizational components.

Five Aspects of Health Information Resources Management (HIRM)

As noted, the concept of HIRM has five aspects.[7] Figure 11–5 shows that these aspects have to do with the organizational environment (health strategic management); organizational products and services (health functional management); organizational infrastructure, that is, information administration and information networking (health distributing management); organizational technology (health

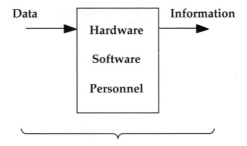

Health Resource Management (HRM)

Figure 11–4 Basic Elements of Health Information Resources: The Health Resource Management (HRM) Aspect

---

technology management); and organizational resources including hardware, software, and personnel (health resource management).

Health strategic management (HSM) outlines the importance for HIRM of providing more than just computer services; in other words, the outcome of HIRM must be information products that will be useful to the strategic positioning of the

---

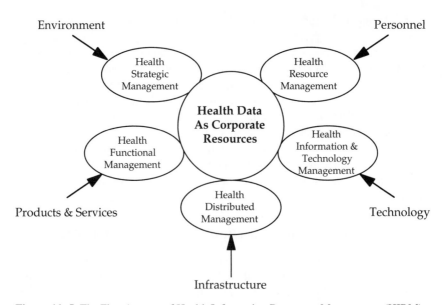

Figure 11–5 The Five Aspects of Health Information Resources Management (HIRM)

health service organization in the external marketplace. Therefore, HSM underlies the overall purpose of HIRM to contribute to the achievement of health service organizational goals and objectives.

Figure 11–6 shows that HSM encompasses the management of corporate as well as HMIS strategies. Essentially, it is aimed at achieving organizational strategic alignment (Chapter 10). Health functional management (HFM) stresses the importance of using managerial techniques in HIRM, for example, management by objectives (MBO), participative management, continuous quality improvement (CQI), and total quality management (TQM). HMIS products and services should no longer be viewed as a special, separate case, but should be managed in the same way as any other functions of the organization. As shown in Figure 11–6, HFM domains include systems development, financial management, and personnel management.

Health distributed management (HDM) domains consist of network administration, database administration, systems integration, facilities administration, and end-user support (see Figure 11–6). The responsibility of HDM should not be delegated solely to the chief information officer (CIO), but to all levels of the organization, as it entails all functions of the organization and requires the commitments of all individuals.

Health technology management (HTM) emphasizes the importance of integrating all technologies that process and deliver information, including telecommunications, office systems, and computer-based information processing. The planning, utilization, and operation of all the information technology of a health service organization should be coordinated for optimal effectiveness and efficiency.

Health resource management (HRM) views health data, information, and computer hardware and software and personnel (Figures 11–4 and 11–6) as valuable resources that should be effectively and efficiently managed. The optimal use and management of health information resources will benefit the entire health service organization.

These five dimensions define HIRM and the philosophy upon which it is based. As a management activity, HIRM regroups a wide range of managerial functions, which in turn summarize and regroup the tasks that are carried out by the health service CEO and CIO. The roles of CEO/CIO with respect to HIRM will be discussed in a later section of this chapter.

Safeguarding Health Information Resources (HIR)

As we mentioned earlier in the chapter, one of the queries arising from HIRM is the security issue, which can be overcome by the implementation of controls at various levels: systems control, procedural control, and facility control (see Figure

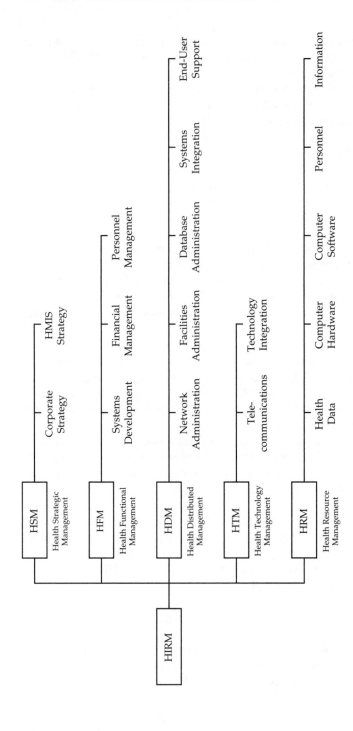

Figure 11–6 Functions and Domains of Health Information Resource Management (HIRM)

11–7). In this section, we concentrate on the means of achieving procedure controls and issues relating to backup, disaster recovery planning, and security of equipment to facilitate effective HIRM.

Procedural controls are an important aspect of systems security. These controls specify how the information services of the health service organization should be operated for maximum security and for high accuracy and integrity of the HMIS functions and operations. There are three major means of achieving procedural controls.

1. Separation of duties
2. Standard procedures and documentation
3. Authorization requirements

Systems development, computer operations, and control of health data and program files should be assigned to separate groups to prevent the possibility that a single group will gain unrestricted access to all related HIRM functions. Development of standard procedures (through manual and software help displays) will promote uniformity and minimize errors and fraud. In addition, to enhance system uniformity and minimize potential destruction, there should be a formal review and authorization on any major system development projects, program changes, or system conversion[8] by the CIO or the end-user departmental head.

Procedures for effective health data backup include regular copying or duplication of programs, files, and databases for disaster recovery; adequate logging of transactions to reconstruct any lost data; detection of missing or incomplete records; and institution of other backup operational procedures for use during system failures such as having an alternative manual or computerized system to be up and running in the shortest possible time. Fault-tolerant procedures, which are designed specifically for fault treatment, error detection, and recovery, provide a high degree of system stability and reliability.[9] Policies governing the process and the frequency of the procedures are also crucial in protecting the health data integrity. For instance, while duplicated data can be secured and stored in a separate location from the central site, procedures must exist for continuing systems operations during downtime experienced at the primary site whether scheduled or unscheduled. In addition, highly sensitive files should be backed up on disks and the disks secured to prevent unauthorized access.

Because of the high cost of computer hardware and software, security measures to protect the investments are essential. Location of terminals, printers, and other accessories in secure areas that can be locked when not in use is advisable. Name tags, access codes, and physical cable-lock systems are examples of inexpensive ways of protecting hardware and software systems.

Viruses, which provide another source of threat, are programs that intentionally try to alter or destroy data or operating system files on computer hard drives or

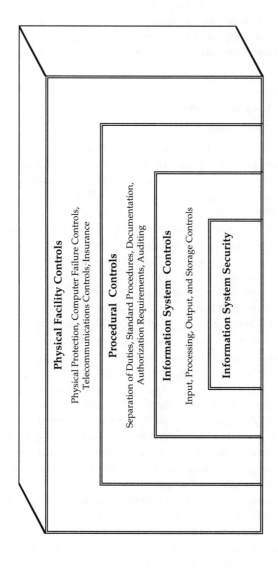

Figure 11–7 Levels of Data Security

floppy disks. Viruses invade a system, usually unintentionally, through a floppy disk or through a network. Security procedures to protect systems from viruses include the following:

- Checking bulletin boards and unauthorized software with an antivirus program
- Using and enforcing effective security codes and passwords for network users
- Periodically running antivirus software programs on network servers, workstations, and nodes without floppy drives

Security, confidentiality, and privacy of clinical, financial, and management health data (whether computerized or not) are major concerns for health service organizations. A balance between restrictive user access and data sharing must be established through the development and enforcement of stringent HMIS policies and procedures. A special case is the management and retention of patient records, which is discussed next.

Management and Retention of Patient Records

One of the high-priority areas requiring strict information management and confidentiality is patient records. Stringent legislative controls govern access to patient records, in particular, mental health records. All health record departments should have specific policies and procedures governing record access, storage, and retention both within the department and throughout the institution since these records contain sensitive information.

All sensitive health information should be maintained in designated areas and be subjected to strict security control. Such information should only be used in areas that are considered private and inaccessible to unauthorized personnel. For example, terminals should shut down automatically when not in use, and mechanisms should be in place to disconnect terminals after a specific number of invalid attempts to access the system. Written policies should delineate who can access what information and for what purpose; for instance, researchers may access a specific population's health information for the purpose of research and education.[10] Health records personnel must be trained experts in aspects of confidentiality, record access, and storage and should become excellent resources in policy development.

The general rule of health service facilities is that no information is released without a written consent from the patient unless otherwise legislated (e.g., emergency or unusual situations). Thus, policies and procedures are essential to guide health professionals and health records personnel in safeguarding confidential information in both normal and emergency or unusual circumstances. Examples of unusual circumstances where access to a patient's record may be requested include

- Review by a coroner in preparation for an inquest
- Litigation against the hospital or physician
- Potential for litigation due to serious misadventure or complication

In general, access to manual or computerized patient health data should be restricted to health providers involved in the patient's care. Patients can legally access their own records provided such an access is requested in writing and, if possible, endorsed by the patient's physician. Policies and procedures should be established to govern these aspects of record confidentiality.

The health service facility must have clear policies delineating who has authority to grant access. Health records personnel are responsible for preventing alteration or tampering of patient records and rely on administrative policies and procedures to support these efforts. The following guidelines may help to safeguard confidentiality and security of information:[11]

- Establishing a formalized mechanism to alert users to an unusual circumstance
- Duplicating and safekeeping a record when an unusual circumstance is identified
- Limiting access to the copied version of this record whenever possible
- Numbering and counting of pages in the record

Facsimile machines are rapidly becoming a popular method to transmit hard copy health information. They present the opportunity for rapid transmission of both written and graphic information that can greatly facilitate health service in urgent or emergency situations. However, this mode of transmission is also open to interception by nonauthorized individuals. Therefore, transmission of patient data or record by facsimile should occur only in urgent or emergency cases and should be conducted between health records departments where there is strict control to ensure the information is received in an appropriate manner. The point is that issues related to confidentiality, security, and privacy should not impede patient care.

Retention of records is another major issue of concern in HIRM since patient records and other information may be needed for legal defense. The retention period should be at least as long as the limitation period during which the organization can be the target of a lawsuit.[12] Retention periods may vary depending on the type of facility and the governing legislation. The courts have also extended limitation periods depending on the patients involved.

Destruction of health information is also controlled by legislation; therefore, written institutional policies must specify

- Methods of destruction to be used such as shredding or burning
- Methods of routine destruction of daily paper accumulation that contains health data
- Periodic destruction of inactive or outdated recorded health data with particular attention to designating personnel who will witness or attest to the destruction in writing
- Erasure of health information recorded or stored by electronic means on tapes, disks, or cassettes[13]

Confidentiality and Control Measures

Computerization adds another layer to the confidentiality issue. The information on computer tapes is no different from the documentation in the patient records. Thus policies, procedures, and guidelines to govern access to information and to maintain confidentiality are just as necessary as they are for written patient records.

Principles of documentation in the context of computerized health information should meet legal and professional standards. Appropriate orientation programs, ongoing educational seminars, and attendance at conferences are essential to ensure that managers, health record professionals, and other hospital staff are fully aware of the policies and procedures governing information access, security measures, and confidentiality expectations.

All employees and health data users should also be asked to sign a pledge of confidentiality that incorporates computerized health information within its scope. As well, reporting of breaches of security should be included in the policies along with a statement of disciplinary measures for violation of the security of computerized data. It may be important to note that the acceptance of the computer signature as a legal signature for admissibility as evidence in court is not yet clearly established.

Finally, essential aspects of computerized health information systems security are the use of audit controls[14] and the enforcement of original policies and procedures regarding systems and information access. For example, users should have authorized access only to data files necessary for accomplishing their work, and breaching of policies must be swiftly and professionally handled to ensure confidence in data integrity and protection of confidentiality.

THE ROLES OF THE CEO AND CIO IN HIRM

The importance of health information as a corporate resource in health services can no longer be denied. Any health service organization looking to survive and grow must recognize the need to treat HMIS as a resource. In this section, we turn to the roles of the CEO and CIO in HIRM.

CEOs, in accepting the challenge of managing health service organizations, must ensure that HMIS are implemented in an orderly fashion with a view to the future and an emphasis on integration (see Chapter 14). The CIOs must expand their role from one of a technical information system manager to one who takes executive responsibility and understands the need to integrate HMIS into the strategic plan of the organization in order to meet its goals, objectives, and strategies (Chapter 10).

Role of the Chief Executive Officer

We begin with a review of Chapter 5 on the emerging roles of the CEO for a health service organization. First, today's health service CEO must be a visionary, particularly one who provides strategic directions and visions, understands the health care environment and its changing marketplace, and recognizes the political and socioeconomic forces that impact on the delivery of health services. Second, the CEO must be a leader, in the true sense of the word. In this role, the CEO plans, organizes, and defines organizational product mix and new programs and services. Apart from retaining the usual planning and control functions, the CEO must form liaisons with various stakeholders in the system to build strategic alliances and ensure a healthy corporate image both outside and inside the organization. Finally, the CEO must be a manager in terms of both managing corporate culture and managing organizational change process. The CEO needs to establish a workplace in which all medical, clinical, and health service support staff can be motivated to provide efficient, effective, and high-quality services. In other words, the CEO must be able to earn the respect of those subordinates and line staff who report to him or her and be able to delegate authority to the right person when the need arises.

In today's turbulent health care environment, the CEO should not be personally responsible for developing and managing information. Instead, he or she must ensure the development of the appropriate infrastructure and the availability of the expertise within the organization and assist in the challenge of positioning the organization in an information system technology (IST) marketplace that is consistent with its positioning in the health care marketplace (see Chapter 10).

In a general survey conducted by Lyne Cohen, the role of the CEO in computerization was investigated through interviewing eight CEOs in various health service organizations throughout North America. All of them had different approaches and insights, and this was reflected in the mix of directions their organizations were taking with respect to HIRM. Although these CEOs exhibited different reactions, all of them felt that they had played a key role in the development or management of HMIS in NAHSDS. The following represents a cross section of some of their comments:[15]

- "Computerization will now involve integration at every turn; information is a key resource that needs more attention from hospital administration."
- "We needed a master plan that would allow us to eventually connect every department and produce excellent management information system information; the key to successful computerization is massive top management involvement."
- "It's really important for hospitals that are computerizing to have a flexible master plan that can be adjusted every year."
- "It's pointless to introduce an information system if it is not done in concert with looking at your organization and how it is structured."
- "One of the biggest challenges is resisting pressure from the individual department to move off the master plan for finance and administration into patient care areas."
- "Practice participative management that involves as many employees as possible in decisions that affect them."
- "You've got to hire people with excellent skills and give them the authority to get the jobs done right."
- "A successful computer system is 80 percent people-dependent and only 20 percent technology-dependent."

As one may conclude, although these CEOs' approaches to HIRM vary dramatically, their concerns cover all of the five dimensions of HIRM discussed previously. For example, HSM, which has to do with strategic alignment, is clearly expressed by several of these CEOs as the need to tie HMIS directions with organizational goals and objectives. Also, from a CEO's perspective, information and people are seen as key resources to successful HIRM. Health technology management (HTM) and health data management (HDM) are highlighted in combination by the need for technological integration and future connectivity, whereas HFM is also emphasized in at least one of the CEOs' comments, indicating the need to practice participative management techniques for effective HIRM. In summary, while there may not be a definitive role for CEO, in general, the pivotal roles of a CEO in HIRM should include the following:

- Having a member of senior management, for example, a CIO, take primary and supreme responsibility for developing and sharing of HMIS within the health service organization
- Acting as a role model (e.g., fostering an HMIS culture throughout the organization; see Chapter 5)

- Working effectively with the CIO to ensure that a state-of-the-art management information technology infrastructure (MITI) is in place as noted in the previous chapters

Having established the significance of health data and all HMIS components, activities, and functions as corporate resources and having acknowledged the role of the CEO in its overall management responsibility for HIRM, we will turn to the role of the CIO, more often known as the information systems (IS) manager, in HIRM.

Role of the Chief Information Officer

A CIO is a senior manager whose responsibility lies solely in the HMIS. In general, a CIO serves two important functions.[16]

1. Assists the executive team and governing board in effectively managing health information resources to support strategic planning and management of the health service organization
2. Provides managerial oversight and coordinating functions in data administration, information processing, and telecommunications throughout the organization

A 1991 study indicated that CIO positions existed in only 10 to 15 percent of all hospitals in North America.[17] This may have been due to the misconception that managing strategic information differs considerably from other, more traditional hospital executive responsibilities. Moreover, the percentage of CIOs may have increased since the study was conducted.

The role of the CIO has significantly changed from that of its predecessors, the manager of management information systems, and the manager of health data processing even before that. The CIO has achieved an increasingly important role and should be positioned in the top management team of an organization. Whereas previous managers of management information systems were seen more as functional managers, CIOs are now considered executive managers who play an important role in the strategic planning and decision-making processes of an organization.

Some of the longer-term responsibilities of CIO may include (1) policies, procedures, guidelines, or standards for information resources; (2) strategic planning for information resources, linked to business planning, to provide improved organization functions and competitive advantage; (3) approval/acceptance of computing technology expenditures; (4) coordination of information technology, functional units, and environments; (5) education of management, especially top management, on uses of technology; and (6) environmental scanning. Short-term responsibilities may include (1) consultations on present problems and (2) day-to-day general managerial work.[18]

For many health service organizations, however, the immediate step required to advance the current state of HMIS for the organization would be a broad-based program using the shared knowledge and skills of technicians, managers, and users. More importantly, this would require the CIO to take the leadership role. The mandate would be to provide the directions toward advancement of the HMIS capacity in the health service organization. These directions will depend largely upon the type of training and experiences of the CIO. In the growing complexity of the HMIS environment in today's health care system, there are eight major functions expected of the CIO: operations management, communications management, corporatewide HMIS planning, information center or end-user computing (EUC) support, data resources management, project management, systems development and maintenance, and quality management.[19] These are shown in Figure 11–8.

Operations management deals with the overall technological context of the health information system. Procedures and methods that deal with the scheduling of hardware and software installation and deinstallation, planning of system capacity, operations security, and recovery from disaster or equipment failure all fall under this function. Communications management involves the collection, relay, and transmission of data between sources in and around the organization, as well as identification of the forms of transmission data to be communicated and reproduced (Chapter 9). Above all, the alignment of the HMIS plan to the strategic plan of the organization is an integral part of corporatewide HMIS planning (Chapter 10).

Data resources management involves the analysis and administration of data and the design and administration of the database. EUC support is the function of the HMIS that responds through staff specialists to the ad hoc requests for data or analyses from end-users. Project management is management toward the effective implementation of a proposed IS project (Chapter 12). Most IS projects, however, are never completed on time, within budget, and according to plans. Systems development and maintenance are integral roles of the CIO involving flexible thinking as well as insightful and broad long-term overviews of the administration and impacts of IS upon the organization (Chapter 12).

Finally, quality management is achieved through a comprehensive approach that entails the structuring of review (audit) and approval procedures for applications, hardware, and software systems; establishment of an HMIS infrastructure supportive of total quality management (Chapter 13); and establishment of the domain of responsibility and authority of the HMIS function.

Each of these functions, therefore, will require more or less specialized training and years of experience of a CIO. And, as future changes in the functions occur,

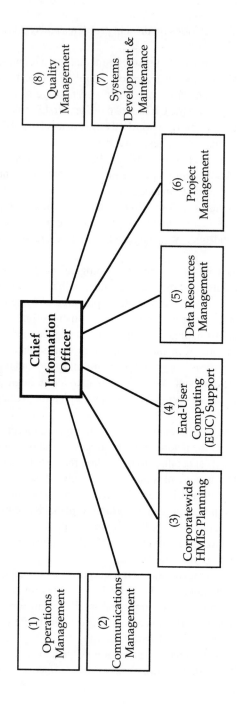

Figure 11–8 Eight Major Functions of the Chief Information Officer (CIO)

the role and outlook of the CIO will necessarily be transformed as well. To put together all of the diverse concepts discussed so far about HIRM, we will use the concept of case management systems (CMS).

CASE MANAGEMENT (CM) SYSTEMS

Today, large health service delivery organizations, with the general teaching hospitals as the prime example, usually have very well developed departmental structures developed along functional lines. As a result, several different departments in areas such as pharmacy and radiology are usually involved in the care of a patient.

From Chapter 3, we note specifically that in an imperfectly organized system, even if every part performs as well as possible relative to its own objectives, the total system may still not perform as well as possible relative to its overall objectives. An implication of this systems perspective is that the quality of care received by an individual patient cannot be assured even if the high quality of services delivered from each separate department (in a health service institution) to the patient is maintained. There needs to be some form of coordination among these various departments to bring about truly effective and high-quality care of each patient. This is where case management (CM) and hence case management systems (CMS) come into play.

The purpose of case management (CM) is to oversee the use of multiple institutional and community resources by the needed clients. Ideally, it is part of a coordinated admission-discharge-transfer (ADT) planning process.

Typically, clients are screened, and usually because of budgetary and procedural constraints only those who may be easily classified into a case-mix (or cohort) are referred to CM.

Essentially, CM is a process that is based on information: it includes clinical assessment, coordinated placement, regular monitoring, periodic evaluation, and follow-up of the patient. Because of the complexity and subjectivity of the different types of data involved, it is not a simple process. It also requires cross-departmental and interdisciplinary efforts to be implemented effectively. Accordingly, CMS may be seen as the future HMIS for use in supporting patient care. More importantly, CMS represents the integration of various health information resources and in this respect serves as a model of HIRM. In this discussion we focus on four aspects of case management systems.

1. Health data
2. Information priorities
3. Technology
4. People

CMS Health Data

CMS involve various aspects of caregiving. As such, the medical records system, billing system, scheduling and productivity analysis system, as well as directories of available community resources should all be part of a CMS. Conceivably, the health data to be captured into the case management systems will be very diverse indeed. The lack of consensus on terminology, coding, and classifying scheme, as well as the lack of standard use of psychosocial language in case management, can adversely affect the quality of health data collected. Common meaning and interpretation of assessment terms and variables will therefore have to be worked out a priori to facilitate effective communications.

Apart from using standardized codes with predetermined definitions, health databases to support CMS must permit the entry of descriptive texts in a word processing format for such items as progress notes. The computer stored ambulatory record (COSTAR) system mentioned in Chapter 2 is an example that uses standardized but changeable codes (with predetermined definitions) for health data entry and at the same time allows the entry of descriptive text. Built-in programs (health database queries) in COSTAR can also search for specific words in the text entry. However, the entry of free text in such systems should be standardized to facilitate clarification and explanation of information captured in such a system.

Above all, the types of health data entered into specific CMS should be compatible with other such systems used outside or inside the institution. This compatibility allows the convenient sharing of data among various departments of a health service organization or across departments among health service organizations. Systems compatibility also permits smooth uploading and downloading of data to and from the primary computer in which the data reside, thus enhancing the potential accessibility to a larger database for further classification and allowing the linkage of information inside and outside the organization.

CMS Information Priorities

In general, the three basic functions (or processes) of CMS are oversight, case tracking, and resource allocation.[20] Oversight is the ability of the system to oversee the use of multiple institutional or departmental resources by the clients. Case tracking is the ability of the system to track health data of each client (e.g., address, marital status, insurance coverage) sequentially, to facilitate the evaluation of long-term multidimensional changes occurring with the clients. Resource allocation is the ability of the system to monitor (and gradually, control) the utilization of various health resources available in the care of a client.

In the late 1980s, Frank Williams of Arizona State University and his colleagues helped to establish and implement CMS in six hospitals in Arizona. Their experience specifically indicates that answers to questions regarding purpose, reimbursement, and outcome measurement greatly determined the information priorities of CMS.[21] Purpose is related to the question of whether case managers function primarily as extensions of discharge planning and utilization control, or whether they serve as longer-term care coordinates and client advocates. Case managers are more likely to have client responsibilities that extend significantly before and after hospitalization in institutions with managed care and those with chronic and ambulatory services for the elderly and disabled.

Reimbursement relates to the means by which the CM programs will be financially supported. Very often, the health data in CMS can help to justify the support for CM; administrators may be able to justify the cost if the health data demonstrate that CM facilitates earlier discharge to less expensive levels of care, or if the program reduces unreimbursed readmissions. To do so, it would have to track and compare utilization and cost health data. Tan et al. discussed the use of the utilization care plan (UCP) system, which can be expanded to facilitate CM.[22]

Outcome measurement is often achieved by evaluating the effect of case-managed services on clients. As more complex cases are assessed, simple outcome evaluations may translate into more frequent assessments that are then expandable to include a broad scope of psychosocial and environmental variables. Generally, this level of CM processing and analysis may require larger capacity hardware and more efficient software so that the records can be maintained as components of health databases rather than as collections of individual documents. This brings us to the technology of CMS.

CMS Technology

In terms of CMS technology, there are a number of well-developed and relatively flexible computer programs. But most of the software available is only applicable to one or two of the many facets of CM needs (e.g., financial, medical, psychosocial, and support service requirements). These programs may take the form of proprietary software, application software, or in-house developed software. However, there is, at present, no single software package that can effectively satisfy all the diversified information needs of CM.

Proprietary software are programs that are commercially available. One of the quickest ways to get a computer system into operation to serve a particular need in a health service setting is by modifying a proprietary software package. However, the modification costs can turn out to be higher than many of the original savings anticipated in choosing proprietary packages, and not all vendors are supportive of (i.e., willing and able to assist in) such changes. Thus, if changes are to be made without the vendor's approval, product warranties may be voided and product patents may be violated.

Application software are mostly end-user developed products written in a popular spreadsheet, health database, or other fourth-generation languages that have been implemented on microcomputers. The Geriatric Patient Information Management System (G-PIMS),[23] for instance, is a program written for a popular PC health database package for collecting numerous variables about patients at Baylor College of Medicine's Geriatric Evaluation Unit. It provides information about patients to physicians, family members, and patients. The system, however, does not replace the chart. The primary advantage of application software is that staff members and personnel from other departments will be more likely to be familiar with the base program, thus making subsequent changes in health data requirements easier to understand. The software, however, may not be adequately sophisticated for management because of the design constraints of the base programs.

In-house developed software has the greatest advantage in terms of customizing the needs and idiosyncrasies of CM programs for a specific health service institution. End-users can be consulted in the planning process to provide input into the design, thus enhancing end-user acceptability. The development of these programs is often placed in the hands of HMIS professionals and may thus be very expensive. Because of the considerable amount of time and support of qualified computer programming staff required, the development and maintenance of in-house programs may in fact be as difficult as creating proprietary software. Accordingly, it is not uncommon to attempt to provide proprietary software through in-house application development for very large health service organizations as a means of adding to the value chain of business services already provided.

In addition to the applications of software technology, user friendliness of the software for CM should also be a major concern of information system managers. For instance, having menus that list possible choices is far more user-friendly than just having a blinking cursor awaiting input in a blank monitor. To minimize errors, special "fail-safe" programs that prompt for missing health data or that only allow the entry of data within a certain range of values that are valid can be included. More importantly, the design of the information system interface language (e.g., database query) should be relatively simple to understand and use.

As for hardware technology, one possible solution to meeting the varied information needs of CM is to include the various softwares as part of the organization's main computer system. This can, however, involve a substantial amount of resources and a number of organizationwide tests that may be disruptive. An alternative approach is to use a separate application system on microcomputers for CM and connect it to the mainframe for downloading patient registration and related information. Again, the choice of equipment should facilitate, and not impede, systems integration.

People

Finally, as for all other HMIS applications, user acceptance can be a problem for CMS. Resistance to using a computer system can occur at two levels: (1) natural resistance and (2) resistance to standardized assessment.[24] This subject is also discussed more fully in the next chapter, Chapter 12.

"Natural" resistance to computers arises from the excessive effort required to learn and use the new technology. Very often, an information system is designed, marketed, and chosen by the HMIS professionals of the health service organization without consulting the actual users of the system. As a result, case managers and other users of the system may not find it particularly useful or suitable for its intended functions. Their traditional methods of record keeping therefore continue, and the addition of such an automated system actually becomes a burden to them. To prevent this from happening, it is essential to include end-users or their representatives in the system design process, thereby building consensus and the commitment to using the system.

Another level of resistance occurs because the computer-based information systems (CBIS) have forced standardization of assessments. Case managers can no longer regard client records as personal notes; rather, they are now compilations of health data collectively determined to be necessary. This level of resistance can be overcome through an understanding of the advantage of standardized recordings. The establishment of protocols for care plans and guidelines can be beneficial, for example, by relating more successful outcomes to particular practice modalities. At the same time, case managers should recognize that client outcomes can be more easily compared by using standardized and automated systems than by using traditional, manual systems.

CONCLUSION

In conclusion, it should now be evident that information resources have to be considered as a critical corporate resource and must be managed using the same basic principles that are used to manage other assets. In the future, as health care facilities increase in complexity, so will the volume of health data. Therefore, it is essential to have a well-organized, integrated, and well-managed information system. An example of this is the evolving case management systems model. Such a model is critical for managing the organization health information resources and ensuring that the organization will thrive in the future.

CHAPTER QUESTIONS

1. Define health information resource management (HIRM) and describe its purpose.
2. What does HIRM provide to managers of health service delivery organizations?
3. What are the five aspects of HIRM?
4. Why should health data be considered corporate resources?
5. What are the uses of information systems in health service delivery organizations?
6. What are the four major aspects of data administration in health database management?
7. Name and describe the three types of health databases.
8. What are the four aspects of case management information systems?
9. Please indicate whether the following statements should be included in the job description of a CEO or a CIO:

_____ He or she should be responsible for developing and managing information.

_____ Ensure that a key executive/manager who has a primary and unmistakable responsibility for developing and sharing information within the organization is appointed.

_____ Act as a role model (e.g., be organized and positive) as all other strata of management and staff within the organization may take their cue from him or her.

_____ An individual within an organization has been given the responsibility to manage the organization's information.

_____ Work effectively with the chief _____ officer to assure that the processes for managing information within the organization are effective.

_____ Assist the executive team and governing board in using information effectively to support strategic planning and management.

_____ Provide management oversight and coordinating information processing and telecommunication systems throughout the organization.

_____ He or she should have an in-depth understanding of the current care giving environment.

_____ He or she should be an active leader in the development of the organization's information systems plans for the future.

_____ He or she should have a sound understanding of the information systems industry, particularly in relation to health care.

_____ He or she must ensure the development of the appropriate structure and the availability of the expertise within the facilities and assist in the challenge of obtaining the right information and interpreting it appropriately.

_____ He or she should be an executive who understands and advocates that information is a corporate asset to be used and protected with the same care as any other corporate asset.

_____ He or she should anticipate the appropriate time for implementing leading-edge technology.

_____ He or she should create a current state-of-the-art management information technology infrastructure that supports the organization's overall plans, goals, and objectives.

MINI CASE 11
BOUNDARY REGIONAL COUNCIL INVESTIGATES
INFORMATION SHARING

The Boundary Regional Council (BRC) is planning to invest in new information technology for five local health service facilities in order to solve problems in the way their information resources are organized. To date, the various facilities have catered to their own specific information systems requirements with a number of different types of hardware and software from a variety of vendors, even though there is a considerable amount of information that overlaps between the systems. Now, it would like to develop a local area network among the facilities within the region with linkages to a wide area network of physicians, hospitals, long-term care institutions, and other health care facilities. It also wants to have the capability to link directly with government and private insurance services. Ultimately, it would like to be able to be integrated with all the major information systems in the regional health service sector to achieve a completely integrated regional health service information system.

The present information systems of the five facilities consist of separate site databases. Each of the sites may also carry a duplicate copy of another site database from which data are being shared. The configuration can be schematically represented as follows:

Site 1: Database 1
(includes DB 2)

Site 2: Database 2   Site 3: Database 3
(includes DB 4)   (includes DB 2)

Site 5: Database 5   Site 4: Database 4
(includes DB 1 & 3)   (includes DB 1)

The money budgeted for a new system is quite extensive, so the council is able to investigate alternatives using the very latest technology and advances in systems software. However, the council is experiencing great resistance to their plan despite the fact that much of the technology is not expensive and readily available to link the various subsystems in the health service system. Other organizations involved, and even the government, are not prepared to allow them access to their individual systems. Moreover, the majority do not have the time and resources necessary to develop an effective way of allowing the systems to be integrated. The Boundary Regional Council is seen as a "fat cat" that can afford all the very latest in technology, and, needless to say, there is a great deal of animosity as well.

MINI CASE QUESTIONS

You are the newly appointed CIO of the Boundary Regional Council (BRC). Your first assignment is to analyze the information systems of the various health service facilities within the BRC mandate so that they can realize their ultimate goal of a completely integrated regional health service information system. During your analysis, the following questions were raised:

1. How can you convince the other parties involved that the development of a completely integrated health service information system is to their advantage? Explain what some of the specific benefits of systems integration might be to a representative of a long-term care facility, an insurance company, and the government.
2. What are some of the problems associated with the current setup of BRC's information systems?
3. What are some of the options for reorganizing BRC's information systems?
4. Suggest some similarities and differences between your role as a CIO and the role of the CEO. Comment on how you and the CEO can and should work together.

Discuss briefly how you would address each of these questions, drawing from the information you have learned from this and previous chapters.

CHAPTER REVIEW

The resources used in the transformation of health data into accurate, relevant, and timely information include the health data itself, the information generated, the computer hardware and software, as well as the information system personnel. The effective and efficient management of the information resources is of vital importance in today's information-intensive health care organizations.

Various aspects of health data administration for effective HIRM include data availability, data quality, data independence, and management control of data. Most HMIS will involve some form of health database programs.

Very often, these programs have an organizational structure of hierarchical, network, or relational format. The relational databases have gained wide popularity among today's health service organizations.

HIRM is a concept that seeks to have information resources recognized as a major organizational asset and managed as such. The five dimensions of HIRM are health strategic management, health functional management, health distributed management, health technology management, and health resource management.

The security of an organization's HMIS can be accomplished by the implementation of controls at three different levels. Information systems controls seek to protect the integrity and confidentiality of health data by using measures such as antivirus programs and passwords. Controls at the procedural level aim to protect the daily operations of the HMIS. Physical facility controls are essential for the physical protection of the information technology.

The CEO and CIO have important roles to play in the management of health information resources. The three main roles of the CEO are to make sure a key manager is appointed to manage the information resources, to act as a role model in the effective use of information, and to work closely with the CIO to establish a management information technology infrastructure. The CIO or information systems manager is the key agent responsible for the management of the health information resources. The two major functions are to assist in the effective use of information and to coordinate all of the organization's information processing and telecommunications. In accomplishing these tasks, the CIO will face various issues relating to health policies applicable to the development and maintenance of HMIS, as well as security and confidentiality of the organization's information.

Interest in case management has grown significantly in recent years. The purpose of case management is to oversee the use of multiple institutional and community resources by the needed clients. It is a process based on information sharing and cross-departmental cooperation. The four aspects of the case management information systems model are health data, information priorities, technology, and people.

NOTES

1. J.H. Murnaghan, Health-Services Information Systems in the United States Today, *New England Journal of Medicine* 290, no. 11 (1974): 603–610.

2. A. Mingione, Search for Excellence within a Systems Development Project, *Journal of Systems Management* 37 (1986): 31–34.

3. C.E. Shannon, A Mathematical Theory of Communication, *Bell System Technical Journal* (1948): 370–432, 623–659.

4. Central Computer and Telecommunications Agency, *Managing Information As a Resource* (London: Her Majesty's Stationery Office, 1990), 4.

5. J.P. Fry and E.H. Sibley, Evolution of Data-Base Management Systems, *Computing Surveys* 8, no. 1 (1976): 7–42.

6. Ibid.

7. F.R. McFadden and J.A. Hoffer, *Database Management,* 3rd ed. (Menlo Park, Calif: Benjamin/ Cummings Publishing Co., 1991).

8. J.A. O'Brien, *Introduction to Information Systems in Business Management,* 6th ed. (Homewood, Ill: Richard Irwin Publishers, 1991).

9. T. Anderson and P.A. Lee, *Fault Tolerance: Principles and Practice* (Englewood Cliffs, NJ: Prentice Hall, 1981).

10. C.J. Austin and W.J. Harvey, Hospital Information Systems: A Management Perspective, *Frontiers of Health Services Management* 2, no. 2 (November 1985): 3–36.

11. P. Freedman, The Role of the Health Record Professional, in *Managing Information in Canadian Health Care Facilities,* ed. M. Ogilvie and E. Sawyer (Ottawa: Hospital Association Press, 1992), 83–98.

12. Ibid.

13. Canadian Health Record Association, *Code of Practice for Safeguarding Health Information* (Ottawa: College of Record Administration, 1988).

14. Austin and Harvey, Hospital Information Systems, 3–36.

15. L. Cohen, Computerization: The role of the CEO, *Dimensions* 66, no. 4 (1990): 28–33.

16. C. Austin, *Information Systems for Health Services Administrators,* 4th ed. (Ann Arbor, Mich: AUPHA Press/Health Administration Press, 1992).

17. R. Hard, CEO's Begin To Share Control of IS Purchases, *Hospitals* 65, no. 1 (1991): 48.

18. C.S. Stephens, et al., The Nature of the CIO's Job, *MIS Quarterly* 16, no. 4 (December 1992): 449–467.

19. J.K.H. Tan, Graduate Education in Health Information Systems: Having All Your Eggs in One Basket, *Journal of Health Administration Education* 11, no. 1 (1993): 27–55.

20. S.R. Rosenthal, *Managing Government Operations* (Glenview, Ill: Scott, Foresman & Co., 1982).

21. F.G. Williams, et al., Implementing Computer Information Systems for Hospital-Based Case Management, *Hospital and Health Services Administration* 36, no. 4 (1991): 559–570.

22. J.K.H. Tan, et al., Utilization Care Plan and Effective Patient Data Management, *Hospital and Health Services Administration* 38, no. 1 (1993): 81–99.

23. Williams, et al., Implementing Computer Information Systems, 559–570.

24. Ibid.

Chapter 12

Health Management Information System Implementation: Guideposts to Success

LEARNING OBJECTIVES

1. Identify critical success factors (CSF) for HMIS implementation.
2. Identify strategic planning and management considerations in HMIS implementation.
3. Illustrate the use of project management tools for HMIS implementation.
4. Identify the major steps of HMIS implementation.
5. Illustrate the use of guidelines and standards in HMIS implementation.
6. Assess the implications of legal issues for HMIS implementation.

INTRODUCTION

Time and time again it has been said that the "people problem" is the major difficulty firms encounter when they attempt to design, develop, and implement management information systems.[1]

The implementation of a health management information system (HMIS) in a health service organization is a process whose success is dependent upon the fulfillment of a number of key activities. These include strategic planning, a thorough preliminary systems analysis, broad and detailed systems design specifications, user training and education, and hardware and software vendor selection.

Success in the implementation of HMIS technology is deeply rooted in organizational strategic planning (Chapter 10). It must take into consideration a comprehensive but operable organizational strategic plan, one that drives the strategic health information system plan. Therefore, there are several aspects of organizational planning and management considerations that must precede HMIS implementation. First, proper implementation of any health information system applications requires a concerted effort to advance an implementation plan, to incorporate designs, and to involve skillful human interactions and liaisons. Second, successful HMIS implementation demands competent health information resource management (HIRM: Chapter 11). Finally, successful implementation can be achieved by utilizing a variety of program management techniques that allow for ongoing monitoring of project progress.[2]

In practice, certain critical factors can influence the success of HMIS implementation. For example, two broad areas that have played key roles are (1) the application of well-tested guidelines and standard protocols and (2) the enforcement of ethical and legal concerns. Figure 12–1 shows that once HMIS planning is fine-tuned to address success factors for HMIS implementation, on the one hand, and organizational planning and management considerations, on the other, the actual steps including specific activities for HMIS implementation can be specified, directed, monitored, and controlled by project planning and management directives.

This chapter serves as an overview of HMIS implementation. It highlights the steps necessary to successful implementation of HMIS in a health service organizational setting. The chapter draws from previous parts of the book, in particular Chapters 10 and 11, to show how HMIS implementation is no more than an outgrowth of strategic planning and health information resource management. Even so, because of the growing complexity of HMIS applications and the huge amounts of investments involved in HMIS projects, all (or most) health service organizations today require that success be a prime criterion in any HMIS implementation effort. We therefore begin the discussion with a look at the critical success factors (CSF) for HMIS implementation in health service organizations and management.

CRITICAL SUCCESS FACTORS FOR HMIS IMPLEMENTATION

To date, a number of critical factors have been found to affect the success of HMIS implementation in health service organizations. Top management attention must be focused on these CSF and seriously consider them before any major HMIS implementation exercise is undertaken. In other words, management should try to position the health service organization to be ready for HMIS technology adoption. More particularly, management must pay special attention to those CSF and also acknowledge factors that are likely barriers or constraints to the implementation process. The minor issues that do not warrant top management consideration can then be delegated to middle managers, who can oversee these issues or control them with inputs from top management on an ad hoc basis during the actual implementation. However, there may be times when minor issues are

Figure 12–1 The Implementation Process

truly major issues in disguise, and if so, they should then be flagged for top management intervention.

In general, the CSF for HMIS implementation falls into one of three broad categories.

1. User characteristics
2. Systems design characteristics
3. Organizational characteristics

Exhibit 12–1 shows specific examples of factors from each of the three categories that contribute to successful or unsuccessful HMIS implementation.

User Characteristics

Among the variety of factors believed to influence HMIS success, user characteristics (i.e., the "people problem") are by far the most extensively studied by both academics and practitioners.[3,4] Examples of factors in this category are individual differences (i.e., cognitive style, personality, demographics, and situational

Exhibit 12–1 Characteristics of Implementation Success Factors

User Characteristics	Systems Design Characteristics	Organizational Characteristics
• Cognitive Style • Personality • Demographics • Situational Variables • Attitudes • Expectations	• Hardware and Software Performance • Learning • Decision-Making Support • Ease of Use • Graphical User Interface	• Organization Structure • Hierarchy of Authority • Organization Culture • Top Management Support • Commitment • Involvement

Implementation Success

variables), cognitive behavior, user attitudes, and user expectations of what the HMIS can do for them.

HMIS implementation often carries with it great expectations. It is not unusual, for instance, to find that users who are not well trained and who have little or no knowledge of system capabilities become disappointed with the final results of HMIS implementation because the HMIS product does not match their expectations. Therefore, it is sometimes important to emphasize and promote HMIS only as a tool rather than as a solution to health service organizational problems, although the ultimate role of HMIS in health service delivery organizations is to support decision-making and problem-solving activities.

The argument that HMIS "is a mirage" is familiar.[5] Clearly, the HMIS itself is not the panacea for all organizational problems, but it will certainly help CEOs and managers make better choices as well as speed up processes that were previously handled manually or by isolated systems. Adopting an attitude that HMIS applications are the "ends" and not the means sets up impossible goals and expectations that can only result in unfulfilled expectations. Consequently, this is another reason to involve personnel from all departments or programs of the health service organization in the planning and implementation of HMIS right from the start. In so doing, one can generate positive attitudes and feelings among end-users, with realistic expectations that can only enhance successful HMIS implementation. Further, the adoption of a comprehensive user education program can serve to increase the likelihood of meeting operational objectives sought in the initial planning of an HMIS.

Among various personal reactions to HMIS, resistance is the most destructive behavior related to HMIS implementation. Dickson and Simmons noted five factors relating to resistance.[6] First, the greater operating efficiency of HMIS often implies a change in departmental or divisional boundaries and a high potential to eliminate duplicating functions. This can create a sense of fear of losing their jobs among operational and clerical workers. Second, HMIS can impact the informal organizational structure as much as it can impact the formal one by creating behavioral disturbances such as doing away with informal interactions. Third, whether individuals will react favorably to HMIS implementation depends on their overall personality (e.g., younger, inexperienced workers are less likely to resist change than older, more experienced ones) and cultural background (e.g., the replacement of interpersonal contacts with human-computer interface). Fourth, the presence of peer pressure and previous experiences with HMIS implementation can also influence the organizational climate for success. Finally, the management techniques used to implement HMIS, for example, the use of project planning and scheduling methodologies, directly affect users' perception of the system.

In summary, the recognition of potential dysfunctional user behaviors is a first step to successful HMIS implementation. User orientation, training, education, and participation are ways to minimize the behavioral problems that may follow the introduction of HMIS in health service organizations.

Systems Design Characteristics

Apart from user characteristics, systems design characteristics also play an important role in determining the eventual acceptability of the HMIS installed. Examples of factors in this category include hardware and software performance, the characteristics of information and decision-making support provided to the user, and systems interface characteristics such as the incorporation of easy-to-use and easy-to-learn features into the HMIS.

The essential ingredients of any computer-based HMIS are the hardware, software, and firmware. Common sense dictates that configuration of wares be applicable to the organizational performance and strategies. In order for an organization's information needs to be satisfied from a systems design perspective, they need to be articulated and documented during the early planning stages and acted upon by using tailored implementation techniques. Further, the reliability of hardware and software is critical to HMIS performance. It is important to acknowledge, for example, that most information needs demand a certain amount of flexibility, notwithstanding the needs for completeness, accuracy, validity, reliability, frequency, and currency (timeliness) of information to be supplied to the user.[7] Flexibility necessitates an ability to cope with growth and variability in an ever-changing health service delivery environment.

Systems interface is a subject that could fill an entire chapter of its own. To relate this topic to HMIS implementation, we will provide several nursing examples to bring home the points. First, HMIS should be designed in the way users (i.e., nurses) organize themselves. For example, nurses organize their thoughts about patients by using patient room numbers as a constant frame of reference.[8] Inevitably, when a dietetics system in a hospital uses the alphabet as an organizing scheme, the systems interface becomes inadequate to support the users in performing their routine activities. This has happened in real life, where a group of nurses and clerks who were exposed to the system complained about the time it took to enter diet orders and changes into the HMIS. They became less efficient and increasingly anxious, frustrated, and dissatisfied with the system. The end result was to abandon or redesign the software to follow through with the patient room number organizing scheme.

Second, HMIS interface design should incorporate favorable factors such as the proper use of graphics and color.[9] One hospital information system (HIS) used bright primary colors that were "hard on the eyes" and thus distracting during prolonged use. The HIS also produced graphics that were difficult to read and interpret. The system was almost abandoned until it was discovered that both the graphics and colors were changeable. Finally, these and many other cases illustrate the significance of human-computer interface in the success of HMIS implementation.

Third, the design of HMIS should consider the previous knowledge of the users. For instance, in a long-time care facility, the nurses who have been acquainted with the "file-drag" iconic-based operation of Macintosh systems for years have found the command-based operation on PC systems extremely cumbersome and incomprehensible. In that case, the incorporation of Windows applications on the PC systems solved a significant part, if not all, of the problem.

Organizational Characteristics

Lastly, organizational characteristics can also influence HMIS implementation success. Examples of variables include organizational structure and power (e.g., the authority hierarchy), organizational culture, and other managerial factors such as top management support, commitment, and involvement.

One of the key areas to affect implementation success is the influence of top management. Exercising sound project control, resolving issues in a timely manner, allocating resources accurately, and avoiding short-lived changes in critical areas are all serious management considerations.[10] The strategic alignment of corporate-HMIS planning and the application of proper project planning and scheduling will together serve to prevent costly delays in HMIS implementation. Such an alignment will also ensure that the organization is not forced into a reactive as opposed to a proactive role.[11] Here, a proactive strategy is one that anticipates industry trends and installs innovative processes for competitive advantages and operational efficiencies, while a reactive strategy is one that has taken into account current industry trends and chooses to adopt a known process developed elsewhere.

Key strategies to achieve successful HMIS implementation include a realistic situational assessment, accurate identification of necessary resources, and development of an action plan (project and business plan).[12] It is therefore critical to provide top management involvement in many areas, and there should be a CIO or another knowledgeable senior member of the management team appointed to take charge of HMIS implementation.

Implementation of HMIS in health service organizations is thus no different than in business organizations. Long-term success is affected by the degree of commitment and involvement of all end-users and especially the support, commitment, and involvement of top management. All users need to invest their energy in the planning and implementation of the HMIS in order to create a system that is capable of providing the necessary information to assist them in performing their duties. Top managers in particular must provide support and act as role models to their subordinates. Potential heavy users such as middle managers, physicians, nurses, and support staff also need to be committed and involved in the process of HMIS implementation in order to improve the likelihood of its long-term success.[13,14] In short, HMIS success requires inputs that come directly from all users, not just systems professionals.

STRATEGIC PLANNING AND MANAGEMENT ISSUES

Our analysis of CSF for HMIS implementation reveals a number of critical considerations involved in the planning and management of an HMIS. Often, careful attention to these details in the early planning stages can facilitate the creation of strategies that will enhance the success of the HMIS implementation process.

Figure 12–2 shows the various types of planning and management issues that will influence the process as well as the strategy chosen to optimize HMIS implementation for a health service organization. Our discussion in the rest of this section will be focused on staffing issues, organizational project management, end-user involvement, and vendor involvement.

HMIS Staffing Issues

Issues associated with HMIS staff can be addressed by first simply asking the question, Do we have the adequate human resources and HMIS expertise to carry out a successful implementation project? The answer to this question will normally require the use of an internal audit of the current HMIS staffing situation. There can also be a projection of future staffing needs if the project has a long-term focus.

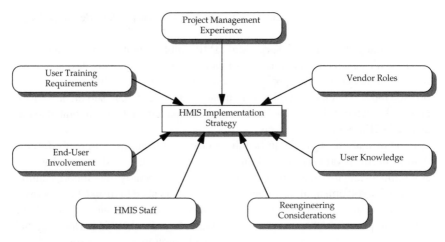

Figure 12–2 Planning and Management Issues

If the organization has to start from scratch, HMIS development is relatively straightforward: all the individuals with the needed skills are simply to be recruited externally. However, once beyond that, it is a more complicated process: it becomes necessary to identify potential knowledge gaps in HMIS staff that need to be filled. The following are more specific questions that need to be answered:

- Are the current staff already working at capacity?
- Is there any IS staff on payroll at this time?
- What level of knowledge do the current staff have, and how does this affect recruitment and training?
- How many new staff will be needed and when will they be needed?

The answers to these questions will enable the planning of staffing strategies to be layered into an HMIS implementation plan. It is critical that these considerations be addressed so that arrangements can be made well in advance to hire the necessary staff or to plan for the needed training. For instance, carrying through with an implementation schedule will require data on the availability of specific trained staff members for certain periods. Conversely, the training of specific staff members and the scheduling of recruitment will depend on the overall implementation schedule. Clearly, a lack of personnel with the necessary skills will slow the process of HMIS implementation, often leading to increased pressure and frustration among the existing staff members and possibly resulting in missed opportunities associated with on-time and "seamless" project completion.

Even though the staffing issues can be resolved at the systems implementation stage, it is also crucial that management of health service organizations establish clear reward policies to encourage the retention of experienced staff members right from the beginning. Gray documented that the demand for new systems personnel of all types grows at a rate of 15 percent per year, while the turnover of IS personnel averages about 20 percent per year.[15] Reducing this high turnover rate will immediately improve productivity and reduce operation costs.

To reward good technical personnel in HMIS, health organizations can consider developing a "dual career path" or adopting a "professional stage model."[16–19] In the dual career path model, a pathway of promotions in the technical level is created to parallel the managerial path in rank and salary. For example, a technical staff member would be promoted from programmer to systems analyst, then to systems specialist, and finally to senior technical specialist. In a professional stage model, the path for promotions can be from apprentice to colleague to mentor to project sponsor.[20] Both models provide significant incentives for the return of experienced staff members past the initial stage of HMIS implementation, thereby sowing the seed for long-term HMIS successes.

After examining various staffing issues on the systems level, we will now touch briefly on an important issue at the individual level: user knowledge. HMIS implementation in health service organizations requires an assessment of in-house systems and expertise knowledge. This assessment should take into account future user needs. Together with staffing needs assessments, management can ascertain the educational requirements of the organization. By doing so, the organization also avoids heavily diverting its resources to educating and training users during and after the on-line implementation of HMIS. Thus, educational planning including general training for managers, technical training for HMIS professionals, as well as specific end-user training to satisfy the needs of various user groups will help ensure a smooth and timely HMIS implementation.[21]

Numerous difficulties, both expected and unexpected, associated with the initial 3 months of on-line operations can be prevented through proper orientation and HMIS staffing training. In certain cases, this responsibility can even be off-loaded to software vendors. This approach may be particularly desirable for "turn-key" systems prepackaged and serviced by a single vendor. However, the costs in the long run can be significant.

Alternatively, if the organizational structure is capable of supporting this role, with an internal training department and knowledgeable personnel, it may be more cost-effective to provide the staff education in-house. If in-house training is to be conducted, the training personnel should be able to distinguish two levels of training: holistic level training and technical level training.

The holistic (or ideological) training here refers to training modules focused on the systems perspective rather than the operational perspective. Systems goals and benefits, systems constraints and limitations, organizational impacts, and functional implications are sample topics of this level of training. In short, holistic training intends to bring the entire system (HMIS) into view and to analyze its relationship with its surrounding elements (the environment). This kind of training should be directed primarily to managerial staff who need to view HMIS in its entirety and secondarily to operational staff who are more concerned with the day-to-day operations.

The technical (or operational) training is aimed at familiarizing the appropriate personnel with the operational aspects of HMIS that pertain to their tasks. This level of training may encapsulate such topics as form filling, report abstracting, data validation, standard data input or update procedures, and introduction of routine tasks. This kind of training is directed primarily to technical or operational staff who are concerned with the day-to-day use of the HMIS and secondarily to managerial staff who also need to know the procedures of their subordinates.

In any case, it should be recognized that the use of a team approach in-house does have the additional benefit of increasing user acceptance and reducing resistance in the long run.[22] Regardless of how a health service organization is planning to conduct the needed training for its staff, the quality of the training should be stressed, since well-managed training for IS operations has the potential to reduce anxiety and potential user resistance and to promote a team approach to improve the implementation of an HMIS, especially if behavioral factors are considered during the process.[23]

Organizational Project Management

The style of project management is extremely dependent upon the organizational culture and on the depth of experienced personnel who are available to manage such a process. In many instances, experienced project managers with technical knowledge and application knowledge are difficult to find. As a result, outside consulting is often used. However, time is needed to educate the consultant on specific situational and historical characteristics, both internally and externally, that can at times be significant enough to make outside consultation counterproductive. As for within the health organization, there is often a tradeoff. While team or committee management of the implementation process provides the benefits of internal knowledge, user acceptance, and overall effectiveness of implementation,[24] the need for a fresh look from an unbiased outside perspective should not be overlooked.

Although it is difficult to make specific recommendations with respect to implementation of HMIS in health service delivery organizations, there are certain techniques that are useful in project management. Here we will take a brief look at some of the techniques for project scheduling and program coding.

To ensure that the implementation of the system is complete by a certain date, a detailed and realistic schedule needs to be prepared and followed at the initial and subsequent planning stages. At the same time, the schedule should be flexible enough to accommodate some unexpected delays. Moreover, a detailed timetable for implementation is often essential to inspire management confidence in the installation plan. We will consider two techniques to assist project scheduling: the critical path method (CPM) and Gantt charts.

When using the CPM, the duration of all the tasks involved and the sequence (indicated by arrows) of all tasks need to be compiled in a network representation, as shown in Figure 12–3. In the figure, the numbers in circles represent different stages of implementation, the letters different tasks involved, and the numbers beside the letters the number of days needed to complete the task.

After translating the implementation schedule into a network representation, we can then determine the critical path of the network. The critical path is the sequence of activities that will take the longest period to complete. The time needed to complete all the activities on this critical path is the minimum period required to complete the entire project. Table 12–1 lists all the possible paths (activities in sequence) and the time needed to complete each. From Table 12–1 we can see that the path through activities A-B-F-J-K is the longest, requiring 15 days for completion. This is therefore the critical path of the project. In other words, the project cannot be completed in less than 15 days unless certain tasks are started early or shortened.

Another way of representing the details in Figure 12–3 and Table 12–1 is to use Gantt charts, which represent projects tasks with bar charts. They are often easier to construct and understand than CPM but may capture and generate less information. Figure 12–4 shows a Gantt chart for the project described earlier. It is worth mentioning that the exact start and end dates of certain noncritical tasks can be moved without causing delay to the overall schedule. For instance, if every other task on Table 12–1 commences and finishes on time, task L can be postponed for a day without delaying the final completion date.

After examining two scheduling techniques, we now turn to program coding techniques. Program coding, or, simply, programming, refers to the process of writing instructions that the computer system can execute directly. This is usually a very labor-intensive task, and as a result coordination among programmers will need to be emphasized. Here we will introduce two useful coordination techniques: data dictionaries (DD) and walkthroughs.

A DD can be computerized or manually compiled and contains definitions and proper uses of entities that are in alphabetical order. A DD should also have the identities of database programs used; the names of all the data fields found in the database, along with the names of the programmers that use them; and descriptions of the data and the personnel responsible for the data. It therefore resembles a regular dictionary. DD are useful in program coding coordination as they allow the names of data elements to be cross-referenced, help programmers to locate

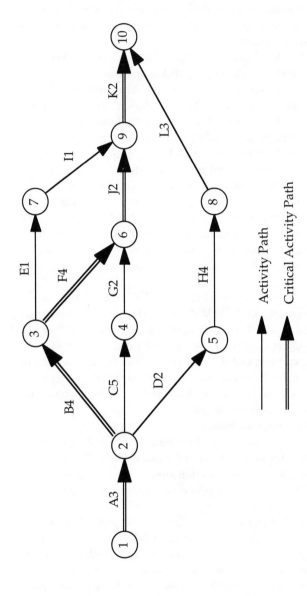

Note: Letter-number pairs represent the name of the path and the amount of time it takes to travel it. For example, "A3" indicates that path A takes 3 days.

Figure 12–3 A System Implementation Schedule in a Network Representation for the Critical Path Determination

Table 12–1 Possible Paths through the Critical Path Network in Figure 12–3

Path	Days Required
A → B → E → I → K	11
A → B → F → J → K	(15)
A → C → G → J → K	14
A → D → H → L	12

blocks of codes that are reusable in new applications rapidly, and ensure that all codes are consistent with the overall application.

Another very useful tool in program coding is conducting a walkthrough (or review). A walkthrough can take place at various stages of program design and development. It is essentially peer evaluation and testing of a programmer's work, with the primary objective of soliciting constructive feedback. In other words, walkthroughs act as control points in programming, making sure that what is programmed is in line with specific goals and objectives, as well as other operational constraints. It is not in any way directed personally at the programmer.

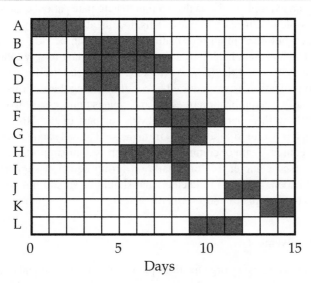

Figure 12–4 A Gantt Chart Representation of the System Implementation Schedule in Figure 12–3

At this point, after discussing issues in staffing and project management, we will briefly touch on some considerations in reengineering.

Reengineering Considerations

Often when new HMIS applications are implemented, work flows and processes change drastically because of the inherent differences of daily operations with the computerization. Without careful consideration of changes to daily operations, users will find their tasks at work gradually changing from time to time. While adequate training initially helps better prepare end-users for some of these changes, end-user involvement in the reengineering process can greatly enhance satisfaction with computerization. This again relates to the importance of the "people aspect" in HMIS.

In order to gain maximum benefit from an HMIS, all operations must be redesigned periodically to accommodate environmental changes and maximize operational benefits, while still maintaining the necessary controls in the process. If the delivery systems are not reengineered to meet new organizational needs, the increase in efficiency brought about by the HMIS may be offset by the unmet demands in the environment.

Often, it is inefficient simply to automate old systems processes, as computerization lends itself to a new work flow, thus demanding extra personnel and resources. A good example of this is the attempt to automate patient charts to mimic paper-based systems currently in place. This document is primarily a legal document on paper, but once in an information system it can become a much more versatile tool. Very often, health organizations are reluctant to rely totally on the computerized system and therefore opt to keep the paper copy for backup. As a result, health professionals are required to continue filling these forms manually, which essentially is a duplication of effort and creates unnecessary workload.

To decide how the operation of the HMIS (or part of the HMIS) is to be reengineered, it is useful to solicit inputs from the staff already acquainted with the existing procedures. Team or committee forums on system-supported group decision settings (see Chapter 14 for details on group decision support systems [GDSS]) are excellent means to decide what should or should not be modified. This leads us to the topic of end-user involvement.

End-User Involvement

In health service delivery organizations planning and development of HMIS are recognized to be slow, compared to their pace in the business world. However, lessons learned in the business sector have been found to be especially useful; one such lesson is the empowerment of end-users through their involvement in systems planning and design.

HMIS planning and development require active (as opposed to passive) end-user involvement throughout the entire process in order for implementation to be truly successful. It has been recognized in health service delivery organizations that unless HMIS staff, physicians, and nurses are involved in systems planning and ongoing evaluation, success will be short-lived.[25,26] In fact, in the health service delivery system, which consists of a much broader group of individuals representing many technical and professional groups, it seems wise to extend this to users of all the different modules or areas of HMIS. For this to materialize, adequate time and resources need to be allotted, and critical committees and internal and external liaisons have to be established,[27] such that all aspects of HMIS can be optimized while generating organizationwide user acceptance.

Specific considerations with respect to acceptance of end-users include

- The effect of the change on the need satisfaction of the affected personnel
- The position of those affected
- The leadership style of those managing the change

In Chapter 5, we noted that beliefs and attitudes, growth needs, and leadership intentions to support the change of an HMIS should be carefully considered in the planning and implementation stages of an HMIS developmental life cycle.[28] In addition, it is important to realize that not all demands from the end-users of the HMIS can always be met: there are technical and financial constraints. Often, simply letting the staff members know about the technical and financial constraints can lead to more realistic requests and reduction in user resistance at the same time. As a result, it is also highly recommended that health organization management be involved in the consultation process. Needless to say, frequent contacts with the management can also significantly improve staff morale as a "spin-off" benefit. Furthermore, direct involvement of application program vendors, which is our next topic of discussion, is often of critical importance.

Vendor Involvement

The traditional view that vendors specialize only in sales of equipment or computer software is fast giving way to the realities of the vendors of today. Although the primary function of computer systems vendors is and will continue to be the actual sale of equipment, there is rapidly increasing emphasis on the sale of "services" beyond the realm of equipment maintenance. In other words, vendors can be and in fact very often are involved in some degree of systems development and implementation, including HMIS implementation.

The options with respect to the roles of vendors vary between two extremes. Here the term "vendor" usually refers only to software vendors, as they dictate much of the implementation. However, the hardware vendor is important when considering outsourcing HMIS services. On the one hand, there can be complete turnkey implementation by the software vendor (turnkey systems are prepackaged, ready-to-go application programs that are often products supplied by a single vendor). On the other hand, there is the option of exercising complete in-house organizational control. Between these extremes lies the most used option, a blend of vendor and organizational responsibilities, with each performing in areas of specialty to tailor the process to the needs of the HMIS implementation.[29] Depending on the strengths of the organization and the vendor, the following areas of responsibility can be shared:

- Analyst support
- Project management
- User training
- Hardware and facilities planning
- Software modification
- Interface development
- Conversion assistance
- Procedure development
- Implementation audits

The means through which vendors can be involved vary from one organization to another. In some cases a single vendor acts as the sole handling agent for all technical problems and even some user training; in others, several vendors may have to cooperate to deal with systems problems.

Nevertheless, there are generally six steps through which a health organization can solicit and apply useful inputs from vendors: initial conceptualization, strategic planning, feasibility study, request for proposals, proposal evaluation and selection, and physical implementation. These, as well as postimplementation upkeep issues, will be outlined later in this chapter. We first take a look at some addition considerations.

Additional Considerations

A few other considerations that are not described often in the literature can help to ensure smooth HMIS implementation. The first of these is related to the concept of quality. There are several methodologies that can be adapted to address quality in health service delivery. The methodology continuum consists of quality control, quality assurance, continuous quality improvement, total quality management, and reengineering (see Chapter 13). Depending upon the organization's information status, implementation may be facilitated by the inclusion of any one of these principles.

Another consideration that needs to be taken into account pertains to the manner in which health service delivery organizations have been changing the way they measure performance. Many organizations are progressing from an efficiency and throughput approach to an effectiveness and outcome measurement approach. Experiencing the economic pressure perceived by many businesses, health organizations are also increasingly being pressured to link the utilization of various health resources to their level of outcome and demand, and, in many cases, to justify the utilization with the outcome produced.

While almost all organizations are run differently with respect to performance measurements, management styles can impact directly on the implementation of HMIS. For example, the structure of management within organizations, such as departmental organizations, program management, matrix design, hierarchical design, and circular design, can influence HMIS implementation. In keeping with the changing priorities in the health service delivery system, there has been a demonstrated need for better integrated information systems.[30] Thus, it is critical to keep these considerations in mind when making decisions regarding the implementation of any HMIS project within an organization.

Finally, it is also crucial to keep in mind that leadership roles exhibited by the CEO and the CIO can also affect the success of HMIS implementation (see Chapter 11). Information technology, therefore, needs to be integrated from the cultural perspective of an organization. In order for this to occur, the CEO and CIO must leverage HMIS in achieving goals and objectives of the organization and communicate this effectively within the organization.[31]

In particular, Austin has called attention to several areas that should be addressed when monitoring and evaluating HMIS implementation: productivity, user utility, value chain, competitive performance, business alignment, investment targeting, and management vision.[32] While it is recognized that these criteria suit profit-oriented organizations, several seem equally applicable to nonprofit health service delivery organizations as well.

SYSTEMS IMPLEMENTATION

Regardless of the strategies utilized in the implementation of an HMIS, there are several steps most health organizations need to take in order to optimize internal and external processes in a manner that ensures an efficient and effective outcome. In general, these steps fall into two broad stages, preimplementation preparation and postimplementation upkeep, each of which will be discussed in greater detail.

Preimplementation Preparation

The stage of preimplementation preparation begins with the initial conceptualization of HMIS and ends with the initial on-line operation of the system. The major steps included in this stage are

- Initial conceptualization
- Strategic planning
- Feasibility study
- Request for proposal
- Proposal evaluation and selection
- Physical implementation

Initial conceptualization of an integrated HMIS can be considered the first step to developing an HMIS in a health service organization. This can take place in a variety of ways. For instance, the CEO of a long-term care facility may be impressed by an HMIS in another health organization in the same community; the board of directors of a hospital may have discussed HMIS in their 10-year plan; staff members of an HMO may complain about their aging islands of technological applications. In short, the initial conceptualization represents a genuine wish to consolidate and improve the information flows and storage in a health organization.

As stated previously, incorporating organizational strategic planning into HMIS strategic plans is a desirable milestone in any HMIS implementation. HMIS development must be based upon a strategic information plan that is aligned with the organization's mission, vision, goals, and objectives. Adopting a strategic approach will help to focus measurable goals and objectives for information technology implementation that best suits internal and external information needs. Only in this way can the necessary factors and considerations, such as outcome measurement, future technological change, networking, and process reengineering, be included.

Once strategic information planning is completed, a feasibility study can be carried out. In general, this study aims to determine the extent to which the implementation and the upkeep of an HMIS are feasible. It includes results from various meetings with the board, middle management, and even staff members who are likely to be affected (user involvement) to solicit their inputs. It also incorporates financial (how much is available) and physical (whether the facility is too crowded for extra equipment) feasibility research. Moreover, the feasibility study can also make recommendations on the schedule of implementation, its speed, and other issues of concern. In many health service organizations, the reports for the feasibility study need to be approved or endorsed by the board of trustees. In these cases, the feasibility study report will also be acting as project proposals subject to extensive inquiries. Always the study reports should be produced professionally and should be subjected to peer review.

After a feasibility study is completed, the detailed goals and objectives of an information systems can be outlined on the basis of an internal and external needs assessment. Needs assessment makes it possible to formulate a request for proposal (RFP) for the various hardware and software vendors to submit bids. The RFP can include details on the organization, its information needs, and the specifics of the organization's goals and objectives that an information system is expected to fulfill. When vendor replies are received, it is then possible to correlate proposals on the basis of such internal objectives as budget and infrastructure compatibility issues in terms of existing hardware and software.

This leads us to the next stage of proposal evaluation and selection, which is followed by physical implementation. We will dedicate a section of discussion to each of these important steps.

Proposal Evaluation and Selection

As soon as all the proposals have been submitted, it is time to evaluate them to make a selection. In the evaluation process, two methods commonly used are benchmark tests and the vendor rating system. In a benchmark test, the health service delivery organization provides the vendors with a set of mock data. This set of data then acts as inputs in a prototype of the proposed system. The prototype system is then asked to perform a list of computations that are expected to be performed by the real system. The actual performance of these prototype systems is then compared with the prespecified standards for evaluation.

In short, benchmark testing attempts to create an environment that is as close to the real clinical setting as possible. Since it is the prototype systems that are being tested, it is not uncommon to find that the real, constructed system may perform at a lower level because of the heavy load of information to be processed in real life. Nevertheless, benchmark testing gives the organization a "concrete" feel for what the system would look like and how it would function (to some extent) in the clinical setting.

In comparison, the vendor rating system is simply a system in which the vendors are quantitatively scored as to how well their proposed systems perform against a list of weighted criteria. Commonly used criteria are

- User friendliness
- Data management
- Graphical and reporting capabilities
- Forecasting and statistical analysis capabilities
- Modeling

- Hardware and operating system considerations
- Vendor support
- Cost factors

As we have seen, the importance of the "people" aspect to the success of HMIS implementation cannot be overemphasized. As a direct consequence, user friendliness should be a prime concern when evaluating system proposals from vendors. User friendliness can be manifested in a variety of ways. The consistency of language command, the use of natural language and command abbreviations, and the availability of the "Help" and "Undo" commands are examples of features of a user-friendly HMIS. Moreover, menus and prompts, novice and expert modes, spreadsheet display of data and results, as well as What-You-See-Is-What-You-Get (WYSIWYG) features also contribute to the user friendliness of the system.

HMIS is designed to be an advanced "data-processing" facility. It therefore should have adequate data management tools to handle the massive volumes of data to be processed in the day-to-day operation of a health service delivery organization. Such features as common database manager, data security measures (log-in password, etc.), simultaneous access (without significant trade-off in performance), data selection, data dictionary, and data validation should be included in the HMIS.

The primary function for an HMIS is to produce timely and accurate information for health decision making. Accordingly, an ideal HMIS should have the capability to generate standard and custom reports, as well as to report variables and computations. In terms of graphical reports, the HMIS should be able to generate basic plots and charts, multiple graphs per page, and a preview of graphical outputs. Moreover, multicolor support, integration of graph and text files, and compatibility with existing graphics devices should be additional assets of an HMIS.

For strategic and tactical planning purposes, the ideal HMIS should be able to support appropriate forecasting and statistical applications. Linear regression, multiple regression, curve fitting, seasonal adjustments in time-series, and multivariate statistics are examples of common forecasting and statistical functions required by health service organizations in higher-level planning. In particular, the HMIS should be able to treat time as a special dimension.

"Modeling" here refers to the ability of the system to comprehend procedural logic (within definitions), to detect and solve simultaneous equations, and to compute mathematical and financial functions and user-defined functions. Functions like these are probably not used in the day-to-day operation of the system, but would come in handy in systems reengineering and reprogramming, probably as a result of periodic evaluation (to be discussed later in the chapter).

Another theme emphasized throughout this book is systems integration. The selection of HMIS should take this into consideration. In practice, this can be viewed in terms of hardware and operating system considerations. Compatibility with various operating systems (icon-based versus command-based), microcomputer support, compatibility with workstation requirements, printer and plotter support, as well as mainframe compatibility should also be considered when selecting an HMIS.

As we have seen in an earlier section, vendor involvement positively influences HMIS implementation. In selecting an HMIS, the amount of vendor support can definitely be a valid selection criterion. Vendor support can be provided in a variety of ways: consultation, training, active research and development, maintenance of local branch offices, technical support personnel, and continuing enhancements. Also, the financial stability and credibility of the vendor should be confirmed before reaching a final decision.

Probably the most important factor for all health organizations is the cost. In evaluating HMIS proposals, it would be very helpful to bear in mind how the costs are calculated and what they include. A modular pricing approach combined with some form of "packaged offer" is one of the more common approaches. In this case, the management should pay particular attention to the initial license fees, license renewal fees, maintenance arrangements, documentation, and resource utilization, as well as hidden conversion costs. Certainly, the cost of training and staffing has to be estimated by the management themselves.

Exhibit 12–2 presents a sample evaluation sheet used in a vendor rating system. Note that although these criteria are generally applicable to all health service delivery organizations, there are specific criteria that are more important to each organization by virtue of its unique environment. These should be specified separately and weighted accordingly.

Physical Implementation

Once the vendor(s) is (are) chosen, a contract is then signed, thereby beginning the physical implementation stage, the stage when the most "action" takes place. The stage of physical implementation actually comprises several steps.

- Recruitment of personnel
- Training of staff
- Acquisition of equipment
- Installation of equipment
- Uploading of initial data
- System testing
- Documentation
- On-line implementation

Exhibit 12–2 A Sample Evaluation Sheet for Health Management Information System (HMIS) Proposals

VENDOR RATING

Vendor: _____   **Proposed System:** _____

Criteria	Weight	Score	Weighted Score	Criteria	Weight	Score	Weighted Score
User Friendliness •Language Command •Help Command •Undo Function •Others: _____				**Data Management** •Common Database Manager •Security •Simultaneous Access •Others: _____			
Reports & Graphs •Report Format •Basic Graphs •Graph Previews •Others: _____				**Forecasts & Statistics** •Linear Regression •Multiple Regression •Curve Fitting •Others: _____			
Modeling •Mathematical Functions •User-Defined Functions •Procedural Logic •Others: _____				**Hardware & Operating System** •Hardware Compatibility •Operating System Compatibility •Workstation Compatibility •Others: _____			
Vendor Support •Consultation •Training •Technical Support •Others: _____				**Cost Factors** •Total Budget •Leveraged Payment •Maintenance Cost •Others: _____			

Total Score:

Additional Comments:

Evaluated By:_____ Signed: _____ Date:_____

All of these steps are performed in a logical progression (some carried out simultaneously) depending on the needs of the organization and how these are reflected in decisions based on the described factors and considerations. The keys to a smooth implementation process are effective planning and project management. (Some useful tools in this area have been described earlier.) Some variations may be necessary, depending on the differences in each organization, but some common steps (including some earlier steps) in initial HMIS implementation are shown in Figure 12–5.

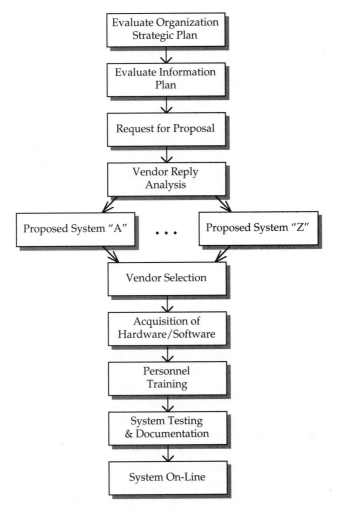

Figure 12–5 Common Steps of Initial Implementation of a Health Management Information System (HMIS)

Among these steps, the recruitment of HMIS personnel and training of existing staff members have been discussed in detail in an earlier section. The modes of acquisition and installation of the equipment are highly dependent on the characteristics of each health organization, as well as on the contract between the vendor and the management. Also, whether the equipment is acquired over some period or at the same time ultimately depends on the payment scheme agreed upon by the vendor(s) and the management.

The uploading of initial data and systems testing are sometimes conducted simultaneously: the initial sets of data are used to test whether the system is functioning at the desired level. If there are any significant discrepancies between the predesignated level of performance and the actual level, the system may have to be modified. Accordingly, there should be ample time allotted to these two steps.

Very often, documentation can proceed simultaneously with systems testing, since the structural layout of the system is already fixed. Any additional modifications along the way can then be documented as updates or memos. Ideally, there should be at least one copy of the master documentation with details on how to operate the system at the technical level and on how to manage the system at the tactical and strategic levels. Periodically, the distributing copies as well as the master copy should be updated, incorporating the ad hoc updates or memos.

We will concentrate here on on-line implementation, which involves four common approaches.

1. Parallel approach

2. Phased approach

3. Pilot approach

4. Cutover approach

In the parallel approach, systems activities are duplicated, as the old (possibly all manually operated) system and the new system are both operated simultaneously for a time, so that their results can be compared. In the phased implementation approach, different functional parts of the new system become operative one after another. This approach is relatively safe and less expensive than the parallel approach since the systems are not duplicated. The pilot approach requires the installation of the new system in sites that are representative of the complete system (e.g., in a small geographical area). This means that certain locations or departments are to serve as "alpha" pilot test sites first, followed by other "beta" pilot sites or departments until all sites operate under the new system. The cutover approach is also called the "cold turkey" or "burned bridges" approach. Essentially, this approach requires the organization to "flip the switch" to the new system all at once. If the results are not satisfactory, the system can be revised and activated again.

Figure 12–6 gives a diagrammatic representation of the four common approaches to on-line implementation. As to which approach is most suitable, it depends directly on the specific environment of each health service delivery organization. For instance, the general level of HMIS knowledge in the staff, the availability of resources for systems implementation, and the amount of data handled per day will and should all affect the choice of on-line implementation approach.

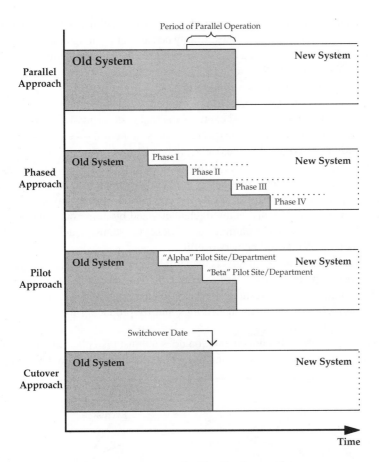

Figure 12–6 Common Approaches to On-Line Implementation

Postimplementation Upkeep

Although full on-line implementation of HMIS is a prominent milestone, it is definitely not the end of the story. Once the new HMIS has been fully implemented, the system operates as an information production and processing facility. Ongoing maintenance is essential to achieve implementation success in the long run.

In general, ongoing upkeep is required because of (1) problems within the system and (2) changes in the environment. Problems within the system may be errors that have not been discovered by previous tests or may develop primarily as a result of unexpectedly heavy work load. Changes in the environment include those in related systems (e.g., inventory order systems) and those in the organization of human resources. In many cases, simply because of the long time it takes to develop an HMIS, there are some deviations between the initial planning and the final product (i.e., the HMIS installed). These deviations also contribute to the need for close postimplementation monitoring.

Regardless of why the system needs to be maintained and modified, the maintenance cycle depicted in Figure 12–7 captures the major steps involved. Problems are usually discovered in either unexpected events or periodic systems evaluations. Postaudits (or postevaluations) are intended to evaluate the operational characteristics of the system, thereby acting as control points throughout the operation of the system. Once the problem is defined, a maintenance project can be initiated. Very often, as a result of creativity and the uncertainty involved, this type of project is relatively unstructured, characterized by numerous attempts to search for the ultimate "ideal" solution. Here, tools in systems modeling and systems thinking (Chapter 3) will be very useful.

After a feasible solution is found, it is then implemented and tested. If the problem is still not completely solved, it may need to be redefined. Attempts to search for the ideal solution are then resumed. If the problem is solved, the project can be completed by recording on maintenance logs and by producing the appropriate documentation for circulation.

It is also worth noting that documentation does not just take place at the end of the maintenance cycle. Rather, it occurs throughout the entire cycle in the form of

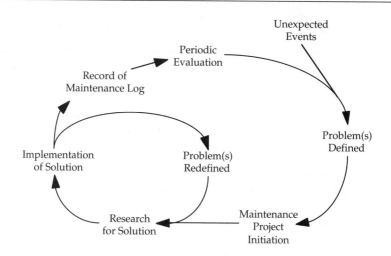

Figure 12–7 A Sample Maintenance Cycle for Health Management Information Systems (HMIS)

documentation of problems, written requests for change, and memos on possible sources of problems and solutions. The documentation at the end of the cycle therefore emphasizes the incorporation of all these forms and memos into a minireport that can be used for future reference or incorporation into the system manual.

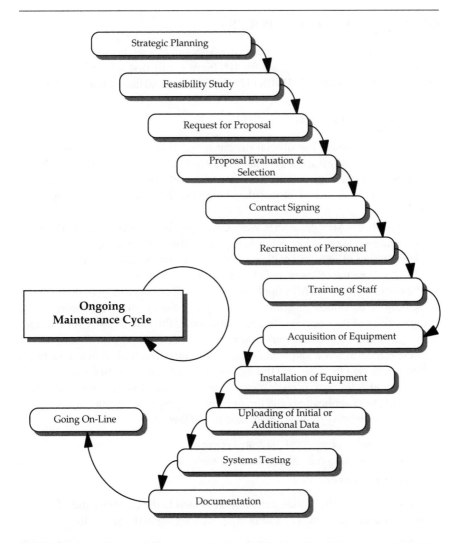

Figure 12–8 The Overall Schema of a Health Management Information System (HMIS) Implementation

Figure 12–8 recaptures the main steps of the overall schema of HMIS implementation. Throughout the entire implementation process (both preimplementation preparation and postimplementation upkeep), active involvement of both the users and the managers cannot be overemphasized, for reasons described earlier.

GUIDELINES AND LEGAL ISSUES

After examining the various steps of HMIS implementation, we now turn to some guidelines and legal issues for HMIS. We will first take a look at some guidelines and standards for HMIS in North America and then certain legal issues.

Guidelines and Standards

At present, there are few official standards and guidelines for the development of management information systems (MIS) in health service delivery in North America. While these guidelines may serve as useful educational and implementation protocols, it is important that they be optimized to meet specific organizational needs.

In general, the MIS guidelines were developed in Canada with a mandate to provide management information and productivity information guidelines for implementation of MIS in health service delivery organizations (in the form of HMIS), to allow the efficient and effective allocation of health service resources. The specific goals of the MIS implementation projects, according to these guidelines, may be described generally as "to improve the timeliness, usefulness, and comparability of data being collected within the health care industry for management, planning, evaluation, reimbursement and research purposes" and "to encourage standardization and integration of administrative and clinical data bases within health care facilities and throughout the health care industry as a whole."[33]

Some guidelines have been developed and delineated from a functional center framework, with applications and limited reporting aspects. Additional features of the guidelines worthy of mention include the following:[34,35]

- Work load measurement systems (WMS)
- Cost accounting (i.e., direct, indirect, variable)
- Service volumes

In fact, the strengths of the guidelines are rooted in the extensive use of definitions and standardization. The following points highlight the strengths:

- Efficiency issues are addressed using accounting measures and principles provided in the *Canadian Hospital Accounting Manual* (CHAM);

- Charting is used to describe accounts and expense-revenue breakdowns to allow statistics and management indicators to be reported.
- Extensive coverage is given to work load measurement.
- A comprehensive road map is used for IS education, planning, and implementation purposes.
- Allowances are made for the quantification and monitoring of several types and amounts of health care services occurring within an institution or organization.

In general, these guidelines, however many are followed, form a good framework for addressing efficiency through the use of HMIS. Yet unfortunately, they lack the ability to deal with the more recent developments in health service delivery and are limited in their scope of applicability; for example, they are meant for Canadian hospitals, just as the Joint Commission on Accreditation of Healthcare Organizations has guidelines that are mainly applicable to U.S. hospitals.

More generally, guidelines are needed for both U.S. and Canadian hospitals and other types of health service organizations to address the following issues:

- The role of top management in HMIS implementation
- The distribution of software and electronic data interchange
- The specification of health status or outcome indicators to allow system performance evaluation (i.e., cost-effectiveness, efficiency measures, and so on)
- The use and access of "information highway" and electronic networking (i.e., a framework for connection to community health information systems or linkage with provider systems)
- The standardization of health records and the use of advanced card technology

It is thus hoped that more guidelines will be developed in the near future to standardize HMIS development and implementation efforts.

Legal Issues for HMIS

To complete our discussion of HMIS implementation, we now focus on some legal issues of HMIS. Medical, legal, and ethical issues are becoming more and more a consideration when developing and implementing an HMIS. Generally, these issues are treated in the same way as paper-based systems are, but it is important to bear in mind that specific legislation with respect to IS systems is in a state of constant flux.

In Canada, patient access to personal health care information is clearly defined by the supreme court ruling of *McIrney v MacDonald,* June 11, 1992, and is further backed by the Freedom of Information Act at the provincial level.[36] The judicial system has established that, in the absence of contrary legislation, patients are entitled to access upon request their personal medical records. The patient is entitled to personal medical record access in order to examine and copy all information pertaining to administering advice or treatment, including that which has been prepared by other physicians. However, it has also been stipulated that the record itself remains the property of the physician, clinic, or institution that compiles the information. Further, it should be noted that physicians may refuse patient access to records in specific circumstances, but the patient has the right to apply for court intervention, whereby the refusal must be rightfully justified. There is simply no reason to believe that these rulings will be different in the United States.

Freedom of information acts and court cases[37] clearly have implications that relate to HMIS implementation. As these acts become effective, data collected will change, physicians will record different data as patient access becomes more commonplace, and charting of sensitive information will tend to occur less often. Likewise, there will be changes in data collection and data destruction methods to make compliance with patient requests and changes brought about by legislation more efficient, in terms of time and expense, when assembling and reviewing data or being excused from providing the data because they have been destroyed. In the end, there is always an increasing danger of greater risk of potential defamation suits as sensitive information is disseminated and construed as defamatory in some circumstances. As a result, it will become crucial to recognize the necessary legal obligations in terms of patient information collection. Typically considerations that will need to be addressed are confidentiality, custody, and administration. Thus the challenge for health service organizations will be to balance the concerns of individuals and society in the daily administration and release of health information.[38]

In terms of broader issues of privacy, "ownership," property, accuracy, security, and access of health information, Chapter 11 provides further, more detailed discussion.

CONCLUSION

Successful implementation of HMIS and its continual evolution into the information backbone of health service delivery organizations are the ultimate objectives of the HMIS discipline. Among the various steps along the path from initial conceptualization to physical operation, the stage when HMIS resides in the spotlight of organizationwide attention seems to be the physical implementation stage.

This chapter has discussed various concerns to be addressed in HMIS implementation, as well as some general steps involved. It is, however, not expected that managers of all health service organizations follow the exact same steps and address the same concerns in identical fashion. Rather, it is hoped that the chapter has provided the "essentials" for health managers and planners interested in HMIS implementation or expansion (e.g., an integration of older systems), who will then be able to adapt this "global" knowledge to schemes that are suitable to the special environment of each health service organization.

As we have seen, long-term success of HMIS implementation depends also on factors external to the IS itself. Among these various factors, the organizational influence (that is, the "people influence") has repeatedly been demonstrated to be one of the most dominant. HMIS planners therefore have to pay extra attention to the "people aspect" in the periodic evaluation and update of the system. Over time, the most successful HMIS is therefore one that responds to both changes in the climate in the organization within which it resides and the global climates of the health service delivery system and the society at large.

CHAPTER QUESTIONS

1. What are some of the critical success factors in HMIS implementation?
2. Why is careful planning so important to the implementation of health management information systems?
3. With respect to HMIS staffing, what are some of the major concerns for HMIS planners?
4. Describe some useful tools in HMIS implementation project management.
5. Why is end-user involvement important in HMIS implementation? How can end-users be involved in the process?
6. What are some common steps in HMIS implementation? What other issues need to be settled?

MINI CASE 12
HMIS IMPLEMENTATION PLANNING

Imagine that you have just been hired as the director of information services for a moderately sized community hospital totaling 400 beds. Half are acute care, half long-term care. As your first order of business, the senior management group has asked you to come up with a preliminary project brief to computerize the organization. They would like to get an idea of what will need to be done, the process they will need to follow to implement such a system, and suggested staffing requirements, time frames, and costs. They also would like an idea as to what will influence the success of implementation. It should be noted that time and money are short, so you'll need to describe what can be done, what should be done, and the bare bones requirements by using the Mini Case questions to guide your responses.

MINI CASE QUESTIONS

1. List the key activities and steps that need to be undertaken in the implementation plan. Outline the steps/activities in logical progression and state which implementation approach you would submit as the most suitable for the hospital.
2. For the purpose of educating the senior management of the hospital, explain how you perceive their role in making the implementation a success.
3. One of the senior managers is worried about the morale of the workers, who fear for their jobs. How would you deal with the potential problem of user resistance?
4. Are there governmental guidelines or standards that need to be followed? If so, can you brief senior management what these might be and what their implications are for HMIS implementation in this hospital?

CHAPTER REVIEW

The purpose of this chapter is to give an overview of HMIS implementation. Success in the implementation of HMIS technology is deeply rooted in organizational strategic planning. Therefore, certain aspects of organizational planning and management considerations must precede HMIS implementation. Moreover, a number of critical factors also influence the success of HMIS implementation. These generally fall into three categories: user characteristics, system design characteristics, and organizational characteristics.

Apart from the critical factors, a number of other issues need to be addressed. The need to assess the level of knowledge of the current staff body, to recruit knowledgeable and experienced staff members, and to provide adequate training of existing staff members may translate into delays in the implementation plan. The appropriate application of such tools of project scheduling and program coding as the critical path method (CPM), Gantt charts, data dictionaries (DD), and walkthroughs will certainly smooth the path of systems implementation and garner confidence from all sides. Considerations for future reengineering, end-user involvement, and vendor involvement will definitely enhance the success of HMIS in health service organizations.

In terms of system implementation (selection of system and inauguration), two stages are involved: preimplementation preparation and postimplementation upkeep. The steps involved in the preimplementation stage may vary from one health organization to another. However, they in general include initial conceptualization, strategic planning, feasibility study, request for proposals, proposal evaluation and selection, and physical implementation. In the postimplementation stage, a maintenance cycle, featuring periodic evaluations (postaudits), problem definition, initiation of maintenance project, research for solution, solution implementation, and documentation, is commonly used by many institutions with HMIS. Throughout these stages, HMIS planners should be aware of the influence of the "people aspects" of the system.

In addition, certain governmental guidelines or standards may have to be followed in designing and implementing an HMIS. Such legal issues as access to patient information and patient privacy rights should be settled before finalizing the implementation plan.

NOTES

1. G.W. Dickson and J.K. Simmons, The Behavioral Side of MIS: Five Factors Relating to Resistance, *Business Horizons* 13, no. 4 (1970): 59–71.

2. J.E. Toole and M.E. Caine, Laying a Foundation for the Future Information Systems, *Topics in Health Care Financing* 14, no. 2 (1988): 17–27.

3. Ibid.

4. R.W. Zmud, Individual Differences and MIS Success: A Review of the Empirical Literature, *Management Science* 25, no. 10 (1979): 966–979.

5. John Dearden, MIS Is a Mirage, *Harvard Business Review* 50, no. 1 (1972): 90–99.

6. Dickson and Simmons, The Behavioral Side of MIS.

7. K. Kropf, *San Bernadino County Medical Center Implementation of a Hospital Information System* (New York: New York University, 1990): 7–8.

8. M. Staggers, Human Factors: The Missing Element in Computer Technology, *Computer in Nursing* 9, no. 2 (1991): 47–49.

9. J.K.H. Tan, The Use of Redundant Codes in Graphing the Graphical Interface: An Extension of the Anchoring Principle in Human Processing of Graphical Information, Working paper (Vancouver: Faculty of Medicine, Department of Health Care and Epidemiology, University of British Columbia, 1991).

10. R. Lemon and J. Crudele, System Integration: Tying It All Together, *Healthcare Financial Management* 41, no. 6 (1987): 46–54.

11. H. Austin, Assessing the Performance of Information Technology, *Computers in Health Care* 9, no. 11 (1988): 56–58.

12. Ibid.

13. R.J. Feldman, System Evaluation and Implementation Strategies, in *Information Systems for Ambulatory Care,* ed. T.A. Matson and M.D. McDougall (Chicago: American Hospital Publishing, Inc., 1990), 67–78.

14. H.W. Ryan, User-Driven Systems Development: Defining a New Role for IS, *Information Systems Management* (Summer 1993): 66–68.

15. S. Gray, DP Salary Survey, *Datamation* 28, no. 11 (1982): 114–128.

16. J. Couger and R. Zawacki, What Motivates DP Professionals, *Datamation* 24, no. 9 (1978): 116–123.

17. K. Bartol and D. Martin, Managing Information Systems Personnel: A Review of the Literature and Managerial Implications, *MIS Quarterly.* Special issue (1982): 49–70.

18. J. Couger and M.A. Colter, *Motivation of the Maintenance Programmer* (Colorado Springs, Colo: CYSCS, 1983).

19. J. Baroudi, The Impact of Role Variables on Information Systems Personnel Work Attitudes and Intentions, *MIS Quarterly* 9, no. 4 (1985): 341–356.

20. K.C. Laudon and J.P. Laudon, *Management Information Systems: A Contemporary Perspective* (New York: Macmillan Publishing Co., 1988), 698.

21. C.J. Austin, *Information Systems for Health Service Administration* 4th ed. (Ann Arbor, Mich: AUPHA Press/Health Administration Press, 1992).

22. Ibid.

23. Ibid.

24. Feldman, System Evaluation, 67–78.

25. Ryan, User-Driven Systems, 66–68.

26. Kropf, *San Bernadino,* 7–8.

27. Feldman, System Evaluation, 67–78.

28. G.J. Mann, Managers, Groups, and People: Some Considerations in Information System Change, *Health Care Management Review* 13, no. 4 (1988): 43–48.

29. Feldman, System Evaluation, 67–78.

30. Lemon and Crudele, System Integration.

31. Austin, Assessing Performance, 56–58.

32. Ibid.

33. *Management Information Project.* Guidelines for Management Information Systems in Healthcare Facilities, Ambulatory Care Services and Implementation Manuals, Circulated report of MIS project, Ottawa, Revised October 1, 1993.

34. B. Lowry, Key MIS Guideline Issues for the Information Planning Process, *Healthcare Communication and Computing Canada* (4th Quarter 1987): 26–28.

35. Forum, MIS Project Guidelines, *Healthcare Communication and Computing Canada* (2nd Quarter 1988): 22–23.

36. D.M. Robinson, Patient Access to Health Records: New Legal Developments and Implementations, *Healthcare Communication and Computing Canada* (4th Quarter 1992): 54–60.

37. Ibid.

38. D.M. Robinson, Health Information Confidentiality: Balancing Extremes, *Healthcare Communication and Computing Canada* (3rd Quarter 1991): 8–9.

Chapter 13

The New Paradigm of Total Quality Management (TQM): The Crossroad between Health Management Information Systems and TQM

LEARNING OBJECTIVES

1. Define total quality management (TQM).
2. Identify principles and philosophies advocated by TQM gurus.
3. Formulate a TQM–health management information system (HMIS) framework for health service delivery.
4. Inventory the spectrum of tools to support TQM processes.
5. Identify critical quality factors linkage with HMIS.
6. Evaluate software to support TQM processes.
7. Identify the future role of HMIS for continuous quality improvement (CQI) in health service organizations.

INTRODUCTION

The paradigm is a cognitive structure or mechanism: however, this set of taken for granted assumptions and beliefs, which is more or less collectively owned, is . . . the organization symbols, . . . a short-hand representation of the nature of the organization.[1]

In today's turbulent health care environment, with various political, economic, and social pressures placed on health service institutions, the processes relating to high-quality health service delivery have now become an organizational paradigm, an integral part of health institution life, maintenance, and sustenance. Quality processes are needed to sustain health service institutions and maintain a viable, efficient, and effective organization that meets the needs of the people it serves.

Total quality management (TQM) processes are instituted within a health service organization in order to review, monitor, and perfect the performance (services) of the organization (structure and processes) along a never-ending cycle. All occurrences within the system take place for the purpose of providing high-quality service (care) to consumers (patients). The health service organization exists for this purpose and its cumulative activities, including data collection, process monitoring, outcome measurement, and performance evaluation, are points where health management information systems (HMIS) enter the TQM equation.

Is the health service organization doing things the right way (service efficiency)? More importantly, is it doing the right thing (service effectiveness)? Are customers (patients) satisfied with the type and delivery of services they are receiving (service excellence)? These and other questions that underlie the TQM concept cannot be adequately answered without the organization's first having a "quality-focus" HMIS.

The significance of such a quality-focus HMIS to the success of organizations in the health service business is clearly brought home in one of the minicases documented by Fuld:

> An information audit and needs assessment for a healthcare company revealed extremely tangled lines of communication which resulted in poor decisions—decisions that were made too late to take advantage of market opportunities. The company had to recall one of its products because its customers were experiencing adverse reactions. The company lost tens of millions of dollars on the recall. Unfortunately, the European parent had information in its R&D files that verified reformulation problems, but this information was misread or ignored by the American subsidiary. The result was a significant misjudgment and an expensive recall.[2]

The point here is that had there been a quality-focus information sharing (i.e., one with clear "lines of communication"), the research and development (R&D) information would have been intelligently shared among the company workers, and the very costly error would not have occurred.

HMIS processes applied to TQM incorporate all of the knowledge gathered in our previous discussions. First, the systems perspective is utilized in understanding TQM processes: a continuous quality improvement (CQI) program for a health service organization must function within an integrated system perspective in order to bring about organizationwide service quality (Chapter 3). In order to ascertain whether quality has been achieved, data on these elements must be collected and processed and performance criteria or indicator measures set in order to aid decision making concerning whether standards of service quality (efficiency, effectiveness, and excellence) have been met (Chapters 4 and 5). This life cycle of organizational learning incorporates the fundamental concepts of data management and HMIS designs and development (Chapter 6). Moreover, the goal of achieving world-class performance for health service organizations in an information era cannot be realized without the support of advancing HMIS technologies and applications (Chapters 7 through 9). Finally, success of TQM or CQI in health service organizations is not possible without a strong corporate vision, an empowered and committed group of frontline workers, and an effective information sharing and communication system, all of which depend critically on the organization's ability to plan, manage, and implement effective HMIS (Chapters 10 through 12).

This chapter attempts to show how HMIS activities, by supporting intelligent information analysis (IIA) and health managerial decision making, can be used to achieve TQM in health service delivery on an ongoing basis. With HMIS intelligently incorporated into a health service organization's data collection, process monitoring, and performance evaluation systems, success with regard to service excellence can keep pace with the high-quality patient services demanded in today's health service delivery industry. The chapter begins with a definition of the total quality management concept, followed by a brief discussion of TQM principles and philosophies from the perspectives of three TQM gurus. The TQM paradigm as viewed from an HMIS imperative and the analytical tools used to support TQM processes are then presented. A review of the five critical factors in the Baldrige Award for quality awareness is used to illustrate how HMIS activities may be applied for quality management (QM) in health service delivery. Software that can be used to support TQM processes is also surveyed, and the chapter closes with a look at the future role of HMIS for CQI in health service organizations.

TQM DEFINITION, PRINCIPLES, AND PHILOSOPHIES

TQM refers essentially to the dynamic perpetual drive to increase focus on constant improvement rather than on minimal standards. The current health care situation can be characterized as an era of change. The implementation of TQM by many health service facilities is seen as a viable means of addressing change in the perception of quality. It is thought that TQM will provide a viable framework for ensuring continued high quality in the health service setting by focusing on customer (i.e., patients, payers, regulators, physicians, etc.) satisfaction despite the threat of budget constraints. TQM consists of a wide array of managerial and organizational activities designed to help management understand and streamline production processes, to eliminate waste and unpredictability, and to achieve previously unprecedented levels of performance in customer service.

For health service organizations, TQM's results are measured in terms of the needs and experiences of customers (e.g., patient satisfaction or any other customer satisfaction). It is thought that by improving processes (process redesign) it is possible to improve the quality of work or performance of the health service providers. This in turn will meet the patient or customer expectations (patient or other customer requirements). Exhibit 13–1 shows this basic conceptualization of TQM.

A current definition of TQM is that it is a structured system for creating organizationwide participation in planning and implementing a continuous improvement process to meet and exceed customer needs. According to the U.S. Federal Quality Institute, it is a "strategic integrated management system for achieving customer satisfaction which involves all managers and employees and uses quantitative methods to continuously improve an organization's processes."[3]

Perspectives from Three TQM Gurus

TQM concepts, principles, and philosophies are the cumulative thinking of many scholars, most notably Dr. Edwards Deming, whose work in the field of management has been recognized as revolutionary. Others include Philip Crosby, whose consulting work on quality is widely acclaimed, and Dr. Joseph Juran, who has published extensively and developed the "Quality Trilogy" as a universal way of applying quality concepts.

Exhibit 13–1 A Basic Conceptualization of Total Quality Management (TQM)

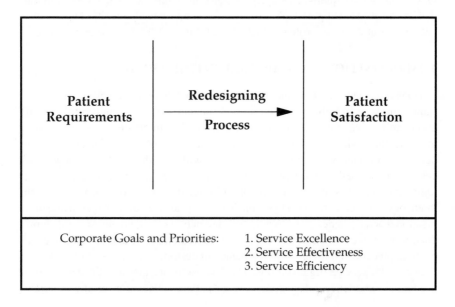

Since the early fifties, Deming has emphasized the significance of quality and helped to educate Japanese manufacturing leaders in statistical quality improvement (QI) methods. Deming's 14 Points embody the concepts, principles, and philosophies related to QM.

1. Create consistency of purpose.
2. Adopt the new philosophy.
3. Cease dependence on mass inspection.
4. End the practice of awarding business on price tag alone.
5. Improve constantly and forever the system of production and service.
6. Institute training and retraining.
7. Institute leadership.
8. Drive out fear.
9. Break down the barriers between departments.
10. Eliminate slogans, exhortations, and targets for the work force.
11. Eliminate numerical quotas.
12. Remove barriers to pride of workmanship.
13. Institute a vigorous program of education and retraining.
14. Take action to accomplish the transformation.[4]

Altogether, the theme of Deming's 14 points for health service delivery is completely reinventing the way management envisions success in health service organizations. In other words, QM involves leaving behind the "old" ways of doing things, redesigning (and, even more radically, reengineering) processes, regularly asking how the current services can be improved, and acquiring new knowledge and skills continually. In Deming's view, health service CEOs and managers must recognize the need to establish the time frame and criteria for managerial performance evaluation, cultivate loyalty and trust among professional workers that will result in long-term relationships, train and educate staff, discover the barriers preventing workers from taking pride in their work, and continually seek ways to empower workers to perform well. To do this, Deming argued that managers must establish an open line of communications with workers and customers (patients) so as to encourage their feedback, participation, and ideas; eliminate goal conflicts among subordinates by enforcing a unified "vision"; delegate as much authority as possible to subordinates; and organize themselves as teams.

Unlike Dr. Deming, who does not believe in the necessity of measuring the "cost of quality," Crosby argues that this in fact is the best measure of quality. Accordingly, Crosby divides this cost into two parts: (1) costs associated with conformance and (2) costs associated with nonconformance.[5]

Whereas the former refers to the cost of normal operation including education, training, inspection, testing, and prevention, the latter refers to the cost of internal and external failures including reinspection, liability and damage claims, replacement cost, and costs associated with legal proceedings and the loss of valued customers. Therefore quality, in Crosby's view, is "conformance to requirements," and he strongly advocates a system of QI that is based on prevention rather than appraisal.

Dr. Juran, founder of the Juran Quality Institute, believes that an organization should begin its focus on quality by planning for it (quality planning). The purpose of this step is to design a process that is capable of meeting quality goals as defined by the needs of internal and external "customers." The next step is quality control, which involves the definition of quality attributes to be monitored, measured, and controlled by focusing on processes (quality monitors). The final step in Juran's "Quality Trilogy" is to study the processes and outcomes thoroughly with the purpose of locating the critical points where quality breakthroughs can be achieved (quality improvement).[6]

In the 1970s and early 1980s quality assurance (QA) was the contemporary mind-set of most health service managers. It was a traditional problem-solving management philosophy, atomistic in its approach in that it focused on specific isolated causes of undesirable outcomes. It was further characterized as primarily reacting to problems (i.e., "find and fix"). Its scope was on the internal, departmental "bad apples." Ultimately, it was thought to encourage mediocrity.

In contrast, TQM is "a conceptual approach different from quality assurance and quality inspection and runs counter to many underlying assumptions of professional bureaucracies."[7] Whereas QA emphasized individual responsibility, professional and managerial authority, quality standards, and rigid objectives and plans, TQM emphasizes collective (team) responsibility, participatory authority, continuous improvement, and flexible objectives and plans. Figure 13–1 portrays the traditional QA versus the contemporary TQM structure and the role of HMIS as it relates to the two different approaches.

Quality in health services has traditionally been defined by physicians and hospitals in professional and technical terms.[8] Today, however, the renewed interest in quality has brought about a new perspective and definition that will necessarily include the perception and satisfaction of customers (patients) receiving the services. Consequently, with the diverse and more externalized demands placed on health service providers, the limitations of traditional managerial approaches such as QA are even more apparent.

Strengths and Weaknesses of TQM

In the context of today's changing health care environment, TQM is therefore seen as a viable alternative to managing change. Moreover, the concept has al-

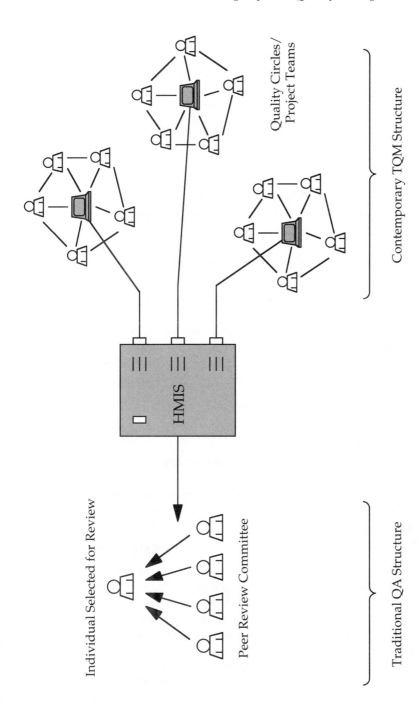

Individual Selected for Review

Peer Review Committee

HMIS

Quality Circles/
Project Teams

Contemporary TQM Structure

Traditional QA Structure

Figure 13–1 Quality Assurance (QA) versus Total Quality Management (TQM) Philosophies

ready proved successful in private sector markets. Its implementation, however, is not without pain; for example, one organization in health service delivery lost several employees including a few of its best workers when attempting to institute a TQM program because the mind-sets of these workers were not accustomed to the radical changes that were occurring within the organization. In fact, recent evidence suggests that in some industries, "TQM appeared to be just one more hothouse Japanese flower never meant to grow on rocky American ground."[9] This entreats us to spell out a list of the strengths and weaknesses of the TQM approach.

On the one hand, the following elements constitute the strengths of TQM:

- TQM places customers first, with their satisfaction as the "gold standard."
- TQM provides a blending of "soft" management techniques with "hard" data and measures.
- TQM encourages participation (teams) in organization problem diagnosis and problem solving although employees still work within traditional job descriptions.
- TQM can be used in large geographically and culturally diverse organizations.
- TQM performance management is a one-on-one activity with individual performance being critical to the success of "quality first."
- TQM requires few or no contractual changes even though labor and management must collaborate.

On the other hand, the following challenges constitute TQM weaknesses:

- TQM is not easy to understand, especially for nonmanagerial workers, making commitment inconsistent.
- TQM is often associated with a "conversion process" analogous to a "quasi-religious" movement.
- TQM requires clear explicit measures that are not always possible.
- TQM can be expensive and does not guarantee success.
- TQM tends to be a one-way communication and education process.
- TQM maintains the traditional hierarchy within the organization.

According to Mathews and Katel, "Two rituals are sacred to the devout TQM congregation. First, managers must act as if they have signs on their backs: HOW ARE WE DOING? ANY COMPLAINTS? CALL 1-800-BLAMEUS. . . . The second ritual is the posse play. When something goes wrong, TQM executives recruit a few managers, clerks, assembly-line workers and even customers to ride off, find the problem and literally analyze it to death."[10]

This discussion of its strengths and weaknesses is meant to provide a clearer understanding of TQM in a real-world context. In short, TQM as a management philosophy is not without problems. However, it does provide a way out from the "business as usual" traditional management philosophies.

A TQM PARADIGM: THE HMIS IMPERATIVE

The TQM approach represents a total paradigm shift in health service management, and the burden of its successful implementation falls squarely on the shoulders of top management.[11] In many organizations, health service organizations included, it is found that TQM implementation begins with CEO interest and curiosity, which evolve into a "conversion process" wherein the CEO internalizes the principles and starts to refocus the organization's management philosophy.[12] From this point, senior management is increasingly integrated into the process. A formal TQM body or council is established with the intended purpose of filtering through the various facets of the organization.

A key question to be answered for health service organizations is therefore, How should the CEO (or the CIO) visualize the TQM process, and what role can HMIS play to promote successful TQM? Figure 13–2 shows a schematic view of the strategic and functional ties between the TQM concept and all HMIS concepts embraced in this book.

Figure 13–2 depicts the two contexts (i.e., environmental and organizational contexts) that continually define and shape the TQM paradigm for the organizational system, but the apparatus for promoting and ensuring TQM success is no more than the organizational HMIS. In short, it is the design of an organizational intelligent information analysis (IIA) system that will continually drive the TQM paradigm top-down through the organization in achieving the goals of service excellence, effectiveness, and efficiency.

On the one hand, an information analysis of opportunities and threats in the environment to shape the strategic understanding of TQM implications for the organization is needed. This will result in asking questions such as, What is it that we produce (outcome)? Are we producing the right things, that is, those products and services that meet customers' (patients') needs?

On the other hand, an information analysis of particular strengths and weaknesses of the system processes within the organizational context will point to areas where the organization might particularly consider applying TQM. Some of the questions to be asked in this realm are, How do we produce what we produce (process)? Are we producing these products (services) in the right way? TQM involves asking whether a health service organization is producing the most needed services in the best possible way, a concept that epitomizes the ideal of system optimization.

In a health service organization, IIA is an information collection, monitoring, and control system that parallels the concepts of Juran's Quality Trilogy:

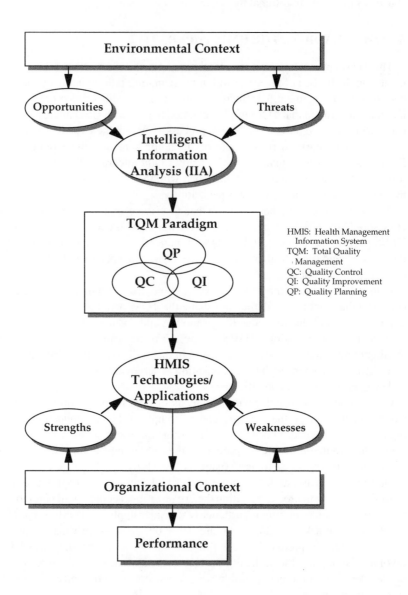

Figure 13–2 The Paradigm of TQM: An HMIS Perspective

- Quality planning: defining quality HMIS input
- Quality control: monitoring and evaluating quality HMIS output
- Quality improvement: monitoring, investigating, and modifying quality HMIS processes

Quality Planning: Defining Quality HMIS Input

Defining quality in health services begins with quality planning. This involves, first, identifying patient or other customer satisfaction, which in turn depends largely on how patient's or customer's requirements are met. In other words, what are the expectations of the customer with respect to service quality? The responses from a customer survey, for example, can be translated into specific individual requirements for the health organization's IIA, a critical HMIS application designed specifically for promoting TQM. This is a direct consequence of the fact that the needed action can be produced only if the right request is heard. Consequently for QM to be operative, high-quality data that are relevant, timely, meaningful, and accurate must be used as input to the system (i.e., quality HMIS input). In addition, data from the evaluation of quality performance (i.e., quality HMIS output) in terms of specific, measurable indicators must be available to generate constant feedback into the organizational QM IIA system. This means that the data derived from these measures, as well as information generated from them, provide additional valuable inputs that are needed for the system to improve its product or service quality. This information processing model pertains to TQM thinking, which will eventually form the mind-set that can be used for redesigning health managerial decision-making processes and for achieving a paradigm of continuous QM in a health service organization.

Therefore, in health service organizations that are trying to put quality first, the ability to define clearly who their customers are is an important first step. For example, in a hospital setting, patients, payers, regulators, suppliers, physicians, and specialists having practicing privileges at the facility may all be considered major customers. The next step is then to identify high-priority customer needs accurately and to match these needs to product (service) characteristics. In this sense, QM can be instituted at various levels and for various departments. The key is to be able to specify clearly which quality data are to be collected; otherwise, the whole exercise is merely rhetoric. In any case, quality HMIS inputs (i.e., relevant and valid data relating to quality indicators and feedback from surveys of customer requirements) are then processed by using appropriate and available HMIS technologies (e.g., TPS, OIS, DBMS, AI, ES, CMIS, C-MIS: Chapters 7 through 9), to give management the information needed for job design (or, redesign) that will produce the needed quality products or services. Hence, it is also equally important for the organization to spell out the types of products and services that are acceptable to the customers, and this is where quality HMIS output comes into play.

Quality Control: Monitoring and Evaluating Quality HMIS Output

The question to ask regarding what outcomes should be monitored in health services has been explained by Donabedian.[13] Health managers and professionals alike (since we are all working together for quality) should ask, If we are successful in the services we are carrying out, what change should we see in the customer (the outcome indicator)? For example, if our customers are patients, then changes could include changes in health state, changes in health knowledge, changes in health behavior pertinent to future health states, or more simply, changes in patient satisfaction with health services.

In conjunction with these outcomes tasks/decisions/processes must be carried out in order to reach the outcome (e.g., test, drug, procedure, education, interaction, etc.). Various chains of events eventually produce an outcome and this chain of events should indicate to health service professionals whether they are on the right track to reaching quality goals. This is the realm of process analysis, which we discuss later. Sometimes, in health service delivery, it is difficult to say where a process ends and an outcome is reached. The problem is amplified when outcomes are multidimensional. Again, in the case of patients as noted in our example, we must ask, When did the patient become different?, in terms of our preset standard for "different."

In this regard, one should keep in mind that outcomes do not directly assess quality of performance.[14] Outcomes only permit an inference regarding the quality of the process that occurred. The degree of confidence in that inference is based on the strength of the (causal) relationship between the processes and the outcome. Only when this relationship is sound can we draw conclusions regarding quality based simply on outcomes. Although the evaluation of process and performance is the entire focus of TQM, here we will simply take a holistic look at the measurement and evaluation of final outcome from a quality HMIS perspective.

First, an issue that deserves mention in terms of quality control is the integrative property of outcomes (i.e., quality HMIS output), which makes it difficult to isolate with certainty the process contributions that lead to negative outcomes. Outcome measures the combined effects of all causes operating inside and outside the system.[15] Differentiating causes of negative outcomes is therefore emphasized in QM performance evaluation. Kritchevsky and Simmons argued that all systems failures to achieve a desired level of quality stem from two sources: "systemic," or common causes that arise from within the system, and "extrasystemic," or special causes that are external to the system.[16]

Figures 13–3 and 13–4 graphically illustrate the characteristics and performance trend of a systemic cause. Figure 13–3 shows that when a systemic cause is

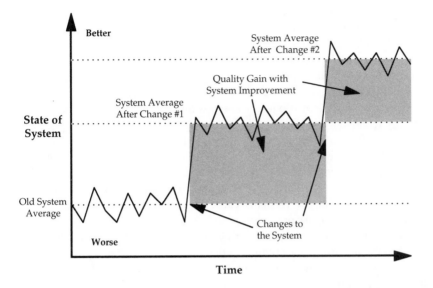

Figure 13–3 An Example of Presence and Trends of Systemic Cause and Improvement

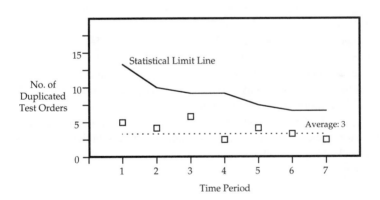

Figure 13–4 A Nonrandom Variation Carried by Systemic Improvement

corrected, the system improvement is a total shift in terms of performance since the cause of the quality problem is really a part of the system. This improvement can be achieved incrementally as the organization becomes more and more quality conscious. Figure 13–4 shows that the presence of a systemic cause in the system is generating a nonrandom variation albeit within reasonable limits from the average of quality performance. A case of a systemic cause would be one in which it was found that the use of triplicates in a test ordering HMIS is responsible for producing redundant (e.g., duplicated) test orders even though the requested test results were often received previously by the ordering physicians. When a duplicate order form is used instead of the original triplicate, for example, it produces a systemic improvement in quality service to the ordering physicians.

In contrast, Figures 13–5 and 13–6 graphically illustrate the characteristics and performance trend of an extrasystemic cause. Figure 13–5 shows that such a cause may either result in a deterioration in quality (shaded trough or valley) or in fact cause an improvement—albeit temporary—in the system (nonshaded bump or hill). The system performance returns to the same average when these causes are either consumed or removed. Figure 13–6 shows that the presence of an extrasystemic cause in the system is generated as an "outlier" of quality performance. The case in which quality improvement is suddenly observed through an influx of a group of "world-class" visiting physicians to the hospital is an example of an extrasystemic cause. Of course, if poorly trained physicians were exchanged into another facility, they would provide a good example of an extrasystemic cause of temporary deterioration of service quality in that facility.

Quality control should therefore focus on both systemic and extrasystemic causes. However, QM effort directed to systemic causes affects the total system (i.e., it affects everyone in the system) and will thus produce a permanent change in the level of quality performance, whereas quality control that focuses on extrasystemic causes alone may produce only temporary improvement and the average of the majority remains the same.

Second, in order for an organization to be able to control quality and produce desirable outcomes, it must also explicitly state two things, both of which require the appropriate design of HMIS:

1. Indicators
2. Measures

Indicators are needed in order to determine what level of performance quality is or is not acceptable. They are set against standards, and if standards are not being met, indicators reflect where the gap in performance exists. Indicators are also useful in that they can detect possible causes of a problem by indicating where these causes may lie. Indicators also provide the necessary feedback to decision making. They show whether or not a manager should continue to use present deci-

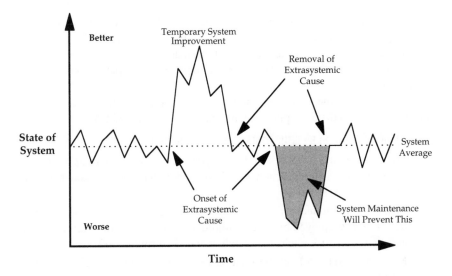

Figure 13–5 An Example of Presence and Trends of Extrasystemic Cause and Improvement

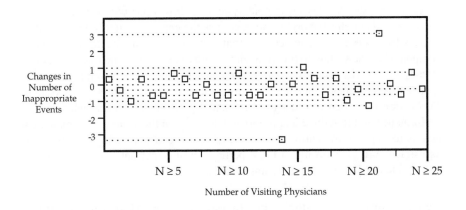

Figure 13–6 Outliers Caused by Temporary Extrasystemic Interventions

sion-making methods because they help detect whether objectives and standards are being reached. Overall, indicators monitor performance, identify causes and areas of deviation, and allow assumptions to be made about process and outcomes. An example of an indicator in health service delivery is the patient mortality rate for a particular procedure and length of stay.

Finison outlines the following criteria for appropriate health service measures related to quality HMIS output (here, a clinical bias is alluded to):[17]

- Measures should be collectible and chartable by line staff.
- Measures should be built into the everyday routine of the staff as monitoring can then occur in conjunction with daily work/service processes, where quality is to be assessed.
- Measures should use technology that is available to line staff. Such technology is to be employed by process improvement teams to monitor daily work and should incorporate data collection and charting methods.
- Measures should reflect the relation between outcome(s) and key process variables.
- Measures should show changes seen in indicator values over a period of time.
- Measures should involve organizational commitment and genuine internal interest.
- The quality measuring process should be simple and carefully planned by using a flowchart.

As we can see, the organizational system described has within it a feedback mechanism that helps the organization control the gap between its desired quality outputs (preestablished) and actual outputs. In order for this feedback or control component of the system to function with regard to QM, goals and objectives must already be set. The corrective action that can subsequently be taken then is a response to a discrepancy between the desired and the actual output in the system. This action is needed in order to bring actual performance in line with desired performance and to reduce inappropriate variations in the system. The main idea here is to improve the entire process continuously and not simply to meet standards. This brings us to the last and perhaps most important component of Dr. Juran's Quality Trilogy—quality improvement.

Quality Improvement: Monitoring, Investigating, and Modifying Quality HMIS Processes

One should note that within the process of TQM the goal is continuous improvement. To this end, the standards alluded to in the preceding framework are broad standards depicting quality states for which monitoring is carried out.

Finison emphasizes that the stages of the process should be a translation of professional standards into operational requirements, and not a translation of current reality into operational standards.[18]

From this framework, a chain of activities leading to a particular quality outcome can then be designed. Undertaking processes (services) that lead to quality can be expressed in the form of an information flow diagram (flowchart). For example, in the case of our patient model, the flowchart is a critical path of all the processes involved in carrying out a service for a patient (or case mix of patients). It is sequential and shows how a patient moves through the procedure or service. At each point in the flowchart, quality criteria, indicators, and measures are included. These steps are outlined so that quality services can be carried out effectively and efficiently or monitored to ensure that they are carried out in such a manner.

TQM advocates the use of a scientific approach to process improvement. Sahney and Warden note that alteration of the process "based on whims and hunches amounts to tampering and destabilizes the process."[19] They suggest using the nine-step process improvement methodology of FOCUS-PDCA recommended by Dr. Batalden and his colleagues of the HCA Quality Resource Group, which incorporates the Deming-Shewhart PDCA cycle:[20]

1. Find a process to improve.
2. Organize a team that knows the process.
3. Clarify current knowledge of the process.
4. Understand sources of process variation.
5. Select the process improvement.

Also called the Shewhart cycle, the PDCA cycle essentially refers to the following four points:[21]

1. Plan: this is to study the process and to decide on what needs to be changed to improve the system.
2. Do: this refers to the gathering and analysis of data or inputs.
3. Check: this refers to the checking of data and the study of the effects of the recommended changes.
4. Act: this is to determine what parts of the improved process should be standardized.

The traditional notion that the management is in charge of "planning," the health professionals in charge of "doing," the supervisors and senior health professionals in charge of "checking," and the nurses and other health professionals in charge of "acting" is fast giving way to the concept that every member of a health service delivery organization must practice the entire cycle in order to make the improvement effort successful. Moreover, the PDCA cycle should be practiced in daily routines, as well as in nonroutine situations. The simple act of self-checking and reflection is expected to bring new insights into currently adopted procedures and organization. As may be seen, the FOCUS-PDCA methodology relies largely on intelligent information processing by every member of the health service organization.

In addition to the FOCUS-PDCA approach, two important principles for quality process improvement are the 4Ms (discussed in relation to the fishbone diagram later in the chapter) and what the Japanese call *Genba, Genbutsu. Genba* means to go see the place where the problem is occurring, *Genbutsu* means to observe the material or product with the defects itself.[22] Too often, managers of health service delivery organizations rely too much on meetings and printed reports to understand the services provided by the organization: that is, they are remote from the "action." The essence of *Genba, Genbutsu* is captured in the saying "Seeing is believing," which is far more effective than presenting information in meetings and reports alone. Health organization managers are therefore encouraged to visit patients and health professionals in the wards and waiting rooms and to communicate directly with them. The same principle applies the collection of firsthand information, which essentially implies a redesign of current HMIS for quality purposes.

Put together, the process improvement methodology implies, first, identifying a critical process in the system, bringing it under statistical control, and eliminating any "undesirable" extrasystemic causes, and, second, using the FOCUS-PDCA cycle and other approaches to improve the process incrementally by eliminating systemic causes one by one. Kuperman et al. outline how the FOCUS-PDCA process is to occur.[23] The authors use a clinical scenario in their example to depict such a process. Health care professionals, working as a team, would be included in this example as they document each stage of the process and its expected outcomes (determining standards to be met). The key steps in the process are emphasized, and in succession they determine the quality of the outcome. The health professionals are reminded that all steps in the process must have measures associated with them. As the process occurs data are collected and analyzed. The final outcome (the stage that is determined to be the outcome) is also measured and evaluated. According to Selbmann and Pietsch-Brietfeld, what is occurring is a quality cycle, where a routine monitoring of quality indicators is taking place and a comparison of these indicators to preset standards is occurring.[24] If these indicators compare unfavorably with the standards, a modification is made to the quality process until the indicator measures compare favorably with their preset standards.

From an HMIS perspective, the IIA system acts as feedback so that corrective actions in response to variations in the system can be used to bring actual performance in line with the desired quality level, if this is not already the case. All subsystems of the system (the organization) function individually in their processes (inputs, processes, and outputs related to quality) and must eventually interact to provide the organization with its overall goals and objectives and mission (quality). The feedback that occurs within the whole system (all subsystems included) is to be seen as a positive progression toward quality, and not as a negative "policing" of organizational processes.

Thus, the system can then see where improvements can be made and where accountability for particular processes can be assigned through the feedback/control loop. Burke et al. give an example that relates to optimization of the system.[25] The authors illustrate that data on key process steps and their outcomes can be analyzed and compared against preset standards. The variation between the actual and the expected can show, through optimization indicators, where quality waste and inefficiency occur in the service delivery process. This information is then relayed to health service professionals so they can change practice/service patterns in order to meet standards. This type of subsystem feedback is part of a greater system feedback that evaluates performance and progress at regular intervals.

Very often, the entire system tries to achieve the best quality while also trying to conserve resources. In effect, certain criteria are to be maximized while cost is to be minimized. As Daigh explains, cost and quality are not conflicting but complementary.[26] High quality need not increase cost but instead should result in improved productivity and reduced waste in the system. The author states that it is poor quality that is expensive. The kind of quality that produces an appropriate service for a patient reduces errors, rework, inefficiency, and waste. All these attributes result in reduced costs.

A health service organization manager can monitor costs associated with service processes leading to quality outcomes through a "quality chain." The chain includes processes that lead to fewer mistakes, effective work, fewer delays, and efficient use of time and materials. Quantifying resources related to quality improvement processes in this chain provides a means of measuring, monitoring, and analyzing the resources used within such a process. The chain can lead to increased quality and decreased cost since series of actions (processes) designed to produce a desired outcome can be changed/modified/redesigned/improved in order to make the quality process more efficient while maintaining effectiveness (performance). The challenge is to reduce total quality costs by better design of the process. Time should be spent on quality planning and design, as well as monitoring and reporting, in order to control costs associated with quality processes.

As we have seen, TQM employs a very different philosophy from QA, namely, decentralization through the use of project teams. Multidisciplinary project teams of frontline employees collect and analyze data from clinical and administrative sources, both internal and external to the organization. The project team determines the type and scope of data to be collected, collects the data itself, and determines how it will analyze the data and how the data will be used to take corrective action. As it is common in TQM organizations to have several project teams working concurrently on different problems, there is often data sharing among the various project teams. This sharing of information eliminates redundancy of collection and analysis and is the key function of an IIA, the central functioning of a quality-focus HMIS in the organization. In other words, organization needs to take a good look at how their design of HMIS can be used to promote QM throughout the subsystems of the total system.

Other significant roles of IIA in promoting TQM are data presentation and dissemination. With the shift from centralization of problem solving to decentralization, the organization must plan and implement strategies to manage the emerging data. Centralized information systems management alone is no longer the ideal means to aid these quality project teams. The transition to TQM necessitates the change from a centralized mainframe information system to an integrated but distributed technology, supported by IIA and other HMIS subsystems, which each project team can readily access and utilize to solve quality problems. Whereas traditional HMIS designs (e.g., QA reports) provided only summaries of counts and percentages that were not widely disclosed, TQM utilizes many graphical tools to demonstrate data that are widely distributed. The next section will discuss some examples of TQM tools.

TQM TOOLS

The focus of TQM is on process, in that the quality of outcome is determined largely by the quality of the process. TQM applies the scientific method to improve processes continually by using data, statistics, and "tools" to search for the underlying causes and determine problem solutions. There are seven tools, used commonly by TQM project teams, which help to identify a problem and then analyze it further so that appropriate corrective action can be identified and implemented. The TQM process consists of two phases: problem finding and problem solving; each of the seven tools fits into one or both of these stages, as depicted in Figure 13–7.

In order to understand the use of these seven tools, each TQM tool will be discussed alongside a case simulation to illustrate the tools and techniques in the context of a realistic health service oriented example—waiting times in the emergency room (ER).

The Metropolitan Emergency Room (ER) Waiting Times Problem

The management of Metropolitan Hospital (MH) came to realize that the hospital has a problem with patient satisfaction in the emergency room (ER). On average it has been estimated that it takes 5 hours from the time patients arrive at the

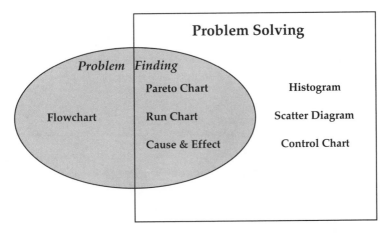

Figure 13–7 A Classification of Total Quality Management (TQM) Tools for Problem Finding and Problem Solving

ER until they are transferred to a bed in the hospital. Further, most of this time (about 3 hours) occurs after the ER physician has made the decision to admit the patient to a hospital bed. This decision is communicated by making the appropriate notation in the patient's chart. The communication process that is involved with admitting a patient from the ER to an inpatient bed is, however, complicated as there are many people involved: ER resident, ER admitting physician, clerks in the admitting department, ER nurses, floor nurses, lab personnel, and so on. As a result of management's finding the problem in the ER, a TQM project team was formed to address the situation.

Before taking appropriate corrective action, the TQM team wanted a clear definition of the problem. A statement explicitly stating that the problem, including its location, time, and scope, was to be written. In order to facilitate this process, the following TQM tools were examined.

1. The Flowchart
2. The Run chart
3. The Fishbone (cause-and-effect) diagrams
4. The Pareto chart

The flowchart (introduced in Chapter 4) is a graphical representation of the steps involved in a process. By "flowcharting" the steps, the chart enables the project team to think clearly through relationships between steps, the dependency of steps, the ordering of steps, and the individuals and departments involved. By examining the completed flowchart, potential or actual sources of trouble can often be identified and redundancy of steps targeted.

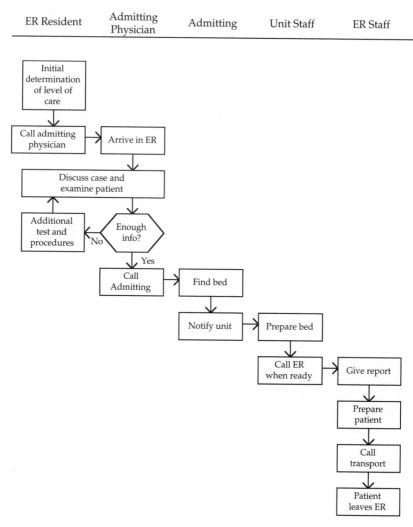

Figure 13–8 Flowcharting a Patient's Path in the Emergency Room (ER) at Metropolitan

The TQM project team started addressing the apparent problem in the ER by flowcharting the steps involved from the decision by the ER resident to admit the patient to the patient's leaving the ER for the ward. The team's flowchart is illustrated in Figure 13–8.

From this detailed flowchart, the TQM Team created their problem statement "to reduce the time needed from the point when the ER resident makes the initial determination of the patient's required level of care to the point when the patient leaves the ER for an inpatient bed."

A flowchart thus defines a service process and its operational requirements. As the patient's condition becomes more complicated, additional sections can be added to the flowchart to reflect the various processes, health professionals, and departments needed to provide quality service for such added complexity.

The run chart is a simple graphical representation of data that allows the project team to identify trends or to monitor processes over a specified period. By using a run chart, not only can trends be identified, but the magnitude of the variation may also be estimated.

In order to identify variations in the time a patient spends in the ER, the team collected data. Twenty patient charts were reviewed for the time spent in the ER. The data were presented in a run chart, shown in Figure 13–9.

The fishbone (cause-and-effect) diagram, also referred to as an "Ishikawa" diagram after Kaoru Ishikawa, who developed it, assists in locating the "causes" associated with the "effect" or problem. Possible causes are exhausted and then grouped according to their similarities. A method commonly used for grouping causes in process control improvement is to attend to the 4Ms, that is men (people), materials, methods, and machines. To locate the true cause and to find the right countermeasure, the 4Ms should first be standardized and staff then asked to follow the standardized procedure in order to stabilize the operation under current conditions. A useful technique to exhaust all possible causes is to ask, "Why?" repeatedly as each potential cause is identified. In using this technique,

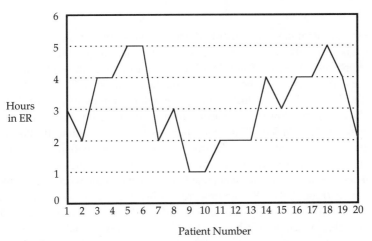

Patient Number

Figure 13–9 A Run Chart Showing the Time Patients Spend in the Emergency Room (ER) at Metropolitan

hidden (less obvious) causes that may have been overlooked are often identified, after the most obvious ones are determined. In creating the diagram, it is important not to consider only the most likely causes. Users should first brainstorm suggestions to complete the diagram, then think through the potential causes. In order to understand the causes associated with the prolonged time a patient is in the ER, the TQM team brainstormed ideas and created the fishbone diagram of Figure 13–10.

The Pareto chart is based on the 80/20 Pareto principle: 80 percent of the trouble arises from 20 percent of the problems. By using it to examine possible causes of the problem, it allows one to determine the 20 percent of the causes on which to concentrate their efforts. The Pareto chart is essentially a bar chart of the possible causes (usually derived from the fishbone diagram) with attached attribute data. Once the chart is completed, it is easy to see which are the "vital few" and the "useful many" suggested causes of the problem. The project team again collected data to determine which of the many causes identified should be the focus of their attention. Figure 13–11 shows the Pareto chart compiled by the team.

Other Useful TQM Tools

In addition to those four tools just described, there are three very useful TQM tools, as shown previously in Figure 13–7. Unlike the earlier set, these latter tools are not suited for problem finding; rather, they are more appropriate for problem solving:

1. The histogram
2. The scatter diagram
3. The control chart

Once the problem has been identified and a clear problem statement has been derived, it is necessary to start identifying corrective actions that will successfully solve the problem. The use of TQM tools can help to analyze the problem further so that the correct action can be chosen for implementation.

Like the Pareto chart, the histogram is a graphical representation of data by means of a bar graph. However, the histogram uses data that involve measurement (e.g., frequency, dimensions, time) and displays their distribution. It allows the project team to see variation in the data and demonstrates the amount of variability in the process. After reviewing information and assessing the data and TQM charts, it became apparent to the team that two distinct processes occurred in moving the patient through the ER. The first process involved the steps and time interval from the ER physician's decision to admit the patient to the admitting physician's call to the admitting department. This process was labeled "Decision to Call." The second process involved the steps and interval from the admitting physician's call to the admitting department to the transfer of the patient from the

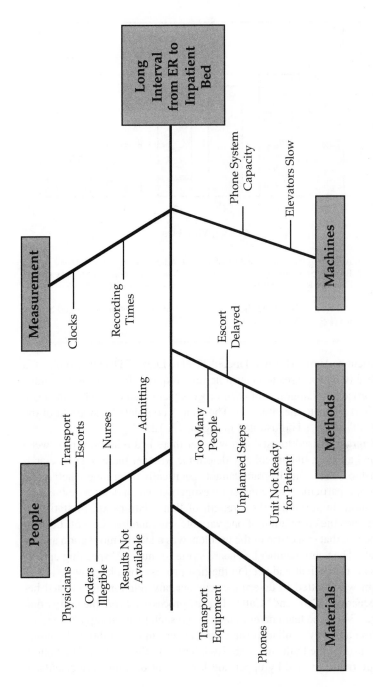

Figure 13–10 A Fishbone (Ishikawa) Diagram Showing Possible Causes of a Prolonged Stay in the Emergency Room (ER) at Metropolitan

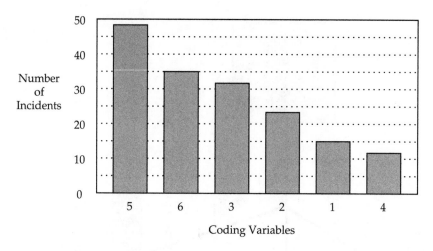

Coding Variables

1. Admitting Physician Not Available   4. Admitting Department Delay
2. Escort Not Available   5. Transport Equipment Not Available
3. Unit Not Ready for Patient   6. Test Results Not Available

Figure 13–11 A Pareto Chart Showing the Frequency of Six Causes of Prolonged Stay in the Emergency Room (ER) at Metropolitan

ER to the inpatient bed unit. This was labeled "Call to Leave." Data were collected on each of these two processes to determine time required for a patient to move through each process. Histograms of each process were then created so the team could review and evaluate the situation. The team's completed histogram of the "Decision to Call" process is illustrated in Figure 13–12.

A scatter diagram is used to establish whether there is a relationship between one variable and another, in particular to determine whether there is a cause-and-effect relationship. While the diagram cannot specifically determine whether the effect is due to the particular cause under investigation, it can determine the relationship and, more importantly, the strength of that relationship. In statistical terms, it determines the correlation of one variable with another. One of the team members suspected that one cause of the problem was a lack of motivation among the nursing staff. The team member had heard stories of nurses' "speeding up" the second process if the patient had been in the first process for a lengthy period. A scatter diagram was plotted to determine whether any relationship existed between the "Decision to Call" and "Call to Leave" processes. From the scatter diagram of Figure 13–13, the team determined that no such relationship existed.

Control charts are very similar to run charts except in one additional feature: they also demonstrate the built-in variability inherent in the process. The boundaries, which are demonstrated by upper and lower control limits, are calculated

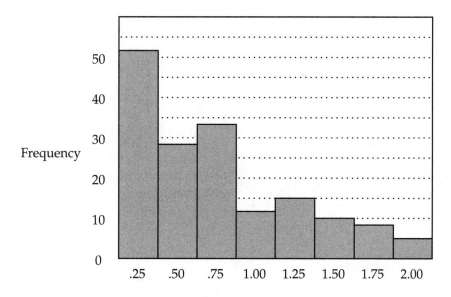

Time To Proceed through Process (Hours)

Figure 13–12 A Histogram To Show Time from Initial Admission to the Emergency Room until the "Decision to Call" at Metropolitan

statistically from data collected on the process under investigation. By examining the control charts, the project team is able to discern whether variability is "systemic" or "extrasystemic." As discussed earlier, systemic causes of variation have data points lying within the control limits set, whereas extrasystemic causes have data points lying beyond the control limit barriers.

Through control charts, the project team continued with their investigation and derived possible modification to the entire ER process. Having implemented the modification, they wanted to monitor the time it took for a patient to move through the ER, to see whether these changes corrected the problem. The team determined that 3 hours was an acceptable and achievable length of time for a patient to travel through the entire process. The team therefore decided that control limits of 2 and 4 hours would be set. The team's control chart is illustrated in Figure 13–14.

Other tools, in particular those that have been used in practice by management for TQM purposes, include the affinity diagram, interrelationship diagram, time log, tree diagram, matrix diagram, prioritization diagram, process decision program chart, and activity network diagram. Because of the limited space in this book, more particularly in this chapter, they will not be discussed here. Interested readers may learn about them through much recent TQM literature.[27]

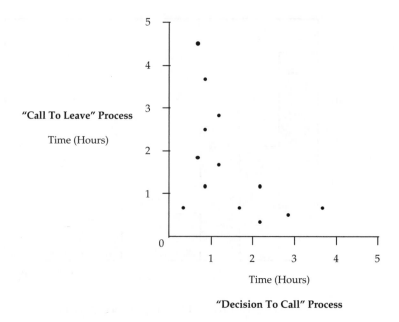

Figure 13–13 A Scatter Diagram To Show the Relationship between Two Processes for Emergency Room Problems at Metropolitan

---

INTEGRATING TQM AND HMIS FOR HEALTH SERVICE DELIVERY

Up until now, we have examined HMIS topics from a theoretical and method-ological perspective and have presented various technologies and applications in HMIS. In our discussion on systems theory (Chapter 3), we argued that the numer-ous interrelated elements of a system are united by a common goal in order for the system to function purposefully. In the same vein, the various components of HMIS we have examined throughout this book must share a common goal in order for the holistic study of these components to be useful and practical.

For example, we note that the ultimate purpose of the existence of the North American health service delivery system (NAHSDS), the environmental context in which our discussion on HMIS is immersed, is simply to improve the quality of life of the general population, in particular, the patient population that is served by health provider organizations in the United States and Canada. Then the ultimate goal of HMIS is really no different from that of TQM, as TQM simply refers to the drive for continual improvement of quality health services. In the longer term, therefore, the application of all aspects of our knowledge of HMIS, in particular the planning and management aspects, can be interpreted as focusing on the same

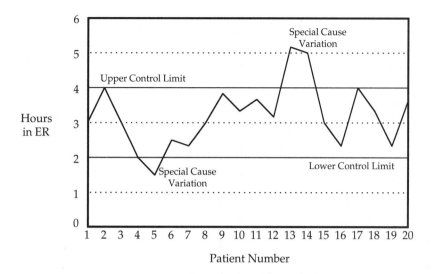

Figure 13–14 A Control Chart Showing the Time Patients Spent in the Emergency Room at Metropolitan

goal as that of TQM: that is, genuine improvement in the quality of life and well-being of the public. In this sense, HMIS and TQM are inseparable.

The Baldrige Critical Quality Factors: Building a Quality-Focus HMIS

In 1987, the Malcolm Baldrige National Quality Award[28] was created to promote quality awareness among U.S. companies and to inculcate the sense of the need for high quality in sustaining global competition as well as the significance of information sharing as a way to meet the competition. Recipients of the awards to date have included such prestigious companies as the Xerox Company and Milliken and Company. According to Fuld, applicants for the Baldrige Award are judged on the following five critical quality factors:[29]

1. Customer focus
2. Meeting commitments
3. Process management and elimination of waste
4. Employee involvement and empowerment
5. Continuous improvement

As depicted in Exhibit 13–2, each of these critical factors relates closely to the way an organization handles its intelligence information analysis (IIA) system.

Exhibit 13–2 Five Baldrige Critical Quality Factors and Health Management
Information System (HMIS) Linkages

Factor	Intelligent Information Capability
1. Customer Focus	Customer-Related Information
2. Meeting of Commitments	Standards
3. Process Management and Elimination of Waste	Information Exchange
4. Employee Involvement and Empowerment	Directory for Information Resources
5. Continuous Improvement	Benchmarking

We will discuss each factor briefly, paying special attention to its implication for HMIS and health service delivery.

First, organizations, including health service organizations, that are striving to rank quality first must demonstrate that customer-related information is seriously being tracked and channeled appropriately as feedback for improving the quality of the organization's products or services. In other words, a quality-focus HMIS must contain a database component for tracking and monitoring patient complaints and thereby allowing various groups of health professionals to improve the kinds of patients services performed by them concurrently or even prospectively. Feedback mechanisms also should be developed for customers other than patients, such as payers, regulators, suppliers, physicians, volunteers, and the general community (e.g., families and friends of patients). Moreover, such feedback should include all aspects of the health services, as well as evaluation of current services provided and ideas and suggestions for improvement.[30] Many hospitals and health service organizations lack the kind of HMIS that would be able to capture such quality HMIS input (i.e., an integrated database of customer-related information); therefore their HMIS must be redesigned.

Second, meeting quality standards or commitments is difficult as it requires the collaboration of all employees in process improvement. Translated into health information systems terms, it implies a certain amount of data standardization through the organization. Thus, in order for an HMIS to provide the same meaningful and useful quality measure data effectively and efficiently (i.e., quality HMIS output) to all service providers involved, a single comprehensive and integrated database with standardized data and their criteria, indicators, and measures must exist. The same database must also be widely distributed through the addition of networking capabilities so as to be accessible throughout the organization (Chapter 9). Common data needed for generating clinical information and facilitating decision making, for example, must be made available and accessible. This database can then act as a common basis on which other patient service information can be compared and evaluated.

As an example, the HMIS would compile, over a period of time, average resource utilization information and patient service guidelines for a standard case load (e.g., a total hip replacement), and any information received in the course of caring for a new patient falling within this case load could then be compared to the baseline. Tan et al. have discussed the use of a computer-based utilization care plan (UCP) system for effective patient data management that is in line with the concept discussed here.[31] Designing HMIS in this way depends on systems integration, which has been described at length in earlier chapters.

Third, a key challenge for quality is to focus on processes, particularly key processes. TQM entails making each key process statistically stable and reducing variability (i.e., eliminating waste). HMIS provide the infrastructure and means through which health service quality data can be handled with speed and in an integrative fashion. The HMIS can collect data in as complex or as simple a form as is required and allow the information to be widely distributed throughout the organization. As such, an HMIS can contribute significantly to "inform" the organization with respect to what goes on[32] as well as foster an environment of data sharing. Consequently, what transpires in the key organizational processes essentially becomes transparent as the organizational HMIS continually monitors predefined indicators of quality performance, audits the ongoing processes of patient care concurrently, evaluates implemented solutions, and provides additional information regarding process management to health professionals on request. Selbmann and Pietsch-Breitfeld note that HMIS can help to identify deviations from preset standards during the care of a patient based on the system's knowledge of the health status of the patient as well as the processes involved in patient care.[33] Moreover, HMIS can not only be designed to track process deviations in patient care but be programmed to monitor the use of resources (utilization management) in the provision of that patient care.[34] This kind of tracking provides a record of where, if anywhere, resources are being wasted or used ineffectively.

Fourth, HMIS in TQM can provide support to employee decision making through intelligent data analysis and empowerment through managerial decision support systems or clinical expert systems (Chapter 8). The HMIS designed to empower workers should not simply be accessible, but also acceptable. This acceptability should be for all health service professionals, for the purpose of direct interactions with the system. If various user groups are involved in the automated TQM processes, the HMIS should be made as user-friendly as possible. HMIS can generate periodic reports on key processes, as well as present the data in graphical forms that are easy to interpret for various user groups or departments. Help facility can assist data entry and retrieval. In addition, a very useful type of IIA is an automated directory of key resources for employees to find the needed information themselves without the need to draw constantly on the limited resources of their immediate groups. Fuld notes that such directories need not be expensive as they can be compiled like internal telephone books with names of individuals indexed according to several keys, including department affiliation and expertise.[35] Not many health organizations provide such a directory, and yet all it takes is perhaps a prepackaged database management system (DBMS) to set one up.

Finally, the underlying theme of successful TQM or CQI is continuous improvement, and one technique to ensure that a health service organization is achieving continuous service quality improvement is realistic benchmarking. This implies knowing one's quality of services and making comparisons with service quality of others who are known to be quality leaders, for example, the quality management process at Henry Ford Health System (HFHS). Other good examples are Hospital Corporation of America (HCA) and Harvard Community Health Plan. In terms of HMIS, this is where the IIA comes in as information on competitors and their service quality must be captured. The threats and opportunities in the environment and the strengths and weaknesses of the organizational processes must all yield valuable information on where management attention should be focused and where employees' efforts should be concentrated. Without an IIA system that is sensitive to both external and internal data, the health organization can only hope to drag its quality improvement program.

If there are such benefits to applying HMIS to institute TQM processes, then why have health facility performance and progress toward patient care goals generally not been actively tracked by using HMIS? Selbmann and Pietsch-Breitfeld believe that up to the early 1990s, most computer-based hospital information systems (HIS) have concentrated mainly on financial and administrative operations, as compared to patient care processes.[36] The reasons for this leaning are that patient management processes are hard to standardize, acquire, document, process, and measure in a timely fashion as compared to financial and administrative operations and that many key processes in clinical activities have not been articulated. As well, TQM processes require advanced HMIS technologies to network and coordinate interdisciplinary inputs adequately. Potential systems technologies related to workstations and networking in QM can promise more support to these TQM endeavors in the future (see Chapter 14).

As we have seen earlier in this book, the prevalence of these rather obsolete HMIS, which are essentially no more than advanced versions of transaction-processing systems, in health service organizations is also partly due to the "technophobia culture" of health professionals in the early days and the resultant lack of an integrated vision for the future of HMIS along a systems perspective. These same old human barriers to integrative HMIS evolution will also hinder the development of the TQM concept. Here, we have only touched on a few issues that should be considered when adopting an HMIS imperative to implementing TQM in health service delivery organizations. In the following section, we briefly discuss the integrative role of HMIS in TQM.

The Integrative Role of HMIS in TQM

Fishbain outlines specific HMIS components required to support TQM initiatives fully.[37]

- Appropriate application software that captures relevant and reliable data on quality
- Appropriate hardware for quality data input, processing, and output
- A system that retrieves, models, and displays quality data rapidly and accurately
- A system that is flexible for different operational setting conditions
- A system that has the capacity to adapt to different quality initiative methodologies
- A system that has the ability to engage in linking and networking
- A system that tracks flowcharting and aids in clinical decision making as processes proceed

Members of the TQM team can then review steps that are taken or not taken and modify their quality processes.

More generally, HMIS can assist in TQM programs through the following:

- The provision of an integrated data storage and computation facility for laboratory test results
- The timely delivery of accurate patient information
- Expert systems to help health professionals decide on medication and protocols
- An efficient means to record health resource utilization
- A communication link for all health professionals to enhance coordination

Specifically, the role of HMIS in TQM includes data collection, process monitoring, outcome measurement, and performance evaluation. A procedure carried out with the patient has to be documented by the health professionals at the closest HMIS workstation soon after it is carried out (e.g., at a nursing unit in the operating room area or an admitting-discharge-transfer area). A comparison of the data entered can then take place vis-à-vis the standardized computer database. Any variance can be flagged and brought to the attention to those health professions involved in the process. Thus, an ongoing review of the patient care process is considered and improvements are made on a regular basis, depending on how often variances are reported. If certain aspects of the process are observed to ameliorate patient care in this type of procedure, then to "hold the gains" would mean working on perfecting those aspects. This amelioration should be shared among disciplines. If certain parts of the process cannot be met, these should be reconsidered and discussed, and new guidelines formulated on these processes.

In addition, HMIS can be used in resource management and coordination. Health resources could also be tracked and evaluated, as the process itself was evaluated. Basically, within flow diagrams, the quality process is broken down into chunks that can be addressed systematically and multidisciplinarily. Note that the whole exercise is process-oriented and can be analyzed as such, in order to preserve the parts of the process that lead to high-quality patient care outcomes. The process has to be timely and must include tracking (i.e., following each measure through to the end) and accountability. Tracking occurs in terms of variances to the preset standards.

HMIS should also be able to organize and integrate the various groups, departments, and variables involved in the TQM endeavor within the organization. An integrated HMIS encourages the subsystems or departments involved to "talk" to one another and share among themselves integrated information. In other words, HMIS is useful in bridging the gap between various health professionals by attempting to speak a "common language" that is understandable to all health service team members in the organization.

Other capabilities required of a quality-focus HMIS include the ability to scan environmental information and to accommodate an ever-expanding database. The system should also be on an open platform in order to interface with data captured in various hardware from different departments and user groups. Eventually, the main challenge in applying HMIS to TQM in a health service delivery setting is related to what, how, and with whom data are collected. A health service delivery organization can only know whether it actually meets or even exceeds the level of quality it defines for itself if it knows (1) where the quality problems arise within the system, (2) how the quality problems arise, (3) what has been done about the quality problems, and (4) whether what has been done is adequate to solve the quality problems. Appropriate designs of HMIS software will assist in all four of these areas. This brings us to the topic of TQM software support.

TQM Software Support

When selecting software to support TQM, there are many considerations that must be factored into the choice. Ideally, a single software platform that is easy to use and flexible enough to meet the needs of TQM teams is the standard to aim for. When evaluating the many software packages available, there are nine key elements which should be given due consideration.[38]

1. Ease of use and learning
2. Flexibility
3. Analytical and graphical capabilities
4. Database management
5. Programmability
6. Portability
7. Network compatibility
8. Affordability
9. Dependable support

If it is difficult to learn a software program, project team members will devote more time to learning it than to solving project problems. This is undesirable as time should be spent in improving processes to ensure quality. If the software program is difficult to use, project teams should avoid using it. This is obviously undesirable as the software program is supposed to aid the project team, not hinder it. The project teams are composed of multidisciplinary members who will have a variety of experience with computer technology. Therefore, software related to TQM purposes must be easy to use and understandable and have special key functions for rapid execution of the programs. The software package that is chosen must also be flexible enough to accommodate the creativity and needs of various project teams. The software must allow the team to do what they feel is necessary and must not dictate to the team how they will proceed with the collection and analysis by limiting their flexibility.

There are three basic tools that each TQM project team will need to use in solving their process problems: TQM charts, statistics, and presentation of results. As noted earlier, these TQM tools can assist project teams in problem finding and problem solving. Most of the TQM tools require graphical support to be used effectively. Although there are specific TQM/CQI programs available, when evaluating software more common programs should not be overlooked if they do provide the basic functions to the project team. TQM stresses the presentation of data for analysis and monitoring. It is common in TQM organizations to see histograms and Pareto charts proudly displayed by departments who are either working through a problem or are keeping a watchful eye and monitoring the process for improvement. The software program should be capable of producing attractive, easy-to-create, easy-to-output, and easy-to-read documents that may be viewed on screen, downloaded to hard copy, or developed into slide presentations.

As the project team will require access to various sources of information, the mainframe system, and other data stored in personal computers and from external sources, it is essential that the software be capable of sorting files and data. The software program should enable the team to verify the accuracy of the data, sort and stratify the data, and group the data from the various sources. The ideal software program will provide basic relational database operations such that data may be combined and edited from these many sources as needed.

Although many project teams will proceed with problem finding and problem solving in a similar fashion, each project will require different data collection methods. If the software program chosen has programmable features, the HMIS department can aid the project team by developing applications that are specific to the data collection and data chart presentation of each team. Doing so may reduce data collection entry and chart creation to a few simple steps, thus reducing time and frustration. As many organizations will have both PC and Apple Macintosh systems, the software program should also preferably be able to be operated on both systems. The software will therefore be able to be accessed by more team members as the dependence on types of computer system will be eliminated.

As the TQM project teams are multidisciplinary, meeting on a regular basis and finding compatible meeting times is often very difficult. By having the software network compatible, several team members may access the data at their leisure on their own computer systems. Network compatibility also facilitates the transfer and sharing of information with other team members and other project teams. When considering a software program that is network compatible, it is essential to choose one that also has a locking mechanism. This prevents two users from opening the same file and making their own changes.

As organizations are becoming more cost conscious, affordability of software is another major consideration. This cost factor supports the argument for a single software program, as one site license will be required for the program. Should several different software programs be purchased to fulfill all these criteria, the cost of the license for these programs may be considerable. As the software program is being implemented, help will be required with the operation of the program. The software chosen should therefore be from a well-established, dependable vendor that provides support to the organization.

From these nine elements, we can break down the software needs into three broad categories. Fishbain speaks of three types of systems that are needed to support TQM initiatives:[39]

1. Database systems
2. Analysis systems
3. Decision support systems

Database systems are transaction systems that include clinical systems (e.g., lab, radiology, pharmacy), financial systems (accounting, materials management, etc.), and administrative systems (admitting, registration, medical records, etc.). Analysis systems are developed through and for the database systems. They provide standard outcome measurers and rates (utilization rates, outcomes related to diagnosis, resource utilization by treatment, etc.) and can also compare facilities by peer groups. Altogether these systems can help TQM project teams carry out their work effectively.

In terms of decision support systems technologies that are available to support TQM endeavors, Pryor et al. have documented a few examples.[40] Within the quality management realm of identifying deviations from standards during patient care processes, such systems as the HELP system and the COSTAR system remind health professionals of needed patient care that is based on professionally preset standards. The reminders relate to the appropriate recording of clinical findings, the proper ordering of tests, and the proper altering of therapies. An example would be that of professionals caring for a patient in need of diuretic therapy. These systems can remind, say, the physician to order serum potassium tests and digitalis medication for the patient's congestive heart failure, keeping in mind the outcome of the lab test.

In terms of software application programs that are on the shelves, it is convenient to have a single platform with all the essential functions needed by TQM, as shown in Figure 13–15. In particular, Excel 5.0 for Windows, a spreadsheet program produced by Microsoft Corporation, can be used as an ideal platform for TQM as it consists of a rich set of tools for data collection, storage, and manipulation; reasonable statistical analysis, graphical display, and diagram drawings (TQM tools). It is relatively affordable and has dependable support from vendors. The program's major drawback is the lack of value-check functions. Coming close to Excel for Windows are Quattro and Paradox by Borland International. These two are not Windows-based but have excellent presentation tools and relationship database support. The external database access and statistics applications, however, are limited.

Moreover, Lotus 1-2-3 version 3.4 would also be a good TQM platform, with some limitations on diagramming, value-checking, and presentations. As well, the program is not as easy to use as Excel, Quattro, and Paradox, and its statistics applications, data entry, and relationship database support are also limited. SAS/QC, published by the SAS Institute, comprises a set of specialized tools that operate as part of the extensive SAS software system. It is traditionally a mainframe computer program, though current versions also run on high-performance PCs. It is primarily run for sophisticated statistical analysis but also can be adapted for data management functions. Similar to SAS/QC is Epi-Info; published by the Centers for Disease Control in Atlanta, this program is available free of charge. It offers the essential database, statistical, and graphics capabilities but is less easy to use than the other programs mentioned.

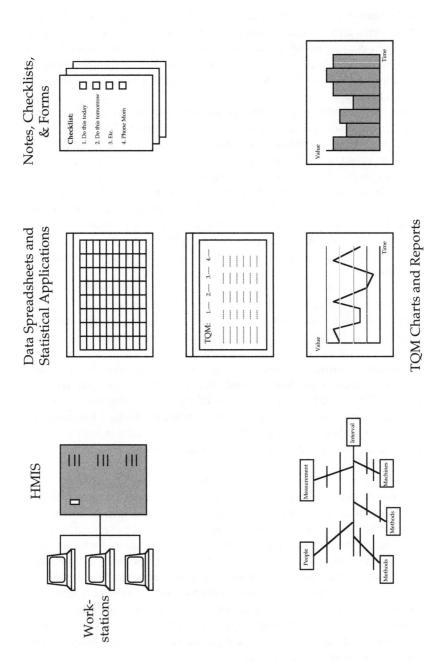

Figure 13–15 An Ideal Software Platform for Total Quality Management (TQM)

CONCLUSION

The information systems (IS) department is traditionally staffed with individuals who possess many skills and expertise in the collection and management of information. This role will continue for the HMIS department, particularly in the domains of financial and administrative data. The requirement, however, for decentralized data collection and management by TQM project teams will likely alter the role HMIS departments play. In line with the philosophy of TQM, HMIS departments that act as information resource centers that support the TQM project teams to complete their tasks will emerge.

Although the current function and purpose of the HMIS department are also in a state of transition, their presence in the TQM process is essential to the success of the organization. Traditional roles may be lost or lessened; however, new responsibilities and roles will take their place.

As the reader comes to the close of this chapter, he or she will find it evident that TQM processes, as they can be carried out in dynamic health care settings, are enhanced when combined with HMIS. Monitoring the degree of quality in patient services is integral in any health care facility. A health care facility exists to provide high-quality care to patients, and the measurement of that quality is a measurement of the facility's effectiveness in doing just that.

An understanding of TQM processes allows an understanding of how HMIS can be applied to quality management. With the use of the quality management framework described in the chapter, the standards, criteria, indicators, and measures collected with regard to quality flow processes can be tracked by HMIS and used for decision making. Health professional teams and administrators alike should now be able to follow how and why organizational goals with respect to quality are being reached or not being reached. In short, the principles of TQM ideally should be practiced by all members of health organizations, ultimately resulting in solid long-term improvements in health service delivery.

CHAPTER QUESTIONS

1. What are the seven tools of total quality management (TQM), and how can they be used to improve quality?
2. With organizations moving to the implementation of TQM, what transitions in information management do you see occurring?
3. What do you see as the new role for information systems departments in TQM organizations?
4. What roles does HMIS have in supporting TQM initiatives in health organizations?

5. What key elements must be given consideration when selecting software to support TQM project teams?

MINI CASE 13
DESIGNING TQM HMIS FOR A TOTAL
HIP REPLACEMENT SURGICAL PROCEDURE

The setting of this case is a hospital where a conscious male patient, 73 years of age, has been admitted for a total hip replacement (THR) surgical procedure. This patient's admissions and his THR procedure represent a patient care process that is open to improvement and quality management. The process of TQM in this case is outlined in the following:

1. Determine the key steps in the process, from time of admission to time of discharge.
2. Choose outcomes of each step in the process (process outcomes) and the outcome(s) of the entire process, all with criteria, indicators, measures/ standards.
3. Choose a means of collecting the data for each of these steps.
4. Compare the collected information to a preset standard for each step.
5. Relay favorable as well as unfavorable comparisons to the health service team responsible for the patient.
6. Use feedback information to improve the manner in which patient care is provided.

It should be emphasized that in the quality management process, the patient is the focus, whereas in quality patient care, it is the services delivered to the patient that are the main focus. This quality patient care can then be related to such outcomes as decreased morbidity and/or mortality.

The patient care process (THR procedure) is followed through by using a quality flow diagram (also called a clinical path development or process improvement) as shown in Figure 13–16. The ultimate objective here is to provide the best care to the patient and to measure its quality while he or she proceeds through all these stages, from admission to discharge. To achieve this, the outcome measurement of quality of the services provided at each stage must be designed. Let us take the preoperative phase (Stage III) as an example. By the end of this stage, the preparation of the patient for surgery should be completed in the following areas:

• Physical aspect
• Emotional aspect

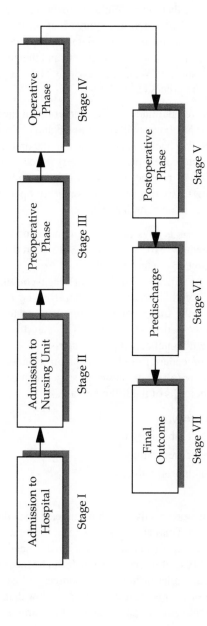

Figure 13-16 Quality Management Patient Care Process for Total Hip Replacement Surgery

- Intellectual aspect
- Legal aspect

Physical preparation entails that the patient's preoperative area is ready for the surgical procedure. Emotional preparation requires that the patient's fear, concerns, and questions be responded to or alleviated appropriately. Intellectual preparation demands that the patient be able to understand the general procedures and likely outcomes of the surgery. With regard to the THR surgery, the patient should be able to describe the process as follows:

> I will be anesthetized (or "put under"). The surgeon will then cut open my skin at this hip. . . . My bones will be removed and replaced by artificial bones. I will be sewn back up and returned to the unit. On the unit I will be in pain and can request painkillers every 4 hours by injection for the first 2 days. I will resume my diet slowly, starting with clear fluids and progressing to solid food. I will keep my operated hip/leg turned outward in order to prevent dislocation. . . .

To make sure that the patient is physically, emotionally, and intellectually prepared for the surgical procedure (expected outcome of the preoperative phase), a checklist as shown in Exhibit 13–3 can be used.

Legal preparation refers specifically to the patient's legal consent to the surgical procedure. The "quality" of this process can therefore be evaluated by the patient's comprehension of the true meaning of this legal statement and health professionals' answers to the patient's questions. This can, to a large extent, be counted as part of the patient's intellectual preparedness.

Generalizing the entire procedure from the preoperative phase, we see that the quality of the entire procedure (all seven phases or stages) can be measured, from the patient's perspective, in terms of the following areas:

1. "Smoothness" of procedures
2. Comprehensiveness of laboratory testing
3. Choice and efficacy of medication
4. Attentiveness of health professionals
5. Timeliness

Adding the management's perspective, we have at least one other criterion: efficiency of the resources used. This can be stated in terms of the number of person-hours (from a particular group of health professionals) needed to achieve a predesignated level of quality health services (which can be measured in terms of the four criteria listed). In a similar fashion, the resources utilized can be tracked and evaluated, as the process itself is evaluated, by using flow diagrams. The quality process can be broken into smaller parts that can be addressed systematically

Exhibit 13–3 Checklist for the Outcome Measurement of the Preoperative Phase of a Total Hip Replacement (THR) Surgery

Preparedness of Mr./Mrs./Ms. _____		Checked
Physical	•Surgical area sterilized with Hibitane •Hair completely removed •Taken nothing by mouth for ___ hours •Serum range normal •Glucose range normal •Calcium range normal •ECG results normal •Urinalysis results normal •Liver test results normal •Urination/defecation 24–48 hours prior to surgery •IV therapy •Sedation with Valium/Demerol 2–5 hours prior to surgery	____ ____ ____ ____ ____ ____ ____ ____ ____ ____ ____ ____
Emotional	•Voice of fears from surgery responded to •Questions of concerns on surgery answered •Voice of fears from surgical failure responded to •Questions on postoperative states answered	____ ____ ____ ____
Intellectual	•Surgical procedures understood •Can relay in layman's terms the surgical procedures •Likelihood of failure understood •Possible surgical outcome understood	____ ____ ____ ____
Legal	•Legal consent read and signed	____

Time taken for this phase:_____   Hours (Nurse): _____
                                            Hours (Physician): _____

Comments by patient:

Comments by patient's visitors:

Documented by: _____   Signed: _____   Date: _____

and multidisciplinarily and then they can be pieced together to illustrate the over-all effects.

MINI CASE QUESTIONS

1. Describe the features of an ideal HMIS that would facilitate the processes of (a) quality patient care and (b) quality management with respect to this total hip replacement surgical procedure.
2. List and describe some TQM tools applicable in this case.
3. With the help of the appropriate personnel, design the outcome measurement of quality of the seminar provided at (a) the postoperative phase and (b) the predischarge phase. Also try to organize your design in a tabular format as in Exhibit 13–3.
4. With respect to your answers to the preceding questions, generalize the role(s) of HMIS in TQM processes.

CHAPTER REVIEW

On applying HMIS to TQM processes, this chapter in fact brings all previous concepts together. The concepts of systems thinking, data, information, decision support, systems methodology, and information management are all pertinent to this chapter's topic. For instance, the concepts of data input and decision making with output information, as well as feedback controls, all within the systems framework, are part of the understanding of HMIS in TQM processes. HMIS support of TQM endeavors provides decision support for health professionals as well as administrators, to make decisions regarding high-quality patient care outcomes.

A current definition of TQM is that it is a structured system for creating organizational participation. For health service organizations, TQM essentially refers to the dynamic perpetual drive to achieve continual improvement in all clinical work processes. In today's changing health care environment, TQM, despite its weaknesses, is seen as a viable alternative for managing change.

TQM concepts, principles, and philosophies reflect the cumulative thinking of many scholars, most notably Edward Deming, Philip Crosby, and Joseph Juran. TQM concepts, principles, and philosophies, including quality planning, quality monitoring, and quality improvement, are embodied in Deming's 14 Points, Crosby's measure of the cost of quality, and Juran's Quality Trilogy.

In all TQM processes, the indicators and measures of improvement have to be defined in a feedback system context. Moreover, an array of tools, including flow charts, run charts, fishbone diagrams, Pareto charts, histograms, scatter diagrams, and control charts, are useful in TQM. In particular, in quality improvement processes, the Deming-Shewhart PDCA cycle and the principle of *Genba, Genbutsu* can be applied. The Baldrige National Quality Award was created to promote quality awareness among U.S. companies. Applicants for this award are judged on five quality factors: customer focus, meeting of commitments, process management and elimination of waste, employee involvement and empowerment, and continuous improvement.

As for the HMIS, there are specific roles that the HMIS has to fulfill in order to support the TQM initiatives in health organizations fully. As with the implementation of HMIS, the implementation of TQM with the support of HMIS also involves a few concerns that need to be addressed.

NOTES

1. G. Johnson, Managing Strategic Change: Strategy, Culture and Action, *Long Range Planning* 25, no. 1 (1992): 28–36.

2. L.M. Fuld, Achieving Total Quality through Intelligence, *Long Range Planning* 25, no. 1 (1992): 109–115.

3. R.L. Chaufournier, et al., Quality Management, Deming Principles, and Clinical Engineering, *Biomedical Instrumentation and Technology* (1991): 441–449.

4. W.E. Deming, *Out of Crisis* (Cambridge, Mass: MIT Press, 1986).

5. P.B. Crosby, *Quality Is Free: The Art of Making Quality Certain* (New York: Penguin Books, 1979).

6. J.M. Juran, *Juran on Planning for Quality* (New York: Free Press, 1989).

7. C.P. McLaughlin and A.D. Kaluzny, Total Quality Management in Health: Making It Work, *Health Care Management Review* 15, no. 3 (1990): 7–14, 12.

8. R.F. Casalou, Total Quality Management in Health Care, *Hospital and Health Services Administration* 36, no. 1 (1991): 134–145.

9. J. Mathews and P. Katel, The Cost of Quality, *Newsweek* (September 7, 1992): 48–49.

10. Ibid.

11. Casalou, Total Quality Management, 134–145.

12. V.K. Sahney and G.L. Warden, The Quest for Quality and Productivity in Health Services, *Frontiers of Health Services Management* 7, no. 4 (1991): 2–40.

13. A. Donabedian, The Role of Outcomes in Quality Assessment and Assurance, *Quality Review Bulletin* (November 1992): 356–360.

14. Ibid.

15. S.B. Kritchevsky and B.P. Simmons, Continuous Quality Improvement: Concepts and Applications for Physician Care, *Journal of the American Medical Association* 266, no. 13 (1991): 1817–1823.

16. Ibid.

17. L.J. Finison, What Are Good Health Care Measurements? *Quality Progress* 25, no. 4 (1992): 41–42.

18. Ibid.

19. Sahney and Warden, The Quest for Quality, 11.

20. B.C. James, TQM and Clinical Medicine, *Frontiers of Health Services Management* 7, no. 4 (1991): 42–46.

21. Chaufournier et al., Quality Management, 441–449.

22. L.J. Kerr, Achieving World Class Performance Step by Step, *Long Range Planning* 25, no. 1 (1992): 46–52.

23. G. Kuperman, et al., Continuous Quality Improvement Applied to Medical Care: Experiences at LDS Hospital, *Medical Decision Making,* no. 11 (supplement) (1991): S60–S65.

24. H.K. Selbmann and B. Pietsch-Breitfeld, Hospital Information Systems and Quality Assurance, *Quality Assurance in Health Care* 2 (March/April 1990): 335–344.

25. J.P. Burke, et al., The HELP System and Its Application to Infection Control, *Journal of Hospital Infection* 18 (Supplement A) (1991): 424–431.

26. R.D. Daigh, Financial Implications of a Quality Improvement Process, *Topics in Health Care Financing* 17, no. 3 (1991): 42–52.

27. W. Leebov and C. Ersoz, *The Health Care Manager's Guide to Continuous Quality Improvement* (Chicago: American Hospital Publishing, Inc., 1991).

28. E. Riddle, *Xerox Leadership through Quality* (Presentation made to Henry Ford Health System executive management staff, 1990).

29. Fuld, Achieving Total Quality, 109–115.

30. Sahney and Warden, The Quest for Quality, 2–40.

31. J.K.H. Tan, et al., Utilization Care Plan and Effective Patient Data Management, *Hospital & Health Services Administration* 38, no. 1 (1993): 81–99.

32. S. Ziboff, *In the Age of the Smart Machine: The Future of Work and Power* (New York: Basic Books, Inc., 1988).

33. Selbmann and Pietsch-Breitfeld, Hospital Information Systems, 335–344.

34. Tan et al., Utilization Care Plan, 81–99.

35. Fuld, Achieving Total Quality, 109–115.

36. Selbmann and Pietsch-Breitfeld, Hospital Information Systems, 335–344.

37. K. Fishbain, The Interrelationship between Quality and Information Systems, *Topics in Health Care Financing* 18, no. 2 (1992): 85–88.

38. D.C. Kibbe and R.P. Scoville, Computer Software for Health Care CQI, *Quality Management in Health Care* 1, no. 4 (1993): 50–58.

39. Fishbain, Quality and Information Systems, 85–88.

40. D.B. Pryor, et al., Clinical Databases: Accomplishments and Unrealized Potential, *Medical Care* 23 (1985): 623.

Part V

Epilogue: The Future of HMIS

Chapter 14

Road Map to the Future: HMIS in the Twenty-First Century

LEARNING OBJECTIVES

1. Identify trends for the health service delivery industry.
2. Anticipate future health management culture and processes from a systems perspective.
3. Relate emerging computing technologies to health service delivery.
4. Project the implications of remote computing to health service delivery.
5. Project a role for HMIS in the twenty-first century.

INTRODUCTION

The hospital of the future will be by its pattern, not by its structure; by its function, not by its form.[1]

Imagine compressing all of the technological advances that have occurred during this century into a period of about 20 years and you'll begin to see what the rest of this century and the beginning of the next century will be like in the realm of information systems technology. Old health management information systems (HMIS) and technologies will pave the way for new and advanced HMIS applications, leading health service organizations to rethink their current operational processes and communications structure. Health service organizations, especially hospitals, may literally be without walls. Michael McDonald and Henrich Blum in their recent position paper *Health in the Information Age* describe the impact of emerging information technology on health service as follows:

Telecommunication in the form of telephone service and elementary data communication is already critical to the operations of all aspects of the health care system. Yet this role is dwarfed by the emerging tele-

447

communication applications that will become widely available to the health sector in the upcoming decade. . . . Presently, health care institutions and practitioners still view themselves as recipients and consumers of telecommunications. However, a new information infrastructure with a strong public network platform would recast the health sector's role in the Information Age from solely a consumer of telecommunications to a central provider of information and facilitator of health information exchange within their community. The health care institutions with which the practitioner is associated could be networked to make most or all the necessary connections for its "practicing partner." This would entail access and use of the world's medical and scientific data bases, access to his or her patients' institutional records, decision-support software, communications structure for expert consultation (on a nation-wide or international basis, when needed), electronic inventory control, supplies purchasing, prescription order, and so on.[2]

As we approach the twenty-first century, hospitals and other health service organizations alike will face increasing pressures to redefine their roles and operations in the continuum of health service delivery. Computer hardware and telecommunication systems will continue to improve with increased emphasis on the networking of computers, linking of software from multiple vendors, and development of high-capacity information storage media. A complete digital record system would allow patient records to be electronically available around the clock to the practitioner whether the information request were initiated from an office, a home, or anywhere else, such as in a hospital or health organizational facility.

Meanwhile, the organizational level in the North American health service delivery system (NAHSDS; see Chapter 3) may also witness fundamental changes. In fact, many of these changes will be further manifestations of various trends already taking place in the 1980s and 1990s. For instance, traditional management styles will be replaced by total quality management (TQM) and reengineering concepts (Chapter 13). As a consequence, sweeping changes will likely be evident in other related areas as well, including the extensions of health information concepts; HMIS development methodologies; and health computing technologies such as artificial intelligence (AI), expert systems (ES), group support systems (GSS), and electronic data interchange (EDI), all of which we have already discussed to some extent in earlier chapters. Amid all these changes, health management information systems (HMIS) will present many new challenges as their role gradually evolves from that of a vehicle for service provision to that of a facilitator of change.

This chapter attempts to rationalize various trends already occurring in the past few decades and then projects a view of the NAHSDS into the near future, thereby strengthening our understanding and imagination about the future of HMIS. Briefly, we will begin with a look at some far-reaching trends in the health service delivery system, including changes in the organizational structures and management styles and culture specifically relating to health service organizations. The discussion will then be followed by a broad survey of health computing technological advancements and some glimpses of the health service delivery mechanisms in the twenty-first century. Theories, methods, and applications discussed in previous chapters will now be discussed from an integrated perspective, with the assumption that the reader already has been exposed to these concepts.

THE NAHSDS IN THE NEXT CENTURY: A SYSTEMS PERSPECTIVE

Changes in the NAHSDS, like those in many other such systems, are likely to be multifaceted and will be considerably diversified; some will be relatively short-lived, and others will be more far-reaching. At times, some changes may even seem to be opposed to each other. In examining these changes, a systems perspective helps to provide a general context.

Before we go on any further, let us take a brief but expanded view of the NAHSDS introduced in Chapter 3. We may divide the entire NAHSDS into three major realms.

1. The general public
2. Health professionals
3. Environmental health (public health)

As shown in Figure 14–1 the general public is the most fundamental part of the health service delivery system. Almost all of the first line of health-related decision making is in fact carried out in the home or in the workplace, by individuals acting on their own or with the help of family and friends. A body of uninformed or poorly informed population under the NAHSDS therefore is more likely to generate more health service claims than are necessary, translating the system into an extraordinary waste of all kinds of resources. Until recently, the interface between the general public and health information has not attracted much attention from the government or academics. Now, as individuals are encouraged to take a more active role in their own health, this interface is gaining new importance. In the distant future, the development of a national or North American information infrastructure for interactive telecommunications would very likely make health information and health decision-making tools more available and accessible to the general public.

Most health services to the general public are provided by traditional institutionalized health professionals. These professionals, together with their associated hospitals and universities, are the primary destination of most scientific research

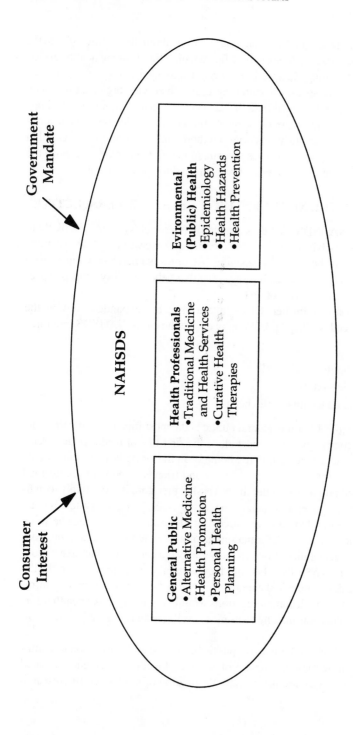

Figure 14–1 A General Systems Perspective of the NAHSDS

grants and government-allocated health resources. Incidentally, this realm is the main focus of this book, where HMIS development will likely be most conspicuous. Throughout various chapters, we have seen that far-reaching changes will likely render many facets of traditional health service areas as far different from what they used to be. The development of advanced telecommunication networks with the latest technology, for instance, will definitely amplify some of the trends already in place at the organizational level (which will be discussed in the next section).

Environmental health, traditionally called public health, is a realm of the entire health service delivery system that is often regarded as "behind-the-scenes." Its main responsibilities include measurement of group health status, discovery of patterns of ill health in society, determination of generative factors of diseases, and intervention to alleviate health problems through education and biomedical and environmental measures. In addition, this field is also taking on a broader meaning as a result of shifts in culture, demography, epidemiology, technology, and knowledge of population health and human potential. Directed at improving the public's health, this broader scope includes actions by groups of individuals as well as established health institutions. The actions of key individuals, groups of concerned citizens, and communities therefore play a critical role in shaping public health policy and decision making at both the government and health institutional levels. This brings us back to the importance of maintaining a broad perspective of the NAHSDS, including an understanding of trends development in all three realms: the general public, health professionals, and environmental health.

Trends Toward Organized Delivery of Health Services

In this section, we will first take a look at various trends that have already been taking place in the NAHSDS and that will likely continue in the near future. Our discussion will then concentrate on future changes likely to be observed in the management and development of health service organizations and on the rising importance of systems thinking amid these organizational and managerial changes.

Just a few decades ago, the independent practitioner and the freestanding voluntary hospital used to be the dominant forms of health service provision in North America. Today, physicians affiliated with numerous specialized organized delivery systems (ODS) and multihospital corporations are fast becoming the major sources of health services. Consistent with this apparent dramatic change, which has occurred in the North American health care scene, several megatrends and more specific trends occurring at the broad organizational level may be observed, as documented by Scott[3] and by Naisbett and Elkins.[4] These trends include:

- Increased scale
- Increased concentration, diversification, and specialization
- Increased linkages among health service organizations
- Expanded role of government
- Increased managerial but reduced professional influence
- Increased privatization and market orientation

Regardless of how we decide to measure the size (scale) of the health service delivery system (e.g., number of professionals, number of health service organizations, or amount of resources employed), the NAHSDS has grown tremendously in the past half decade. In the United States, for example, health care costs in 1990 consumed about 11 percent of the gross national product, up from the 4.6 percent in 1950.[5]

Increased concentration and diversification of alternative health service mechanisms are manifested in several different ways and are generally seen in the broadening of service domains: (1) it is more common nowadays for physicians to work in multispecialty clinics, health maintenance organizations (HMOs), hospitals, or other health institutions; (2) individual hospitals have expanded, both because of the growth of individual units and because smaller hospitals are more likely to fail;[6] (3) health service organizations today are more likely to operate as part of a corporation or consortium than on their own (at least this appears to be the trend in the United States);[7] and (4) service expansion can occur through the addition of services that are closely related (e.g., ambulatory care programs) or simply unrelated (e.g., management of real estate).[8] In addition, health service providers (physicians and nurses alike) have become more specialized. The number of recognized medical specialties, as well as the proportion of full-time physician specialists, has increased in North America since the 1930s.[9] Specialized facilities and providers have proliferated over the past few decades.

Increased linkages among health service organizations have appeared in a variety of ways. More hospitals than ever before are managed under contracts, with more specialized management systems.[10] A variety of alliances have also been developed among different types of health service institutions to coordinate certain facets of their activities without giving up independent status.[11] Several research-oriented networks have been established and funded by federal agencies to direct the activities of independent physicians and health organizations.[12]

The trend of the expanded role of government is more evident in the United States than in Canada. In the United States, the government has increased its role from merely providing certification to medical professionals in the 1930s to planning and aggressively marketing some form of national health coverage in the 1990s. Across the border, the Canadian federal government in conjunction with provincial governments has long since established a national health coverage plan and in recent years has taken an expanded role in the definition and funding of a new dimension of health and well-being, including health promotion and preventive care.[13]

While practitioners continue to fill a powerful role in health service organizations, their influence is now beginning to be challenged by an increase in the influence of managerial groups. As mentioned in Chapter 3, the notion of "technological imperative," that is, the belief that all physicians should have available for their patients every technology of medicine, regardless of cost, questions of priority, or the optimal allocation of resources,[14] is now increasingly challenged in view of pressing cost-containment measures and tightened budgets. This is most apparent in the recent outgrowth of interest in medical and health technology assessment and evaluation among health service researchers.

In the United States, increased privatization is seen in the number of for-profit hospitals doubling between 1975 and 1985. Today, 35 percent of HMOs are operating for profit, as well as 80 percent of nursing homes.[15] In Canada, a significant number of physicians in British Columbia and Ontario, for example, have opted out of the medical service plan and have been trying to bill their patients privately (and separately from the universal health care plan). Although health care services remain under the discretionary control of providers and governments (provincial in Canada), such services have become more market-oriented in recent decades as consumer influence has intensified. For instance, the rights of patients to health service information have been extended, as encouraged by a number of health-related movements.[16]

Alongside these far-reaching organizational changes, Colin predicts that alternative medicine and health service approaches, encompassing, for example, such diverse topics as holistic medicine, herbal-based medicines, faith healing, acupuncture, and homeopathic healing techniques that differ from traditional, "established" medical technologies, will receive more attention in the future, thus positioning themselves to be complementary to traditional medicine.[17] Translated to the individual level, these alternative approaches also include an increased awareness of illness prevention and the importance of a healthy lifestyle.

We have just seen numerous changes that have been taking place and will continue to do so in our entire health service delivery system. As Scott has noted, "Trends in the medical care sector have operated to reduce the uniqueness of organizational arrangements that had long distinguished this field from other economic sectors."[18] It is worth noting that "concentration, specialization, diversification, managerialism and market orientation are the familiar hallmarks of modern industrial and commercial practice" in North America. These trends are not significantly limited by the role of the individual health organization as they occur at the broader organizational level of the NAHSDS. We now try to explore some manifestations of these changes on the management level, that is, within a health service organization setting.

Strategic Group Thinking: The New Management Culture

We have just taken a brief overview of some of the mega and specific trends occurring in the NAHSDS at the broad organizational level that will also likely continue in the near future, including increasing concentration, diversification, and specialization. This has given rise to two main implications for the management of health service organizations in the future. First, there will be a dramatic increase in information flow, brought about by the organizational changes described and by the rapid technological advancements (e.g., the information highway) that will occur in the near future. Second, there will be an increasing need for health professionals from different specializations to work together as a group to provide a "managed" form of care, as opposed to the long-held belief in "technological imperative." Let us examine each of these implications in detail.

With the dawn of the information age, information will become the currency of the next century. This applies to hospitals and other health service delivery organizations just as much as it applies to any other institution. We can therefore expect to see a significant increase in the emphasis on HMIS as part of the agendas of health planners and managers. Evidently the impact of HMIS theories, methods, technologies, applications, and activities on the management of health service institutions in the coming decade will become significant. This trend is greater sharing and exchange of information.

In an increasingly competitive health care environment, management of information to support strategic planning, control costs, improve quality of information for health managerial decision making, improve quality of health service, enhance productivity, and redesign products and services will become a central (core) management function. Austin suggests that "financial information systems developed during a period of cost-based reimbursement are not adequate to the task of cost and profitability analysis necessitated by prospective payment and competition among providers. Competition will demand continuous quality improvement, and sophisticated management information systems will provide data for monitoring progress toward accomplishing this goal."[19] We thus anticipate many older-generation HMIS, which are essentially financial information systems, to either require significant expansion or be replaced by more advanced electronic data interchange (EDI) systems in the near future. The HMIS in the future will be able to generate a database of clinical and organizational performance indicators at broader and more specific levels of the organization from which quality will be assessed and measured and accountability will be monitored.

In the meantime, priorities in HMIS development will shift from routine operational data processing to analytical group decision support. Expert systems that employ artificial intelligence techniques will be applied to management problem solving and strategic planning in new areas such as impact analysis, market analysis, and productivity improvement. Expert systems will have the ability to draw upon "the knowledge and experience of key people from within the organization and external to it."[20] Considerable benefits will be derived from capturing experience and making it available organizationwide. The new technology will move to an integration of various domains within AI (Chapter 8). We will discuss expert systems and artificial intelligence in the health service delivery scene more fully later in this chapter.

Admittedly, traditional management structures have tended to provide relatively routine departmentalized information management. For each department, information is separately filtered across various management levels, often producing "fragmented" and "marginalized" data. Data collection and preparation tend to be inconsistent because of duplications, allowing for several potentially conflicting versions of the same information. In the future, a new level of management information technology infrastructure (MITI) may be implemented to coordinate the collection of a "centralized" database. With accurate, reliable, timely, consistent, and valid information, the role of the administrator will change from one who has to screen and scrutinize fragmented data continually to one who can spend time using the shared information and knowledge network in productive analysis, thus allowing for direct feedback, enhanced strategic management performance, and results.

While much technology and software will be highly advanced in the future, all projects will still rely on human skills for successful implementation. As technologies and new forms of health service organizations continue to evolve, the skills required for health managers to complete their tasks successfully will change and expand accordingly. In general, strategic group thinking, interdisciplinary skills, and capability to self-learn continually will be among the most sought-after skills in health organization management in general and health information management in particular.

In addition, health service managers in the next decade will also continue to experience challenges in the development and the use of their skills in negotiated strategic planning and management. These skills are expected to be in high demand in the near future primarily for two reasons. First, as mentioned in Chapter 10, hospitals and other health service delivery organizations nowadays are more involved in forming strategic alliances. This will not only enhance communications with sources external to the organization but will also provide new opportunities for finding better ways of sharing limited resources. For example, interorganizational project teams are becoming a trend in the rapidly changing health service delivery environment. Projects such as community healthy lifestyle ventures that are guided by such teams will usually take on a life of their own. These interdisciplinary teams comprising various professionals will have access to vast networks of resources and information that would not have been accessible within the framework of a single health organization. New skills are therefore required to create and maintain a climate for teamwork that fosters creativity and innovation, leading to an increased exchange of knowledge and ideas.

Second, as noted previously, technological advancements will play an increasingly important role in health service delivery. Already health service professionals are becoming more familiar with the use of new information technology and this trend will surely continue in the future. With interactive systems and rapid access to fountains of information via CD-ROM technology, for example, health professionals from all specialties and different disciplines will be brought together, enhancing the integrated managed care concept that is evolving very quickly. However, not all these changes will be pleasant. Greater emphasis on interdisciplinary and multidisciplinary approaches may in fact sow the seeds for "turf battles" and a general "weeding out" in health service organizations.[21] For instance, neurologists and radiologists in a hospital may fight over who should read computed axial tomography (CT) scans; cardiologists and radiologists may disagree on who should interpret echocardiograms and deliver echocardiography services. Similarly, because of the lack of medical standards and guidelines for certain professional duties and performance accountability in hospitals, health administrators will have to resolve disputes about who should perform specific procedures and use medical equipment or devices. This implies the continuing need for good interpersonal and negotiation skills. Health service managers who choose to live in the past and those who will experience difficulties in keeping up with these changes will be repositioned into other sectors. As technology further diffuses into the health service delivery industry, future health service managers will thus likely face more challenges (for example, the need to position their organization in a balanced fashion in both the health service industry marketplace and the information technology marketplace.

Altogether, we have seen that as a result of the changing organizational structures and the advancing of information technologies the roles of health service management will need to evolve accordingly. In particular, the need for group strategic thinking, interdisciplinary skills, the capacity for continual self-learning, and the ability to mediate and negotiate among conflicting parties will be in great demand in the next few decades.

Systems Thinking: The New Management Process

We have just examined the changing needs for health service managers in the near future. As we have seen, numerous issues will arise with the advent of technology and changing organizational structures. When dealing with these issues, it is important not to lose sight of the big picture, that is, how things are placed in perspective. In this regard, the significance of systems thinking should not be underestimated.

Figure 14–2 shows how the concepts of systems thinking have penetrated our discussions from Chapters 3 through 5, and even more extensively in Chapter 6. As we can see, systems perspective is one of the main themes of this book. The systems approach is valuable in that it facilitates two important aspects of the functioning and structure of HMIS in health service organizations: problem finding and problem solving. Problem finding allows for a new viewpoint that encompasses systems thinking and its implications for the hospital's role in providing future health programs and services. It embraces the idea that without the inputs from the health care environment and without a strategic overview of the different levels of operation in a health service organization, the problem of providing a broad continuum of care will never be totally resolved. The implications of advancing technology for problem finding will also be essential in future health service systems since information technology will be the "strategic enabling ingredient"[22] in the redefinition of the role of health service organization. Given that a trend in health service organizations is a movement away from large-scale institutionalization and toward alliances and a variety of diversified facilities, HMIS will likely become the key to transforming health service from institutional and rather segmented delivery to ambulatory and integrated global systems.

Systems thinking will also have implications for management concepts. Problem solving within the framework of systems thinking enables health service providers and new technologies to work together in the delivery of services. Murray and Trefts suggest several problem-solving strategies that will govern this new process of management with linkages to strategic alignment between organization and HMIS strategy (see Chapter 10), a clarification of roles and responsibilities for HMIS managers, and a management information technology infrastructure (MITI) being most relevant to health service delivery.[23] They define strategic alignment as an organizationwide HMIS initiative that is driven by vision and strategy, tied to specific quantifiable benefits, and based on the redesign of cumbersome processes. Such strategic linkages clarify what problems may be solved by HMIS solutions and how performance success may be measured. After strategic alignment, vision and strategy are then translated into conceptual statements of

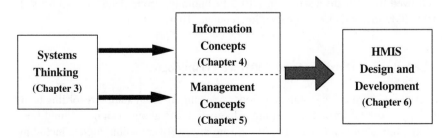

Figure 14–2 Concept of Systems Thinking in This Book

specific tasks that the health service providers must perform exceptionally well to achieve goals and objectives. In this way, the new goals trigger a process of re-evaluating the health managerial roles and responsibilities. In terms of systems thinking, this element of the new management concepts will explicitly indicate what is truly important, so that individuals may become aware of and accountable for their contributions to the whole.

An MITI provides a basis for understanding information sharing concepts. Such an infrastructure is needed to coordinate and integrate efficiently and effectively individual departments or programs over extended periods. Murray and Trefts explain it as follows:

> The new management process embraces the concept of architectural standards to organization-wide information technology to guide the development of new system capabilities. These standards, as they relate to technologies, data, communications, applications, and systems, are analogous to the plumbing, heating, ventilation, air conditioning, and electrical systems standards for a new residential construction project. Without these standards a house is apt to run on the wrong voltage or be missing drainage pipes. Similarly, without IT [information technology] architectural standards, organization wide systems become yet additional islands of automation, akin to existing departmental solutions in that they are useful only to a limited segment of the business.[24]

HEALTH COMPUTING TECHNOLOGIES

As we have just seen, advancements in technology will play an important role in health service organizations of the future. Throughout earlier chapters, we have examined numerous technological applications in the health service delivery field, as shown in Figure 14–3.

Here, we will briefly describe the trends of computing technologies, thereby enabling ourselves to project how future health service delivery could benefit from these changes. We shall first start with hardware and software technologies, followed by brief discussions of AI/ES technology, group decision support systems (GDSS), and electronic data interchange (EDI) technology.

The Future of Hardware and Software Technologies

Already, hard drive storage methods are changing from analog recording technology to digital format. The future is likely to bring about even more mind-boggling innovations in the arena of hardware and software technologies, including peripherals such as storage mediums and input devices.

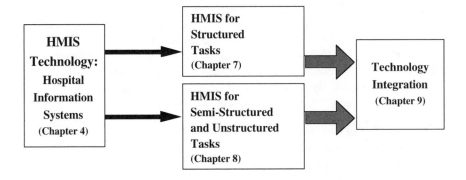

Figure 14–3 Concepts of Health Computing Technology in This Book

---

"The new technology, called digital read channel, will at least double the amount of information that can be packed into each square inch of a platter, and there's no reason to doubt that further advances will produce even greater improvements in density."[25] Such improvements in density are needed to store increasingly complex software systems, to store and index a large number of data files that are maintained on-line for immediate user access, and to manage communications and transfer of files in networks. Digital storage will also be necessary as desktop machines move to include applications that employ such rich data types as voice and video.

Currently, most hospitals use mainframes for a large part of their information processing activities. However, the migration from mainframes to client-server architecture in certain areas, as a guidepost to establishing compatibility between systems and applications, has already begun. At the heart of the change is an efficient transmission medium such as fiber optics, which will be capable of meeting virtually any information-handling need. Powerful computer hardware will reshape the way that information is stored, retrieved, and used. For example, binary file transfer capabilities will allow users to send faxes (even those with video and sound) from one computer to another in an editable format, as opposed to the current "bit-map" fax images. This could potentially change the document-image-communications loop to simple document communications.

As health service organizations leave their mainframes behind, microprocessors will be increasingly used as input-output terminals for large HMIS. Where once "dumb" terminals were used to link users to mainframes, processor-based "smart" terminals will become the standard in the years ahead. Such "smart" terminals will allow user input data to be validated before transfer to the hospital information system for processing and storage. This validation process provides two benefits: (1) data entry speed is increased because validation occurs at the source with a device dedicated to a single user and (2) the operation of the HMIS is more efficient because work load is completely managed at the terminal.[26]

With regard to the long-term adoption of technology, software will be the prime determining factor because it is an area that will see the greatest changes in the future, with interactivity driving its development. McDonald and Blum suggest that future systems will have several layers of complexity.[27]

- Navigational transparency
- Referential transparency
- Decision-support transparency
- Programming transparency
- Virtual reality

Navigational transparency, the first layer of complexity, refers to the ease with which users can locate the needed information. This can be achieved by navigational aids (search capabilities by key word or menus) that allow users to find the information they seek quickly without spending time looking through a stack of information that is irrelevant. Referential transparency, the second layer, refers to the listing of the (alternative) sources of information, so that references can be reviewed by those who would be concerned about the credibility of such information or who might want to see the spectrum of different perspectives. Decision-support transparency constitutes the third layer. In expert and heuristic systems, the logic of all the steps necessary to reach a decision to support a specific activity may not be readily apparent to the reader. This layer of transparency refers to the provision of this kind of background information. Programming transparency is the fourth layer of complexity. Although the programming dimension of the information an average individual is consuming does not always need to be transparent to the user, in some cases the ability to examine the programming script would be helpful. Programming transparency will provide this capability. Virtual reality constitutes the final layer. This refers to the experience created by the software such that real-life perception is technologically enhanced, reshaped, or replaced. Simulation programs such as fighter pilots and flight simulators are examples of virtual reality that is an important component of the software.

Transparent interactivity of information is crucial to the general public as well as to professionals using the system for purposes such as personal health information access. Whereas the dominant media today (i.e., television, radio, newspapers, books, magazines) are by nature passive, the emerging media will engage the user in decision making on an ongoing basis. This phenomenon can be illustrated by an example of a patient who has just been diagnosed with high blood pressure and is concerned about salt in the diet. It would be difficult to find information on salt levels in the current media quickly. The patient would have to travel to a library or bookstore to find the information. In a future HMIS, this information can be instantly accessed through an interactive network with a personal health information system by using a keyword search or menus. Hypertext search capabilities would further expedite the information extraction process. In many situations, this search can be accomplished with simple question-and-answer sessions that would, in effect, provide the end-user with computer-assisted self-learning experience.

Hypertext is an emerging technology that is expected to have a significant impact on the structure of information as it is presented to the public. Leary notes, "This software technology will work very much like the human brain. It forms associations among similar subjects, topics or ideas and links them together. When someone wants the latest information on a specific topic, he merely specifies that topic. He can also call up related information if he desires. The hypertext software will gather all of the related information and present it almost instantly. The information gathered also does not have to be located in the same document."[28]

In terms of the overall development, two distinct trends emerge: (1) the use of applications generators, 4GLs, and computer-aided software-engineering tools (CASE) and (2) the use of object-oriented programming (OOP). The use of a spreadsheet to develop a forecasting support system for pharmacy drug usage is an example of an application programmed in a 4GL.[29] But the success of current efforts has been limited. Along with being restricted to simple applications, 4GLs are sometimes at a disadvantage because the automatic linkage of databases and report-generation capabilities produces a system performance penalty. In contrast, advances in OOP will allow designers and programmers more rapidly to create a highly flexible system that does not require much programming of users. Users can manipulate objects without knowledge of the database internal structure. "Data–rich" information such as images can also be stored. Objects can easily be arrayed into complex data structures, and complex interrelationships can be easily defined. Object-oriented databases will allow optimization of disk data storage: that is, data accessed at the same time can be stored in a single segment to constitute a single unit in memory. Productivity is a major benefit of object-oriented development because it will facilitate software changes, and code reusability automatically becomes a time-saving exercise.

In object-oriented technology, an "object" is data about some entity in the system and the code (called methods, rules or procedures) that knows how to manipulate that data. In limiting the knowledge of how a particular function is performed to one routine, the impact of change is greatly limited. A working function can also readily be reused. Another mechanism for promoting reuse is "inheritance," a property enabling the programmer to define a new object in terms of an existing object by specifying only how the new object differs from the existing one.[30] OOP will open up a world of integrated information management by allowing objects to be moved around the system through networked computers. When using OOP to model a personnel (e.g., patient) record, for example, it will be able to create discrete elements that can be supported on a variety of computers specialized for tasks, such as imaging, but accessible by other systems. Figure 14–4 provides an example of an object "participant" in a community health promotion program (CHPP). An application would then be able to access information distributed over many databases and collect it in the distributed data. Hospital applications are candidates for using this technology since it is superior in designing complex information systems while making the software easier to write.

In summary, future distributed systems that allow powerful PCs, mainframes, and minis to be linked in a network will become a dominant force, leading to decentralized computing that will have many advantages such as speed and increased information sharing. New software production technologies and new processors that are the basis of operating PCs or using them as parallel processors in large-scale computer setting will be key to future HMIS development. Such advances in HMIS technology will facilitate the transformation of hospital applications from single departmentalized systems to a total integrated organizational system.

In addition, programs that specialize in modeling intelligent processes in a narrow field, called artificial intelligence (AI) and expert systems (ES), are about to give future health services a new dimension.

Artificial Intelligence and Expert Systems

Riding along the waves of fifth generation computing, AI and ES will play pivotal roles in the production and delivery of health information and knowledge in the future. Future generations of computers will use AI heavily to manage the information and knowledge diffusion revolution. Computers will be able to interact with users in humanlike fashion. They will be able to interpret natural languages and voice commands as well as interact with other devices such as robots to perform complex procedures. Machines will be able to handle heuristic processes and to learn. Holographic images will add a new dimension to current diagnostic images that is not now available through computer simulations.

Information technology will have the greatest impact on direct patient care in the decade ahead. Advances in data input such as voice recognition coupled with high-capacity, low-cost mass storage for both digital information and medical images will make the paperless medical record a reality. Generalized knowledge bases of current clinical information will be available in most, if not all, of the major medical specialties. Clinicians will routinely use expert systems for combining patient specific information from an institutional automated medical record with generalized knowledge bases to support diagnosis and treatment planning.

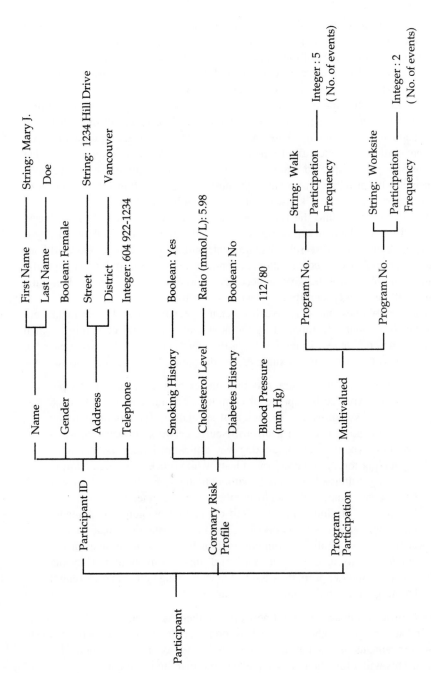

Figure 14-4 An Example of Using Object-Oriented Programming (OOP) To Model a Patient Record

Computer aided diagnosis (CAD) and computer aided medicine (CAM) will become so sophisticated in the coming century that physicians will probably not need to remember some of the traditional ways of practicing medicine. AI-based CAD/CAM will give the physician the ability to integrate and review all of the relevant data from different sources such as past patient records, current progress charts, test results, and patients' symptoms. Further, the system would then process the physician's data using a knowledge-based algorithm electronically linked to a medical information database. With access to the medical literature, the CAD system could then match all of a patient's symptoms with all known causes that are present in a suspected diagnosis. In this way, the computer would act as a consultant by providing a possible diagnosis and pinpointing future sources of information about what is known about the patient's condition.

When projecting into the future, we can see the emergence of an AI-based HMIS. First, all the data can be instantly related and be made available to physicians, including new research data and contributions from around the world, allowing for professional consultation. Second, the ability to narrow in on a specific cause will eliminate expensive, unnecessary, and uncomfortable tests. Third, the cause will be quickly identified, allowing timely treatment.

The technologies that will make this scenario possible are still experimental but will be well under development by the next century. Neural computing, which consists of neural networks modeled loosely after the neurons and synapses in the human nervous system, is an example. Aeh describes neural networks as follows:

> In the connectionist [neural network] model, biological neurons are polarized, active cells capable of complex communications with each other, and synapses are the region of specialized interconnection and communication between neutrons. Neural networks process information in a dynamic, self-organizing way typical of living systems. Self-organizing refers to the ability to learn while processing, e.g., learn to recognize patterns in input data without being given the correct answer beforehand. Once a threshold number of interconnections exists between a set of simple neurons, self-organizing phenomena spontaneously emerge. These networks can learn to associate one pattern with another, to generalize a common pattern from a large number of examples and to distinguish one pattern of input from another. They can also exhibit other properties associated with living systems: preferential learning, optimization and fault tolerance.[31]

The significant impact of neural networks is, therefore, that they will also offer several advantages in other areas such as robotic applications. They will be able to learn movements or orientation from example and not from programmed procedures. This will allow them to operate in unfamiliar environments.

Group Decision Support Systems (GDSS) and Electronic Data Interchange (EDI)

Group decision support systems (GDSS) and electronic data interchange (EDI) are two applications of network technologies that will likely change the way health institutions function in the future, at least to a significant extent. We will take a look at both now, starting with GDSS.

By definition, a GDSS in an interactive, computer-based system that facilitates the finding of solutions to unstructured and semistructured problems by a set of decision makers working as a group. GDSS are particularly useful to solicit inputs from several decision makers in committees, review panels, board meetings, task forces, and decision-making sessions. A model of GDSS (in a local decision network) is shown in Figure 14–5. Also shown in the figure are some of the main components of a GDSS, which include

- A database as a data repository
- A model base with modeling capabilities
- A dialog management with multiple-user access
- An actual group facilitator or a specialized application program to facilitate group access
- General purpose input/output devices (e.g., terminal, voice input/output)
- A central processor
- A common viewing screen
- Individual monitors (for each participant)
- A network system linking the different sites or participants to one another

In the health service delivery and HMIS settings, GDSS are ideal for soliciting inputs from HMIS users in association with managers in the evaluation and selection of vendor proposals and even strategic planning for HMIS. Moreover, the actual architecture of a GDSS varies according to geographical distribution. Shown in Figure 14–5 is a GDSS in a decision room (e.g., board room) setting. Alternatively, a local decision network (LDN) can be used for participants dispersed in a limited geographical area. For decision makers in scattered geographic locations, teleconferencing and remote decision making can be applied.

EDI is another application of the network technology. Electronic data interchanges (EDI) are interorganizational systems (IOS) that allow business partners to exchange business information electronically. IOS is simply defined as an automated system used by two or more organizations that allows users to share in the utilization of a particular application program. Figure 14–6 is an example of an EDI connection.

Pfeiffer has provided a list of four essential features of EDI.[32]

1. At least two organizations (not necessarily ownership-independent) having a business relationship must be users of the system.
2. Data processing tasks at both or all organizations pertaining to a transaction are supported by independent application systems.
3. The integrity of the data exchange between application systems of trading partners is guaranteed by agreements on data coding and formatting rules.
4. Data exchange between the application systems is accomplished via telecommunication links.

In a health organization, EDI may replace manual or telephone links between the organization and its drug and inventory suppliers. For instance, the drug-inventory monitoring system in the organization may be directly connected to an EDI with a supplier, so that a reorder of drugs that have fallen below a predetermined inventory level can be automatically issued and electronically transmitted to the supplier.

Pfeiffer also identified some benefits to health organizations with such an EDI.[33]

- Reduced transaction costs due to the elimination of paperwork and savings on manual data input
- Improved cash flow due to faster processing of transaction and exchange of information
- Reduced inventory levels due to shorter order cycle and reduced ordering costs
- Increased operational efficiency by improvement of the internal operations due to reductions in time and cost and better information management

In addition, having an EDI between a particular health organization and drug/inventory suppliers will definitely give these suppliers a competitive edge over future market entrants. Another example is the hospital-physician link, which allows the patient information to be transferred directly between the parties. As a result of all these perceived benefits, EDI is expected to play a major role in the daily operation of future health organizations.

HEALTH ORGANIZATIONS IN THE TWENTY-FIRST CENTURY

After taking a look at the various trends in the NAHSDS at the organizational level and the various technological advancements, we can now attempt to visualize what health service organizations will be like in the twenty-first century. The most obvious trends of health service reorganizations in the near future seem to be decentralization,[34] emergence of alternative medicine, and formation of alliances such as organized health delivery systems. We shall therefore take a closer look at

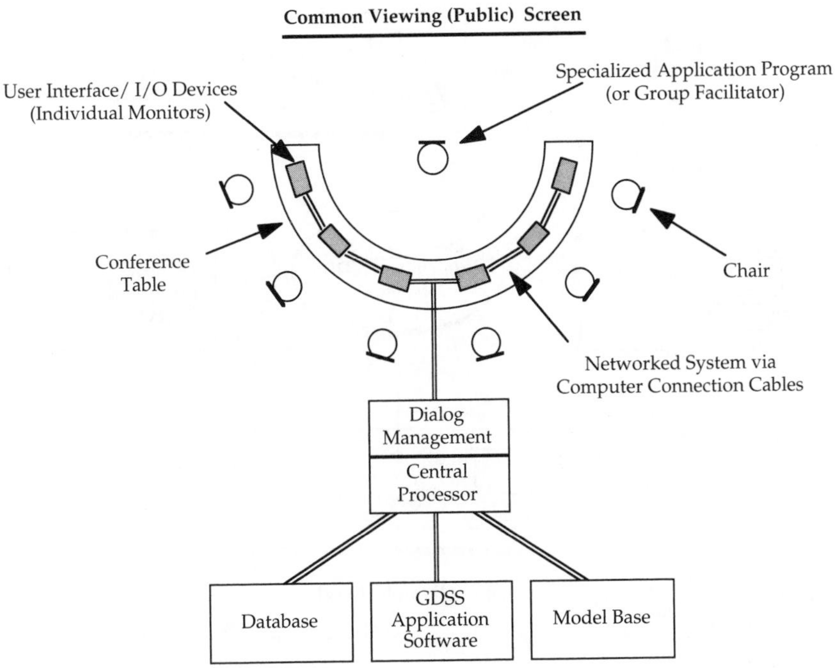

Common Viewing (Public) Screen

Figure 14–5 A Model of a GDSS (a Local Decision Network)

the technology that makes these three trends possible: remote computing. To bring the book to a close, we will then briefly discuss the future HMIS, then follow with some anecdotes that will expand our imagination of what health service organizations will be like in the coming century.

Health Remote Computing

Briefly, health remote computing will extend the reach of the hospital or the traditional means of health service delivery (e.g., physician offices). Employees who work at home can remain "connected" as if they had never left the office. Patients and the public in general will have access to information they could not have reached before. Figure 14–7 shows an example of remote computing network in a distributed HMIS.

The key to this new accessibility is electronic and satellite communication. Where once the flow of data was constrained by the span of cable, and then by the limits of dedicated data circuits, now nearly anything goes. Computers will communicate through a variety of media, including telephone lines, cellular communi-

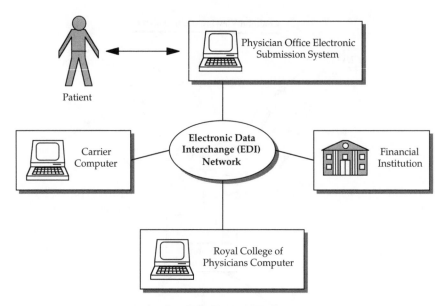

Figure 14–6 An Example of a Health Claim Network

cation, ISDN cables, and even laser communications. Health service organizations of the future will likely have a high-speed backbone network with LAN and WAN capable of handling many different networking protocols. The backbone will also be capable of supporting data, voice, graphics, and video transmissions.

This infrastructure will evolve from the current, rather embryonic state of network usage to an expanding horizon of multidevice support; the end result will be an improvement in management solutions. New health computing technologies will encompass all these aspects and will become the single most important issue in the future. The driving factor in future intelligent networking is open systems. "Open systems" is a broad term that encompasses many aspects: portability of applications software, data accessibility and compatibility, and multivendor interconnectivity. The vision of open systems, and all the benefits that such interconnections and compatibilities promise, are dependent on the creation of and conformation to standards.

Meanwhile, networking and integration will be the glue that will hold future technologies together. In particular, the future will see the development of an intelligent infrastructure that is characterized by

- Internetworking capabilities
- Optimal software and data distribution capabilities

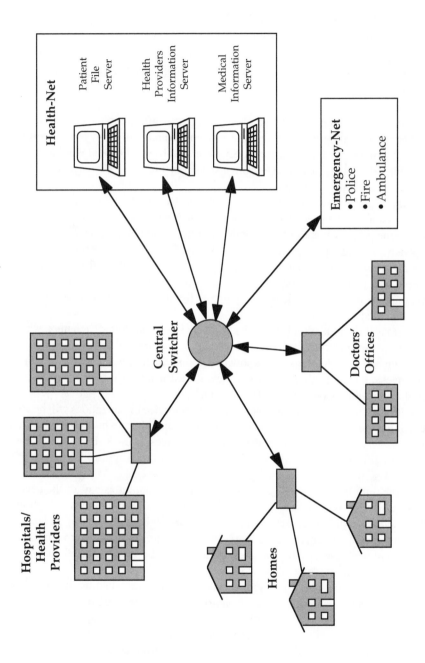

Figure 14–7 An Example of Remote Computing Network in a Distributed HMIS

- Media and topological independence
- Open systems interconnection (OSI) standard-based
- Device independence (the ability to utilize peripherals units of any type)
- Remote capable (the ability to control remote peripherals as if they were local)

Network technologies will lead to changes in the information age. Of immediate benefit to health services is digital switching, which will allow more information to be transmitted at higher rates. So, for example, one hospital will be able to transmit a digital CT scan image from a specialized imaging database to another hospital in a matter of seconds.

With all these new technologies, a sophisticated and high-capacity means of transmission will be needed to carry the information that is generated. Fiber optics will be the primary means of accomplishing this. Although at present it is still too expensive for linking hospitalwide networks, the future will see its price dropping. Fiber optic's extensive bandwidth, which allows it to carry more data at increased speed, will facilitate the delivery of full-motion audiovideo, on-line real-time communications, remote viewing via high-definition monitors, and higher levels of distributed processing.

There is little doubt that fiber optics will be a key future foundation upon which intelligent networks will be built. The new infrastructure will use every wide-area communication technology now known, including fiber optics, satellites, and microwaves, and connecting users to the new infrastructure will be fiber optics, coaxial cable, and copper and wireless technology.

With such a substructure, hospitals and health service organizations will be able to manipulate a new type of patient records, including those which contain digital images. Magnetic resonance imaging (MRI) images, X-rays, ECGs, and other forms of film media will all be able to be viewed digitally through interactive videos. Essentially, if it can be digitized, it can be shared.

At the intraorganizational level, the "remote" computing as part of the decentralization trend will probably be manifested in the proliferation of workstations. Workstations will be used extensively in the future for both patient care and record keeping. The next generation of workstations will be distributed throughout the hospital or health service organization from portable bedside workstations to central, clinical, and home or office workstations.

The workstation combined with specialized hardware, such as imaging systems, will become an important new platform in the future—particularly because of its ability to support high-resolution graphics and multitask applications. The key to the power of these workstations is how they will be networked to access information from centralized, decentralized, and distributed databases.

Planning for the Future HMIS

Building on the concept of technology as a strategic weapon, the book began Chapter 5 by discussing the management aspect of an information infrastructure and its strategic implications. The need for a solid infrastructure, driven by the dynamics of the environment, was examined. The intricacies of strategic planning and critical success factors in forming a cohesive management information infrastructure were then explored in Chapters 10 through 13. Figure 14–8 shows how the concepts on the planning and management for future HMIS are developed throughout this book.

In Chapter 12, HMIS implementation was examined in detail. The need for a comprehensive implementation plan was stressed and the system's goals and objectives were seen as key components during the implementation process. By exploring early efforts in HMIS analysis and design, it was observed that most systems design was carried out by in-house staff consisting of systems analysts and professional programmers. As a result, these systems were tailored to meet the needs of a single organization and in general were not transferable to other institutions. Future systems will move toward the increased use of generalized software available from commercial sources or the employment of "turnkey" systems in which a vendor provides software, training of personnel, and systems installation. This trend toward increased use of software generalized applications will continue in the future as in-house designs decline in popularity. In-house efforts will be

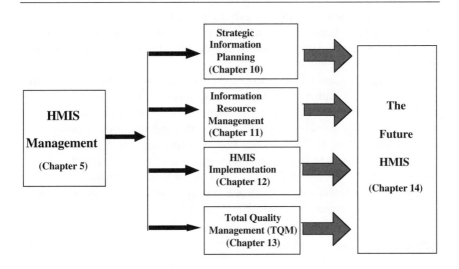

Figure 14–8 Concepts on the Planning and Management of HMIS in This Book

directed to establishing communications and linkages between software packages and databases within and across departments of organizations and across organizations in the local health care system.

Technology will dominate hospital strategy and decision making in the decades to come. Every significant hospital decision will have a technological component but not without a human factor component. The technological advantage with the human factor consideration will allow the health service delivery industry to apply HMIS technology as its business counterparts do. Aside from contributing to patient care technology, HMIS will also become an image builder for hospitals and health service organizations. Coile's view of this aspect of health technology is, "Technology is a market magnet that will attract physician referral and patient self-referral. Consumers equate high-tech equipment and modern facilities with quality. A growing percentage of consumers believe they know the 'best' hospitals providing specialized services, from obstetrical care to cardiology. . . . Top-rated Mayo Clinic for example, enhances its image with the latest and best technology."[35]

The health care sector in the future will see information as a valuable corporate resource and not as isolated departmentalized data as they do today. Technology will become a strategic factor and technologically driven planning will become the trend of the future. As a result, there will be a new type of senior manager, the chief information and technology officer (CITO), who will be responsible for strategically linking corporate information through new technologies with the hospital's long-range plan. Essentially an internal consultant, the CITO will work to advance the state of the art in health information computing by continuously scanning for new technology in the marketplace and advising in areas such as advanced diagnostic devices, genetic engineering, bionics, robotics, and new pharmaceuticals.

Health organizations will have to be dynamic to manage in this changing environment, and information technology will require even more of the hospital's or health service organization's share of financial resources. For example, in terms of the SOG curve discussed in Chapter 2,[36] we would expect health service organizations to double their HMIS spending from an estimated 4 to 5 percent of their budget to a possible 8 to 10 percent. This suggests that information will become a decisive factor in achieving desired results. To achieve competitive advantage through the use of information, health service organizations will therefore have to increase their investments in HMIS.[37]

Glimpses from the Next Century

In order to give the reader a more concrete vision of what health service organizations will probably be like in the next century, this section describes some aspects of the health service delivery system in the future, based on the trends discussed. It is hoped that through these illustrations, the reader will gain a more concrete grasp of the role of HMIS in the future.

Case 1: Attending to Richard Smith with the Aid of Cutting-Edge Technologies

Richard Smith has just had a heart attack and is rushed to the emergency room of a local hospital. In this situation time is critical. The doctor has to assess the extent of the damage quickly and determine whether the patient has had previous heart attacks.

Mr. Smith's smart card, with its own processor and memory, is found in his wallet. After inserting the card into an optical reader connected to the emergency room workstation, the patient's records are accessed from the network server and displayed. Figure 14–9 gives an example of a possible workstation screen for a patient. While continuously monitoring Richard, the physician is linked to the emergency room workstation via a wireless microphone. This allows doctors to transmit information to the patient's file continuously.

Noninvasive monitors are attached to Mr. Smith. These devices, such as ultrasonic transducer and pulse oximeters, that utilize wireless technology are able to capture information and merge it with measurements in Richard's record. This allows the doctor to view the data once the computer-aided analysis begins.

Richard has had previous cardiac workups, and this information is critical for comparing the current measurements. The combined benefits of future HMIS and intelligent networks are seen as the team of clinicians access and retrieve a baseline ECG from Richard's record. Once the doctors are able to access Richard's existing patient record electronically, all the previous cardiac results such as angiograms and vascular echoes can be displayed. Once instructed, the workstation begins a comparison and interpretation of current cardio measurements to previous ones, allowing it to provide a computerized diagnosis and speeding up treatment. Then on the screen a distinct color and flashing highlight the problem area: "Probability of acute MI, 87%."

Richard's own physician, Dr. Akawi, has received an alert message that her patient has been admitted to the emergency room (ER). She calls the ER via the interactive video capability in the workstations, and the attending physician in the ER is able to share with her on her workstation the results of the three-dimensional (3-D) ultrasound. The ultrasound indicates that the anterior wall is not moving. Using an ultrasonic pencil, the technologist who is with her at the workstation highlights a suspected artery as the probable cause.

Dr. Akawi, who knows Richard's history, suggests that they pull up the record of a CT procedure from the prior year. This, too, is displayed and now the two

The screen gives the physician immediate access to all of the patient's records, including images and charts. By clicking on the "eye" icon, the doctor can video conference with another physician anywhere in the world

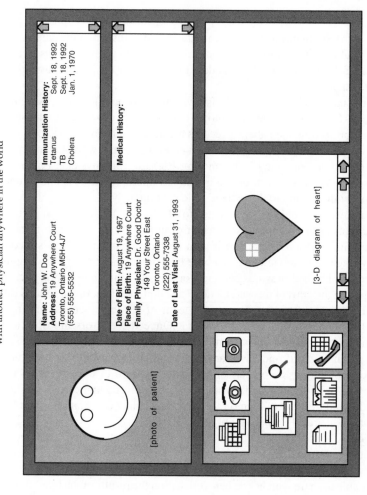

Figure 14–9 A Possible Workstation Screen for a Patient

conferring doctors and the technologist begin to narrow in on the problem—an occlusion in the left anterior descending artery. Medication is prescribed and Dr. Akawi initiates a consultation with the cardiologist on duty, Dr. George Hanlon, while Richard is moved to the cardiac care unit (CCU).

Dr. Hanlon is able to do his consultation from the catheterization lab between procedures because Richard's records are also available to him, via his workstation display. It is less than 2 hours since Richard was admitted, and Dr. Hanlon has already reviewed Richard's chart electronically and sent video e-mail to Dr. Akawi.

Meanwhile, at the central station console in the CCU, Dr. Akawi reviews Richard's progress on an electronic sheet that automatically is updated with the new lab test results. The wireless transducers on Richard's chest continue to send a 3-D ultrasound for the doctors to monitor the anterior wall. The computer analysis confirms that the probability of reperfusion is high. As Dr. Akawi orders the appropriate tests, the nurse checks off the requests on her slate computer for electronic transmission to the lab.

Five hours later, Richard has another episode. An alarm is transmitted to the CCU central station and to Dr. Akawi's workstation. The nurses' personal data assistant (PDA) shows ventricular tachycardia and the red alert is sounded. All the relevant critical readings are displayed at the workstations and on the PDA along with a suggested course of action. After the intervention, Richard's heartbeat returns to normal and the intervention is documented on his electronic record. When a new group of nurses come on shift, they are able to check the historical progress notes on Richard's therapies and other documented procedures. The chart also gives the nurses a current status of vital signs and medications, including analysis of medication level and recommendations for adjustments.

Case 2: A Session with a Humanlike Computer Assistant

Imaging that you are a doctor entering your office in the morning. By voice command, you turn your computer on by saying something to the effect of "COMPUTER ON." You'll want to name your computer so that it recognizes when it is being addressed. So, if your computer's name is Kay, you can then issue a command like "KAY, OPEN PATIENT FILE FRANK CALIDAY."

The computer will recognize that it is being addressed. It recognizes that a command (OPEN FILE) has been issued and that the file to open is for a patient named Frank Caliday. If you want to modify the patient's file, you can dictate an entry to the computer by issuing another command such as "DICTATE," followed by your dictation.

Through text-to-speech capability, Kay will be able to speak back to you as well. Current video animation technology will be so advanced that a video image of Kay will be indistinguishable from a real person, giving it the look and feel of a true assistant. As an assistant, Kay will be able to remind you of important tasks such as meetings and other calendar events.

Kay informs you that while you were out you received a message from a colleague in Australia. Today's voice mail will make way for video e-mail, which will allow you to issue the command "KAY, PLAY NEW VIDEO MESSAGE." Kay complies and instantly a full-motion video playback of your colleague's message appears. Full-motion video will add immeasurably to the productivity of electronic communication by allowing for a more natural "face-to-face" discussion.

Case 3: Combining KNOWLEDGE with Group Decision Support for Cindy

With access to the medical literature, the KNOWLEDGE system, an expert system with clinical group decision support capability, will link all of Cindy's symptoms with all known causes to present a possible diagnosis. Cindy's doctor becomes more concerned about the growing severity of her symptoms and requests a consultation with Dr. Lam, a leading expert in kidney disorders. Dr. Lam, located in China, and Cindy's doctor consult via interactive video workstations. Dr. Lam is able to view Cindy's record as they confer. All the lab results are also available on-line. As both doctors find more clues, they are entered into the KNOWLEDGE system in hopes of getting a diagnosis. The KNOWLEDGE system eventually provides a new diagnosis and pinpoints a dramatic possibility. On the basis of the new diagnosis, Dr. Lam suggests a new test.

The test result comes back positive for a poisonous substance in the kidney. The two doctors reconvene while Dr. Lam consults a toxin specialist in Zurich. Dr. Heinlich is experimenting with a newer and safer treatment protocol for toxic substances. Results of all of Cindy's tests, including images, are transmitted to Zurich. The specialist reviews the case and transmits back the details of a treatment regimen.

CONCLUSION

In the next few years there will certainly be unforeseen technological advances that will represent fundamental departures from the current technology. The continuation of the numerous trends in the health service delivery industry in fact depends heavily on technological advancements. Advances in computer hardware, AI and ES, computer networks, robotics, and more will drive health organizations' strategic and decision-making processes clear into the next century.

We are now in an information and electronic revolution that parallels the industrial revolution. It has been suggested that just as the industrial revolution and its social implications changed the way of life not only of workers but of the family and of society in general, so may the information revolution have similar effects. Where once computers and information technology were needed by only a few people with redundant information needs, the potential for applying information technology to every department and every level of hospital operation now exists.

Technology will infuse every imaginable component of health care, from medical research to patient care to housekeeping. With all the glory that technology promises, many challenges will arise. The new technology will require an assortment of new health care experts and as medical technology becomes more sophisticated it will also become more expensive.

Computer systems will continue to support noninvasive techniques of diagnosis and treatment, offering the dual benefits of improved patient care and reduced costs through the elimination of costly and potentially dangerous surgical procedures. Generalized databases of clinical information will be available in most of the major medical specialties. Clinicians will use expert systems that combine information from the automated medical record of the individual patient with information from the specialty database to aid in diagnosis and treatment planning.[38]

As the hospital's information needs change and computer hardware and software make striking advances, complex, diverse, intelligent, and organized information infrastructures will be the cornerstone of the exchange and integration of knowledge. Advances in technology will radically reconfigure the way health services have been rendered. A completely digital patient record will allow practitioners to view a record electronically whether they are calling in from their office, home, or various locations within the organized health service delivery system. Interactive personal health systems will allow individuals to assess their problems and concerns as if they were conversing with a physician. Such systems will empower the public to become partners in their own care.

CHAPTER QUESTIONS

1. What are some of the trends faced by NAHSDS at the organizational level?
2. What kinds of skills should health information systems managers in the future possess?
3. What significant changes will occur in future computing technologies?
4. Discuss how some technological advancements can facilitate certain changes at the organizational level of the NAHSDS.
5. Discuss some specific applications of AI in future scenarios.

MINI CASE 14
THE PERSONAL HEALTH NETWORK

The year is 2005 and homes, hospitals, and other health providers are all linked on a high-speed information network that has been constructed. This infrastructure allows every household, for a small fee, to have access to unlimited interactive health information. Homes are installed with interactive computers as part of the Internet communications system. The interactive machine is as easy to use as the telephone. Various menus can be easily accessed as well as the health menu that links you up to the health net. The patient file server, health provider information server, and medical information server are all found on the health net. These servers comprise massively paralleled supercomputers. The health net allows one to seek advice for a complaint about one's health, about any given disease, or about what to do when an inheritable disease is identified in one's family. One can ask questions about one's own health concerns, whether hereditary, habit related, or environmentally influenced. The user can even learn of options for treating one's own illness. In every case, the medical information server is kept updated with new procedures, treatments, symptoms, literature, and diagnosis.

The system is entirely voice and touch screen driven. This makes it enjoyable and easy to use. The ease-of-use factor minimizes apprehension, while allowing the user to reach deeper into the health network. Information is presented in terminology that is augmented with images. This allows the user to "drill down" into a level that would be useful to both the professional and the lay person. With population demographic information, the health network will be able to provide a multiple language option.

The system is linked via satellite to hospitals and health provider networks, doctor's offices, and the 911 fire, police, and ambulance network. The health net is an integrated health network, and the emergency network allows automatic calls to the police, ambulance, or fire fighters. The medical information service contains extensive health sciences databases, which are constructed specifically for the purpose of general public use. Different databases are called upon, depending on the user's needs, so that the responses are uniquely tailored to each inquiry. The medical information server is also able to deliver customized information based on the user's personal characteristics such as age, sex, race, and occupation. The health network is able to offer many features that are valuable to the public, one component of which is health and lifestyle.

The health and lifestyle assessment module is the most valuable to users. It is able to identify behavioral, genetic, and environmental forces that may be causing an adverse effect on an individual lifestyle. Upon identifying the prioritized risks, it is able to provide greater information depth through specialized loops or algorithms before returning to complete the general assessment. As needed, further algorithms that explore other potentially problematic areas are utilized as the inquirer indicates their possible importance. Through this interactive means, the inquirer is "conversing" with the software as if talking to a real doctor. At the end of each session the program is able to provide an audio as well as visual list of steps the user can follow to alleviate an aliment such as diet change, smoking habits, and alcohol intake along with an explanation as to why it is worth making these changes. It is also possible to get a personalized copy of the session both printed on paper and electronically stored on a smart cards, optical disk, or some other medium. Such flexible storage and updating can be done at home, in the office, at public terminals, or in a health institution. The health and lifestyle assessment mode is also able to assess the inquirer's complaint in order to determine how critical the person's condition appears to be. It can advise the user to seek help immediately or later. If a condition appears truly urgent, the user will be able to seek immediate care and the program will give the user the opportunity to call 911 automatically.

At the conclusion of the interaction, the program is able to make several suggestions to the inquirer. It may suggest that all is well and refer the inquirer to the health maintenance module, which indicates the key risk factors that are present and suggests what their implications may be. If further information is requested, the user is linked to a specialized database that will provide more specialized information. For any problem that is found, the health and lifestyle assessment module offers a full description of the relevant resources and is able to access the health provider's database to see what is available (i.e., smoking control workshops, dietary advice, general counseling services) or what is relevant to the condition.

The general health treatment adviser module is another mode that inquirers can access. This area of the health net advises users on how to carry out various prescribed treatment regimens. It explains what is prescribed by physicians or other health practitioners. Upon request, it displays a detailed or summarized outline of the treatment, including side effects and probabilities of successful outcomes. Essentially, this module enforces what the health service provider may have had only limited time to explain.

MINI CASE QUESTIONS

1. What organizations do you think would be involved in the creation of the health information data required to support the health net system described? What changes would these organizations have to face in the near future?

2. There have been suggestions of using computerized "infomercials" as a means of funding the health net. What do you think?

3. Discuss ways in which the health net can affect the health care of the population.

4. Discuss several computing technological advancements that have made the scenario possible.

5. Discuss some management issues that would arise according to the previous scenario that are not as significant as in today's health organizations.

CHAPTER REVIEW

As we approach the next century, hospitals and other health service organizations alike will likely face more pressing budget-control measures. Their roles and operations in the delivery of health service may have to be redefined.

At the same time, some far-reaching trends are expected to continue to change the face of health organizations in North America. These include increased scale, concentration, specialization, diversification, alliances, governmental influence, privatization, managerial influence, and market orientation. Health management culture, structure, and process will also change accordingly. The structure of management may have to be modified to coordinate the collection of the "right" data. Health administrators will also likely spend more time using the data in various analyses. Group strategic thinking, interdisciplinary skills, and the capability to learn will be the key characteristics that are expected to be eagerly sought after in a health information systems manager. In rationalizing all these changes, it is crucial that the big picture is not lost: systems thinking should be applied, particularly in health service organization problem finding and problem solving.

Both hardware and software will see tremendous developments in the near future. The trends of development ultimately favor decentralization of HMIS. Advances in end-user computing and human-computer interface technologies will also be realized. The overall organizational trends of health organizations, coupled with the technological advancements and the increased use of artificial intelligence, group support systems, and electronic data interchange, will ultimately facilitate the adoption of distributed HMIS. Various remote computing technologies will come into play. In the changing NAHSDS, the role of HMIS will become central rather than peripheral.

NOTES

1. G.L. McManis, Are You Ready for the Next Revolution?, *Healthcare Executive* (November/December 1988): 40.

2. M. McDonald and H. Blum, Health in the Information Age: The Emergence of Health Oriented Telecommunication Applications (Berkeley, Calif: Environmental Science and Policy Institute (1992), 23.

3. W.R. Scott, The Organization of Medical Care Services: Toward an Integrated Theoretical Model, *Medical Care Review* 50, no. 3 (1993): 271–303.

4. J. Naisbett and J. Elkins, *Megatrends: Ten Directions Transforming Our Lives* (New York: Warner Books, 1982).

5. O.W. Anderson, *Health Services As a Growth Enterprise in the United States Since 1875,* 2nd ed. (Ann Arbor, Mich: Health Administration Press, 1990).

6. D.R. Longo and G.A. Chase, Structural Determinants of Hospital Closure, *Medical Care* 22 (May 1984): 38–40.

7. S.M. Shortell, The Evolution of Hospital Systems: Unfulfilled Promises and Self-Fulfilling Prophesies, *Medical Care Review* 45, no. 2 (1988): 177–214.

8. S.M. Shortell, et al., *Strategic Choices for America's Hospitals: Managing Change in Turbulent Times* (San Francisco: Jossey-Bass, Inc., Publishers, 1990).

9. American Hospital Association, *Physician Characteristics and Distribution in the U.S.: 1992 Edition.* (Chicago: American Hospital Publishers, Inc., 1992).

10. M.A. Morrisey and J.A. Alexander, Hospital Acquisition or Management Contract: A Theory of Strategic Choice, *Health Care Management Review* 12, no. 1 (1987): 21–30.

11. T.A. D'Aunno and H.S. Zuckerman, The Emergence of Hospital Federations: An Integration of Perspectives from Organization Theory, *Medical Care Review* 44, no. 2 (1987): 323–370.

12. M.L. Fennell and R. Warnecke, *Diffusion of Medical Innovation: An Applied Network Perspective* (New York: Plenum Publishing Corporation, 1988).

13. J. Epps, *Achieving Health for All: A Framework for Health Promotion.* (Ottawa: Ministry of Supply and Services, 1986).

14. I.L. Bennet, Jr., Technology As a Shaping Force, in *Doing Better and Feeling Worse: Health in the United States,* ed. J.H. Knowles (New York: W.W. Norton & Co., Inc., 1977): 125–133.

15. B.H. Gray, *For Profit Enterprise in Health Care* (Washington, D.C.: National Academy Press, 1986).

16. P. Hamilton, *Health Care Consumerism* (St. Louis: C.V. Mosby Co., 1982).

17. D.W. Colins, Future Health Care: Increasing the Alternatives, *The Futurist* (May-June 1988): 13–16.

18. Scott, Organization of Medical Care Services, 275–281.

19. C.J. Austin, *Information Systems for Health Services Administration,* 4th ed. (Ann Arbor, Mich: Health Administration Press, 1992), 162.

20. Ibid.

21. S.L. Bloom, Hospital Turf Battles: The Manager's Role, *Hospitals and Health Administration* 36, no. 4 (1991): 590–599.

22. R. Murray and D. Trefts, Building the Business of the Future: The IT Imperative, *Information Systems Management* (Fall 1992): 54–59.

23. Ibid.

24. Ibid.

25. R. Wayner, Digital Hard Drives, *Byte* (March 1994): 91.

26. F.M. Frankenfeld, Trends in Computer Hardware and Software, *American Journal of Hospital Pharmacy* 50 (April 1993): 707–711.

27. McDonald and Blum, Health in the Information Age.

28. E. Leary, Amino Acids: The Future of Computing in the 1990s? *Journal of Systems Management* 40, no. 12 (1989): 23–30.

29. M.M. D'Sa, et al., Exponential Smoothing Methods for Forecasting Drug Expenditures, *American Journal of Hospital Pharmacy* 51 (1994): 2581–2588.

30. R. Aeh, Technology's Impact on Organizations and Their Structures, *Journal of Systems Management* (December 1989): 20–30.

31. Ibid.

32. H.K.C. Pfeiffer, *The Diffusion of Electronics Data Interchange* (New York: Springer-Verlag, 1992).

33. Ibid.

34. Naisbitt an Delkins, Megatrends.

35. R.C. Coile, Jr., Strategic Technology Plan, *Healthcare Executive* (January/February 1990): 21–22.

36. R.L. Nolan, et al., Computers and Hospital Management: Prescription for Survival, *Journal of Medical Systems* 1, no. 2 (1977): 187–203.

37. K.K. Kim and J.E. Michelman, An Examination of Factors for the Strategic Use of Information Systems in the Healthcare Industry, *MIS Quarterly* (June 1990): 201–214.

38. Austin, Information Systems, 162.

Index

483